AIR BATTLE FOR
LENINGRAD
—1941-1944—

AIR BATTLE FOR LENINGRAD
—1941-1944—

★

DMITRY DEGTEV AND DMITRY ZUBOV

AIR WORLD

AIR BATTLE FOR LENINGRAD, 1941–1944

First published in Great Britain in 2023 by
Air World
An imprint of
Pen & Sword Books Ltd
Yorkshire – Philadelphia

Copyright © Dmitry Degtev and Dmitry Zubov, 2023

ISBN 978 1 39906 123 0

The right of Dmitry Degtev and Dmitry Zubov to be identified as Authors of this work has been asserted by them in accordance with the Copyright, Designs and Patents Act 1988.

A CIP catalogue record for this book is available from the British Library.

All rights reserved. No part of this book may be reproduced or transmitted in any form or by any means, electronic or mechanical including photocopying, recording or by any information storage and retrieval system, without permission from the Publisher in writing.

Typeset by SJmagic DESIGN SERVICES, India.
Printed and bound in the UK by CPI Group (UK) Ltd, Croydon, CR0 4YY.

Pen & Sword Books Limited incorporates the imprints of Atlas, Archaeology, Aviation, Discovery, Family History, Fiction, History, Maritime, Military, Military Classics, Politics, Select, Transport, True Crime, Air World, Frontline Publishing, Leo Cooper, Remember When, Seaforth Publishing, The Praetorian Press, Wharncliffe Local History, Wharncliffe Transport, Wharncliffe True Crime and White Owl.

For a complete list of Pen & Sword titles please contact

PEN & SWORD BOOKS LIMITED
George House, Units 12 & 13, Beevor Street, Off Pontefract Road,
Barnsley, South Yorkshire, S71 1HN, England
E-mail: enquiries@pen-and-sword.co.uk
Website: www.pen-and-sword.co.uk

or

PEN AND SWORD BOOKS
1950 Lawrence Rd, Havertown, PA 19083, USA
E-mail: uspen-and-sword@casematepublishers.com
Website: www.penandswordbooks.com

Contents

Introduction vi

Chapter 1   They'll be here soon! 1
Chapter 2   Hitler's bombers get to work 31
Chapter 3   Bay storm 46
Chapter 4   Deadly lake 62
Chapter 5   Aerial war of attrition 79
Chapter 6   The Schmidt's wasteland 93
Chapter 7   Operation Eisstoss 126
Chapter 8   German air attacks against 'Ladoga battleships' 151
Chapter 9   Operation Froschlaich 168
Chapter 10   'Natural coffee' by Generaloberst Alfred Keller 188
Chapter 11   Third Sinyavino meat grinder 201
Chapter 12   Operation Brazil 216
Chapter 13   'Hydra' of Ladoga against 'mosquitoes' and 'bedbugs' 228
Chapter 14   Operation Iskra 239
Chapter 15   The Luftwaffe's last futile efforts 258
Chapter 16   Mission impossible 279

Conclusion 308
References and Sources 310
Index 315

Introduction

The Battle for Leningrad has not become such a well-known topic for research by military historians as Moscow, Stalingrad, or Kursk. Very few books have been written about it, both in Russian and in English. There are a number of objective reasons for such a lack of attention by historians. Despite the occupation of Leningrad being one of the objectives of Operation Barbarossa, after the initial successes of the German Blitzkrieg the offensive slowed down, and the Germans could not take the city on the move. From the autumn of 1941, the front in the Leningrad area stabilised, and the war on this section of the Eastern Front began to develop on the model of the First World War. Despite the ferocity of the fighting, and the great attention of Hitler and Stalin, the military actions in the Leningrad area did not significantly affect the course of the war. Thus, the development of military events in the north of Russia made Leningrad one of the many secondary sections of the huge Eastern Front.

Usually, at the mention of Leningrad, the image of a city dying of hunger arises in the minds of Second World War history lovers, whose defenders heroically repelled the endless attacks of the besieging Wehrmacht for 900 days and nights. This truthful, but extremely schematic image does not reveal even 1 per cent of all the details of the grandiose scale of the battle going on simultaneously on land, on water and in the air. The lack of information about the events of the Leningrad siege has been distorting reality for more than eighty years and does not allow us to get an objective idea of this important battle of the Second World War.

In the Soviet Union, the blockade of Leningrad became an important component of the sacred Soviet myth of the Great Patriotic War. Despite all the efforts of Stalin's propaganda, the defeat of the Red Army in 1941 and the subsequent humanitarian disaster in Leningrad could not be turned into a victory for the 'wise' leader. They tried to forget about the defeats of 1941 in the Stalinist Soviet Union, and the authorities focused on the victories of 1945. In this regard, the events that took place on this section of the Eastern Front were described very sparingly in official Soviet sources. Any criticism of the Soviet leadership and Stalin personally, who was objectively guilty of the monstrous

INTRODUCTION

sufferings of the Leningraders, was strictly prohibited. The main emphasis in the official Soviet history was placed on a completely plausible version of the atrocities of the Nazi army, which led to the death of hundreds of thousands of Leningrad residents from hunger and disease. Thus, the total secrecy and politicisation of the Eastern Front theme prevented Soviet and foreign historians from understanding the complexity of this deadly confrontation between the Wehrmacht and the Red Army.

The collapse of the 'Red Empire' opened access to classified archives, but contrary to expectations, the topic of the battle for Leningrad did not cause much excitement among Russian and foreign researchers. In addition to the above-mentioned secondary importance of this section of the Eastern Front, the emotional background of the Leningrad Holodomor tragedy plays an important role. This monstrous humanitarian catastrophe obscures the military aspects of this confrontation between the two totalitarian regimes. All the complexity and diversity of events in this sector of the front complicates the compilation of a generalised view of the battle for Leningrad. These difficulties encourage researchers to highlight only certain aspects of this extensive research problem. Historians usually focus on studying only certain aspects directly or indirectly related to Leningrad, namely numerous land operations on the front line of Army Group North or events related to the actions of the Soviet Baltic Fleet. However, these important branches of this vast problem have not yet been studied sufficiently. The aerial component of this protracted battle is even less represented in historical literature. Therefore, it was the description and analysis of the air battle for Leningrad that was chosen as the key topic for this book.

The authors, due to the above circumstances, do not claim to fully document the stated topic within the framework of one book. However, they will try to reflect all facets of the Luftwaffe and Red Army Air Force air confrontation over Leningrad in connection with military events on land and water.

Welcome to the brutal reality of the aerial battle for Leningrad!

Chapter 1

They'll be here soon!

'German planes are dropping some objects ...'

The beginning of Sunday afternoon on 22 June 1941 at the main Soviet Baltic Fleet naval base in Kronstadt did not portend anything bad. The weather was warm and windless over the sea, the water was completely calm. The most powerful ships of the Baltic Fleet – the battleships *Marat* and *Oktyabrskaya Revolutsiya* – had recently returned to the harbour after exercises and were quietly anchored. However, the premonition of an imminent war did not leave the Soviet sailors. On the eve of the day of the German attack on the USSR, the ships of the Soviet Baltic Fleet were ordered to operational readiness No. 1, which preceded the state of full combat readiness. But neither the sailors nor the senior officers knew about the reasons for this decision, although it certainly testified to the preparation of the USSR for war. Yesterday they read the newspaper *Pravda*, in which it was printed that all the rumours about the upcoming war between Germany and the Soviet Union were fake and provocation by the enemies of these countries. According to the Soviet government, Great Britain was particularly hostile to the fraternal alliance of Hitler and Stalin.

The city of Kronstadt was located on the small Kotlin Island, in the eastern part of the Gulf of Finland 21.5km west of Leningrad. This gloomy, rocky piece of land measures 10 by 3km. Kronstadt – translated from German as 'Crown City' – was founded by the cruel Tsar Peter the Great in 1710. Powerful forts, coastal artillery batteries, warehouses, berths and repair shipyards were built there. The island became a shelter for Russian warships and reliably protected St Petersburg, the new capital of the Russian Empire, from the sea. For 200 years, Kronstadt served as the main navy base. During this time, the city witnessed the successes and defeats of the Russian fleet, and periods of prosperity and desolation of the Russian Empire. The Bolsheviks, who destroyed tsarist power in Russia, adopted from their predecessors the pernicious idea of military domination at sea. The new 'Tsar' Stalin spared no expense to modernise the surviving tsarist battleships of the First World War. In the 1930s, an ambitious programme for the construction of new warships was adopted on his orders. By 1941, the Soviet Baltic Fleet posed a serious threat to Hitler, which he wanted to end as soon as possible.

On 22 June 1941, at about 03.00, a phone rang at the command post of the main navy base of the Soviet Baltic Fleet. It was a call from the attendant at Coastal Artillery Battery No. 413, located at Fort Obruchev,[1] 7km north-west of Kronstadt. He reported that the noise of engines approaching from the north-west could be heard in the sky. The attendant asked for instructions on further actions. The Head of the Kronstadt Air Defence Captain Sergey Kushnerev gave the order to turn on the searchlights and illuminate the unidentified planes. Soon the searchlights beams struck into the brightening sky, and observers were horrified to see twin-engine planes with crosses on their wings flying over the water at a low level. At that moment, an urgent message came from another observation post in Kronstadt: 'German planes are dropping some objects on parachutes in the area of the Tolbukhin lighthouse.'[2]

In the next few minutes, Captain Sergey Kushnerev had to make a very difficult decision, on which not only did his future military career depend, but possibly his life. The day before, all Red Army commanders received Stalin's categorical order: 'Do not succumb to German provocations!', which meant a ban on any retaliatory actions. For several weeks before the war, Soviet anti-aircraft gunners had been forced to look silently at German planes invading Soviet airspace. Following Stalin's orders, they did not dare to shoot at them. Taking advantage of this impunity, the Germans flew over Soviet military facilities at a low level, photographing everything they considered necessary. Captain Kushnerev bitterly recalled his passivity in front of the enemy:

> We, the anti-aircraft gunners, who were directly confronted with examples of brazen aerial reconnaissance of the Germans, accumulated anger ... I could not raise our fighters to intercept, and our planes would not have had time to catch up with the Germans. And, the enemy, having done his dirty deed, would have gone unpunished. And it happens again and again!

---

1. Fort Obruchev is one of the northern forts of the Kronstadt Fortress. It was built on two artificially created islands. The construction of the fort was carried out in the period from 1896 to 1913. The length of the fort's battle front was 950m. In the 1930s Fort Obruchev underwent modernization. By the beginning of the German invasion of 1941, 254mm, 203mm (mounted in turret installations), 152mm, 120mm and 45mm guns were installed on it.
2. The Tolbukhin Lighthouse was located on an island 3km west of Kronstadt.

THEY'LL BE HERE SOON!

Meanwhile, the German planes continued to confidently carry out their combat mission. Captain Kushnerev understood that if he opened fire on the Germans, he could be accused of violating Stalin's order, court-martialled and shot. On the other hand, the same sad consequences could occur in the event of his inaction in response to the German attack. Many Red Army officers found themselves in such an ambiguous position at that moment. Finally, after agonising reflection, Captain Kushnerev gave the command: 'The batteries on duty, open fire on enemy aircraft! To all other air defence units, declare a combat alert!'

At 03.40, the commander of the Anti-aircraft Battery from the 11th Separate Anti-aircraft Division (11th OZAD), Senior Lieutenant Yakov Dmitriev, also received a report about the approach of German aircraft. Running up to the optical rangefinding telemeter, he quickly became convinced of the correctness of the report. In the predawn darkness, Dmitriev saw in the eyepiece of the telemeter a large group of aircraft that seemed to him like German Do 215s. The bombers flew at an altitude of 300–400m in a long, stretched column. Flying up to the fairway, they dropped some rectangular objects, which then parachuted slowly into the water and sank. Since the actions of the German aircraft were clearly hostile, the commander of the anti-aircraft battery ordered firing to begin. The gunners, who were running through the dawn fog to their anti-aircraft guns, did not yet know that they would now fire the first shots in the upcoming long and terrible war!

Specialists in the fight against the Soviet Baltic Fleet against Kronstadt's air defence

The aircraft 'similar to the Do 215' were actually fourteen Ju 88 A-5s of 1./KGr. 806 and four Ju 88 A-5s of 1./KGr. 506. They took off from East Prussia and, flying over the Baltic Sea and Gulf of Finland, approached Kronstadt Naval Base from Finland. Each aircraft carried two BM1000 parachute bottom mines equipped with the latest magnetic fuse. The fact that the bombers were flying at a low level, about 500m, was explained by the restrictions on the height of dropping mines of this type. When dropped by parachute from a height of 2,000m, the minimum water depth at the drop site should be 12m, when dropped from a height of 1000m it should be 8m, and at a height of 500m, at least 6m. The eastern part of the Gulf of Finland was very shallow, so the Germans needed to dump the parachute mine from the lowest possible height. The shallow depths were the reason that Russian ships could only move between their bases along narrow fairways, which could be blocked with bottom mines.

The Germans, reassured by the prolonged impunity, did not expect the Soviets to start shooting so quickly. To avoid hits, the surprised Ju 88 pilots even had to perform flak evasion manoeuvres. However, not a single German plane was hit by ground fire, although the Russians claimed to have shot down two of them. After dropping mines in fairways on the approaches to Kronstadt, the German bombers turned towards Finland and after a short flight landed at Utti Air Base, near the Finnish city of Kouvola.

It should be noted that the first blow to the Soviet Baltic Fleet infrastructure was inflicted not by ordinary bombers, but by aviation units specially created for attacks on such non-standard targets.

Coastal Aviation Group KGr. 806 Major Hans Emil was part of the Baltic Sea Aviation Gruppe (Flugzeugüberführungsgruppe Ostsee, Fl. F. Ostsee). On 1 April 1941, it became part of Luftflotte 1 and was designed specifically to fight the Russian fleet in the Baltic. In addition to KGr. 806, the Fl. F. Ostsee included the 1st Squadron Combat Training Group JG 54 (Erg.Gr./JG 54) commanded by Oberleutnant Eggers (Bf 109 E fighters), the 125th Naval Reconnaissance Air Group (Aufkl.Gr. 125), under Oberstleutnant Gerhard Kolbe (seaplanes He 114, He 60 and Ar 95 A), and the 9th Naval Search and Rescue Squadron (9.Seenot-staffel), which used Do 23 flying boats and He 59 seaplanes.

KGr. 506 was formed in August 1939 also in the format of a Coastal Aviation Group. It was originally intended to make torpedo attacks on ships and was armed with He 115 seaplanes. Shortly before the start of Operation Barbarossa, KGr. 506 was re-equipped with Ju 88 A bombers. This aviation unit was planned to be used as a universal Gruppe capable of laying various types of parachute mines from the air, bombing ships and naval bases, and so on. During the period described in the book, its commander was Oberstleutnant Weygold.

By the beginning of the war, Kronstadt's air defences consisted of the 1st Anti-aircraft Regiment under Major Sergei Ignatovsky, which had twelve anti-aircraft batteries with 76mm M1938 anti-aircraft guns. In addition, the regiment consisted of three anti-aircraft batteries of the 27th Separate Anti-aircraft Division, Anti-aircraft Searchlight Company and Anti-aircraft Machine gun Company, located on Koivisto Island, 75km north-west of Kronstadt. The southern approaches to Kronstadt, as well as ships and coastal artillery batteries on the shore of the Gulf of Finland, were protected from air attacks by the 2nd Anti-aircraft Regiment under Major Nikolai Rychkov. It consisted of ten anti-aircraft batteries with 76mm M1938 anti-aircraft guns, an Anti-aircraft Searchlight Battalion and Anti-aircraft Machine gun Battalion. All these units were part of the Air Defence Sector of the Kronstadt Naval Base, whose command post was located in the town of Petergof. Before the war, it was considered a rear area, so the air defence of the Kronstadt area was quite weak. The main forces of the Soviet Baltic Fleet were located at the forward bases on the Hanko Peninsula and in the Baltic ports of Estonia and Latvia recently occupied by the USSR. More impressive air defence forces were located there to protect them.

THEY'LL BE HERE SOON!

The tasks of air defence of the fleet and its coastal facilities were also assigned to the Air Force Soviet Baltic Fleet under the command of Major General Mikhail Samokhin. By the beginning of the war, they included the 61st Fighter Aviation Brigade (5th Fighter Aviation Regiment, 13th Fighter Aviation Regiment and 71st Fighter Aviation Regiment) and two Separate Fighter Aviation Squadrons. In total, there were 368 I-16, I-153 and I-15bis fighters in these units.

Dangerous 'walk' by Leutnant Hans Turmeier and its consequences

On the night of 22–23 June 1941, Ju 88 A bombers from KGr. 806 reappeared over Kronstadt Naval Base. This time they took off from Utti Air Base and flew up to the target from Finland. The factor of surprise and indecision was absent this time, and the Russians promptly opened fire on the German planes, which were flying at an altitude of 500m. In the area of the town of Sestroretsk, German bombers came under heavy fire from anti-aircraft batteries of the 115th and 194th Anti-aircraft Regiments. As a result of fire from the ground, KGr. 806 lost four aircraft:

> Ju 88 A-5 W.Nr. 6357 'M7+DH' of 1./KGr. 806 was shot down near Uskela (Finland). After making an emergency landing, the crew under the command of pilot Hauptmann Seedorf managed to escape from the Russians and on 26 June reached Finnish territory in the area of settlement Reboly;

> Ju 88 A-5 W.Nr. 4186 'M7+FK' from 2./KGr. 806 was damaged by anti-aircraft fire and made an emergency landing at Utti Air Base. One member of the bomber's crew was killed. The aircraft was declared beyond repair (60 per cent of damage) and written off;

> Ju 88 A-4 W.Nr. 4577 'M7+FH' of 1./KGr. 806 was damaged by anti-aircraft fire and made an emergency landing at Utti Air Base. The aircraft was declared beyond repair (60 per cent of damage) and written off;

> Ju 88 A-5 W.Nr. 6300 'M7+GL' from 3./KGr. 806 at 00.10 was shot down by anti-aircraft fire near village Yukki and made an emergency landing on its fuselage on Soviet territory. The air gunner and flight engineer were killed, and pilot Leutnant Ernst Satorius and navigator Leutnant Hans Turmeier were captured by the Russians.

AIR BATTLE FOR LENINGRAD, 1941–1944

Soon the German pilots were sitting in the Soviet commandant's office and waiting for interrogation. At the same time, their behaviour did not correspond at all to the usual image of a captive humbly awaiting his fate. According to the Leningrad writer Vissarion Sayanov, who was present at the interrogation of Leutnant Turmeier, he mockingly told the Russians that he flew out for a walk, got lost in the fog, and then accidentally ended up in the Kronstadt area. He further claimed that he had never dumped mines into the Soviet fairways. Apparently Leutnant Turmeier was so confident of an imminent German victory that he did not consider it necessary to show at least some respect for the Russians who had captured him. The adventures of the German pilots did not go unnoticed by the Soviet press. On 24 June, the newspaper *Leningradskaya Pravda* published a message: 'On 23 June, six German planes that took off from Finnish territory tried to bombard the Kronstadt area. The planes were driven away. One plane was shot down and four German officers were captured.'

German mine installations created serious difficulties for the Soviets. Already on the morning of 22 June, minesweepers based at Kronstadt Naval Base began reconnaissance minesweeping on the entire fairways network. However, the Russians did not know anything about the existence of a new type of German bottom mine with a contactless fuse. This innovative weapon was detonated in the event of a change in the parameters of the magnetic field when a ship passed near it! Until the beginning of August 1941, Soviet Baltic Fleet engineers believed that the Germans and Finns used only contact fuses on naval mines. Only thanks to information received from the Allies at the end of the summer of 1941 were they were able to understand the principle of operation of the hi-tech German magnetic fuse. Therefore, the mine clearance conducted by the Soviets in July 1941 using contact sweeps turned out to be completely useless. Soon the first sad confirmation of this fact appeared.

On the morning of 24 June 1941, the Soviet minesweeper *T-208 Schkiv* with a displacement of 450 tons was blown up by a naval mine near Kronstadt Naval Base. From a powerful hydrodynamic impact, large cracks formed in the hull of the ship, and despite the operation of all pumps, the minesweeper sank after forty minutes. At the same time, some sailors noticed that the explosion occurred not directly under the bottom of the ship, but away from it. This was the first evidence that the Germans were using fundamentally new weapons against Soviet warships. However, the 'wise' Soviet admirals reacted sceptically to such evidence from poorly educated sailors and ignored the important message. Meanwhile, the number of victims of the German innovative naval mines continued to grow. On 7 July, opposite the Tolbukhin lighthouse, the minesweeper *TSCH-39 Petrozavodsk* was blown up. In this case, the explosion also occurred away from the side, however, the official cause of the loss of the ship was again declared to be a 'moored contact mine'. After that, the fairways in the Kronstadt Naval Base area were closed to navigation and mine clearance was carried out again by conventional contact sweeps. As expected, such tactics did not produce any results and the German naval mines again failed to neutralise. Special devices for the distant sweep of German naval mines only appeared at the disposal of Soviet Baltic Fleet much later. Before the advent of new mine clearance tools, the only method of dealing with German bottom mines with magnetic fuses was dropping depth charges in the fairway. However, the probability of destroying bottom mines in such a crude way was small.

Hitler's 'wonder weapon'

The decision of the Germans to start a war against the Soviet Baltic Fleet with the help of bottom mines looks very strange. Probably, a sudden torpedo attack or the bombing of large ships would have caused more damage. This is exactly what the Japanese did when they attacked the American naval base at Pearl Harbor on 7 December 1942. However, the Luftwaffe command was apparently still under the influence of Hitler's speech on 23 November 1939, during which he announced the Luftminen as the new 'wonder weapon'. The Führer believed that with the help of bottom mines dropped from aircraft it would be possible not only to destroy enemy fleets, but also to win the war. Speaking in his habitually very emotional manner, Hitler inspired his military: 'The constant mining of the English coast will force England to kneel!' Thus, it was the Führer, who constantly rudely interfered with the Luftwaffe leadership, who determined the strategy of German aviation against the Soviet Baltic Fleet in the summer of 1941.

The Luftwaffe arsenal included four types of parachute mine. The smallest, Luftmine A (LMA), had a mass of 500kg and an explosive charge of 300kg. Luftmine B (LMB), with a total weight of 920kg, contained 680kg of explosives. The third type of bottom parachute mine, Luftmine F (LMF), could be used at depths up to 300m. The fourth type, Bombenmine (BM1000), nicknamed 'Monika', was a hybrid of a bottom mine and an aircraft bomb. It was filled with 700kg of explosives and could be equipped with both magnetic and acoustic fuses and even contain multiple types of sensors. In addition, the BM1000 could be equipped with a conventional contact fuse and used as a particularly powerful aircraft bomb. Unlike high-explosive bombs of similar mass (SC1000), which went deep into the ground when falling, Bombenmine 'Monika' exploded on the surface and caused much more damage to industrial and residential buildings. One BM1000 explosion could destroy an entire city block. All four types of aviation mines could be dropped both by parachute and without it, from a low altitude.

The very fact that the Germans had innovative types of mines was insufficient for their effective use. It was necessary to develop tactics and choose a means of delivering mine weapons to the sea area of the alleged enemy. The Luftwaffe leadership was preoccupied with the technical equipment of the bombers and the appropriate training of the crews intended for such missions. Setting up a naval mine from the air was a very difficult task that only a specially trained bomber crew could handle. Therefore, the Germans created special aviation groups (Gruppen) and separate squadrons (Staffeln) to perform such missions. The first such units were II./KG 4 and III./KG 4. Then the crews of II./KG 26 and KGr. 806, who had previously specialised in bombing enemy warships and merchant ships, were also trained in minelaying.

In 1940–41, the Luftwaffe actively used Luftminen in the area of ports and rivers in the UK, in the Mediterranean Sea and in the Suez Canal. The German invasion of the Soviet Union was also accompanied by the laying of parachute mines around the main navy bases of the Soviet fleet.

The British Royal Navy was the first to feel the power of the new German 'wonder weapon'. At the initial stage of the Germans using mines with magnetic fuses, the British suffered heavy losses. However, a lucky break in the form of the capture of two intact German naval mines on a coastal shoal allowed English scientists to study their design in detail. Soon the UK had an effective means of dealing with the new 'wonder weapon', which they later passed on to the Soviets.

'The Germans threw down their weapons, surrendered ...'

Residents of Leningrad knew nothing about these disturbing events. The headlines of local newspapers in the early days of the war were full of belligerence: 'The anger of the Soviet people is terrible!', 'Nazi robbers will pay cruelly!', 'Nazi obscurantists will be destroyed!', 'We will have straitjackets for fascists!', and so on. Newspaper publications were full of traditional propaganda pathos. *Leningradskaya Pravda* wrote on 23 June 1941:

> Dawn and morning were sunny. And the city, which had been waiting for a warm summer day for a long time, gave itself up to the festive bustle of Sunday. Crowds of people flowed through the streets and avenues. Their way lay to the train stations and parks, there, outside the city, to the seashore and rivers, to the coolness of forests and the expanse of fields. Our beloved city is always beautiful and doubly good on such a clear day, with its liveliness, the flashing of sails over the water surface, the splash of oars on rivers and canals, music that does not cease over

THEY'LL BE HERE SOON!

gardens and parks, the fullness of rest that only people who enjoy all the benefits of freedom know. And suddenly, a vile attack by the Germans! But the news was not unexpected. Our people are ready for any eventuality. And even this 'accident', for all its enormity, had historical analogies. It is not the first time the Russian people have met with enemies!

On 24 June, the first summary of the Red Army command was published in Soviet newspapers:

> During the day, the enemy sought to develop an offensive along the entire front from the Baltic to the Black Sea, directing its main efforts in the direction of the cities: Shyaulyai, Kaunas, Grodno, Volodymyr-Volynskyi, Rava-Ruska and Brody. But he had no success. All enemy attacks in the direction of the cities of Volodymyr-Volynskyi and Brody were repulsed with heavy losses for him. In the direction of the cities of Shyaulyai and Rava-Ruska, the enemy, wedged into our territory in the morning, was defeated and thrown back over the state border by counter-attacks of our troops in the afternoon, while 300 enemy tanks were destroyed by our artillery fire in the direction of the city of Shyaulyai ...

Deceived by many years of Stalinist propaganda, the residents of Leningrad were confident of an early victory. From day to day they were expecting reports about how the Red Army had entered the territory of the Third Reich and was moving towards Warsaw and Konigsberg. Soviet citizens had no doubt that battleships and cruisers of the Soviet Baltic Fleet were already sailing into enemy waters: to Danzig, Stettin and rapidly destroying the Nazi fleet.

In June 1941, none of the Soviet citizens could even think that German troops could reach Leningrad. However, the deceitful Stalinist leadership nevertheless cautiously prepared city residents for Luftwaffe air attacks. Recent publications in newspapers about the bombing of Warsaw, Rotterdam and London by the Germans encouraged citizens to take this threat very seriously. The militarised Soviet society had long been ready for a possible war and obediently fulfilled all the instructions of the Soviet authorities. Exercises were held regularly in residential areas and factories, and training air alarms were announced.

Leningradskaya Pravda wrote:

> This is an ordinary Leningrad apartment block. It faces Zhelyabova Street. And ordinary people live in this apartment block – doctors and nurses, engineers and accountants, families of commanders

and Red Army men. Today in this apartment block, as in thousands of others, outwardly everything is the same as yesterday. Children are playing in the yard, the sounds of the radio are coming from the open windows, and housewives are peacefully talking at the porch. There is only one difference between today and yesterday. It has become calmer, more serious, stricter in this apartment block, where a thousand Soviet citizens live.

The apartment block is ready for defence. Even from the street you can see the following inscriptions:

'Air-raid shelter',
'Headquarters',
'Medical aid point',
'Public order guard post'.

Before the war, these inscriptions would have been considered conditional. The apartment block has long been equipped with a spacious air-raid shelter. Hundreds of people have already visited it during training air alerts. And everything has been prepared at the medical centre for a long time in case of an enemy air attack.

However, despite the belligerence and 'seriousness', almost none of the Soviet citizens believed that air-raid shelters would have to be used for their intended purpose. For many years, Soviet propaganda had inspired Leningrad residents that 'Stalin's Falcons' and Soviet anti-aircraft gunners would not allow an insidious enemy into the Leningrad sky! The war would only go on in enemy territory!

Meanwhile, the real situation at the front continued to deteriorate rapidly. Stalin's Red Army, the largest in the world in terms of the number of soldiers, already at the beginning of the war began to need additional human resources. An urgent mobilisation of the male population was announced. On 27 June, the *Leningradskaya Pravda* published a report from Tikhvin, a town 170km east of Leningrad. The correspondent wrote:

> On the day of sending those mobilised to the Red Army, a vegetable grower, a participant in the battles with the Finns, an order-bearer, Comrade Kuzmin spoke at a rally in the kolkhoz [collective farm] 'Red Way'. On behalf of the soldiers leaving for the front, he said:

> 'We are going to defend the Homeland from the invasion of enemies. We will selflessly fight for the motherland.'

THEY'LL BE HERE SOON!

> Comrade Kuzmin called on all kolkhozniks [members of the collective farm] to work hard, strengthen the military power of the country.

The vegetable grower Kuzmin, as well as his listeners – residents of the forest and swampy region stretching to the south-east of Lake Ladoga, certainly could not have thought that the enemies would be there in just four months, and Tikhvin itself would have to be protected from the invasion of the Germans ...

After reading the latest newspaper on 28 June, the residents of Leningrad were once again convinced about the imminent victory of the Red Army. On the second page of *Leningradskaya Pravda* there was a pretentious headline: 'The enemy could not bear the all-crushing blow'. Further, in the same cheerful propaganda style, it was written:

> For over two hours the Germans attacked the positions, but the Red Army company calmly repelled their assault. The ranks of the enemy thinned, the forces began to weaken.
>
> – Go ahead! For Stalin, for the Motherland! The company commander shouted and was the first to rush at the enemy with a rifle at the ready. Following the commander, the fighters rose up in an all-crushing avalanche. Bayonets flashed. Dozens of grenades exploded among the enemies. The Germans faltered, could not bear the bayonet strike of Red Army men.
>
> The outcome of the battle was decided by a bold and decisive manoeuvre of Comrade Gordienko's platoon. Entering the enemy's rear, Soviet soldiers cut off his escape route. The Germans threw down their weapons and surrendered. The state border was again in the hands of Red Army men.

In the following days, the militant tone of *Leningradskaya Pravda* did not change. On 29 June, an article titled 'Hitler's Finnish henchmen will get what they deserve' stated:

> The Soviet Union has long endured unheard of provocations by the reactionary, fascist government of Finland and the military on which it relies. But the long patience of the Soviet people is coming to an end. It's time to teach the arrogant executioners of the Finnish people a lesson. The Finnish military – Hitler's hired agents – already know from their own experience what a cruel and bitter fate will befall those who encroach on the Soviet borders, on the city of Lenin. The new lesson that the arrogant Hitler's

henchmen will receive will be a hundred times more convincing. Hitler's vassals of Finland will not recover from this lesson. The Red Army will forever ensure the safety of Leningrad with all the power of its weapons.

However, the victorious mood in the Soviet mass media suddenly stopped on 3 July. It was on this day that Soviet citizens heard on the radio the half-dead and tragic voice of Joseph Stalin: 'Brothers and sisters. I am addressing you …'. The bloody dictator, who had exterminated millions of his citizens, had to admit the collapse of the Red Army. On that black day, for the first time, Stalin asked his people to protect him and the Red Empire he had created from the Germans.

The Wehrmacht[3] offensive is going according to plan

According to the plan of Operation Barbarossa, Army Group North under Generalfeldmarschall Wilhelm Ritter von Leeb was supposed to liberate the Baltic coast from the Red Army, destroy the Soviet Baltic Fleet, capture Leningrad and connect with the Finnish army. The German 18th Army was to advance along the Tilsit–Riga highway and further on the cities of Tallinn and Pskov, and the 16th Army was to advance through the city of Daugavpils in the direction of Lake Ilmen and the city of Novgorod. The main strike force of Generalfeldmarschall von Leeb was Panzer Group 4, which included the XXXXI Army Corps (mot.) under General der Panzertruppen Georg-Hans Reinhardt and LVI Army Corps (mot.) under General der Infanterie Erich von Manstein.

At the initial stage of the invasion of the USSR, the Wehrmacht offensive developed according to plan. On the morning of 26 June 1941, General von Manstein's tanks captured bridges over the Western Dvina River near Daugavpils. The next day, the first navy base of the Soviet Baltic Fleet, Liepaya and Ventspils, fell. On 4 July, just twelve days after the start of the invasion, the Military Council of the Northern Front received a directive from Stalin on preparing defences on the approaches to Leningrad: 'In connection with the clear threat of an enemy breakthrough in the Ostrov–Pskov area, immediately take the line of defence on the towns of Narva, Luga, Staraya Russa, Borovichi …' The next day, People's Commissar (Minister) of the Navy

---

3. In this and other books by the authors, the German term 'Wehrmacht' is often used as a synonym for 'German Army' (land forces).

THEY'LL BE HERE SOON!

Admiral Nikolai Kuznetsov issued an order on measures to create the defences of the city of Leningrad from Lake Ladoga. According to the order, it was necessary to immediately begin deploying the Ladoga Military Flotilla and prepare for the creation of Military Flotilla on Lake Onega.[4]

However, people in Leningrad were still unaware of the impending danger. Sovinformburo[5] reports hid the true state of things on the fronts. The population of Leningrad was informed mainly about minor details of the war. Soviet propaganda continued to focus on the 'reports' about a mass surrender of the Germans. At the beginning of July 1941, the huge city was still living its usual life. The disturbing attributes of the war included a night blackout, and emotional scenes at Leningrad train stations, where thousands of women saw off trains with men mobilised to the front every day. But at the same time that many of the people of Leningrad were leaving for the front, Soviet sailors and soldiers fleeing from the German offensive had already begun to arrive from there. Deserters could easily be distinguished from the crowd of citizens by their slovenly appearance and frightened faces. They left their units in a panic, and delivered the latest, and most importantly, truthful information to Leningrad. Numerous deserters everywhere told the surprised people of Leningrad about the complete collapse of the Soviet defence, the chaotic retreat, the abandonment of the navy bases, and finally, about the incredible power of the Wehrmacht. But, most importantly, they brought the terrible news that the Germans would be here soon!

The scale of panic at the front turned out to be so great that the top military leadership of the USSR was forced to react to the situation and take urgent measures to combat desertion from the Red Army and Red Fleet. Admiral Nikolai Kuznetsov wrote in an order of 9 July 1941:

> There are cases when whole groups of Red Fleet men and even some commanders independently 'evacuate' from the front line, sometimes seizing cars, in which they freely and uncontrollably come directly to Leningrad, where they spread false, obviously provocative rumours with impunity. Some 'commanders' even change into the uniform of ordinary sailors, destroying personal documents.[6]

---

4. TSAMO RF. Foundation 3. Inventory 11556. Case 1. Sheet 71.
5. Sovinformburo (Soviet Information Bureau) – the main information and propaganda agency of the Soviet Union during the war.
6. TSVMA. Foundation 216. Case 12490. Sheet 246.

AIR BATTLE FOR LENINGRAD, 1941–1944

There were though reasons for panic. On 10 July, German tank divisions, having broken through the front south of Pskov city, rushed to the town of Luga. They had only 180–200km to drive to Leningrad. With such a rapid pace of attack, which Army Group North took from the beginning of the invasion, it took only nine to ten days to reach Leningrad.

Luftwaffe strategic intelligence

Since the beginning of the German invasion of the USSR, German reconnaissance planes had been appearing regularly in the Army Group North offensive zone. They flew to Tallinn, Kronstadt, Leningrad and Lake Ladoga. Most of these missions were carried out by crews from 2./Aufkl. Gr.Ob.d.L. (2nd Squadron Separate Long-range Reconnaissance Air Group Commander-in-Chief of the Luftwaffe) under the command of Oberst Theodor Rowehl. This unit was engaged in strategic intelligence and carried out particularly important missions, the results of which were reported directly to the Oberkommando der Luftwaffe (OKL), Abwehr and personally to the Führer. Some of the reconnaissance flights in the Leningrad area and its environs were carried out by another German aerial reconnaissance unit, 2 (F)./Ob.d.L. Hauptmann Klaus Pritzel, which was based at Insterburg airfield in East Prussia.

Unteroffizier Max Lagoda, who served as a radio operator in a reconnaissance aircraft flown by Oberleutnant Walter Froschauer, recalled:

> On 21.06.1941, we learned that war with Russia was beginning! In the morning, the first planes flew to the east. Our crew went on a mission on the second day. We were well prepared, and everyone knew their job. The order read: to control the movement of ships to the Baltic Sea from islands Ézel and Dago to Reval (Tallinn), as well as to photograph all transport vessels. The first flight took place over Reval. Part of the Soviet Baltic Fleet was located here in the port … We photographed the harbour and the city. Then we continued the flight at an altitude of 7,800 metres above the airfields surrounding the Naval Base.[7]

---

7. Lagoda, M., *Ein Blick in die Vergangenheit. Kriegsernnerungen eines Fernaufklarers aus Russland und dem Orient*, Helios, 2011, p.36.

THEY'LL BE HERE SOON!

The first flight of Lagoda and his crew to Eastern Front lasted 245 minutes. At the same time, almost throughout the flight, due to the high altitude, the pilots used oxygen masks.

To do their job and avoid encounters with Soviet air defence fighters, German reconnaissance planes flew mainly at high altitude and above the clouds. However, this was not always possible. On 29 June 1941, 2 (F)./Ob.d.L. suffered the first combat loss on the Eastern Front when a Ju 88 A-5 flown by Leutnant Dietrich Albrecht made a long-range flight to the Lake Ladoga area. Flight engineer Unteroffizier Otto Gustaw reported by radio to his base that the plane had been intercepted by a Russian fighter, and all the crew members had been seriously injured. It should be noted that radio conversations during the execution of the reconnaissance mission were prohibited. It was permitted to transmit messages in plain text only in emergency situations. The Ju 88 was able to fly to East Prussia, but crashed during an emergency landing. The entire crew was killed and soon the German pilots were buried with military honours at the military cemetery in Insterburg.

On 6 July, 2 (F)./Ob.d.L. suffered a second loss. On this day, the Ju 88 D-2 'VB+KM', flown by Leutnant Karl Neelmeier, was to take photographs of Leningrad. Navigator crew commander Leutnant Ditrich Willms recalled:

> At an altitude of 8,000 metres, the plane flew up to the city on the Neva. It was midnight sun, and aerial reconnaissance was conducted for eighteen hours a day. When Kronstadt Bay appeared on the left, the winding ribbon of the Neva River and hundreds of houses of the three-million city appeared in front, our VB+KM plane descended and 'opened the eyes' of its photo cameras.

Lieutenant Willms began service in Aufkl.Gr.Ob.d.L. at the end of the 1930s. He flew as a navigator and crew commander in an unmarked Do 215 over France, Great Britain, Yugoslavia, and later over the Soviet Union. On 12 June 1941, Willms attended a secret meeting held at Luftflotte 1 headquarters. There the pilot was informed about the imminent outbreak of war against the USSR and the tasks of strategic intelligence. Leutnant Willms took this message with optimism, as it seemed to legalise his position. Now, if his reconnaissance aircraft was shot down over the enemy's rear, he would become not a spy and a saboteur, but a serviceman participating in combat operations. On the eve of Operation Barbarossa, Leutnant Willms and his crew underwent retraining on the new reconnaissance aircraft Ju 88 D-2, which until recently was an experimental model.

AIR BATTLE FOR LENINGRAD, 1941–1944

A decision to descend to an altitude of 4,000–5,000m was a fatal mistake for Leutnant Neelmeier, an experienced pilot. As a result of this manoeuvre, before the plane had time to start its photography, a Soviet fighter appeared nearby. Leutnant Willms described the subsequent events as follows:

> There's a fighter behind, – navigator Leutnant Karl Neelmeier reported.
> Surprised! This is truly terrible! I replied mockingly.
> 'He's coming up to meet us, Mr Leutnant! It's not 'Rat'[8] at all. – someone shouted from behind.
> As soon as the flight engineer and navigator managed to take their places at the machine guns, the Soviet aircraft rushed to attack from the direction of the sun. It was a Yak-1 fighter of the latest modification. The first burst from the rapid-firing cannon hit the target, oxygen cylinders shattered with a whoosh, the plane was engulfed in flames.[9]

In fact, the attacking fighter was not the latest Yak-1, but a MiG-3 of Senior Lieutenant Dmitry Titorenko from the 19th Fighter Aviation Regiment Air Defence. What Leutnant Willms took to be firing from a cannon was apparently shots from a large-calibre 12.7mm BS machine gun, since the MiG-3 fighter did not have cannon armament.

After the shelling, the Ju 88 was severely damaged and began to fall. Leutnant Willms ordered all crew members to jump with parachutes. Soon he himself was slowly descending by parachute on the enemy city. The German pilot understood that soon he would inevitably fall into the hands of the 'enemy who knows no mercy'. It even crossed his mind that the best outcome was to shoot himself before he landed on enemy territory! But the desire to live won out, and after a couple of hours Leutnant Willms was interrogated at the Soviet headquarters. Leutnant Neelmeier saved his own life in the same way. The other two crew members were unable to leave the burning plane and died. MiG-3 pilot Senior Lieutenant Dmitry Titorenko, who shot down a German reconnaissance aircraft, observed the details of the death of one of the German pilots. He claimed that one of the crew members opened the parachute prematurely, and as a result the slings caught on the tail and carried him away with the falling plane.

---

8. 'Rat' – nickname of the Soviet fighter I-16.
9. Khazanov D.B., *The Battle for the Sky, 1941: from the Dnieper to the Gulf of Finland*, Moscow: Yauza, 2007. p.124.

THEY'LL BE HERE SOON!

The next day, 7 July 1941, Ju 88 D-2 'VB+KL' flew to Leningrad, flight engineer Unteroffizier Max Lagoda part of the crew. The crew was tasked to photograph Leningrad, Kronstadt navy base and all the Soviet airfields in the area. Before the flight, the pilots were seized with anxiety, as they were afraid to meet the sad 'military fate' of the previous crew. The flight turned out to be very dangerous. In the Kronstadt area, dozens of anti-aircraft guns opened fire and the aircraft barely escaped being hit. Unteroffizier Lagoda recalled: 'We were only there for twenty minutes, but they seemed like an eternity.' However, with every minute spent in Soviet airspace, the danger continued to grow. Soon, the Ju 88 was attacked by several MiG-3s at once. Fortunately, the Soviet fighters were spotted in time by navigator Manfred Pohl, after which the reconnaissance aircraft began to perform evasive manoeuvres. To break away from the Soviet fighters, the crew commander Oberleutnant Walter Froschauer performed a sharp right turn, then began to dive. At the same time, the crew of the Ju 88 fired at the MiG-3s with their on-board machine guns. After that, some of the Soviet interceptors fell back, but the remaining fighters continued their pursuit. Then Oberleutnant Froschauer started a sharp dive for the second time. Due to the greater mass and power of the engines, reconnaissance aircraft gained much more speed during a dive than an opponent. Unteroffizier Lagoda recalled: 'The end was very close. I have remembered this moment on the verge of death for the rest of my life.' The fight lasted about twenty minutes. Finally, over the Gulf of Finland, the Ju 88 was able to break away from the Soviet interceptors, but it used up a lot of fuel while manoeuvring. It could no longer return to East Prussia and landed at Helsinki airport in Finland.[10]

According to Soviet information, the reconnaissance aircraft Ju 88 appeared in the area of the town of Petergof at 12.00. First, it was intercepted by MiG-3s patrolling in the air from the 7th Fighter Aviation Corps Air Defence (7th IAC PVO), which unsuccessfully shot all their ammunition at the target. Then, over the Gulf of Finland, the reconnaissance aircraft was pursued by three MiG-3s from the 19th Fighter Aviation Regiment Air Defence (19th IAP PVO). Soviet fighters chased the Ju 88 to Fort Grey Horse,[11] after which the German broke away from the pursuers and went to the north-west.

---

10. Lagoda, M., *Ein Blick in die Vergangenheit. Kriegsernnerungen eines Fernaufklarers aus Russland und dem Orient*, Helios, 2011, pp.36–39.
11. Fort Grey Horse is part of Peter the Great's Naval Fortress, a complex of coastal defences built to protect the coast and waters of the Baltic Sea. Fort Grey Horse was built in 1911 on Cape Grey Horse near the village of Chyornaya Lakhta.

AIR BATTLE FOR LENINGRAD, 1941–1944

Hornets' nest of Soviet fighters

The episodes described above showed how dangerous it was to fly over Leningrad and Kronstadt in the early days of the war. At the beginning of July 1941, the 7th Fighter Aviation Corps Air Defence (7th IAC PVO), commanded by Colonel Stepan Danilov, included ten fighter aviation regiments, which were based at Gorskaya, Levashovo, Uglovo, Manushkino, Lezya, Schum, Pushkin, Gorelovo, Ropsha, Vitino, Sivoricy and Siverskaya. There were 408 fighters in the regiments, including 260 I-16s, 101 MiG-3s and 47 I-153s. Thus, there was a real 'hornets' nest' of Soviet fighters in the vicinity of Leningrad! These forces were quite enough to fight single reconnaissance aircraft and repel daytime bomber raids, but the Germans did not undertake any air attacks against Leningrad at the beginning of the war.

By mid-July 1941, the situation in this area began to change dramatically. The front line was rapidly approaching the city, and German bombers began to appear frequently in the Leningrad area. On 12 July, 7th IAC PVO fighters conducted five air battles and reported four downed German aircraft. For example, at 11.30, Lieutenant Antonov's MiG-3 from the 19th Fighter Aviation Regiment Air Defence (19th IAP PVO) in the area of the city of Krasnogvardeysk (now Gatchina) rammed a Ju 88 at an altitude of 7,600m and brought it down. After that, the Soviet fighter returned safely to its airfield. An I-16 from the 157th Fighter Aviation Regiment Air Defence (157th IAP PVO) piloted by Lieutenant Nazarova attacked a Ju 88 at low level near Torfyanaya railway station. According to the Soviet pilot, the Germans were afraid of him and began a sharp U-turn, after which the enemy bomber crashed into a telegraph pole. The third Ju 88 was shot down near Lyuban railway station by a pair of MiG-3s flown by Captain Andreev and Lieutenant Budnikov from the 44th Fighter Aviation Regiment Air Defence (44th IAP PVO). Another downed Ju 88 was recorded on the combat account of Lieutenant Aksenov from the 157th IAP PVO. Lieutenant Aksenov in his I-16 attacked German bombers bombing Babino railway station. The next day, pilots of the 7th IAC PVO reported two downed Bf 110s near the town of Narva and one Finnish Bristol Blenheim near Lake Svirsky.

However, these turned out to be the last days when 'Stalin's Falcons' operated in comfortable conditions around Leningrad. On 14 July, German bombers raided Sivoricy airfield, 35km south of Leningrad. Several Soviet aircraft were destroyed and two pilots were killed. On 16 July, for the first time the 7th IAC PVO fighters had to launch assault strikes on ground targets, advanced German units approaching Leningrad. Such missions resulted in numerous losses of Russian fighters. They were completely devoid of armour, and, therefore, were very vulnerable to fire from the ground.

THEY'LL BE HERE SOON!

7th IAC PVO against Zerstörers

In the period from 15 to 20 July, the 7th IAC PVO fighters conducted fifteen air battles and reported eleven downed aircraft (seven Bf 110s, three Ju 88s and one Bf 109). For example, on 20 July at 10.00 twenty Zerstörers ('destroyers') from ZG 26 raided the city of Krasnogvardeysk. The main targets were the railway station and the nearby airfield. When ground-attack Bf 110s finished bombing and shelling ground targets, they turned west to return to their airfields. At that moment, the German planes were attacked by four MiG-3s from the 44th Fighter Aviation Regiment Air Defence (44th IAP PVO). Lieutenant Golovin, piloting the MiG-3, shot down one Zerstörer with a sudden attack, after which the rest of the German aircraft formed a defensive circle and began to withdraw gradually to their territory. At the same time, Lieutenants Pakhomov and Antonov from the 19th Fighter Aviation Regiment Air Defence (19th IAP PVO) attacked another group of Zerstörers consisting of three Bf 110s. Two of them switched to low-level flight, while the third began a sharp climb. Lieutenants Pakhomov and Antonov went in pursuit of the third Bf 110. Approaching it, MiG-3s fired simultaneously from two sides. After that, the Bf 110 began to fall randomly, and two crew members jumped out with parachutes.[12] According to German data, two Zerstörers were indeed shot down by Russian fighters near the city of Krasnogvardeysk: Bf 110 E-2 W.Nr. 2379 '3U+LH' of 1./ZG 26 and Bf 110 W.Nr. 4094 '3U+KH' of 9./ZG 26. The crew of Unteroffizier W. Hahn was killed, and the crew of Unteroffizier H. Vogelsang was recorded as missing.

The 7th IAC PVO's own losses during these six days amounted to nine fighters (five I-16s, two MiG-3s and two LaGG-3s). In addition, the commander of the 7th Fighter Aviation Regiment Air Defence (7th IAP) Major Sinev was killed. After take-off, his MiG-3 crashed into a telegraph pole, apparently due to a technical malfunction. Fighters of this type were equipped with a very poorly manufactured engine, which often unexpectedly lost power. During take-off, such a malfunction often led to MiG-3s accidents.

On the morning of 21 July, a group of Bf 110 from ZG 26 raided Gorelovo railway station and a nearby airfield. Since the target was in the immediate vicinity of Leningrad (10km from the Leningrad port of Torgovyi), this event caused a big stir in the city. Many high-ranking Soviet commanders thought that the long-awaited Leningrad bombing attack had begun. Therefore, eighty-seven Soviet fighters were scrambled to intercept German aircraft. The first group of eight MiG-3s from the 19th IAP PVO entered the battle at 04.38. This happened at a time when German planes were already preparing to attack the

---

12. TSAMO RF. Foundation 20506. Inventory 1. Case 40. Sheets 21-25.

selected targets. However, the Soviet pilots had no success. Then six slow I-153 biplanes went on the attack, but the Bf 110s easily broke away from them. After dropping their bombs, the Zerstörers group set off on a south-westerly course. Thus, the large-scale use of Soviet fighters controlled by poorly trained pilots ended in complete failure. Most of 'Stalin's Falcons' could not even detect a target, and only interfered with each other in the air. Only the pilots of the 44th IAP PVO reported that they caught up with the enemy in the Lake Samro area (120km south-west of Leningrad) and shot down four Bf 110s there. In fact, only one Bf 110 E-2 W.Nr. 3892 '3U+GL' of 3./ZG 26 was shot down by Soviet fighters. The crew of the German plane was killed.

During the implementation of Operation Barbarossa, Bf 110 twin-engined heavy fighters were usually used in the ground attack role. They attacked cars, trains, railway stations, airfields, artillery positions and crossings, dropping bombs on them and firing cannon and machine guns. The ZG 26 'Horst Wessel' used a new modification of the Bf 110 E, which was equipped with two Daimler-Benz DB 601 N engines. These Zerstörers could carry 1,200kg of bombs and a droppable external fuel tank with a capacity of 300 litres. In addition, the ground-attack Bf 110 E had reinforced armour protection. The Zerstörers' attack was not accompanied by the eerie howling of sirens and a dive at an angle of almost 90 degrees. Therefore, Zerstörers did not produce such a stunning audio-visual effect as the Ju 87 dive bombers. However, the lack of sound and visual special effects did not prevent the Bf 110 E from playing a big role in the successes of the German troops.

The ineffectiveness of the actions of the 7th Fighter Aviation Corps Air Defence (7th IAC PVO) can easily be explained by the extreme haste in the formation of this aviation unit. Stalin's ambitious plans for the multiple growth of Soviet fighter units in 1940 and 1941 completely failed. To somehow ease the anger of the cruel 'Red Tsar', the leadership of the Red Army Air Force was forced to engage in falsifying data and compiling bravura reports for Stalin. An attempt to re-equip Soviet Fighter Aviation with fighters of the 'new type' (Yak-1, LaGG-3 and MiG-3) also failed miserably.[13] Thus, the 7th IAC PVO hastily formed on 19 July 1941, that is, three days before the start of the war, had a bizarre collection of motley Soviet fighters of the 'old type' (I-16 and I-153) and 'new type' (MiG-3). The qualifications of the 'Stalin's Falcons' flying these fighters were also extremely low. The fact is that the programme of accelerated

---

13. A detailed review of the process of creating Soviet fighters of the 'new type' (Yak-1, LaGG-3 and MiG-3) can be found in the book: *Zubov, Dmitry Stalin's Falcons: Exposing the Myth of Soviet Aerial Superiority over the Luftwaffe in WW2*, Barnsley, UK: Air World/Pen & Sword, 2023.

training of tens of thousands of new Soviet pilots, begun shortly before the start of the war, also failed. As a result of Stalin's incompetent interference in the leadership of the Soviet Air Force, by the beginning of 1941, beginners prevailed among the pilots of Soviet fighters, who at best had experience of piloting UT-2 trainer aircraft for only a few hours.

It should be explained to readers that the artificially inflated 7th IAC PVO, equipped with poorly designed and poorly manufactured fighters, was not intended by Stalin for defence at all. The 'Red Tsar', who dreamed of the domination of the communist regime in Europe, had completely different plans for 1941.

By the beginning of August 1941, the consequences of the total failure of Soviet Fighter Aviation tactics and development strategy began to clearly manifest themselves throughout the vast Eastern Front. The 7th IAC PVO was no exception. The number of fighters in this aviation corps had almost halved in a month of combat operations and amounted to only 213 units at the beginning of August 1941. In the future, due to breakdowns, accidents and huge losses, the combat capabilities of the 7th IAC PVO continued to steadily decline.

And how did the great Stalin allow all this?

The residents of Leningrad, meanwhile, were preparing for defence. Now no one in the city had any doubt that the enemy was at the gate. It was no longer fully fledged troops that were sent to the front, but improvised units assembled from poorly dressed and almost unarmed men of different ages. For example, on 10 July 1941, the 'soldiers' of the 1st Kirov Division of the People's Militia were sent to the Luga defensive line.[14] Subsequently, nine more similar 'Divisions', formed in an incredible hurry, were sent after them to certain death. These units, resembling the German Volkssturm of the 1945 model, had a very motley composition. Most of the 'soldiers' of the Divisions of the People's Militia naturally consisted of two groups of the population who were not drafted into the regular army because of their age: young people who picked up a rifle for the first time and older people who had experience of participating in the Russian Civil War of 1918–22. Among them were both the physically strong and people who had poor health. Hastily trained and poorly

---

14. Luga defensive line is a system of Soviet fortifications with a length of about 300m, built in June–August 1941 in the Leningrad region. It continued from Narva Bay, along the rivers Luga, Mshaga and Shelon to Lake Ilmen. The main goal of the Luga defensive line was to create obstacles for the breakthrough of the troops of the German Army Group North to the north-east in the direction of Leningrad.

armed, these 'soldiers' had to literally use their bodies to plug numerous gaps in the crumbling Soviet defence.

Other types of improvised military units were also hastily created. Brigades of Naval Infantry numbering 80,000 people were formed from the personnel of ships, naval units and cadets of military schools. Unlike the 'soldiers' of Divisions of the People's Militia, these servicemen at least had minimal military service experience. However, there is no doubt that the worst sailors were sent to such units, and the most trained and prepared were left on ships.

Simultaneous with measures to replenish military units, almost half a million residents of Leningrad, mainly women, teenagers and the elderly, were sent to build defensive obstacles on the outskirts of the city. At the factories, workers who had not yet been sent to the front or evacuated from their factories to the Urals and Siberia manufactured reinforced concrete pillboxes and concrete Dragon's teeth anti-tank obstacles. These means of defence were transported and hastily installed in the defensive obstacle strip around the city.[15]

Many residents of Leningrad still had newspaper issues from the first days of the war with their militant and pretentious headlines. Now, three weeks later, the reality had changed beyond recognition. Most people were depressed. In the minds of most residents, who until recently were firmly convinced of the wisdom of Stalin, seditious questions involuntarily began to arise. Where did our 'invincible Red Army' go? How did the vile Nazis manage to reach Leningrad so quickly? And how did great Stalin allow all this?! Euphoria and confidence in victory were quickly replaced by fear, panic, and complete disappointment in his army and the leadership of the country. Many citizens became hostile to Soviet soldiers and pilots, accusing them of cowardice and inability to defend their country.

The 'awl' in Hitler's ass

In mid-July 1941, it seemed to many commanders of the escaping Red Army that the Germans would soon reach Moscow and Leningrad, after which they would continue to move towards the Ural Mountains. But at that moment, the Wehrmacht offensive suddenly slowed down on all fronts. Fortunately for the defeated 'Great Commander' Stalin another 'Great Commander' – Hitler – rudely intervened in the management of the German troops! The fact is that after the first breakthrough deep into the Soviet Union, the troops of Army Group North, by order of Führer, were sent in three divergent directions – to the city

---

15. Pavlov, D.V., *Leningrad is Under Siege*, Leningrad, Lenizdat, 1985, pp.10–11.

THEY'LL BE HERE SOON!

of Tallinn, the town of Luga and the Valdai Hills. Instead of rapidly advancing towards the main strategic goals, as required by the Blitzkrieg strategy, Hitler constantly sent his troops on detours into deep forests and wastelands to cover the flanks from non-existent threats. This led to numerous delays and downtime, the dispersal of forces over vast territories and delayed decisive success. As a result of the 'wise leadership' of the Führer, the German offensive slowed down, and the Soviets were able to organise a new line of defence 12–130km from Leningrad. A similar situation developed in the offensive zone of Army Group South.

After that, Hitler made another mistake. He decided to temporarily suspend the offensive against the main target of Operation Barbarossa, Moscow, and transfer part of the troops from the central direction to the north and south. After long fruitless discussions with his generals and field marshals, on 30 July Hitler signed Directive No. 34. According to it, XXXXI Army Corps (mot.) General der Panzertruppen, commanded by Georg-Hans Reinhardt, and VIII. Fliegerkorps, under Generalmajor Wolfram von Richthofen, were temporarily transferred to Army Group North. Generalfeldmarschall Wilhelm Ritter von Leeb was ordered to surround Leningrad within a month and a half, link up with the Finnish army and destroy the Soviet Baltic Fleet.

On 8 August 1941, after resting and regrouping, the German 18th Army and Panzer Group 4 launched a decisive offensive. But instead of a concentric movement towards the main goal, the offensive was again conducted in divergent directions – to the cities of Narva, Krasnogvardeysk and Novgorod. At the same time, the Soviet troops, contrary to the expectations of the Germans, put up fierce resistance along the entire front. As a result, instead of the planned Blitzkrieg, they progressed slowly at only about 2–2.5km per day. On 14 August, the Germans reached the Krasnogvardeysk–Kingisepp railway. Two days later they captured Volosovo railway station (55km south-west of Leningrad), and on 17 August the towns of Narva and Kingisepp were captured. At the same time, on the right flank of the offensive, the German I Army Corps broke into the city of Novgorod and captured the first bridgehead on the eastern bank of the river Volkhov.

During this period, the Luftwaffe mainly operated on the right flank of the offensive, in the Lake Ilmen area. Stukas from StG 2 and Zerstörers from ZG 26 attacked Soviet troops near the city of Novgorod and the town of Staraya Russa.

Soon, the fumes from the fires on the battlefields began to reach the suburbs of Leningrad. The city was filled with a huge number of refugees from the Soviet territory captured by the Germans. It was no longer possible to hide the true state of affairs at the front from the Leningrad population.

AIR BATTLE FOR LENINGRAD, 1941–1944

The enemy is at the gate!

Stalin entrusted the leadership of the Leningrad defence to the First Secretary of the Leningrad Regional Committee of the Communist Party, Andrei Zhdanov. He was one of the closest servants of the 'Red Dictator', distinguished by his absolute devotion to Stalin. He was ready to carry out any order of the Red Tsar, regardless of any victims. On 20 August 1941, Zhdanov made a speech at a meeting of Bolshevik bosses and senior officials of Leningrad. He honestly admitted that the situation was critical and there might be street battles in the city soon. In this regard, the entire population should be involved in defensive work, including young people and teenagers. At the end of his speech, Zhdanov addressed those present with an alarming statement: 'The enemy is at the gate. The question is about life and death.'[16] Thus, Stalin's faithful servant hinted that it was necessary to either win or die in Leningrad. Of course, when talking about death, he did not mean himself, but meant his subordinates and ordinary residents of the city!

On the morning of 21 August 1941, an appeal of the heads of the executive and legislative authorities of Leningrad and Leningrad Region was published in newspapers and also pasted up in the form of leaflets throughout the city. Two months after promising to quickly defeat the insidious enemy, the authorities honestly admitted to the population that the situation was catastrophic. The proclamation stated:

> An immediate threat of an attack by German troops is hanging over our native and beloved city. The enemy is trying to infiltrate Leningrad. He wants to destroy our homes, seize factories and plants, plunder the national heritage, flood the streets and squares with the blood of innocent victims, abuse the civilian population, enslave the free sons of our Motherland ... Let's stand up as one to defend our city, our hearths, our families, our honour and freedom.[17]

The version that the goal of the Wehrmacht offensive was precisely the robbery of the Soviet Union and all its inhabitants was invented by Stalin in August 1941. In the course of an extensive propaganda campaign, it was methodically instilled into Soviet citizens that the Germans wanted to steal their land, factories, furniture, shoes, outerwear and even underpants with socks. This

---

16. Pavlov, D.V., *Leningrad is Under Siege*, Leningrad: Lenizdat, 1985, pp.21–22.
17. K. Voroshilov, A. Zhdanov, P. Popkov, *Krasnaya Zvezda*, No. 196, 12 August 1941.

primitive propaganda ploy was targeted at those who were waiting for the arrival of the Germans with joy (there were quite a few of them) and hoped for improvements in life after the fall of the Bolsheviks. Stalin effectively told people from whom the Soviets had already stolen absolutely everything: do not hope for a good life under the Germans, Hitler will take off your last piece of underwear and take it away!

Meanwhile, the Germans on both sides bypassed the heavily fortified town of Luga. They were advancing in two directions at once: directly to Leningrad, as well as to the north-east to Lake Ladoga. On 21 August 1941, Chudovo railway station was occupied and the Moscow–Leningrad railway was cut. On 30 August, with the continuous support of German aviation, XXXIX Army Corps (mot.) under General der Panzertruppen Rudolf Schmidt reached Mga railway station. From that moment, the last connection of Leningrad by rail with the main part of the Soviet Union was lost. On the same day, the advanced German units reached the river Neva near the village of Ivanovskoye. The leadership of the Leningrad defence was completely unprepared for such a rapid development of events.

On the evening of 30 August, a phone call was made on a regular city telephone line to the Smolny Institute building (office of the Bolshevik Party of Leningrad). It was a young girl calling. She said that German troops were on the southern bank of the Neva, 20km from Leningrad. The headquarters staff of the newly created Leningrad Front considered this message fake news and a manifestation of panic. However, they did not completely ignore it. To verify the information, two Ladoga Military Flotilla vessels, submarine chasers *MO-202* and *MO-174*, were sent to the Ivanovskoye area. When these ships reached the mouth of the River Tosna, guns, mortars and machine guns were fired at them from the southern shore. Hit at point-blank range, the submarine chasers sank with almost the entire crews.[18] After that, it became clear to the Soviet commanders at the headquarters of the Leningrad Front that the girl who called on the phone was telling the truth!

The next day, Ladoga Military Flotilla ships (the gunboat *Selemdzha* and the armoured boats *BK-99* and *BK-100*) opened fire on the shore near Ivanovskoye. Patrols (posts) were set up on the northern bank of the Neva to counter the attempts of the Germans to force the river and penetrate to the northern bank.

The main base of Ladoga Military Flotilla during this period was Shlisselburg, a town fortress located at the head of the Neva, which flows out of the huge Lake Ladoga. By the beginning of September 1941, a lot of passenger,

---

18. Rusakov, Z.G., *Our Sea was Ladoga*, Leningrad: Lenizdat, 1980, p.51.

cargo ships and barges had accumulated in the harbour of Shlisselburg as they did not have time to evacuate inland.

The Germans did not fail to take advantage of this. On the night of 2 September, He 111 bombers from KG 4 raided the town of Shlisselburg. The main targets were Ugolnaya (coal) Pier and the port of Shlisselburg, where there were many different ships. In addition to bombing, some of the German planes dropped parachute Luftmine B (LMB). Soon the German mine weapons began to operate. At 08.37 in Shlisselburg Bay opposite Ugolnaya Pier, a powerful explosion thundered under the boat *R-34*. As a result, it broke in half and sank quickly along with the entire crew. The mine threat brought additional chaos to the port of Shlisselburg, which was seriously damaged by German bombs. Most of the ships began to leave the harbour in a hurry and go to Novaya Ladoga (the port at the mouth of the river Volkhov).

Has the goal been achieved?

At this time, Hitler was rejoicing and was already preparing to celebrate the victory. On the evening of 5 September 1941, he held a meeting at the Wolfsschanze (Wolf's Lair), his top-secret headquarters in East Prussia. One of the participants of the meeting, Chief of the General Staff of the Army High Command (OKH) Generaloberst Franz Halder, wrote in his diary:

> Leningrad. The goal has been achieved. From now on, the area of Leningrad will be a 'secondary theatre of military operations'. The town of Shlisselburg is extremely important. For the complete encirclement of Leningrad along the outer ring (to the Neva), 6–7 divisions will be required. Strong infantry units should be concentrated, if possible, behind the Neva. Encirclement from the east and connection with the Finns. Tanks (Reinhard corps) and aircraft (Luftflotte 1 units) are returning to their former subordination. It is necessary to clear the coast from the enemy. The connection with the Finnish troops should be attempted in the area of the town Lodeynoye Pole.

Well, in the 'achieved goal' itself, that is, in Leningrad, Stalin's envoy Marshal of the Soviet Union Kliment Voroshilov at that time gave all sorts of threatening orders. The poorly educated and simply stupid Marshal demanded from the bleeding army 'concerted actions', 'steadfastness', 'to fight like honest Red Army soldiers'. However, despite a lot of stupid orders, Voroshilov was not able to change the situation around Leningrad for the better.

THEY'LL BE HERE SOON!

'Stalin's Falcons' defend Leningrad

By the beginning of the autumn of 1941, only a faint shadow remained of the once numerous Soviet air forces in the Leningrad area. The 7th Fighter Aviation Corps Air Defence (7th IAC PVO) had ten fighter aviation regiments for air defence, but this grouping looked impressive only on paper. In most of the regiments there five to seven, up to a maximum of ten to twelve combat-ready fighters. The usual army fighter aviation regiments, which were not formally part of the city's air defence forces, were in a similarly deplorable state. For example, the 8th Fighter Aviation Division (8th IAD), which defended the south-eastern approaches to Leningrad, included the 15th Fighter Aviation Regiment (15th IAP), 46th Fighter Aviation Regiment (46th IAP) and 121st Fighter Aviation Regiment (121st IAP). The 46th IAP had just seven LaGG-3 fighters, and the 121st IAP had nine Yak-7UTIs.[19, 20]

The sad combat path of the 8th IAD was typical for Soviet aviation units in 1941. On 22 June, the division was based at the Soviet Kaunas Air Base in Lithuania and had 316 fighters in its composition. But by 4 July, fighter aviation division, under pressure from the Germans, retreated far to the rear, and the number of aircraft in it decreased to twenty-nine! As a result of the huge losses, the 8th IAD completely lost its combat capability and was sent for re-formation on 13 July. This unit returned to the front only at the end of August 1941.

In the autumn, due to a shortage of aircraft, the Soviets began to use their few fighters to carry out a huge number of various missions. They replaced the missing tactical reconnaissance planes and ground-attack aircraft. Although when designing them, Soviet designers formally tried to take into account the requirements of the military to create multi-purpose aircraft of the 'new type' (Yak-1, LaGG-3 and MiG-3), in reality, the new fighters were poorly suited to perform such a variety of missions. In addition, the distraction of fighters from their direct functions led to the fact that 'Stalin's Falcons' no longer had time and energy for aerial combat. Therefore, in early September 1941, air battles of Soviet fighters with enemy aircraft were a very rare event.

For example, on 1 September, at 15.10, a pair of LaGG-3s from the 46th IAP took off on a reconnaissance flight. The pilots then compiled a report: 'The Andreevo–Larionovo road found 20 cars. Railway: Volkhov–Kirishi, Podgorst'e–Kirishi – movement of freight trains. Railway station Tosno is protected by 8–9 Bf 109. They didn't join the battle.' At 18.45, the same pair of LaGG-3s participated in a strike group (four I-16s and three MiG-3s from

---

19. The Yak-7UTI was a 1941 training aircraft hastily converted into a combat fighter.
20. TSAMO RF. Foundation 22020. Inventory 0445249s. Case 0001. Sheet 21–22.

the 7th IAC PVO) for an air attack on Lezya airfield. 'Stalin's Falcons' did not find any enemy aircraft there, but an air battle took place over the airfield with three Bf 109 fighters and Hs 126 tactical reconnaissance aircraft. Russian pilots claimed the destruction of one Bf 109 and one Hs 126. According to German information, the damaged Bf 109 F-4 of 4./JG 52 made an emergency landing on its fuselage on German territory, and Hs 126 B-1 W.Nr. 4007 '4E+FP' of 6.(H)/13 was recorded missing in the area of Sencovo and Kokorevo villages.

On 3 September, MiG-3 fighters fired at a column of German troops on the Elizavetino–Volosovo road and other targets. During the attack, one MiG-3 disintegrated in the air when exiting a dive and the pilot, Senior Lieutenant Pastukhov, parachuted over territory occupied by the Germans. Another MiG-3 was shot down by German anti-aircraft artillery and the pilot, Lieutenant Nikiforov, was killed. In the village of Koncy LaGG-3 Junior Lieutenant Yanishevsky was shot down and killed by a German fighter. Another LaGG-3 crashed while landing at its airfield. In another incident, the engine broke off one Yak-7UTI during take-off. The plane was completely smashed and the pilot was killed. As a result, by the evening, only twelve aircraft remained in the 8th IAD (five Yak-7UTIs, three MiG-3s and four Il-2 ground-attack aircraft[21]).[22]

The Luftwaffe continued to build up its forces in the Leningrad area. Since 5 September, all units of Jagdgeschwader 54 'Grunherz' (JG 54) under Major Hannes Trautloft had relocated to the Siverskaya Air Base, just 67km from the centre of Leningrad. Aircraft from III./JG 27, commanded by Hauptmann Max Dubislav, also flew to Lyuban airfield, 85km south-east of Leningrad, on 6 September. Fighters from II./JG 52, under Hauptmann Erich Woitke, and II./JG 53, commanded by Hauptmann Walter Spies, were also based there.

The first major air battle on the outskirts of Leningrad took place on 6 September 1941. On this day, Luftflotte 1 aircraft attacked the Soviets on several sectors of the front at once. For example, thirty-six Ju 88 A bombers raided the town of Shlisselburg. As a result, the Ladoga Military Flotilla headquarters building was destroyed. Bombs also hit nearby houses, causing numerous civilian casualties.

On Lake Ladoga, German bombers attacked a caravan of seven barges carrying wounded Red Army men and the evacuated population of Shlisselburg and sank three of them. As a result of the bombing, hundreds of people were killed. At the same time, Ju 87s from StG 2 attacked Soviet troops in at Power

---

21. Due to the organisational chaos caused by the rapid German offensive, at that time the Soviets often included armoured Il-2 ground-attack aircraft in the fighter aviation regiments.
22. TSAMO RF. Foundation 22020. Inventory 0445249s. Case 0001. Sheet 24–29.

plant No. 8, Otradny village and on the outskirts of Shlisselburg. Do 17s of I./KG 2 and III./KG 3 supported the offensive of the 20th Infantry Division (mot.). They bombed the villages of Nevsky Dubrovka, Kelkolovo, Annino and other targets on both banks of the Neva. In total, on 6 September Luftflotte 1 aircraft carried out over 1,000 sorties, with 600 by bombers and Stukas.

On that day, Soviet aviation responded to the enemy with 339 combat sorties. As a result, 'Stalin's Falcons' claimed eleven aerial victories. For example, in the morning a pair of LaGG-3s from the 46th IAP flew to intercept German aircraft near the village of Novaya Dubrovka (25km east of Leningrad), where they shot down one Bf 109. At 08.50, a group of I-153 and MiG-3 fighters from the 7th IAC PVO attacked a group of German aircraft, which the Russian pilots identified as '17 Ju 86 and 12 He 113'. 'Stalin's Falcons' reported to their command about one downed 'He 113'.[23]

The Luftwaffe really suffered a lot of losses that day. Three Bf 109 F-4s from 4./JG 53 and two Bf 109 F-4s from II./JG 52 were shot down. Two German pilots were killed, the rest survived. The Red Army Air Force lost twelve aircraft that day.[24]

Zhdanov's phalanx

Meanwhile, German troops were inexorably approaching the town of Shlisselburg, where the last road connecting Leningrad with Russia passed. The approaches to the town were defended by fanatically minded soldiers of the 1st Rifle Division NKVD. On 6 September, the positions of the Soviet troops were subjected to German air attacks, which lasted from early morning until late evening. As a result of the bombing, the 1st Rifle Division NKVD suffered heavy losses in men and artillery. The next morning, the German bombing resumed with relentless force. By 11.00 on 8 September, the surviving soldiers were already retreating randomly. One group crossed to the northern bank of the Neva, the second group of NKVD soldiers retreated to the east. As a result, by

---

23. The He 113 type was a phantom that never existed. The 'He 113' was actually the He 100 D fighter, which had not gone into production. On the orders of Göring, in the spring of 1940 a disinformation campaign was launched. Photographs of nine experimental He 100 Ds were printed in magazines and newspapers. They were painted with various emblems and serial numbers and then repainted, creating the illusion of 'mass production'. Then came the misinformation: the new fighter was called the He 113. The British did not believe this 'leak of information', but in Russia they took it seriously.
24. TSAMO RF. Foundation 22020. Inventory 0445249s. Case 0001. Sheet 30–41.

the evening of that day, German troops had captured the town of Shlisselburg. Shortly before that, the last vessels, tugboats and barges left Shlisselburg Bay for the port of Novaya Ladoga. From that day on, Novaya Ladoga became the new base of the Ladoga Military Flotilla.

German infantrymen and crews who got out of their tanks saw the huge dark Lake Ladoga stretching to the horizon. To many soldiers, this achievement seemed to be the winning point in the Army Group North offensive, which had lasted two and a half months without a break. The huge city of Leningrad was cut off from the rest of the Soviet Union and was soon to undoubtedly fall to the boots of the Wehrmacht.

In reality, things were not so good for the Germans. Despite the land blockade, Leningrad, due to its specific features, was well adapted for defence. The relief of the Neva delta was ideally suited for the construction of defensive obstacles. There were over sixty-five rivers and canals within the city limits. Combined with granite embankments, large buildings turned into fortified strongpoints, and water barriers were powerful lines of defence.

Leningrad had a wide network of underground and sewer passages that could be used to maintain stable communication/and deliver the necessary equipment to the defending troops. The several million people who made up the city's population were also a powerful resource for fighting the enemy. Stalin's servants, party boss Andrei Zhdanov and Marshal Kliment Voroshilov, planned to use the entire combat-ready population for the defence of Leningrad. In case of a shortage of rifles and machine guns, they ordered the formation of working battalions armed with hunting rifles, grenades, bottles with a combustible mixture, as well as ... sabres, daggers and spears. It was such an improvised Zhdanov's phalanx, modelled on the armies of the time of Alexander the Great, that was supposed to protect the cowardly Stalinist servants from the Germans.

Chapter 2

Hitler's bombers get to work

Death from starvation, bombs and shells, that's what awaits the residents of Leningrad

In Leningrad, from the very beginning of the German invasion, aerial bombardment was expected. A blackout was introduced in the city, while to prevent the scattering of glass fragments when exposed to an explosive wave, all windows of buildings were sealed with paper strips. A huge number of earth bomb shelters were dug up in courtyards, squares and numerous factories to provide hiding places from German bombs. The soldiers of the Soviet Local Rescue Service (MPVO) had to monitor all protective measures in the city to minimise the consequences of bomb attacks. They were on duty at their posts around the clock. The population had been tirelessly taught how to hide in bomb shelters and defuse incendiary bombs. However, week after week went by, and there were no bombings of the city. Even when the Wehrmacht was already standing at the walls of the city, Luftwaffe bombers did not appear in the Leningrad sky. Until the beginning of September 1941, the huge city lived an almost peaceful life. Leningrad seemed absolutely safe to many residents and refugees from the German-occupied neighbourhoods.

But on 4 September, trouble came from where no one expected. In the evening Leningrad was shaken by powerful explosions of artillery shells. They came as a complete surprise to the population. Everyone knew that the front was close, but they did not believe that the Germans would be able to fire howitzers at the city. As it turned out, the shooting was conducted by 240mm high-explosive shells from Tosno railway station in the south-east.

The targets of the German artillery shelling were power plant No. 5, Vitebsk-Sortirovochnaya railway station, the No. 232 Bolshevik plant,[25] Krasny Neftyanik and Salolin. In the period from 4 to 6 September, the German long-range artillery fired eighty-two shells at Volodarsky, Frunzensky

---

25. The main products of the No. 232 Bolshevik plant were artillery shells.

and Moskovsky districts. At the same time, fifty-three people were killed and another 101 residents were injured. The Red Army Air Force received an order to locate a German artillery battery, however, due to bad weather, it turned out to be impossible to do so. But the worst was yet to come ...

The most terrible threat to the residents of Leningrad was not from German bombs and shells, but in the very fact of the land blockade of the city. The monstrous inefficiency of the Stalinist regime manifested itself not only in the flight of the Red Army, but also in the complete helplessness of the Leningrad civil administration. Stalin, concerned about the collapse of the Red Army on all fronts, was not sure that Leningrad could be held. The population of a huge city, in fact, was abandoned by frightened Stalinist servants to the mercy of fate. In his memoirs, commissar of the State Defence Committee for Food Supply of Leningrad Front Troops and Leningrad Population Dmitry Pavlov[26] writes:

> Most residents of Leningrad in June to the first half of August did not know exactly where the enemy troops were. The city had not yet been bombed, and this created a calming mood. As the course of developing events showed, steep administrative measures were needed so that people left the city. However, such measures were resorted to very carefully. As a result, 2.54 million civilians, including about 400,000 children, turned out to be in the blockaded city. In addition, 343,000 people remained in suburban areas (in the blockade ring). In September, when the systematic bombing, shelling and fires began, many thousands of families wanted to leave, but the evacuation routes were cut off.[27]

Stalin, resigned to the loss of Leningrad, tried to save the complex technical equipment necessary for the production of weapons. He was literally obsessed with the idea of evacuating military factories from territories that, in his opinion, would inevitably be captured by the enemy. That is why all the efforts of Stalin's servants were directed to the evacuation of the valuable industrial equipment of Leningrad factories. While there was a stable connection with the central regions of the USSR, multi-ton industrial presses and machines bought in the West for gold were taken out of the city by rail on hundreds of trains. Meanwhile, the formal head of the city, Andrei Zhdanov, and his officials

---

26. Dmitry Pavlov served as commissar of the State Defence Committee for Food Supply of Leningrad Front Troops and Leningrad Population from September 1941 to January 1942.
27. Pavlov, D.V., *Leningrad is Under Siege*, Leningrad: Lenizdat, 1985. pp.81–82.

simply forgot about the multimillion population of Leningrad. Before the establishment of the land blockade, only qualified workers who accompanied the evacuated military factories managed to be taken out of the city.

Extraordinary efforts and a large number of vehicles were required to supply food to the huge population of the blockaded city. The experience of the first months of the war showed that the Soviet people were able to cope with the most difficult problems and could do the impossible. However, Stalin, convinced that Leningrad would inevitably fall, did not show the expected firmness and did not give an emergency order for immediate food supplies. Despite extremely economical use, food supplies in the city gradually dried up. The supply of food from outside was extremely irregular and insignificant in volume. The huge population of Leningrad was waiting for a slow but imminent death from starvation.

Pre-emptive strike by 'Stalin's Falcons'

On 8 September at 07.00 during a reconnaissance flight of LaGG-3s, Captain Osipov from the 46th Fighter Aviation Regiment (46th IAP) discovered a 'cluster' of fifty German Ju 87s and Bf 109 aircraft at Lyuban airfield. Having received this information, the Headquarters of the Leningrad Front Air Force immediately ordered an air strike. At 10.00, a strike group consisting of four MiG-3s from the 15th Fighter Aviation Regiment (15th IAP), three Yak-7UTIs from the 121st Fighter Aviation Regiment (121st IAP), three LaGG-3s from the 157th Fighter Aviation Regiment Air Defence (157th IAP PVO) and three Il-2 ground-attack aircraft from The 175th Ground-attack Aviation Regiment (175th SHAP) attacked the airfield. The tactics of the Soviet raid were standard. Ground-attack aircraft Il-2 were the first to appear over the German airfield. After launching rocket-powered projectiles, they began dropping high-explosive and fragmentation bombs. The fighters flying in the second wave lined up in a circle, after which they alternately descended and fired at the German planes standing on the ground. 'Stalin's Falcons' claimed twenty-six German aircraft destroyed on the ground. These included four Do 19s and Fw 200s, allegedly 'preparing for take-off'. In addition, Soviet fighters shot down a Ju 88 bomber that was trying to land at the airfield. This is how this attack was described in the 157th IAP PVO combat log:

> Three LaGG-3s attacked the Lyuban airfield together with a group of aircraft from the 8th Fighter Aviation Division (8th IAD). There were fifty planes at the enemy airfield: Ju 52, Ju 87, Bf 110, Bf 109. The planes were in a row. After the

attack, our ground-attack aircraft and fighters noted up to 15–16 fires at the aircraft parking lot and one large explosion with a fire in the eastern part of the airfield. During the attack, Lieutenant Yuryev shot down one Bf 109 trying to enter the tail of Captain Zverev's plane. At the end of the attack, six Bf 109 aircraft appeared in the sky. Our planes evaded the battle, went into the clouds.

The losses of the Soviets in this raid amounted to one fighter. A Yak-7UTI from the 121st IAP did not return to its airfield and the fate of the pilot was unknown. In reality, no damage was inflicted on the Germans in this raid. Apparently, all the supposedly destroyed German planes again turned out to be a figment of the rich imagination of 'Stalin's Falcons'.

At 13.15, six LaGG-3s from the 44th Fighter Aviation Regiment (44th IAP) repeatedly attacked Lyuban airfield. The leading pair of fighters, breaking ahead, made the first attack on German aircraft standing on the ground. The rest of the Soviet fighters also fired at the aircraft parking lots several times. 'Stalin's Falcons' reported to their superiors that they also carefully shelled the bushes along the borders of the airfield (pilots and technical personnel were 'presumably' hiding in them). Due to the heavy smoke in the target area, the Soviet pilots did not observe the results of the shelling.

Russian pilots always colourfully described their air attacks against German air bases and reported on the great damage caused by their actions. These fake reports impressed their commanders so much that they, confident of success, repeatedly sent their planes to the same targets. In fact, such missions rarely led to serious results. The losses of the attacking side usually significantly exceeded the number of destroyed enemy aircraft on the ground.

In addition to the attacks on German airfields, 'Stalin's Falcons', acting as ground-attack aircraft, tried to carry out air strikes on other ground targets. At 18.10, a group of eight I-16s from the 26th Fighter Aviation Regiment (26th IAP), seven I-153s from the 194th Fighter Aviation Regiment (194th IAP) and five LaGG-3s from the 157th IAP PVO attacked ground targets in the villages Yam–Ijora–Popovka sector. At 18.30 over the village of Pushkino, a pair of LaGG-3s flown by Lieutenants Ivan Lagutenko and Smirnov, returning from a mission, shot down one fighter from a pair of Bf 109s accidentally encountered during a combat sortie. The second German fighter disappeared into the clouds. However, during the air battle, one LaGG-3 was also shot down. According to German information, at 18.35, Leutnant Hans Beisswenger from 6./JG 54 shot down the I-18 (this is how the Germans sometimes identified the Soviet LaGG-3 fighter).

HITLER'S BOMBERS GET TO WORK

Luftwaffe's first raid on 'the city of Lenin'[28]

In embarking on useless missions to attack German airfields, Russian fighters forgot their main function! When 'Stalin's Falcons', satisfied with their victories, were returning to base, they suddenly saw a large group of Ju 88 dropping bombs on Leningrad ...

In fact, these were not Ju 88s, but twenty-three Do 17 Zs from I./KG 2, which at 18.55 made the first raid directly on the 'city of Lenin'. On 8 September, 178 fires broke out in Leningrad as a result of the German bombing. The biggest blaze occurred at the Badayev warehouses,[29] where foodstuffs, stock, spare parts and other property of Leningrad trade organisations were stored. After being hit by incendiary bombs filled with thermite mixtures, the wooden buildings of the food warehouse quickly ignited. The distance between the buildings was only 10m. The fire easily spread to neighbouring sections, turning the warehouses into one big bonfire. According to eyewitnesses, the flames rose hundreds of metres, illuminating everything around. As a result of the fire, which lasted five hours, 3,000 tons of flour and 2,500 tons of refined sugar were burned. Although such a quantity of food would be enough for a multimillion-dollar city only for a few days, this fateful event was remembered by all residents of Leningrad as a harbinger of a future humanitarian catastrophe.

Late in the evening of 8 September, the Leningrad bombing baton was taken up by the KG 4 'General Wever' bomber squadron under the command of Oberst Hans-Joachim Rath. One of the goals of KG 4 was administrative buildings in the central part of the city. Major General Alexander Novikov, who held the position of Commander of the Leningrad Front Air Force at that time, recalled:

> The Smolny Institute[30] area was particularly badly affected during the evening raid. I was on my way to a meeting of the Military Council of Leningrad Front amid smoke and burning buildings. Bombs and anti-aircraft guns were roaring all around, searchlights were feverishly darting in the sky. Dark silhouettes of houses and smoky caps of anti-aircraft shell bursts loomed in

---

28. 'City of Lenin', so it was pathetically called in Leningrad Soviet propaganda.
29. Badayev warehouses are wooden sheds that were built in 1914 by merchant Rasteryaev. After the end of the Russian Civil War, the warehouses were named Badayev in honour of the Bolshevik A.E. Badayev, who made a great contribution to the food supply of the city during wartime.
30. The Smolny Institute building at that time housed the office of the Bolshevik Party of Leningrad.

their light. The picture was fantastic and depressing. I was late for
the meeting. When I entered, there was already a discussion of
cases. Everyone was sullen, spoke little and sparingly – the heavy
news had just come to the city – the Nazis ... captured the town
of Shlisselburg. Leningrad found itself in a blockade.[31]

The experienced crews of KG 4 once again showed excellent accuracy of bombing. The hotel Peasant's House was destroyed. It was just 100m from the Smolny Institute, from which Andrei Zhdanov and Kliment Voroshilov led the defence of the city. He 111s from KG 4 dropped forty-eight high-explosive bombs on the Krasnogvardeysky, Moskovsky and Dzerzhinsky districts. The main water supply station and twelve residential buildings were destroyed. Moscow railway station and Torgovyi port were seriously damaged by the bombs. According to official data, civilian casualties amounted to twenty-four people killed and 122 people wounded.

As a result of the first air raids on Leningrad, there were interruptions in the supply of water and electricity, trams stopped running and panic began among part of the population. Oleg Kobranov, an eyewitness to the events, who was twelve years old in 1941, told one of the authors of this book:

> During the first bombing, people (apparently out of curiosity)
> had a desire to look at the destroyed houses. There were literally
> crowds coming to them. However, the affected neighbourhoods
> were quickly cordoned off by the police, and all curious people
> were driven back. Probably, the authorities were afraid that panic
> would begin, so they did not let them look at the dead bodies
> and blood. Already after the first bombing, there were no whole
> windows left in the city. The broken windows were covered with
> plywood or plugged with some rags.

Despite the presence of powerful air defences in the city, the Germans did not suffer any losses during these raids. By the beginning of September 1941, the 2nd Leningrad Air Defence Corps under Major General Mikhail Procvetkin, had 543 anti-aircraft guns of different calibres to defend the 'city of Lenin'. However, when the German troops came close to the city, many artillery batteries were transferred to the front line to fight tanks. The airspace surveillance system, the Soviet Air Surveillance and Communication Service (VNOS), practically

---

31. Novikov, A.A., *In the Sky of Leningrad (Notes of the Commander of aviation)*, Moscow: Nauka, 1970, p.88.

collapsed during the retreat of the Soviet troops. Soviet RUS-2 'Redut' radar stations were located on flat terrain and could detect aircraft flying at an altitude of at least 1,500m. This meant that the six new radar stations were used by the Soviets extremely inefficiently. Thus, in September 1941, the air defence of the second largest city in the USSR, in the creation of which large resources has been spent, showed in practice monstrous inefficiency.

'Military fate' of Kampfgeschwader 4

The combat path of Kampfgeschwader 4 on the Eastern Front of the Second World War deserves closer consideration. By the will of 'military fate', it was KG 4 that had the 'honour' of being the first to launch military operations against the Soviet Union. On the night of 22 June 1941, He 111s from KG 4 took off from Romania to drop bottom mines in the harbour of Sevastopol, the main Soviet Black Sea Fleet base. By this time, the Kampfgeschwader was mainly armed with He 111s of H-4 and H-5 models. The He 111 H-5s were powered by two Jumo 211 F-2 engines with a capacity of 1,350hp (the standard He 111 Hs had 1,200hp engines at that time), as well as equipment for external suspension of bombs weighing up to 2 tons. The inner bomb bay was occupied by an additional fuel tank designed to increase range. Thus, the He 111 H-5 was created specifically for the delivery of a high-explosive bomb of special power, the SC 2500 General Purpose 'MAX'.

The headquarters Gruppe KG 4 (Stab./KG 4) still operated older He 111 P aircraft. The use of rare aircraft modifications in KG 4 was due to the special missions performed by the pilots of this Kampfgeschwader. During the Battle of Britain, its crews specialised in hitting particularly important targets with large-calibre bombs, as well as mine laying from the air.

The main part of KG 4 (Stab./KG 4, I./KG 4 and III./KG 4) only arrived at the Eastern Front on 19 July 1941. It flew to the large air base of Prowehren in East Prussia. Two days after their arrival, the bombers participated in the first major raid on Moscow. The crews were ordered to drop high-power bombs (including several SC 2500 General Purpose 'MAX' weighing 2.5 tons) on bridges in the western and northern parts of the city and other important targets. On 22 and 26 July, KG 4 bombers participated in two more raids on the Soviet capital. During the last raid, sixty-five He 111s dropped heavy high-explosive bombs and about 150 incendiary bombs of different designs on Moscow. They completely or partially destroyed a shoe factory, the electric machine-building plant Dynamo, Plant No. 93, Plant No. 239, the No. 1 People's Commissariat of Defence of the Soviet Union repair shop and ten residential buildings. Thirty-one people were killed and almost 300 people were injured and concussed.

Despite heavy anti-aircraft fire, the mission passed without loss for the German bombers.

At the end of July 1941, the II./KG 4 under Major Gottlib Wolf was involved in mining fairways in the Baltic Sea. Its crews had extensive experience of mine laying off the east coast of England, the ports of Alexandria, Tobruk, in the Suez Canal and near the Soviet Sevastopol. According to the initial plans, sending this unit to the Eastern Front was considered temporary by the Luftwaffe command.

Shortly after completing these missions, KG 4 was to return to France in August 1941 to continue military operations against Great Britain. But at that time it became clear that Operation Barbarossa was being delayed and was not developing according to Hitler's scenario at all. As a result, the German command decided to concentrate its maximum forces against the Soviet Union. For this reason, the 'business trip' of Kampfgeschwader 4 under Oberst Rath to the Eastern Front continued indefinitely.

On 6 August, KG 4 was transferred closer to the front line to Korovye Selo Air Base (near the city of Pskov). From now on, the crews of the specialised Kampfgeschwader began to be involved in ordinary missions. In particular, He 111s from KG 4 provided direct support to the advancing troops of Army Group North. However, as already noted above, the He 111 H-4/H-5, which KG 4 was equipped with, did not have internal bomb compartments, so carrying small SC50 and SD70 bombs was impossible. Therefore, bombers from KG 4 dropped large-calibre fragmentation bombs on the defence lines and transport communications of the Soviet troops. For example, He 111s from KG 4 together with diving Ju 88 A bombers from KG 77 struck the Moscow–Leningrad railway.

On 29 August, nine He 111s from I./KG 4, led by Hauptmann group commander Klaus Noske, participated in the attack on Soviet ships breaking through from Tallinn to Kronstadt.[32] The bombers appeared over the Gulf of Finland in the afternoon. They found a group of about thirty vessels. After detecting the target, the bombers one by one began to descend and approach the ships, attacking them from a low altitude. Leutnant Siegfried Rothke dropped bombs on the already damaged transport ship *Vtoraya Pyatiletka*. A huge column of fire shot up over the stern of the ship, which had a displacement of 4,000 tons. Water gushed into the engine room, breaking bulkheads. A few minutes later, *Vtoraya Pyatiletka* sank 4 miles from Rodscher island. In total,

---

32. The so-called Tallinn disaster. During the Soviet evacuation of Tallinn in the period from 28–30 August 1941, sixty-two ships of the Soviet Baltic Fleet were killed by Luftwaffe aircraft strikes and explosions on sea mines.

in this attack, I. /KG 4 aircraft sank three Soviet transport ships with a total tonnage of 6,000 gross tons and damaged three more.

From the beginning of September 1941, Leningrad became the main target of KG 4 for a long period. This Luftwaffe unit was to play a big role in the air battle for this city.

New 'Stalin's Falcons' strikes on German air bases

In response to the first Leningrad bombing, the Red Army Air Force launched new attacks on German air bases. At dawn on 9 September, three Il-2s from the 175th Ground-attack Aviation Regiment (175th SHAP), six LaGG-3s from the 157th Fighter Aviation Regiment Air Defence (157th IAP PVO) and four MiG-3s from the 15th Fighter Aviation Regiment (15th IAP) raided Siverskaya Air Base.

Despite the early morning, when approaching the target, the group was met with powerful anti-aircraft fire and was unable to carry out an organised attack from a low altitude. The Soviets lost three aircraft. One Il-2 went missing, while a second made a crash-landing on Soviet territory. The LaGG-3 of Lieutenant Ivan Lagutenko was seriously damaged by a pair of Bf 109s near the city of Krasnogvardeysk. He made an emergency landing near the town of Pushkin. The results of the Soviet attack on the German airfield were negligible. According to German information, only one Bf 109 F-4 fighter from St./JG 54 was slightly damaged (20 per cent on the German damage scale) at Siverskaya.

At 16.15, seven LaGG-3s from the 44th Fighter Aviation Regiment Air Defence (44th IAP PVO) conducted an air battle with two Bf 109s while patrolling over the towns of Krasnoye Selo and Uritsk. Lieutenants Zaramensky and Savushkin were credited with one joint aerial victory.[33] In fact, a Bf 109 F-2 W.Nr. 9602 'RL+IB' was shot down in this battle. It was piloted by commander 5./JG 54 Hauptmann Hubert Mutherich. The German pilot tried to make an emergency landing, but he crashed and died. Hauptmann Mutherich became the first known German ace to die in the Leningrad area. He had forty-three aerial victories to his credit and was awarded a Knight's Cross.

Captain Nikitin and Senior Lieutenant Rudenko from the 5th Fighter Aviation Regiment Air Force Soviet Baltic Fleet (5th IAP VVS KBF) also achieved success in their LaGG-3 fighters when they shot down Ju 88 A-5 W.Nr. 4411 of 7./KG 1. Another aerial victory was claimed by the pilots of the 7th Fighter Aviation Regiment Air Defence (7th IAP). The downing of

---

33. TSAMO RF. Foundation 22020. Inventory 0445249s. Case 0001. Sheet 56–57.

Ju 88 A-5 W.Nr. 2202 of 8./KG 1 was recorded on the combat account of all fourteen pilots (a 1/14th aerial victory each) who participated in this battle!

A heavy loss for Soviet aviation was the death of Senior Lieutenant Mikhail Bagryantsev from the 5th IAP VVS KBF. After a fight with four Bf 109s his LaGG-3 was shot down near the village of Vladimirovka. By that time, this Air Force Soviet Baltic Fleet pilot had claimed several aerial victories and was awarded the Order of Lenin.

At 19.26 on the same day, six LaGG-3 fighters from the 44th Fighter Aviation Regiment Air Defence (44th IAP PVO) made a second raid on Siverskaya Air Base. The attack of 'Stalin's Falcons' again did not cause any damage to the Germans. A combat sortie by seven I-153 biplanes from the 195th Fighter Aviation Regiment (195th IAP) and three LaGG-3s from the 157th IAP PVO also ended in failure. They were supposed to attack Lyuban airfield, but near Tosno railway station they were fired at by German anti-aircraft guns, after which they lost orientation and visual contact with each other.[34]

Both sides suffer losses and change tactics

Meanwhile, Luftwaffe air attacks on Leningrad continued. During 9 September, the 'air alert' signal sounded eight times in the city. On the night of 9–10 September, the city was attacked by twenty German bombers. As a result of the bombing, eighty fires broke out in Leningrad, and the confectionery factory and the Zhdanov shipyard were destroyed. One BM1000 exploded at the Kirov Factory No. 100.[35]

During 10 September, Luftwaffe planes dropped sixty-nine high-explosive bombs and about 1,800 small incendiary bombs on Leningrad. There were twenty-eight large and fifty-five small fires in the city. Many incendiary bombs fell on the surviving buildings of the Badayev warehouses, where three more buildings burned down as a result. In two days eighty-four people were killed in Leningrad, while 622 were injured and concussed. During these attacks, for the first time the Germans used incendiary bombs of a larger calibre: 50kg, of the C50A brand. A bomb of this type is filled with a mixture of oil, gasoline, rubber (or polystyrene) and phosphorus.

This combustible mixture created a huge flame temperature and could not be extinguished with water. The usual practice of defusing German bombs was

---

34. TSAMO RF. Foundation 22020. Inventory 0445249s. Case 0001. Sheet 59.
35. Kirov Factory No. 100 was the largest military factory in Leningrad, which produced tanks, artillery pieces and shells.

that specially trained people lifted the bombs with metal tongs and lowered them into barrels of water or covered them with sand. Part of these incendiary bombs held explosives that exploded at the end of the combustion. This led to numerous deaths among Soviet Local Rescue Service (MPVO) fighters and civilians who tried to extinguish them.

German artillery continued to brutally bombard the city. From 8 to 15 September, 550 shells fell on Leningrad, mainly of 210mm and 240mm calibre.[36] As a result of artillery shelling, dozens of buildings were destroyed, and many mutilated corpses of people lay on the streets.

Luftwaffe also suffered losses. On the night of 15–16 September, He 111 H-4 W.Nr. 4137 of 4./KG 4 was shot down by anti-aircraft fire in the Leningrad area. The burning plane crashed into the Neva river, and four days later German soldiers fished out the corpse of the pilot Hauptmann Helmut Schwanhausser. Since January 1940, he had headed the 4th Staffel KG 4 (4./KG 4). Hauptmann Schwanhausser's glorious combat career included the invasion of France, day and night bombing attacks against Great Britain, and dangerous and exciting bombing missions in the Mediterranean. In May 1941, aircraft from 4./KG 4 participated in the short Iraqi campaign. This Staffel supported Iraqi insurgents who were trying to expel the British from the country. The campaign against Soviet Russia also began successfully for Hauptmann Schwanhausser, and he had participated in air attacks against Moscow and minelaying.

Hauptmann Reinhard Graubner took over as commander of 4./KG 4. He was one of the best aces of German bomber aviation. During the war, Hauptmann Graubner went from an ordinary pilot to commander. Like many other famous pilots of German bomber aviation, he began his combat career in the position of a 'chain dog'. This was the name of the bombers that were on the edges of the formation and were the first to take on the attacks of enemy fighters. This position in the battle formation was the most dangerous test, in which many young crews died. Pilots who passed through the position of 'chain dog', subsequently received a higher status and became commanders of Staffeln and Gruppen.

On the night of 17 September, KG 4 suffered another loss when He 111 P-4 W.Nr. 2977 from the 5th Staffel (5./KG 4) went missing. As it turned out later, the entire crew of the German aircraft died under unknown circumstances.

Unpunished German bombing and the obvious weakness of Leningrad's air defence provoked the anger of the First Secretary of the Leningrad Regional Committee of the Communist Party, Andrei Zhdanov, who was the 'party

---

36. The blockade of Leningrad in the documents of declassified archives. Moscow: AST, 2004. p.681.

leader' of Leningrad's defence. Stalin's servant decided to intervene directly in the activities of the military. The Red Army Air Force command received an order from Zhdanov to use the fighters only for their intended purpose. They should have attacked German bombers, patrolled their flight routes and fought for 'air supremacy'. And only after completing these priority missions were valuable fighters allowed to be used to attack ground targets!

The Germans also changed tactics. On 17 September, the commander of JG 54 Major Trautloft decided to switch from escorting bombers and Stukas to searching for and destroying Soviet fighters in the Leningrad area. The new tactic immediately produced good results. 1./JG 54 shot down two I-16s, and 7./JG 54 and headquarters Gruppe (III./JG 54) eight MiG-3s and LaGG-3s. Feldwebel Karl Heinz Kempf achieved especially great success in the air war, and during two combat sorties won five aerial victories at once.[37] The losses of the 7th Fighter Aviation Corps Air Defence (7th IAP PVO) amounted to ten fighters, including three MiG-3s, three I-16s, three Yak-1s and one LaGG-3. Seven Soviet pilots were killed or went missing. Among the dead was Soviet ace Junior Lieutenant Egor Novikov from the 191st Fighter Aviation Regiment (191st IAP). His I-16 was shot down near the town of Krasnoye Selo. By this time, Junior Lieutenant Novikov had eight personal and two joint aerial victories. He was later posthumously awarded the title Hero of the Soviet Union.

'All commanders, political commissars and soldiers are subject to immediate execution …'

Soviet aviation continued to suffer heavy losses and by mid-September 1941 was in a deplorable state. By the morning of 18 September, only thirty-eight serviceable fighters remained in the 7th IAC PVO. The new Commander of the Leningrad Front General of the Army, Georgy Zhukov,[38] reported to Moscow:

> I have only 268 aircraft on the Leningrad Front, of which only 163 are combat-ready. The situation with bombers and ground-attack aircraft is very bad. There are six Pe-2, two ground-attack aircraft Il-2, two Ar-2, eleven SB. Such a number will not ensure

---

37. Weal, J., *Jagdgeschwader 54 'Grunherz'*, Osprey Aviation, Great Britain, 2001, p.167.
38. Stalin, who was in a panic from the rapid advance of the Germans, tried to influence the situation by constantly changing commanders. Zhukov commanded the Leningrad Front from 14 September to 10 October 1941, that is, less than a month. Despite the Soviet myths about 'Stalin's great commander', the presence of General of the Army Zhukov in this post had no effect on the catastrophic situation on the Leningrad Front.

that the task is completed. I really ask Comrade Stalin to give me at least one bomber aviation regiment equipped with Pe-2, one ground-attack aviation regiment equipped with ground-attack aircraft Il-2.[39]

The situation in this sector of the front also continued to deteriorate. Without undertaking a decisive assault on Leningrad, the Germans and Finns tightened the noose of the land blockade around the city. The towns of Slutsk and Krasnoye Selo were captured on 12 September, and five days later German tanks left for the Gulf of Finland around the settlement of Strelna and the town of Uritsk. From here to the centre of Leningrad was only 14–15km away. German soldiers examined the outskirts of the city, factory smokestacks, port cranes and the dome of the huge Isaakievskiy Sobor (Saint Isaac's Cathedral). Soon the 18th Army captured the towns of Pushkin and Petergof. Meanwhile, the Finnish army advanced along the eastern shore of Lake Ladoga and captured Olonets on 5 September. Two days later, the advanced units of the Finns reached the river Svir, which connects Lake Ladoga and Lake Onega. On 12 September, Finnish troops crossed the Svir and captured the settlement of Podporozhye (230km north-east of Leningrad). There they stopped, waiting for an early meeting with German troops.

In Leningrad, residents were preparing city blocks for street battles. Barricades and anti-tank obstacles stretching over 25km were erected on the streets and intersections. Some 4,100 wood-earth blockhouses and reinforced concrete pillboxes were built, while over 20,000 defensive fighting positions were equipped in city buildings. Factories, bridges and administrative buildings were mined and in the event of a German breakthrough into the city would be blown up. Leaflets hung all over the city called on residents to fight for every house and every yard. Commander of the Leningrad Front General of the Army Georgy Zhukov, in his characteristic cruel manner, gave orders for the execution of alarmists and cowards. In one of the orders it was reported:

> To announce to all commanders, political commissars and the soldiers defending the specified line that for leaving without a written order of the Leningrad Front Military Council and the armies of the specified line, all commanders, political commissars and soldiers are subject to immediate execution.[40]

---

39. TSAMO RF. Foundation 217. Inventory 1221. Case 174. Sheets 58–69.
40. TSAMO RF. Foundation 249. Inventory 1544. Case 112. Sheet 144.

German air attacks remained a serious threat to the city. The Luftwaffe grouping around Leningrad continued to strengthen. On 17 September, units from KG 77 Oberstleutnant, under Joachim Reitel, equipped with Ju 88 A dive bombers arrived at Siverskaya Air Base. This allowed the Germans to significantly strengthen their bombing attacks on the 'city of Lenin'.

'It was a heartbreaking tragedy …'

Friday, 19 September, became one of the hardest days experienced by the residents of Leningrad. The bombers and Zerstörers of Luftflotte 1 carried out about 500 sorties, including 170 to bomb the city. Twenty-eight Ju 88s from I./KG 77 took to the air first (around 08.00 Berlin time) accompanied by Bf 109 fighters, and headed for Leningrad. The main landmark for the aircraft crews was the Oktyabrskaya Railway, the tracks of which brought them to the centre of the city. Then Leningrad was attacked by bombers from II./KG 77. Soon they were joined by Stukas from I./StG 2 Major Hubertus Hitschhold, III./StG 2, led by Hauptmann Ernst-Siegfried Steen, and Zerstörers from ZG 26.

In total, on that day more than 500 high-explosive bombs and about 3,000 small incendiary bombs were dropped on Leningrad. As a result of the bombing, the Great Gostiny Dvor shopping centre, a hospital on Suvorovsky Prospekt and eighty residential buildings were destroyed. The Economizer and Proletarsky plants and Kirov Factory No. 100, as well as the opera theatre, were severely damaged. According to various estimates, from 540 to 700 people were killed, while hundreds more were injured and concussed. The greatest number of victims was in the hospital on Suvorovsky Prospekt. Commissar of the State Defence Committee for Food Supply of Leningrad Front Troops and Leningrad Population Dmitry Pavlov, recalled:

> The floor structures of the upper floors collapsed, and there were many wounded under their debris. It was a heartbreaking tragedy. Around the burning hospital, the air was so hot that window frames flashed in neighbouring houses, the fire threatened to engulf the whole area.[41]

The scale of the German raids is evidenced by the fact that 103 fire trucks, seventy ambulance cars and 18,000 Soviet Local Rescue Service (MPVO) soldiers were out on the streets.

---

41. Pavlov, D.V., *Leningrad is Under Siege*, Leningrad: Lenizdat, 1985, pp.52–53.

HITLER'S BOMBERS GET TO WORK

Simultaneously with the execution of the main missions, Bf 109 F and Bf 110 aircraft attacked Kasimovo, Levashovo and Uglovo air bases. Lieutenant Yashin's LaGG-3 was shot down at Manushkino airfield during take-off and he was killed. At 10.40, eight LaGG-3s engaged a large group of German fighters near the Soviets' Uglovo air base. As a result, LaGG-3 Captain Pauzul was shot down. Following the results of the air battle, Russian pilots and anti-aircraft gunners reported to their command they had shot down about nineteen German planes! In fact, the Luftwaffe suffered minimal losses. MiG-3 fighters shot down Ju 88 A-4 W.Nr. 8034 of 2./KG 77 over Leningrad. The crew left the burning plane over the location of German troops and soon returned to their airfield. Bf 109 E-7 W.Nr. 5039 Feldwebel Ernst Rippe of 9./JG 27 was shot down near the town of Kolpino. A German pilot jumped out with a parachute and was captured by the Russians.

Meanwhile, the situation in Leningrad was getting worse every day. Funerals of the dead, mostly civilians, including women and children, were held daily. People who had recently boldly walked the streets, sat in horror in basements and trenches, praying that another bomb would not fall directly on them. The Soviet press and radio hid from the population the true situation at the front and the terrible results of the German bombing, but this only made it worse. The news was transmitted in trams, in bazaars, in shops, often in a distorted and greatly exaggerated form. Ominous rumours were spreading around the city about thousands of German spies and saboteurs and about future horrors in store in the event of the capture of the city by the Germans. However, only very few people guessed that a third of Leningrad's population would soon die of hunger.

Chapter 3

Bay storm

Soviet Baltic Fleet on the protection of Leningrad

On Monday, 20 September, there was a sudden lull in the sky over Leningrad. This was due to the fact that, at Hitler's whim, the Luftwaffe suddenly had a serious new goal.

When the German and Finnish troops came close to the city, they faced an unexpected problem, namely the firing of large-calibre naval guns. After the tragic evacuation of ships from the main Soviet Baltic Fleet Tallinn naval base for the Soviets, carried out on 28–29 August, all the surviving ships of the Russian Soviet Baltic Fleet were concentrated at Kronstadt, west of Leningrad. The Soviet squadron gathered there was a ridiculous collection of different types of ships. The battleships *Marat* and *Oktyabrskaya Revolutsiya* were dreadnoughts of the Sevastopol class with a displacement of 27,000 tons, built in 1909–14. After the October Revolution of 1917, these ships went to the Bolsheviks and received pretentious revolutionary names. Subsequently, they were modernised and their appearance significantly changed. The main armament consisted of twelve 305mm guns.

The cruisers *Kirov* and *Maxim Gorky* were built in the late 1930s according to an Italian design and were the largest new ships of the Bolsheviks. They had a total displacement of 9,500 tons, a length of 191m (more than battleships!) and a powerful armament of nine 180mm and six 100mm guns. Their cruising range was 3,750 miles. *Kirov* was Joseph Stalin's favourite ship. It was the high-speed cruisers of this type that were to become the basis of the future Red ocean fleet. On 27 August, while fleeing from Tallinn, *Kirov* was subjected to numerous attacks by German bombers. However, despite the danger, the cruiser still managed to reach the new main navy base of the fleet in Kronstadt almost unscathed.

'Military fate' was not so favourable to sister ship *Maxim Gorky*. On the second day of the war, 23 June 1941, while covering Soviet minelaying, the cruiser was blown up by a German mine near the lighthouse at Cape Tahkuna.

BAY STORM

A powerful explosion tore off the bows up to the 47th frame. Thanks to the bulkhead remaining intact on the 61st frame, the cruiser was able to reach the island of Vormsi on its own. There, hasty work began to rescue the ship and prepare it for transportation to Tallinn for inspection to determine the possibility of rebuilding it. First, work was carried out to temporarily fill the holes and lighten the ship. To do this, ammunition from the powder chambers in the turrets of the main-calibre No. 1 and No. 2 guns and all the torpedoes on board were unloaded onto the shore. In parallel with this work, the ship's crew and specialists began to construct a false bow made of wood and canvas. After performing these emergency works, *Maxim Gorky*, as part of a caravan of three destroyers, a salvage ship and tugboats, reached Tallinn. On 27 June, the heavily damaged cruiser left for Kronstadt, where it was put into the Veleschinsky dry dock for repairs. After an inspection by plant No. 189 engineers, it was decided to restore the severely damaged cruiser. A new bow was hastily built for the cruiser at slipway plant No. 189 and then docked to the stump of *Maxim Gorky*. The repair was completed in forty-three days. Also during the repair, the catapult was dismantled and the anti-aircraft artillery was upgraded. The obsolete 45mm anti-aircraft guns (21-K) were replaced with ten 37mm automatic anti-aircraft guns (70-K).

The cruiser *Petropavlovsk* was bought from the Germans in February 1940 in an unfinished form. Initially, it was a heavy cruiser of Nazi Germany's Kriegsmarine called *Lützow*. This was the last ship of the Admiral Hipper class of heavy cruisers. In 1940, during the culmination of friendly relations between Stalin and Hitler, the Third Reich had profitably sold an unfinished cruiser to the Soviet Union. Since then, it had been in the process of completion at the Leningrad shipyard.

The destroyer leaders *Minsk* and *Leningrad* were new ships built at Soviet shipyards in 1938–39. They had a total displacement of 2,237 tons and were armed with five 130mm guns of the main calibre.

After the shameful defeat of the first months of the war, the Soviets did not dare to use their largest fleet for its intended purpose. Instead of attacking the enemy fleet and its bases, large Soviet ships began to be used as floating artillery batteries. At the beginning of September 1941, the large Soviet Baltic Fleet ships began systematic shelling of the Baltic Sea coast occupied by the enemy. For example, on the night of 3–4 September, the cruiser *Kirov* opened fire on Finnish troops on Karelian Isthmus, significantly slowing down their offensive. Since 5 September, the battleship *Oktyabrskaya Revolutsiya* had joined the shooting. The fire was conducted directly from the Srednyaya harbour of Kronstadt, as well as from the roadsteads of Kronstadt and Petergof. Then the battleship *Marat* began firing at the German positions. Since 9 September, its 305mm guns had been firing at several targets daily, and the daily consumption of shells reached 177 pieces. Also, the coast occupied by the enemy was shelled by the cruiser *Maxim Gorky*, the destroyer leaders *Minsk* and *Leningrad* and several destroyers. Even the unfinished cruiser *Petropavlovsk*, which fired from two towers of the main calibre, participated in the shelling. It was in Leningrad's port of Torgovyi, but the proximity of the Germans to Leningrad allowed it to conduct fairly effective fire from the long-range guns.

The order of the Führer is to strike at the ships of the Russian fleet!

Powerful explosions of shells from Russian ships and the huge craters that remained after them had a strong psychological effect on the German infantry. The soldiers were afraid to advance and panicked when they heard the next shots. After numerous complaints from the German 18th Army and from Finnish troops, Hitler personally ordered the Luftwaffe to destroy the large Soviet ships and their Kronstadt base.

Luftwaffe headquarters immediately began planning an operation against the Soviet Baltic Fleet. German aerial photography revealed that in mid-September 1941 there were two battleships, two cruisers, thirteen destroyers and forty-two submarines in Kronstadt. Most submarines were submerged in the daytime and were on the bottom at a depth of 10–15m. In addition, Kronstadt had twelve minelayers, thirty-eight torpedo boats, nine gunboats of various types, sixty-two minesweepers and many other auxiliary ships. To this large number of warships could be added three unfinished destroyers: *Opytnyi*, *Strogyi* and *Stroinyi*. Thus, the piers, harbours and roadstead were literally packed with Soviet ships, so there was no shortage of targets for the Luftwaffe.

On 16 September, the Commander of VIII Fliegerkorps, Generalmajor Wolfram von Richthofen, flew to Tirkovo airfield, south of the town of Luga. Stukas from StG 2 'Immelmann' under Oberstleutnant Oskar Dinort were based there. Von Richthofen personally gave Oberstleutnant Dinort the Führer's order – to strike at the ships of the Russian fleet!

On the same day, twenty-seven Ju 87 Rs from III./StG 2, led by Hauptmann Ernst-Siegfried Steen, took to the air. Their first target was the battleship *Marat*, which was located in the Morskoy channel[42] and from there fired at German positions. However, the weather conditions were unsatisfactory, with dense clouds hanging along the flight route at an altitude of 800m to 1,800m.

---

42. The Morskoy Channel is a narrow deepened part of the Gulf of Finland connecting Leningrad with Kronstadt.

However, over the Gulf of Finland, the clouds began to dissipate a little. Soon the German pilots noticed a large ship below, which they identified as a battleship. Hauptmann Steen immediately gave his subordinates the order to attack. The Ju 87s split into two groups, attacking the target simultaneously from the bow and stern. As a result, three 500kg bombs hit *Marat*. Two of them penetrated the upper armoured deck and exploded on the lower armoured deck, which was bent and depressed by 30cm as a result of the explosion. The third bomb exploded on the stern. Another 500kg bomb cut off the barrel of 120mm gun No. 13 and exploded at the side of the ship.

The stern group of 76.2mm guns was disabled by the powerful concussion and the impact of fragments, while No. 4 turret of the main calibre, several 120mm guns and rangefinding telemeters were damaged. Diesel generators and several auxiliary mechanisms located in the aft part of the ship also failed. But the biggest danger was the penetration of fire through the ventilation system in the powder chamber of No. 4 turret. For this reason, there was a real threat of explosion and sinking. Two sailors, suffocating from smoke, closed the vent of the ventilation pipe with their bodies and thus blocked the access of the flame to the shells. As a result of this attack by Luftwaffe aircraft, twenty-five sailors on *Marat* crew were killed.[43]

Immediately after the end of the attack *Marat* raised its anchors and under its own power went to the Malyi roadstead of Kronstadt. While moving, it continued to shoot at visible targets on the southern shore of the Gulf of Finland. The next day, the battleship moved to the Bolshoi roadstead of Kronstadt. On 18 September, tugboats conducted it to the Srednyaya harbour of Kronstadt, where it was installed in the Ust-Rogatka[44] berth for repairs.

On the evening of 19 September, the He 111s of 5./KG 4 made a new raid on Kronstadt. However, on the approach to the target, the bombers came under heavy anti-aircraft fire from the cruiser *Kirov*, the battleships *Marat* and *Oktyabrskaya Revolutsiya* and coastal anti-aircraft batteries. As a result, the attack did not cause serious damage to Soviet warships. However, despite concentrated anti-aircraft fire, the German bombers did not suffer. One He 111 P-4, W.Nr. 2996, was damaged by anti-aircraft shell fragments, but was able to return safely to its airfield.

On 20 September, during new Luftwaffe attacks on Kronstadt, the tugboat *Krasnyi flot* and the barge *KP-15* were sunk and the transport ship *Maria*, with a displacement of 1,485 tons, was heavily damaged. The crew of *Maria* fought for a day to save it, but their efforts were in vain.

---

43. TSVMA. Foundation 401. Case 401879. Sheets 2–3.
44. Ust-Rogatka is the berth for large warships in Kronstadt.

AIR BATTLE FOR LENINGRAD, 1941–1944

The end of the destroyer *Steregushchy*

On 21 September, at 11.44 hrs, twenty-five Ju 87 Rs from III./StG 2 appeared over Kronstadt. Soviet anti-aircraft gunners opened fire on them. The guns of the destroyer *Steregushchy*,[45] in the Vostochnyi roadstead of Kronstadt, were the first to start firing. However, its anti-aircraft shells exploded far away from the rapidly approaching German dive bombers. Above the target, the Ju 87 Rs lined up in a circle, after which the sailors and residents of Kronstadt could see the impressive spectacle of the classic dive bomber attack. One by one, the Stukas turned over and, with howling sirens, dived almost vertically down. Despite the frenzied firing of anti-aircraft guns, they stubbornly attacked their targets and the naval base was shaken by powerful explosions. After dropping their bombs, the Stukas exited the dive over the water.

Later, *Steregushchy*'s commander, Captain 3rd Rank Evgeny Zbritsky, recalled:

> I heard the report of chief mate: 'Four Ju 87s to the right astern.'
> The boatswain on duty was constantly at the anchor lifting mechanism all the time, so when he heard the combat alarm signal, he immediately began to lift the anchor. A minute later, the ship was already moving. Even before the anchor was lifted, anti-aircraft gunners opened fire on the dive bombers. Sixteen Ju 87s formed up in a circle and began to dive onto the ship. The first bombs fell astern and hit the boat standing next to the destroyer. The bomb broke the boat in half and, exploding at the bottom, threw it to the height of the masts of the ship.
> One by one, the Ju 87s broke off in a dive, waddling over the wing [the aileron roll]. Bombs continuously exploded near the destroyer but, covered by fountains of water from the explosions, stubbornly continued to go forward, firing back with all guns. Finally, one of the planes managed to cover the ship with a series of bombs. From close explosions, some anti-aircraft gunners on the destroyer were wounded, shell-shocked or dropped by the blast wave into the sea. Some of the dive bombers flew at low altitude along the ship and fired at it with machine guns. The dead

---

45. *Steregushchy* was incorporated into the Soviet Baltic Fleet on 30 October 1939. The destroyer had a standard displacement of 1,612 tonnes and was armed with four 130mm, two 76.2mm and two 45mm guns. There were also two triple 533mm torpedo tubes on board.

and wounded appeared. The left 12.7 mm machine gun DShK on the bridge went silent. Political commissar Malyavkin, wounded in the head, took the place of the machine gunner. The chief mate had already been killed. More and more dead and wounded ...[46]

After another bomb attack, *Steregushchy* completely disappeared behind columns of water, fire and smoke. The destroyer was hit by three bombs: one in the non-commissioned officers' quarters, the second in the area of engine room No. 1, and the third in the mess deck area. Hundreds of fragments literally riddled the deck and hull. According to German data, the bombs that hit the warship were dropped by Oberleutnant Hans-Ulrich Rudel, the most famous Ju 87 pilot.

The most severe consequences for the destroyer were caused by the explosion in the engine room. The ship's mechanisms were torn from their foundations and most of the pipelines were broken. A fire broke out near steam turbine No. 1, but it did not have time to spread through the ship as it was flooded with water gushing through the holes. Engine room No. 1 and boiler room No. 3 were flooded, and a strong roll to starboard developed. But, despite the rapidly falling steam pressure, *Steregushchy* still managed to reach the shoal on one steam turbine. A quarter of an hour after the attack began, the destroyer fell to the starboard side and sank at a depth of 5.5m.[47] Soon, a high-speed staff boat approached the crash site, which picked up the few surviving members of *Steregushchy*'s crew. All the rescued were shivering from the cold and were black with soot. Among the survivors was the commander, Captain 3rd Rank Evgeny Zbritsky.

During the attack on the Soviet ships, the commander of 7./StG 2, Hauptmann Ernst Kupfer, also distinguished himself. He achieved a direct hit on the destroyer *Grozyashchiy*, which was under repair in the Pamyati treh esmincev dry dock. The bomb dropped by Hauptmann Kupfer exploded on the upper deck of the ship, making a hole in it measuring 2 m by 3 m. However, his Ju 87 R was damaged by anti-aircraft fire as he flew away. Shrapnel shells chopped off half the blades of his propeller, and a huge hole in the rudder almost deprived him of the ability to control the aircraft. With great difficulty, Hauptmann Kupfer managed to fly to German-held territory and make an emergency landing near the city of Krasnogvardeysk.

---

46. *Military Chronicle of the Navy, 1941–1942*, Moscow, Voenizdat, 1992, p.87.
47. On 20 June 1944, *Steregushchy* was lifted from the bottom and put into a dry dock. Despite the damage, the Soviets managed to repair it. However, the work continued until 1948.

In addition to the sinking of the destroyer *Steregushchy* and damage to other warships, the Ju 87s sank the icebreaker ship *S.A. Levanevsky*, with a gross register tonnage (brt) of 2,333, in Voennaya harbour at Kronstadt.

Ju 88 A bombers from KG 77 take up the baton of air attacks

Even before the smoke from the explosions had dissipated, fifteen Ju 88 As from KG 77 appeared in the sky above Kronstadt Naval Base. Their targets were the battleships *Marat* and *Oktyabrskaya Revolutsiya*. German bombers used proven tactics to attack the ships from several directions at once. Several powerful explosions thundered near the sides of *Marat*, and the water literally boiled from the explosions of bombs. Columns of water with bottom silt flew up tens of metres and then crashed down on the deck of the ship. However, in this attack, *Marat* avoided being hit by German bombs. Three 250kg bombs fell on *Oktyabrskaya Revolutsiya*, which continued to shell German positions. They penetrated the upper 37mm armour deck and exploded inside the ship, completely destroying several compartments. The electric lighting in compartment No. 1 and No. 2 went out and a fire started on board. The shared cabin No. 14 and ship's shop were on fire. The flames engulfed a chemical post and a medical cabinet.

On the upper deck of the battleship, the wooden planking was ablaze. An emergency team led by Captain-Lieutenant Kakstov joined the fight against the fire. In addition to the fire, important communications of the ship were damaged, and steam was escaping from the depths of the hull. In total darkness, the sailors had to look for a place where the steam pipelines had broken. After they had extinguished the fires, the crew began to assess the damage. After sustaining direct hits, the bow of the ship to the main calibre turret No. 1 was almost completely turned into scrap metal, but the vital components of the ship were not damaged. The armour protection of the ship's decks resisted the German 250kg bombs.

Also during this attack, the minelayer *Marti*, docked in one of the berths, was damaged. Its hull was ruptured in several places, and the minelayer fuel tank was holed.

Following this, twenty-two Bf 109 E-4s and E-7s of 9./JG 27 appeared in the sky. The fighters carried one SC250 high-explosive bomb under their fuselages. Their pilots managed to damage the destroyer *Gordy*. At the same time, two German aircraft were damaged by anti-aircraft fire. Leaving behind smoky plumes, these Bf 109s flew at low altitude towards the open sea. The comrades of the pilots of the damaged aircraft immediately radioed to the command post of their group a message about the need to organise a rescue operation and rescue planes took off from the base near Helsinki. Soon both pilots were picked up at sea by He 59 B-2 seaplanes of 9. Seenotstaffel.

After a pause, several more German air attacks followed. At 13.15 a German bomb fell on the destroyer *Silnyi*. The bomb exploded in the stern, and several more detonated 10–15m from the ship, showering it with fragments. The destroyer's stern was severely damaged and a fire broke out. Seven crew members were killed and twenty-seven people were injured. In order to avoid an explosion, the commander of *Silnyi*, Captain 3rd Rank Alexey Shomrakov, ordered the aft powder chambers to be flooded immediately. At the same time, stocks of anti-aircraft shells, depth charges and torpedoes were thrown overboard. In the evening, *Silnyi* moved from the roadstead to the harbour and moored at the berth of the Kronstadt Marine Plant.

One German bomb exploded near the port side of the newly repaired destroyer *Slavnyi*, located in the Morskoi roadstead of Kronstadt. Two boilers in boiler room No. 2 failed due to the concussion. A pipe carrying superheated steam was damaged by shrapnel and as a result three sailors received extensive burns. Three more crew members were wounded by shrapnel from the bombs. Later, one of the sailors burned by the steam died from his injuries.

On the evening of 21 September, Kronstadt Naval Base was attacked again by dive bombers from 7./StG 2 led by Hauptmann Kupfer. Their target was *Marat*, but all the bombs exploded near the sides of the ship without causing damage. When exiting the attack, the Ju 87 R of 7./StG 2's commander was again damaged by anti-aircraft fire. This time, Hauptmann Kupfer's aircraft suffered wing damage and was forced to make an emergency landing near the front line.

At dusk, Kronstadt was attacked by Ju 88 As from I./KG 77 and II./KG 77. The leading aircraft were piloted by the group commanders, Hauptmann Joachim Potter and Hauptmann Dietrich Peltz. As a result of the attack, the transport ship *Barta*, with a tonnage of 2,324brt, three auxiliary vessels and three port barges were sunk. The cruiser *Kirov*, minesweeper *TSCH-206*, submarine *Shch-302* and gunboat *Pioner* were also damaged. The upper deck of *Kirov* was bent from close explosions, the hull of the ship received holes, but the cruiser continued to fire at the German troops blocking Leningrad, not stopping even at night.

The infrastructure of the Kronstadt base itself also suffered a lot of damage. The water supply network and electric power transmission lines, ammunition depots and other naval property were destroyed, as were oil storage facilities, a dry dock pumping station and six residential buildings. Kronstadt Naval Hospital, Marine Plant and Artillery Repair Plant Kronstadt were damaged. In all 135 people were killed, while another ninety-five were injured and concussed.

Such civilian casualties could easily have been avoided as many of the victims neglected their safety and did not take refuge in air-raid shelters. Kontr Admiral Yuri Panteleyev recalled: 'During the air raids, crowds of onlookers stood at street intersections and watched the bombs fall.' Fires burned in Kronstadt until late at night, while moaning from the wounded could be heard and boats scurried around the harbours in search of surviving sailors.[48]

On 22 September, at 05.15, a German reconnaissance aircraft flew over Kronstadt. Such a flight gave the residents of the city and the crews of warships a bad feeling. The morning at the navy base was spent in tension, which was felt everywhere: in the casemates of old forts, in residential buildings, factories, berths, lighthouses, the positions of anti-aircraft batteries and on numerous ships. Submarines submerged again and lay down on the bottom, while some of the ships changed positions. Dozens of observers with binoculars and binocular telescopes peered into the sky.

At 15.00, the hum of approaching planes was heard from the south again. These were thirty-eight Ju 88 As from KG 77 accompanied by fighters from JG 54. Having come from the direction of the sun, they dived in several groups in the direction of the berths of ships and port facilities. Due to the lack of electricity, the 'air alert' signal was given in a very archaic way, namely by ringing the bells of the naval cathedral. Closer to night time, another air raid followed.

As a result of these two attacks, two auxiliary vessels were sunk, and several other ships were severely damaged. The minesweeper *TSCH-206* was literally riddled with shrapnel, and later the sailors counted more than 300 holes in it. The Marine Plant hull shop and two dry docks were damaged.

For the Luftwaffe, the raids on Kronstadt from 19 to 22 September ended with almost no losses. An anti-aircraft shell exploded next to Ju 88 A-5 W.Nr. 2153 of 4./KG 77 and navigator Feldwebel Schlachter died on the plane, but the damaged bomber returned safely to Siverskaya Air Base.

The end of the battleship *Marat*

The attack on 23 September 1941 was the culmination of the Luftwaffe operation against the Soviet Baltic Fleet. It was on this day that the Germans were finally able to use a truly effective weapon to destroy armoured ships. Even before the air attacks began, it was clear that it was extremely difficult to

---

48. *The Red Banner Soviet Baltic Fleet in the Battle for Leningrad, 1941–1944*, Moscow: Nauka, 1975, pp.208–209.

destroy old battleships with conventional high-explosive bombs. The thickness of their upper armoured deck was 37mm, and the lower armoured deck was 25mm. Therefore, headquarters VIII. Fliegerkorps requested the supply of PC1000 armour-piercing explosive bombs, which were specifically designed to destroy well-armoured targets.

The case of the PC1000 had a monolithic construction and was made of forged steel. The thickness at the front reached 34cm. This was a guarantee that due to the kinetic energy acquired after the drop, the bomb would be able to penetrate the armour deck of any ship.

On 21 September, several armour-piercing explosive bombs arrived at Tirkovo airfield. Since there was no equipment on the airfield designed to transport and lift bombs weighing 1,000kg, the gunsmiths had to drag them to the aircraft parking areas. Then they manually lifted them and hung them under the fuselage of the Ju 87s. Each such operation was performed by at least twelve people. By the morning of 23 September, everything was ready. Two PC1000 bombs were suspended from the Stukas of Hauptmann Ernst-Siegfried Steen and Oberleutnant Hans-Ulrich Rudel. Their target was *Marat*, standing at the entrance to the Srednyaya harbour in Kronstadt.

At 11.30 Russian radar stations detected a group target approaching from the south. Soon the most powerful barrage firing began, including from ships. *Marat*'s No. 4 turret of the main calibre fired several volleys of 305mm shrapnel shells with distance fuses. They exploded high in the sky, forming huge smoke balls. Then 76mm and 45mm anti-aircraft guns opened fire, and the whole sky was painted with multicoloured clouds. Russian sailors with binoculars saw Stukas approach the Srednyaya harbour of Kronstadt, line up in a circle, and then start diving in turn.

Oberleutnant Rudel recalled:

> Meanwhile, the middle of the ship is exactly in the centre of my sight. My Ju 87 continues to dive, but the target still remains in the centre of the sight. I feel that it is simply impossible to miss. Now I can clearly see the battleship *Marat* right in front of me. Sailors are running along its deck ...[49]

Senior master of Leningrad Baltic Shipyard A.M. Gorchanikov was inside the battleship at that moment. He later recalled:

---

49. Rudel, H.U., *Stuka pilot*, Moscow: Centerpoligraph, 2009, p.48.

> On the morning of 23 September, hull repair specialists went to the bow of the ship, where electricians repaired a damaged cable bundle. We mechanics worked aft, in the engine room. Chief mechanic Alexander Abramov instructed me to determine the nature of the damage and repair the speaking pipes coming out of the bridge, and our mechanic Barabash to fix the drainage pump. At about 10 o'clock we heard a combat alert and at the same time an air alert. According to the combat schedule, the armoured hatch above us was immediately closed. We clearly heard the wail of dive bomber sirens.[50]

Meanwhile, the German pilots, one by one, pressed the release buttons, and the bombs rushed down. The first bomb dropped by Hauptmann Steen fell into the water near the port side of *Marat*. There was an explosion, and the huge ship, under the influence of the resulting wave, began to list to starboard. At that moment, a second bomb dropped by Oberleutnant Rudel hit the deck in front of the forward superstructure with the foremast. Its explosion caused the detonation of ammunition in the powder chamber of the No. 1 turret of the main calibre. A gigantic explosion followed, instantly claiming the lives of 326 of the crew. Among the dead were the commander, Captain 2nd rank Pavel Ivanov, chief mate Captain 3rd Rank Sergey Chufistov, a political commissar and several other senior officers. Only one person miraculously survived, Alexander Ivashchenko. Together with the 76mm anti-aircraft gun, he was thrown on the forecastle to the No. 2 turret of the main calibre.

The commander of the submarine *L-3*, Captain-lieutenant Pyotr Grishchenko, who was standing on the pier near *Marat*, recalled:

> Continuous fire engulfed the ship in a few seconds. Deafening explosions followed, one, two. Huge clouds of smoke and fire enveloped the bow of the battleship. Then there were two explosions again. It was clearly visible how the massive metal foremast with all the superstructures, bridges, platforms, completely filled with figures in white sailor uniforms and blue commander's uniforms, slowly separated from the battleship and, falling apart on the fly, fell into the water with a crash. The bow of

---

50. *The Red Banner Soviet Baltic Fleet in the Battle for Leningrad, 1941–1944*, Moscow: Nauka, 1975, pp.214–215.

the ship completely disappeared, and with it the turret of the main calibre with three 12-inch (305mm) guns.[51]

Alexander Gorchanikov, who was in the aft part of *Marat* at the time of the explosion, experienced very unpleasant sensations at the time of the ship's sinking. He later recalled:

> There was such a strong explosion that we, who were in the ship's workshop, were thrown almost to the ceiling, many were bruised. From the concussion, the pulley fasteners at machine tools in the ship's workshop burst. At this moment, the electric bulbs began to dim quickly, and then completely went out. We were left in the dark, helped by pocket electric flashlights. The young commander of the post who was with us tried to make phone calls, but no one answered him. Then I suggested opening the entrance hatch a little and looking around. When the locks of the armour cover were opened and the lid was lifted, we saw the sun's rays.[52]

Of course, the destruction of *Marat* was the most serious loss of the Russian Soviet Baltic Fleet in 1941. The bow part up to frame No. 20 was separated from the battleship and lay on the seabed with a roll to port. The main part of the battleship was afloat with a roll to starboard. However, the water quickly filled the internal compartments and after a while the remains sank to the bottom. However, since *Marat* was 14m tall and the depth at this point was just 11m, the upper deck, along with superstructures and the surviving gun turrets, remained above water. Later, the Russians began work on converting the remains into a stationary artillery battery.

The slaughter of Soviet Baltic Fleet ships continues

As soon as the Stukas disappeared in the distance, twenty-four bombers from KG 77 appeared over Kronstadt. They had already habitually dropped bombs on the large Soviet Baltic Fleet ships. Two SC250 bombs fell on the battleship *Oktyabrskaya Revolutsiya*. One crashed into the deck above casemate No. 10, and the second pierced the roof of turret No. 3 of the main calibre. As a result of

---

51. Grishchenko, P.D., *Fight Under Water*, Moscow: Molodaya gvardiya, 1983, p.85.
52. *The Red Banner Soviet Baltic Fleet in the Battle for Leningrad, 1941–1944*, Moscow: Nauka, 1975, p.215.

the explosion, a hole of 60cm by 70cm was formed in this turret, and the plate of the side wall of the turret shifted by 3cm.

The destroyer *Grozyashchiy*, in the Pamyati treh esmincev dry dock, was damaged again. Russian anti-aircraft gunners managed to damage Ju 88 A W.Nr. 4330 of the commander of the 7./KG 77, Oberleutnant Joachim Gunther. However, he was able to recover the damaged aircraft to his airfield.

Later in the evening, it was the turn of dive bombers from III./StG 2 again. Now the main target was the cruiser *Kirov*, moored at berth near the stump of the battleship *Marat*. Hauptmann Steen, who had previously failed to hit *Marat*, certainly wanted to repeat the success of his subordinate. His Ju 87 with a 1,000kg bomb began to dive on *Kirov*, but at an altitude of 1,500-2,000m, an anti-aircraft shell hit the plane, destroying the elevator. A few seconds later, the dive bomber crashed into the water next to the cruiser and there was a powerful explosion. Together with Hauptmann Steen,[53] who was performing his 301st combat mission, air gunner Feldwebel Scharnowsky also died. The commander's comrades who saw this dramatic episode later suggested that he deliberately tried to ram the cruiser in the spirit of a Japanese kamikaze, but missed!

At the same time, the Stukas attacked the destroyer leader *Minsk*, anchored on the Bolshoi roadstead of Kronstadt. Six Ju 87s simultaneously dived at it from a height of 1,000-1,500m from different angles. As a result, three SC50 bombs hit the ship. The first bomb crashed into the aft superstructure closer to the starboard side. Exploding on the upper deck, the bomb made a hole in it with a diameter of 11.5m. The second bomb hit the middle of *Minsk*'s hull closer to the port side. During the explosion, it formed several dozen holes in the upper deck, boiler casing and aft smokestack. The third bomb exploded near the side near boiler room No. 3 and damaged the main boiler. A fire started and part of the compartments began to fill with water quickly. Many auxiliary mechanisms and fuel tanks were destroyed. Having rolled 8 degrees to port, the destroyer leader began to drift slowly in the direction of Leningrad lighthouse. The struggle to save *Minsk* was conducted primitively, and the chaotic sealing of holes led to an increase in the roll. It turned out that there were not enough drainage facilities, especially those that could work autonomously; and there were not enough fire hoses and fire extinguishers. An hour later, a tugboat approached the destroyer leader. It dragged the ship into Voennaya harbour and

---

53. Ernst-Siegfried Steen was born on 25 September 1912 in Kiel. In the 1930s he joined the Luftwaffe and served in dive bombers units. Steen was a member of the Polish and French Wehrmacht campaigns. On 1 August 1941, he was appointed commander of III./StG 2. On 17 October 1941, Steen was posthumously awarded the Ritterkreuz des Eisernen Kreuzes (Knight's Cross of the Iron Cross).

moored it in a berth. There, the sailors tried to pump out the water with salvage ships and tugboats, but this process dragged on until the evening.

At 21.30 Ju 87s from III./StG 2[54] appeared over Kronstadt again and several bombs fell around *Minsk*. The nearest one exploded 40m from the ship. As a result, the outer skin of that side was deformed and destroyed, and new holes were made in it. *Minsk* was strongly rocked by the explosion and was flooded by the resulting wave. The combination of these factors proved fatal for the ship. Half an hour later, *Minsk* began to dive into the water with a roll to port and, breaking the mooring cables, sank at a depth of 8.5m. By 01.00 on 24 September, only part of the superstructures, smokestacks and masts remained above the water.

After a two-day break, air attacks against the navy base continued. On the morning of 26 September, Kronstadt was bombed by twelve Ju 88 As. As a result, the oil storage facility was destroyed and caught fire. Soon the fire spread to the transport ship *Biruta* moored next to it. It was not possible to extinguish the fire quickly and the *Biruta* completely burned out.

The next day, 27 September, the Luftwaffe launched another raid. Ju 87 B/Rs from III./StG 2 and Ju 88 As from KG 77 took part, forty-two aircraft in total. They appeared over Kronstadt at 17.32. The main target of the air attack was the battleship *Oktyabrskaya Revolutsiya*, which received new damage. For example, SC500 bombs pierced bridges near the foremast and exploded on the deck in front of turret No. 2 of the main calibre, whose barbettes and mechanisms were damaged. As a result, the turret completely lost its combat capability. However, the most terrible threat to the ship was another bomb. Oberleutnant Rudel was able to place an armour-piercing explosive bomb PC1000 in the bow. However, unlike a similar hit on *Marat*, the bomb only penetrated the armoured decks and did not explode! Otherwise, Oberleutnant Rudel could have become a real undertaker to the Stalin fleet, destroying two of the three Russian battleships. In addition, *Oktyabrskaya Revolutsiya* was exposed to the non-contact effects of ninety-eight bomb explosions at a distance of up to 25m from the side. From the blast wave and concussions inside the hull, many mechanisms were torn from their fastenings, the skin and bulkheads were dented. Pumps pumped water out of the holds almost continuously. As a result of this damage, the old battleship was disabled and lost the ability to move independently. But it didn't drown!

In addition to strikes on large ships, Luftwaffe pilots paid attention to other targets. During the raid, the gunboat *Pioner* was severely damaged and soon sank, while berths and port facilities at Kronstadt received new damage.

---

54. After the death of Hauptmann Steen, the command of III./StG 2 was temporarily taken over by Commander 9./StG 2 Hauptmann Gunther Schwarzel.

AIR BATTLE FOR LENINGRAD, 1941–1944

Despite the frenzied firing of Russian anti-aircraft guns, almost all the Stukas returned safely to base. Once again, only the commander of 7./StG 2, Hauptmann Ernst Kupfer, was unlucky. For the third time, his Ju 87 was damaged by anti-aircraft fire, when a Russian shell hit the engine. Kupfer was able to return to German territory, but this time his emergency landing ended in disaster. The reason for the complete destruction of the aircraft was a small forest, which unexpectedly turned out to be on the approach to the landing site. Hauptmann Kupfer and his radio operator, Feldwebel Barnebeck, were seriously injured. The pilot was diagnosed with a skull base fracture, severe concussion, and several limb fractures. Hauptmann Kupfer's head was particularly badly damaged,[55] and he lost his eyesight for several weeks.

Has the Russian fleet been destroyed?

From 19 to 27 September, Luftwaffe aircraft destroyed eighteen ships and vessels, including one battleship, one destroyer leader and one destroyer. Thirteen other ships received various heavy damage, including a battleship, cruiser and four destroyers. Three more ships were sunk in the Gulf of Finland in the vicinity of Kronstadt and Leningrad, including the minesweeper *TSCH-33*. If we consider that from 22 June to 27 September 1941 the Soviet Baltic Fleet lost ninety-two ships of various types (from boats to battleship) from bombing attacks and sea mines installed by Luftwaffe aircraft, then we can conclude that Stalin had almost lost his most numerous and beloved fleet. However, the leadership of Soviet Baltic Fleet, frightened by the complete defeat, took the opposite point of view. Fearing imminent execution for the loss of the warships, they continued to send cheerful messages to Stalin. As will be noted later, Hitler also believed that the Luftwaffe had not fully fulfilled its mission and that the Soviet Baltic Fleet still existed as a fully fledged combat force at sea.

As already noted above, after the losses suffered, the command of the Russian fleet was in a state close to panic. Evidence of this was the hasty evacuation of the remnants of the fleet to Leningrad. Commander of the Soviet Baltic Fleet Vice Admiral Vladimir Tributs ordered the transfer of all ships capable of moving to the mouth of the Neva. On 24 September, the cruiser

---

55. On 23 November 1941, Ernst Kupfer was awarded the Ritterkreuz des Eisernen Kreuzes (Knight's Cross of the Iron Cross) for his bravery. After recovering on 1 April 1942, he was promoted to Major and appointed Commander of II./StG 2. On 8 January 1943, Kupfer was awarded Eichenlaub (Oak Leaves) to Eisernen Kreuzes (Iron Cross) and on 1 March, with the rank of Oberst, he became commander of StG 2. Ernst Kupfer died on 6 November 1943 in an He 111 crash.

Kirov, three surviving destroyers and several auxiliary vessels sailed there. The fleet command believed that Leningrad's air defence was stronger than in Kronstadt, and they would be safer there.

On 24 September, the 71st Fighter Aviation Regiment Air Force Soviet Baltic Fleet (71st IAP VVS KBF) arrived at Bychiy Pole airfield (in the western part of Kotlin Island) to protect the ships remaining in Kronstadt. It was armed with I-16 and I-153 fighters. Also the next day, anti-aircraft batteries of the 6th Anti-aircraft Regiment (6th ZenAP) were relocated to Kronstadt. In parallel with the active defence, the Soviet command tried to hide the surviving ships by means of passive camouflage. These efforts by incompetent Soviet commanders looked like obvious manifestations of idiocy! For example, the battleship *Oktyabrskaya Revolutsiya* was supposed to look like a huge grain silo after camouflage work! Obviously, the Soviets considered German pilots to be fools capable of believing that a 'grain silo' would be built in the water at the pier, or standing in the roadstead in the harbour.

The Soviets continued to relocate all the surviving large ships to Leningrad. On 30 September, the destroyers *Gordy* and *Silnyi* sailed from Kronstadt to the mouth of the Neva; the next day, the destroyer *Surovyi*. On 5 October, the destroyer *Grozyashchiy* relocated to Leningrad. On 23 October, the battleship *Oktyabrskaya Revolutsiya* sailed there. By early November 1941, only four damaged destroyers remained at Kronstadt, unable to move even by tugboats.

In just a few months of the war, Stalin's Baltic Fleet had lost all its numerous navy bases (Tallinn, Liepaya, Ventspils, Triigi and Hanko) and now had even had to leave Kronstadt. From now on, the only navy base was St Petersburg, founded by Peter I, renamed Leningrad by the Bolsheviks. The fate of the ships trapped in the Neva was inextricably linked with the fate of the city. If Leningrad fell, then the remnants of the fleet were doomed to perish.

Meanwhile, VIII. Fliegerkorps's time in the front sector of Army Group North had come to an end. The Wehrmacht was preparing for a 'decisive offensive' on Moscow, so the experienced pilots of Generalmajor Wolfram von Richthofen had to return to the subordination of the Army Group Centre. However, Generalfeldmarschall Wilhelm Ritter von Leeb and the Commander of Luftflotte 1, Generaloberst Alfred Keller, strongly delayed the transfer of aviation units and repeatedly petitioned for a change in terms. As a result of these efforts, the dates for the redeployment of more VIII. Fliegerkorps units were shifted from 23 to 25 September, and then to 28 September. This allowed Luftflotte 1 to carry out another 3,500 sorties in the Leningrad sector in a week.

Chapter 4

Deadly lake

How to protect Leningrad's supply waterways by Lake Ladoga?

After the establishment of the land blockade, the situation of the huge city became critical. The Soviets had only one option left for action – to supply Leningrad by water, through the treacherous and gloomy Lake Ladoga. This huge reservoir of glacial origin is the largest lake in Europe and one of the deepest reservoirs of this type on the planet. The depth of Lake Ladoga ranges from 20 to 230m. Even among medieval traders and travellers, this lake was considered a dangerous and perilous place. Strong winds and storms with waves 5–6m high were common there.

Ladoga Military Flotilla carried out the protection and air defence of convoys of ships crossing the lake. In August 1941, it included sixty-six ships and boats. The main striking force consisted of six gunboats: *Bira*, *Bureya*, *Nora*, *Olekma*, *Selemdzha* and *Sheksna*. They were armed with 76mm, 100mm and 130mm guns, as well as 37mm and 45mm anti-aircraft guns. All of these ships, with the exception of *Sheksna* (the former Finnish icebreaker ship *Aallaks* with a displacement of 150 tons) were converted from self-propelled hopper barges.[56]

Interestingly, five of these vessels – *Bira*, *Bureya*, *Nora*, *Olekma* and *Selemdzha* – were built by order of the Soviet government in 1939–41 at the German shipyard Deutsche Werft AG in Hamburg. Before the war, these ships belonged to a special structure, Spetsgidrostroy NKVD.[57] The main Punitive Service of the Soviet Union had its own flotilla to service facilities built by

---

56. Self-propelled hopper barges were designed for transporting soil extracted by dredging vessels from the bottom of the reservoir. When dredging, the self-propelled hopper barge was moored to the dredging vessel, which loaded the extracted soil mass onto it for further delivery to a specially designated underwater landfill.
57. Spetsgidrostroy NKVD was a special unit created within Gulag. It was intended to provide technical support for the construction of various hydraulic structures by prisoners.

Gulag prisoners. All five vessels were built with excellent German quality and a large margin of safety. In the autumn of 1941, self-propelled hopper barges were converted into warships with crews of approximately 110. After such modernisation, the Russians began to informally call the clumsy slow-moving self-propelled barges 'Ladoga battleships'. On the lake, the gunboats really looked impressive. The length of their hull was 60m, the width was 12m, and the total displacement was 1,140 tons. 'Ladoga battleships' reached speeds from 6 to 8 knots.

The Ladoga Military Flotilla also had two large patrol ships, *Constructor* and *Purga*. *Constructor* was an old torpedo gunboat built in 1906. Before the Bolsheviks seized power, it served in the fleet of the Russian Empire under its original name *Sibirsky Strelok*. *Constructor* was armed with three 100mm and two 45mm guns. *Purga* was a modern warship built in 1936. It had a length of 71m, a displacement of 600 tons and was armed with two 102mm guns, two M1939 (61-K) 37mm automatic anti-aircraft guns and one torpedo tube. It was the fastest ship on Lake Ladoga, capable of speeds up to 21 knots. The crew of patrol *Purga* numbered 114.

In addition, the Soviets on Lake Ladoga had six MO-class submarine chasers, two armoured boats, sixteen minesweepers and other ships that were also part of Ladoga Military Flotilla.

The first delivery of goods by water for the besieged Leningrad

The North-Western Shipping Company (SZRP) had about 120 vessels with which to organise transportation on Lake Ladoga in order to supply Leningrad. Among them were five lake and seventy-two river tugboats, and forty-nine lake and river wooden barges. Most of them were only marginally suitable for swimming on such large bodies of water as Lake Ladoga, especially during autumn storms.

However, before starting large-scale transportation on the lake, the Soviets had to determine the places to load and unload supplies. The north-western regions of Russia were deserted. The monotonous landscape, the eternally gloomy sky, deep forests, and swamps were only cut through by bad roads in some places. At first, there were no major ports on the shores of the huge lake, there were only berths designed to receive one or two lake transport ships. However, even the presence of such a primitive port infrastructure only slightly accelerated the process of sending cargo ashore. Due to the shallow depths, the heavily loaded barges could not approach the berths. Therefore, the cargo had to be loaded onto boats or simply dumped into the water, and then manually dragged to land.

The most suitable place to build a port on the western shore of the lake was around the village of Osinovets, on Cape Osinovets. A dense forest grew there, which made it possible to hide warehouses, access roads and air defence facilities from aerial reconnaissance and German bombers. In addition, Lake Ladoga railway station was next to Osinovets. The movement of cars and people from the lake to the railway station was also masked by the crowns of trees. These favourable factors became decisive when making a decision and hasty work on the construction of an improvised lake port began in Osinovets.

However, there were obvious obstacles to the organisation of the port in this place. On the western shore in the Osinovets area, a sandy and rocky low shore prevailed, and the depth was insufficient even for vessels with a shallow draft. An old stone mole, built of cobblestones, formed a small Osinovets harbour, protected from storm waves. Due to shallowing, the entrance to the harbour was only possible for vessels with a small draft. However, the main obstacle to the creation of a port on the western shore was the complete lack of developed infrastructure for organising the transport of large volumes of cargo.

A similar situation developed on the eastern shore in Novaya Ladoga harbour, from where cargo was to be shipped to the besieged Leningrad. However, in order to deliver supplies even to this intermediate point, considerable difficulties had to be overcome. At first, goods from the centre of Russia were delivered by rail to the railway junction at Volkhovstroy. From there, the railcars were moved to berths at Gostinopolye harbour, where the loads were manually dragged to river barges. Then small tugboats dragged the barges to the mouth of the river Volkhov at Novaya Ladoga harbour. There was a transshipment of goods to lake barges, which was also accompanied by overcoming all kinds of difficulties. In particular, the berths at Novaya Ladoga were too short to receive several vessels. Even the most primitive lifting devices were missing, and the roads were in terrible condition and required constant repair. In addition, due to heavy rain, lake barges could not enter the mouth of the Volkhov, so they had to be loaded at a considerable distance from the shore.

Zinovy Rusakov, an officer of Ladoga Military Flotilla, recalled:

> If you look to the east from the shore in the Osinovets lighthouse area, the boundless expanse of Lake Ladoga opens. But this 'space' is deceptive. Each ship could make its way, especially when approaching ports, only along a single winding fairway, the width of which did not exceed 20–25 metres, and the depth – no more than 2.5–5 metres. In storm conditions it is difficult to do this. The slightest deviation from the course and the ship will run aground or stumble upon some dangerous underwater obstacle. The route along the open part of the lake – from Novaya Ladoga

harbour on the eastern shore to Osinovets on the western shore – with a length of 115 kilometres was also dangerous for slow-moving vessels because it took place in close proximity to enemy positions. The entrance to the river Volkhov from the lake due to the underwater shoal had a depth of only 160 centimetres. For this reason, only river tugboats could approach berths in Novaya Ladoga harbour. The rest of the transport vessels and barges were loaded on the external roadstead using shallow-seated river barges.[58]

The hastily organised lake supply line operated with heavy losses from the very beginning. The journey along the waterway across Lake Ladoga took an average of sixteen hours. Moreover, in order to reduce losses from Luftwaffe air attacks, it was necessary to sail across the ferocious lake mainly at night.

To increase the volume of cargo delivered, the Soviets had to use all available lake barges. At the same time, the gunboats and patrol ships guarding the barges were themselves loaded to the top with cargo and also performed the role of tugboats. After arriving on the west coast – at the port of Osinovets – carts and trucks, and often people were sent to Lake Ladoga railway station. There, the supplies were reloaded into railway wagons and taken to the Finlyandsky railway station in Leningrad. There was no mechanisation in the places of cargo transshipment; the whole burden of loading and unloading lay on the shoulders of people. A significant part of the huge contingent of movers was young girls. It is easy to imagine how hard this work was for them, especially in the conditions that included autumn rains, the cold of the approaching winter and, most importantly, hunger!

On 12 September 1941, two barges arrived at Osinovets, delivering 800 tons of grain. It was the first cargo delivery for the besieged Leningrad. On the same day, the patrol ship *Purga* delivered 60 tons of ammunition to Osinovets. Thus began the functioning of the so-called Road of Life, which in fact became for many Soviet people the road of death ...

The First Luftwaffe attacks against the Road of Life

The delivery of cargo by the Soviets on Lake Ladoga was quickly discovered by German reconnaissance planes. On 11 September, Luftwaffe aircraft carried

---

58. Rusakov, Z.G., *Our Sea was Ladoga*, Leningrad: Lenizdat, 1980, p.60.

out the first air attacks against the port infrastructure under construction on the lake.

On 15 September, the dredging vessel *Severo-Zapadnyi-7* came under attack by German aircraft. The ship's engine was disabled, and many crew members were injured. However, the sailors managed to plug the holes, repair the damage and soon put the dredging vessel into operation.

On the same day – 15 September – a Luftwaffe reconnaissance plane discovered a caravan of three barges and a tugboat on Lake Ladoga, approaching the western coast. Several Ju 87s from III./StG 2 were urgently sent from Tirkovo airfield and the dive bombers discovered the barges unloading at Osinovets harbour. Experienced Stukas pilots did not miss. After the air strike, all three barges sank along with 3,000 tons of wheat. The tugboat managed to transmit a distress signal on the radio, and the patrol ship *Constructor* hurried to the scene of the tragedy.

The inspector of the Main Political Directorate of the Soviet Army and Soviet Navy, Alexey Karavaev, who was on the ship, recalled:

> When we arrived at the bombing area on the patrol ship *Constructor*, we saw a terrible picture. Barges were smashed. People were holding on to wreckage and floating bags of flour, at whom Nazi planes fired machine guns from a strafing flight ... Gunners on *Constructor* opened fire on the planes from all guns and paired anti-aircraft machine guns. The Germans flew away.
>
> After that, the patrol ship *Constructor* team started rescue operations. Large waves made it difficult to lower boats and approach the wreckage of barges. As a result, the sailors began to tie lifebuoys to a hemp rope and throw them into the thick of people. They rarely got caught. Exhausted people disappeared one by one into the dark abyss. As a result, only a few people were saved. The next morning, some of the bodies of the victims, along with bags of flour, washed ashore 10km west of Novaya Ladoga.[59]

Records from the logbook of the commander of the gunboat *Selemdzha*, Captain 3rd Rank Mikhail Antonov, testify to the precarious situation in which the Road of Life operated:

> 16.09.41. 21.00. Novaya Ladoga roadstead. We were given a barge to tow to the port of Osinovets with a cargo of 400 tons of

---

59. Ibid., p.62.

flour and 460 soldiers to replenish the troops of the Leningrad Front.

22.00. Our ship weighed anchor and set sail for the port of Osinovets.

17.09.41. 03.25. The wind force is 6 points. The cargo hold hatch cover has been torn off. 03.50. Water flow in cargo hold. A squall with a wind force of 9 points. The wave on the barge breaks the bollards, the hull cracks, the water in cargo holds is added. People with barge are asking for help. Rifle fire is heard.

It is impossible to pull up the barge to remove people. The roll reaches 35 degrees. The tow ropes snapped. The barge was carried to the shore to Severnaya Goloveshko bank (shallow). Ordered the barge to lower the anchor. I stayed anchored until dawn.

Since dawn, apart from the wreckage from the barge and floating bags of flour, there is nothing in the Severnaya Goloveshka bank area.

At the same time, gunboat repelled air attacks by aviation.

The Dark Abyss of Lake Ladoga

On 17 September, a terrible tragedy occurred on Lake Ladoga. Due to the fear of Luftwaffe raids, the old tugboat *Orel* with wooden barge *No. 725* in tow left Osinovets harbour at night. The barge was overflowing with refugees and soldiers. According to the most conservative estimates, there were more than 1,200 people on the half-rotted vessel.

At the beginning of the journey, a storm broke out on Lake Ladoga, and in the area of the Severnaya Goloveshka bank, the hull of the old wooden barge could not withstand the blows of the waves and broke. The barge began to gradually sink and one by one, the passengers were washed overboard by the waves and they immediately disappeared into the dark depths of the lake. Some tried to escape by swimming, but also died. Cold dark waves were taking away more and more victims. The despair of the people on the sinking barge reached the point that one Soviet officer who had evacuated with his family from Leningrad, out of desperation first shot his daughter and wife, and then shot himself.

In the midst of the disaster, an attack by German aircraft began, and as a result of nearby bomb explosions, the barge received additional damage. The bridge and part of the upper deck broke off but, miraculously, the skeleton of the barge, which remained afloat, continued on its way to the eastern shore of Lake Ladoga.

A witness of the events, Vladimir Solontsov, who was escaping on the roof of the deckhouse of the barge, recalled these terrible minutes:

> Being on the roof of the deckhouse of the barge, I did not immediately realise that this water shaft tore the deckhouse off the deck and carried it overboard. No one could even imagine such an option. The deckhouse began to sink quickly with almost no roll. The remaining people on deck were shouting. Inside the deckhouse, everything was somehow quiet – the women and children probably didn't even realise what had happened at first. The deckhouse of the barge sank to the bottom in less than a minute, and when the water rushed into it, the mothers most likely only had time to hug the children to themselves. Their personal struggle for life was lost ... These were terrible moments in my life. I – a strong man – was standing on the deckhouse going under the water and could do nothing to save people. When the water reached my waist, I pushed off and swam towards the *Orel* tugboat. It's hard to say for how long, but I still managed to get to the tugboat. A sailor threw me a rope and helped me up on deck.

When the barge finally disappeared under the water, *Orel* and the gunboat *Selemdzha*, which happened to be nearby, began rescuing people. In total, about 240 passengers were rescued. At the same time, the minesweeper *TSCH-122*, under the command of Senior Lieutenant Fyodor Khodov, rushed to the rescue. Before becoming a 'warship', the *TSCH-122* was the flat-bottomed tugboat *Som*, built in 1913. Despite the lack of time to save the dying people, the worn-out minesweeper hardly rolled from wave to wave. Approaching the crash site, the sailors saw the wreckage of a broken barge ahead. In the waves of the raging elements, exhausted, numb people clung to it. It was impossible to lower the boat in a storm. The minesweeper sailors tied themselves with cables and jumped overboard, pulling out the victims. As a result, another 130 people were saved by heroic efforts.

Soon the position of the minesweeper itself became critical. The seams parted from the blows of the waves, and water began to flood the boiler room. The captain, Senior Lieutenant Khodov, immediately headed straight for the shore, in order, as a last resort, to put the sinking ship aground. Struggling with the elements, the minesweeper drifted until dawn. However, Khodov failed to reach the shore safely ... The sailors and rescued passengers from the drowned barge *No. 725* were horrified to see four planes fall out of the clouds.

DEADLY LAKE

In desperation the *TSCH-122* crew opened fire with a machine gun and a single 45mm gun. But the German planes continued to dive on the minesweeper and drop bombs. Two bombs exploded next to it, raising huge fountains of water, and two more hit exactly on target. The explosion literally tore out a piece of the left side of the minesweeper and *TSCH-122* began to sink rapidly. Soon the deck of the minesweeper disappeared under the water, but then a thud followed – the ship sat on the bottom.

After that, the German bombers flew away, and the surviving crew members and the rescued passengers of barge *No. 725*, grasping the bridge, smokestack and mast sticking out of the water, began to wait for their fate. Periodically, someone lost consciousness, slid into the water and immediately disappeared from sight. The others prayed for help to come. Thirteen hours later, the gunboat *Nora* and the lake tugboat *Orel* approached the sunken minesweeper. Their crew rescued the surviving sailors and several passengers from barge *No. 725*.

After the completion of the rescue operation, it turned out that about a thousand of barge *No. 725*'s passengers drowned in the cold waters of Lake Ladoga. Thirteen sailors from the minesweeper *TSCH-122* were also killed, including chief mate Lieutenant Rostovtsev and Military technician of the 2nd Rank Mishukov.

On the same night, due to a storm, the transport ships *Kozelsk*, *Voima* and *Michurin* sank. Huge waves of the raging Lake Ladoga threw *Michurin* on the rocks. The destruction of lake vessels soon became a sad pattern as storms and German bombing disabled one ship after another. As a result, just two weeks after the start of cargo transportation to supply Leningrad, only nine lake and thirteen river barges remained afloat.

Who will save the crew of salvage ship *Vodolaz*?

On 4 October 1941, the salvage ship *Vodolaz* and the transport ship *Stalinets* went in search of another barge in distress on the lake. A storm was raging on Lake Ladoga, and huge grey waves were beating against the sides of the ships. Despite a long search, it was not possible to find the shipwreck. Due to poor visibility and lack of radio communication, salvage ships lost sight of each other. Soon *Stalinets* turned back to Novaya Ladoga harbour, and *Vodolaz* continued the search. At about 21.00, despite the bad weather, a twin-engine plane fell out of the dark clouds in the Severnaya Strelkovaya area and flew straight over the waves to *Vodolaz*. The German Ju 88 A bomber roared over the ship, dropping four bombs. The first bomb pierced through the lifeboat and exploded in the boiler room. Two other bombs hit the stern of the ship. The damage was fatal. *Vodolaz* immediately began to sink on the starboard side and plunge into the gloomy raging waters. Steam from the boiler burst into the air with an ominous whistle, like a death scream. The survivors among the ship's crew somehow lowered the remaining boat and immediately sailed away. Those who did not have time to get into the boat jumped straight into the water. *Vodolaz* soon sank together with its Captain Vladimir Zenin. However, the trials of the surviving crew members did not end there. The Ju 88 bomber turned around and fired at the boat and people floating in the water on its second approach. Only six people were able to bring the boat to the shore with great difficulty. More than sixty sailors were swallowed up by an insatiable lake ...

Bombers from KGr. 806 over Lake Ladoga

On 5 October 1941, German bombers achieved major successes at Lake Ladoga. They attacked and damaged the gunboat *Olekma*, which was shelling the positions of Finnish troops in the Verhnie Nikulyasy settlement area. The damage received by the gunboat was so severe that the next day the warship sank near Cape Mar'in Nos.

On the same day, Ju 88 A-4 from KGr. 806 commanded by Major Richard Linke attacked the improvised port of Osinovets. The planes approached the target at an altitude of 2,000–3,000m, then dived and dropped bombs. Each bomber performed several approaches to the target. As a result, two boats were destroyed, a dredging vessel and a floating crane. The gunboat *Bira* had its stern destroyed by an explosion. Water poured through holes and filled the stern compartments. However, the gunboat remained afloat and returned to service a few days later. Four railway wagons with flour were destroyed on the shore. Five people were killed and twelve were injured.[60]

It is not surprising that the Luftflotte 1 command chose KGr. 806 to carry out attacks against Osinovets harbour and ships on Lake Ladoga. The pilots of this Gruppe had already demonstrated their developed competencies during air attacks against Soviet Baltic Fleet ships. They perfected them in the Gulf of Riga, near the Moonsund archipelago and in the Gulf of Finland. During these missions, KGr. 806 bombers sank the destroyers *Serdityi* and *Karl Marx*, and heavily damaged the destroyers *Engels*, *Strashnyi* and *Surovyi*. They also sent many other small warships and transport vessels to the bottom. Although there were few military ships that corresponded to their competencies on Lake Ladoga, the crews of KGr. 806 nevertheless began hunting enthusiastically for Ladoga Military Flotilla ships.

---

60. TSAMO RF. Foundation 217. Inventory 1221. Case 103. Sheet 203.

On 7 October, four bombers from KGr. 806 suddenly appeared in the south-eastern part of the lake, over Novaya Ladoga harbour. Their main goal was the patrol ship *Constructor*. At an altitude of about 800m, four bombs separated from one of the Ju 88s. They exploded among the ships standing on the roadstead. As a result of an explosion close to *Constructor*, part of the team led by the commander, Captain 2nd Rank Georgy Zeland, was killed. After that, a fire broke out on the ship. However, despite the damage *Constructor* remained afloat. Also during the German air attack, the minesweeper *TSCH-127* and the transport ships *Stalinets* and *Sovet*, with a tonnage of 300brt were damaged, and the patrol boat *KM-1403* and a barge with flour were sunk.

The degree of intensity of the Luftwaffe attacks can be judged by the entries in the logbook of the gunboat *Bira*, which constantly escorted convoys to Lake Ladoga. On 9 October, six air attacks by German aircraft were recorded, on 10 October – six, on 11 October – five, on 12 October – four, on 13 October – five, on 14 October – four, on 17 October – five.

On the night of 11 October, a German night reconnaissance aircraft flew over Osinovets harbour several times. The next day, the Luftwaffe carried out another air attack. But this time the German bombers were met by intense anti-aircraft fire, and in the sky they were attacked by Soviet fighters. At the cost of losing one Yak-1 and one LaGG-3, the Soviets managed to prevent the Germans from dropping bombs with precision.

This modest success allowed the Headquarters of the Air Defence Forces of the Leningrad Front to draw optimistic conclusions:

> The low accuracy of dropping bombs by German aircraft during the daytime raid on Cape Osinovets (all bombs fell into the lake without causing harm) was the result of measures taken to strengthen the air defence of this sector and increase the effectiveness of our Fighter Aviation and anti-aircraft artillery.[61]

Subsequent events showed that the Soviet air defence really worked, but its high efficiency is a myth.

On the morning of 16 October, four Ju 88 As appeared over Osinovets, accompanied by four Bf 109 Fs. The Headquarters of the Air Defence Forces of the Leningrad Front reported:

> The planes flew up to the object behind the clouds, and when bombing they dropped to 400–700 metres. A total of 16 bombs

---

61. TSAMO RF. Foundation 217. Inventory 1221. Case 103. Sheet 217.

were dropped. Despite the firing of anti-aircraft artillery and repeated attacks by Fighter Aviation, enemy aircraft as a result of the bombing managed to destroy one barge with cargo, sink four boats and damage one boat. One person was killed and four people were injured.[62]

During the raid, anti-aircraft guns mounted on the shore and on the patrol ship *Constructor* simultaneously fired at the diving Ju 88s. In addition, over the roadstead of Osinovets, one Ju 88 was attacked by four MiG-3 fighters from the 124th Fighter Aviation Regiment (124th IAP). In front of hundreds of sailors and anti-aircraft gunners, one German bomber caught fire and crashed into the water near the harbour, raising a huge column of water. It was Ju 88 A-4 W.Nr. 1180 'M7+AL' of 3./KGr. 806. One of the German pilots managed to jump out with a parachute and descended into the water. Soon the Russians caught him and hoisted him on board *Constructor*. Now the German pilot was able to examine in detail his recent goal. After strict interrogation, he was sent to a prison camp, of course, in Siberia. The group aerial victory was recorded on the combat account of Captain A. Beliy, Senior Lieutenant V. Koren and Junior Lieutenant M. Barsov.

On 17 October, during another mission over Lake Ladoga, another Ju 88 A-4, W.Nr. 3570 from KGr. 806, was damaged by anti-aircraft fire. But this crew was luckier than the previous one. The bomber was able to fly to Siverskaya Air Base and made a wheels-up landing. The damage to the aircraft was estimated at 50 per cent on the German damage scale.

In the following days, the actions of German aviation over Lake Ladoga were limited due to cloudy and snowy weather. On the morning of 25 October, five Ju 88s from KGr. 806, accompanied by four Bf 109s from JG 54, raided Osinovets harbour, dropping thirty-two high-explosive bombs on it. This time, the achievements of the Germans turned out to be modest: a fishing schooner was damaged and six people were injured.

The next air attacks against the improvised port of Osinovets were carried out four days later. On 29 October at 13.00, eight Ju 88 A-4s appeared over Osinovets harbour. They flew from Lake Ladoga at an altitude of 3,000m, then dived rapidly, dropped bombs from the first approach and went west. Of the twenty bombs dropped, sixteen fell into the water, the rest near a berth and the anti-aircraft battery position. As a result of the air raid, six Red Army soldiers were killed and twenty-two people were injured. At 16.20, four Ju 88s appeared over Osinovets again. The results of this air attack were even more modest.

---

62. TSAMO RF. Foundation 217. Inventory 1221. Case 103. Sheet 238.

Seventeen bombs fell into the water near the berths, while three exploded on the shore away from the target.

The Luftwaffe attack on Lake Ladoga was repeated the next morning. The Headquarters of the Air Defence Forces of the Leningrad Front report contained the following information: 'At 9.40 the enemy raided the port of Osinovets with six Ju 88 aircraft. Diving planes from a height of 200–300 metres dropped 12 bombs on the port. There is no destruction and no casualties. The planes approached from the north and went south.'[63]

Poor organisation, difficult weather conditions and Luftwaffe bombing hindered the effective functioning of the Road of Life. Leningrad's supply was usually carried out inefficiently. Instead of the planned four days, in reality the cargo turnover of one barge on average took at least eight, and sometimes twelve days. The shortage of vessels forced the Soviets to urgently organise a repair point for barges in the Syasskie Ryadki settlement area, on the eastern shore of Lake Ladoga. There, nine more river barges were modified for sailing on the lake for ten days. On 26 October, they set off on their first trip, but four barges were immediately destroyed as a result of German bombing and a storm.

The Soviets tried to take organisational measures to improve Leningrad's supply along the Road of Life via Lake Ladoga. For additional control over transportation, the positions of political commissar (politruk) from among the Leningrad Communists were introduced on barges. However, this idiotic measure, applied out of desperation before the impending total famine, did not help. The already modest norms for the distribution of products to the population of the city were steadily declining.

Meanwhile, Ladoga Military Flotilla ships completed another important strategic task. They laid an armoured marine communication cable 43km long along the bottom of the lake, which linked the Soviet Baltic Fleet and Leningrad with Moscow.

Combined combat missions

The priority targets of the German bombers in the autumn of 1941 were important military facilities on the territory of Leningrad: port infrastructure, hydraulic structures, power plants, factories and ammunition depots. However, the limited number of Luftwaffe units in this sector of the vast Eastern Front and the appearance of new targets for attacks every day forced the Luftflotte 1 command to use its bombers universally. In addition to bombing Leningrad,

---

63. TSAMO RF. Foundation 217. Inventory 1221. Case 103. Sheet 284.

the planes had to support Wehrmacht operations from the air and counteract the city's supply via Lake Ladoga. In order to carry out such diverse missions with limited forces, staff officers were forced to increase the intensity and effectiveness of sorties of each combat-ready bomber crew. There were two ways to do this. The first method was to increase the number of sorties flown by the bomber crew in one day. The second method involved adding to the main missions with a number of auxiliary combat missions performed before or after the main task.

A striking example of such an intensification of the use of limited forces were the actions of bombers from I./KG 4. Initially, this Gruppe operated almost as usual and carried out missions to support the offensive of XXXIX Army Corps (mot.) under General der Panzertruppen Rudolf Schmidt on the town of Tikhvin. At that time, I./KG 4 was based at Pleskau-Süd air base in Pskov, where they relocated on 16 October. Soon the Gruppe received a new task related to the bombing of transport communications of the defending Red Army units. Moreover, they had to carry out this mission in parallel with the support of German troops around Tikhvin. On 14 and 23 October, I./KG 4 crews conducted several successful attacks against railway lines, destroying several trains with supplies for the Soviet troops.

In early November 1941, the intensity of the use of crews from I./KG 4 increased again. In addition to its many functions, Hauptmann Noske's He 111s were also supposed to attack ships on Lake Ladoga.[64] To perform these combined missions, the bombers had to relocate to Dno-Griwotschki airfield and undertook at least two combat sorties per day. The combination of flight intensity and the variety of missions required special crew training and a carefully selected bomber bomb load. One heavy high-explosive bomb (SC500 or SC1000) was suspended from the fuselage, as well as several SC250s. Based on this, the combined missions were carried out in the following, strictly worked out sequence. Departing at dusk, He 111 groups first flew to Leningrad and dropped SC500 or SC1000 bombs on power plants on the Neva. Then they turned east towards Lake Ladoga and began searching for Soviet ships. Soon, such non-standard tactics of using German bombers began to bear fruit.

The commander of 1./KG 4 Oberleutnant Eberhard Hennings wrote in a report:

> Wide bands of large fires marked the front line. There are frequent outbreaks on the ground. At the same time, anti-aircraft shells

---

64. Gundelach, K., *Kampfgeschwader 'General Wever' 4*, Stuttgart: Motorbuch Verlag, 1978, p.158.

begin to explode in the sky, we perceive them as a signal from the ground, calling us to fly to the fire, to Leningrad! So the Soviets seemed to show us our way. Leningrad is already under us. The city was perfectly visible on a bright moonlit night: the Neva, the canal with a sharp bend and here is our goal. The navigator is immersed in work, and is on his bed in front of the cabin. After dropping our bombs, a fire starts below ...

And here we are, finally, over the west coast of Lake Ladoga. Now begins the search for enemy ships on the largest lake in Europe. The moonlight is reflected on a huge surface, which allows you to detect any traces on the water surface at a great distance. So far, nothing is visible except floating debris. But we persistently continue the search. We had already gone quite far to the east when we saw something on the surface of the water. Maybe it's a small island with a lighthouse that we already know? Or is it the reflections on the surface caused by the illumination from this island? We very carefully approach closer to examine. And we see a plume of smoke over the water! Then it becomes clear that this is a plume of smoke from a ship going east. We are currently in the most advantageous position and at the right altitude to approach the target. Then comes the attack. Up close we can see that our target is much bigger, it's a gunboat!

We receive an order over the radio: drop the bombs and turn right. To the right, from behind, I see high pillars from the explosions of bombs that fell into the water near the target, as well as a bright white cloud of steam, as when boilers explode. Bullseye![65]

A short respite and discussion of the situation. Now we are going on a second run to see the results of the attack, but we do it with caution, for fear of air defence. We can see how the ship has tilted heavily to one side and its front part is already under water.[66]

The 'gunboat' that was attacked by the He 111 actually turned out to be the patrol ship *Constructor*!

---

65. In the jargon of the crews of German bombers, this expression meant 'the highest accuracy'.
66. Gundelach, K., *Kampfgeschwader 'General Wever' 4*, Stuttgart: Motorbuch Verlag, 1978, pp.152–157.

End of the patrol ship *Constructor*

In early November 1941, the Commander of the Ladoga Military Flotilla, Captain 1st rank Vasily Cherokov, received an order to urgently transport several hundred workers to the eastern shore of the lake, who were subject to evacuation to new military factories in the Urals. Together with the workers, their families also went to the rescue evacuation. For this purpose, the fastest patrol ships *Constructor* and *Purga* were allocated. On the evening of 4 November, as soon as it got dark, patrol ships left Morier harbour one by one and set sail at a speed of 17 knots through the troubled waters of Lake Ladoga. There were 350 passengers on board *Constructor*, and 300 on *Purga*.

When the patrol ships were already far from the shore, the hum of approaching aircraft engines was heard. The moon was shining brightly, so it was not difficult to distinguish quite large ships on the surface of the lake. Soon, the bulk of a twin-engine aircraft, which the sailors themselves mistakenly identified as a Finnish Bristol Blenheim, swept over *Constructor*. And at the same moment, two powerful explosions were heard behind the stern of the ship. The passengers on deck were horrified to see two large columns of water in the light of the moon. Fortunately, the Germans missed, and the bombs did not cause any damage to the patrol ship. However, as soon as the passengers on deck breathed easy, a second German plane appeared and also dropped two bombs. One bomb fell next to the side, while the second bomb hit the bow.

As a result of the explosion that thundered in the cargo holds, all the passengers there were killed. Boiler room No. 1 was also destroyed, and the entire bow of the vessel up to boiler room No. 2 was flooded. Ladoga Military Flotilla officer Zinovy Rusakov, who was on board *Constructor*, recalled:

> The ship shuddered violently from the explosion, the light went out, and at the same moment the siren howled furiously: its drive cable was stretched during the explosion, and the siren came into action. Those who were at the top saw how at one moment the entire bow of the ship with rooms full of passengers – women, children – and sailors off duty fell off. In the place where the bombs exploded, the metal skin of the outer sides fell off, the decks were bent, and the entire bow part of it with the compressed three decks sank into the water.[67]

---

67. Rusakov, Z.G., *Our Sea was Ladoga*, Leningrad: Lenizdat, 1980, p.70.

DEADLY LAKE

In the adjacent boiler room No. 2, the brickwork of the high-pressure watertube boiler collapsed from the concussion, while the mechanic on duty was burned. Steam whistled from the torn pipes. However, the bow bulkhead, although bent, withstood the force of the explosion. This saved the ship from a quick death. Water continued to flow in through seams, rivets and coal bunkers. Rusakov continued his dramatic story:

> The patrol ship *Constructor* began to sink into the water. The water quickly began to fill the part of the upper deck that was not affected by the explosion, causing panic to the passengers who were there. The angle of the trim on the nose increased threateningly. It seemed that the ship was slowly falling into some kind of abyss.[68]

The surviving part of the crew immediately began fighting to save the heavily damaged ship. The commander of *Constructor*, Captain 3rd Rank Konstantin Balakirev, turned the ship towards the shore. Soon the gunboat *Bureya* came to the rescue, to which all the surviving passengers and part of the crew were transferred. Only fifteen people remained on *Constructor*, who continued to try to save the patrol ship. The sailors, being waist-deep in icy water, reinforced the bulkhead with props between boiler room No. 1 and boiler room No. 2. At the same time, another part of the team was trying to pump water out of the flooded compartments of the ship. Their work continued all night.

The position of *Constructor* was critical. The bow of the ship was completely submerged, and the propeller was sticking out of the water. Towards morning the salvage ship *Stalinets* and tugboat *Nikulyasy* approached the vessel. They took the ship in tow and steered it with a slow speed stern-first towards the shore. However, soon the bow, which continued to sink, touched the bottom, and the ship ran aground. After that, it was decided to stop trying to save *Constructor* and leave the ship. The human losses from the German air attack were enormous, with 204 passengers and thirty-four crew members killed.[69]

For three weeks, the half-sunken vessel remained in the same place until another strong storm broke out on Lake Ladoga on 25 November. As a result, the bow of *Constructor* was finally torn off, and the ship, along with the ice, was carried to the shore, where it sank at a depth of 4m.

On the afternoon of 5 November, eight Ju 88 As from KG 77 raided Novaya Ladoga harbour. German pilots reported the sinking of one transport ship and

---

68. Ibid., p.71.
69. TSAMO RF. Foundation 217. Inventory 1221. Case 103. Sheet 321.

fifteen barges. In fact, only one unloaded barge perished in the harbour. Soviet anti-aircraft gunners also exaggerated their successes. They reported that they had damaged four Ju 88s, which were then 'finished off by Soviet fighter aviation'.

During the two and a half months of autumn 1941, the Luftwaffe carried out 127 air attacks against harbours and ships in Lake Ladoga. As a result the Ladoga Military Flotilla lost one gunboat, one patrol ship, two minesweepers and one submarine chaser. Six transport ships and twenty-four barges were also sunk by Luftwaffe aircraft. In addition, twenty-two more barges went down during storms and for other reasons. As a result, by the end of 1941, the Soviets had only seven barges left from the non-self-propelled fleet.

Chapter 5

Aerial war of attrition

Pinpricks for Leningrad

Despite the lack of aircraft, the raids on Leningrad continued. According to Hitler's bloodthirsty plan, continuous air attacks and artillery shelling were supposed to break the morale of the starving population and the troops defending the city.

At the beginning of October 1941, bombing raids on the city were carried out irregularly by individual aircraft and only at night. For example, from 1 to 4 October, there were no air attacks at all. On the night of 4–5 October, German bombers appeared over Leningrad five times in groups of two to four aircraft. They dropped bombs flying horizontally from a height of 5–7km. The effectiveness of such Luftwaffe micro raids was low.

The Soviets were puzzled by such little German activity over Leningrad and came up with unfounded explanations for such amazing tactics. For example, the command of the Soviet air defence claimed that allegedly 'the Germans do not have enough pilots trained for night flights'. In fact, the respite in the air war was explained by the transfer of some Luftwaffe units to other sectors of the front and the relocation of the remaining Luftflotte 1 forces to other air bases. In addition, in early October 1941, diving Ju 88 bombers from KG 77 and KGr. 806 were engaged in supporting the German landing on the Moonsund archipelago islands and air attacks against Soviet railways. In the raids on Leningrad, mainly only aircraft from I./KG 4 took part.

On the night of 7–8 October, this Gruppe carried out, in the words of the Headquarters of the Air Defence Forces of the Leningrad Front, another 'attrition raid'. The first He 111 planes appeared over the city at 19.24. Then, at intervals of ten to fifteen minutes, following groups of German bombers approached. The raid lasted until 01.37 on 8 October. In total, the Soviet Air Surveillance and Communication Service (VNOS) and radar stations recorded thirty-eight flights of aircraft over Leningrad. According to German information, each crew of I./KG 4 performed two sorties during the night. Bombs were dropped evenly on almost all districts of Leningrad, with the exception of Sverdlovsky, Vyborgsky and Volodarsky districts. Basically, He 111s dropped incendiary bombs and canisters of flammable liquid with an incendiary bomb attached to it. The most severe fires occurred at the Podemnik plant and the Kalashnikov warehouses. Along with the bombing, barrage balloons received many bullet holes when crews fired their machine guns.[70]

The next 'attrition raid' on Leningrad was carried out by aircraft from I./KG 4 on the night of 10–11 October. The first bomber appeared over the city at 19.20, and the last at 01.03. The Headquarters of the Air Defence Forces of the Leningrad Front combat report reported:

> The planes flew up to the city in four echelons, at intervals of 30 to 50 minutes, at altitudes of 4,000–5,000 metres and dispersed over the city one by one. In Volodarsky, Moskovsky, Vyborgsky, Krasnogvardeysky, Kirovsky, Leninsky districts of the city, 28 high-explosive and up to 2,000 incendiary bombs were dropped. Nine high-explosive bombs did not explode. In addition, 5 parachute bombs were dropped in the Porohovye district, which also did not explode. During the raid, three people were killed and eleven people were injured. The 'Air alert' signal was announced five times at night, the total duration was 4 hours and 25 minutes.

To repel the raid of German bombers, the Soviet anti-aircraft artillery spent 1,097 shells of 85mm calibre, 180 shells of 76mm calibre and 231 shells of 37mm calibre. Curiously, two barrage balloons, raised by the Russians to a height of 4,500m, burned down after being hit by incendiary bombs.[71]

The impudence of Hauptmann Klaus Noske

German bombers appeared over Leningrad exactly on schedule. The commander of I./KG 4, Hauptmann Klaus Noske, specifically chose the same time as before for the bombing. Thus, he wanted to demonstrate the predictability and impunity of the actions of German aviation, which could bomb Leningrad whenever it wanted. And in general, Hauptmann Noske could afford such impudence. The air defence forces of the city were completely unprepared to repel night raids in conditions of poor visibility and due to a lack of visual contact with the

---

70. TSAMO RF. Foundation 217. Inventory 1221. Case 103. Sheet 204.
71. TSAMO RF. Foundation 217. Inventory 1221. Case 103. Sheets 216–217.

AERIAL WAR OF ATTRITION

targets. The Russian anti-aircraft gunners conducted only disorderly barrage firing. Moreover, due to the shortage of ammunition in Leningrad, they could not create such a powerful light show of mass explosions of anti-aircraft shells, as in Moscow.

On the night of 16–17 October 1941, forty-two high-explosive bombs and over 2,000 small incendiary bombs were dropped on Leningrad. As a result, 108 fires broke out in the city, including thirty-one at industrial plants and sixty-four in residential areas.

The next night, German planes reappeared over Leningrad, dropping ten high-explosive bombs and about 3,000 small incendiary bombs. This time, ten districts of the city were affected. The Znamya truda, Karl Marx, and No. 307 plants, the club of the S.M. Kirov Military Medical Academy and the Old St Petersburg Stock Exchange building were destroyed. Barrage balloons, which the Russians were lifting to a height of 3,600m, were damaged again. Due to the strong wind, four barrage balloons broke their moorings and flew away; two more were pierced by fragments of anti-aircraft artillery shells.

In the evening of 20 October, forty high-explosive bombs were dropped on Leningrad during another air attack. Then, during the week from 21 to 27 October, due to bad weather, enemy aircraft were inactive. Only Luftwaffe reconnaissance planes appeared over Leningrad and Lake Ladoga.

On 28 October, at 18.29, several German planes raided Leningrad, dropping ten high-explosive bombs and about a thousand small incendiary bombs on it. As a result of the air attack on the Nevgvozd plant, the scrap metal recycling shop was destroyed, and the warehouse and technical control laboratory were destroyed at the sewing equipment plant. Two wooden houses were destroyed in the Volodarsky district, and a military bunker was damaged. On Zelenina Street, a bomb destroyed the corner of house No. 226. In addition, fourteen fires broke out in the city. According to the Soviet Local Rescue Service (MPVO), there were no fatalities but twelve people were injured.

On the night of 29–30 October, the Luftwaffe carried out two air attacks against Leningrad with a short break, dropping forty high-explosive bombs and about 1,400 small incendiary bombs. There were fires at the cargo area of the Finlyandsky railway station, and plants No. 77 and 349. As a result of a direct hit by a high-explosive bomb on plant No. 7, workshop No. 3 was destroyed. Ten people were killed and fifty-four people were injured.[72]

In total, in October 1941, the Luftwaffe carried out nine raids on Leningrad, and German long-range artillery fired about 3,300 shells at the city. As a result, 808 people were killed, with another 4,038 injured or concussed. Moreover,

---

72. TSAMO RF. Foundation 217. Inventory 1221. Case 103. Sheets 284–285.

most of the victims were from artillery shelling, and not from the aftermath of air attacks.[73] A resident of Leningrad Oleg Kobranov, who was 12 years old in 1941, recalled:

> Hundreds of people died under the rubble. After all, during the raids, the majority hid in the basements of four-, five-, six-storey apartment buildings, which were the majority in Leningrad at that time. When a bomb[74] hit the building, it usually exploded at the level of the 1st–2nd floor, as a result of which the house collapsed, burying under the rubble all those hiding below. Then everything depended on how quickly the blockage would be dismantled, whether they would have time until people suffocated ... At first, the identification of the dead was carried out, later there were so many of them that there was not enough time and effort for all these procedures. Coffins were simply filled with pieces of bodies and buried in a hurry in the dark. Sometimes they put three heads and two legs in one coffin, without wasting time on the exact definition of who exactly they belonged to.

Soviet night fighters did not take to the skies during these air attacks, 'Stalin's Falcons' blaming zero visibility and the poor condition of airfields.

Soviet Devonshire

Meanwhile, the situation of the Soviet troops in the Leningrad region was gradually deteriorating. Clouds were also gathering over the supply bases of the besieged city. In mid-October 1941, XXXIX Army Corps (mot.), led by General der Panzertruppen Rudolf Schmidt, crossed the Volkhov River and launched an offensive to link up with Finnish troops. The German command believed that this would finally blockade Leningrad and completely deprive it of supplies from outside.

Crossing the Volkhov river, German soldiers and tankers found themselves in a dense, swampy and sparsely populated region overgrown with ancient coniferous forests. There was no highway, even dirt roads were very rare.

---

73. The blockade of Leningrad in the documents of declassified archives, Moscow: AST, 2004. pp.681–682.
74. Most likely, Oleg Kobranov does not mean aviation bombs, but the shells of German long-range artillery.

There was not a single major city east of Lake Ladoga for several hundred kilometres. These forests were only full of wild beasts. All this was reminiscent of Devonshire, enlarged many times – a county in the south-west of England, in which the events of the novel *The Hound of the Baskervilles* unfolded. A terrifying howl was heard constantly from the swamps and dense forests. But it was not a ghostly dog howling, looking for its prey, but very real hungry wolves looking for food!

In the conditions of the autumn Rasputitsa (the season of bad roads), the German operation initially proceeded at a very slow pace. One of the factors of the slow progress of the XXXIX Army Corps (mort.) units was the weak support of aviation. Due to low clouds and fog, Luftwaffe planes only occasionally appeared over this wilderness.

The unfortunate evening of the Luftwaffe officer

As of 1 November 1941, Luftflotte 1 had fairly significant forces in the Leningrad area by Luftwaffe standards:

> Ju 88 As from I./KG 77, II./KG 77, KGr. 806, as well as Bf 109 Fs from JG 54, were based at Siverskaya Air Base;
>
> on Dno-Griwotschki airfield – Ju 88 As from III./KG 77, II./KG 1 and III./KG 1;
>
> at Pleskau-Süd (city of Pskov) air base – He 111 H-5s from I./KG 4 and III./KG 4.

On 8 November, Gruppe I./KG 76, equipped with Ju 88 A dive bombers, also arrived at Dno-Griwotschki airfield.

On the night of 4 November, from 18.39 to 23.48 (Moscow time), the Luftwaffe carried out three consecutive air attacks against Leningrad. The bombers approached the city from the town of Uritsk at an altitude of 5,000m, according to the RUS-2 'Redut' radar stations. The flight path of German bombers passed over the Torgovyi port – the centre of Leningrad – the settlement of Novaya Derevnya, then through Piskarevka[75] and Kupchino districts[76] to the south and south-west.

Nine districts of Leningrad suffered from the bombing at once: Moskovsky, Volodarsky, Petrogradsky, Vyborgsky, Frunzensky, Dzerzhinsky, Smolninsky,

---

75. Piskarevka district – the old name of one of the parts of Kalininsky district.
76. In the south of Leningrad.

Kuibyshev and Krasnogvardeysky. According to the Soviet Local Rescue Service (MPVO), fifty-four high-explosive bombs and 3,200 small incendiary bombs were dropped on the city. The most affected were the Lenin, No. 7 and Krasny Vyborzhets plants, and the Moskovskaya-Tovarnaya station and Finlyandsky railway stations. Seventy-six fires broke out, sixteen people were killed and sixty-three were injured.[77]

He 111s from I./KG 4 under Major Klaus Noske also participated in this raid on Leningrad. That evening, He 111 H-5 W.Nr. 3816 '5J+DM' did not return to base. Oberleutnant Wilhelm Well from 1st Staffel (1./KG 4) and his crew were listed as missing. However, ten days later – on 14 November 1941 – an article entitled 'The Identity of a Nazi Officer' appeared in the newspaper *Leningradskaya Pravda*, which told about Oberleutnant Well!

It turned out that over the city, a German bomber was intercepted by the I-153 of Junior Lieutenant Alexei Sevastyanov from the 26th Fighter Aviation Regiment Air Defence (26th IAP PVO). Patrolling over Leningrad, Junior Lieutenant Sevastyanov noticed the silhouette of a twin-engine aircraft in the crossed beams of searchlights. His first attack ended unsuccessfully as his rocket-powered projectiles and machine gun bursts missed the target. When the pilot tried to repeat the attack, he was suddenly blinded by a searchlight beam, and he instantly lost sight of the German bomber. After some time, having regained his eyesight, 'Stalin's Falcon' again saw an enemy plane; it is unknown whether it was the same one or different. The Soviet pilot started shooting, but it was useless – the bullets were 'melting' in the dark. Having shot all his ammunition, Junior Lieutenant Sevastyanov decided to attempt to ram the bomber. 'Stalin's Falcon' tried to cut off the He 111 empennage with the blades of his propeller. The bomber crew saw a fighter approaching rapidly, and the German pilot turned sharply to the left. But it was too late, and the biplane crashed into the right wing of the bomber.

The report of Junior Lieutenant Sevastyanov states:

> When repelling a night raid by the enemy air force on Leningrad, the pilot Junior Lieutenant Sevastyanov, after firing machine gun fire and launching rocket-powered projectiles, rammed the enemy aircraft He 111 into the right wing, and he escaped by parachute and remained unharmed. The enemy plane fell burning at 22.18hrs on November 4, 1941 in Tauride Garden.[78]

---

77. TSAMO RF. Foundation 217. Inventory 1221. Case 103. Sheets 319–320.
78. TSAMO RF. Foundation 217. Inventory 1221. Case 103. Sheet 320.

AERIAL WAR OF ATTRITION

The I-153 fighter, critically damaged as a result of the collision, fell on Baskov Lane.

The authors have discovered other interesting details about this air battle and its consequences. According to Soviet information, Oberleutnant Well's He 111 H-5 was first illuminated by searchlights and damaged by anti-aircraft fire, and only then attacked by Junior Lieutenant Sevastyanov. As it fell, the bomber hit a cable of a Russian barrage balloon, which was raised to a height of 2km. As a result, the cable broke, and the balloon flew away.

Oberleutnant Well managed to jump out of the plane and open his parachute. But there were few reasons for joy! A few minutes earlier, Oberleutnant Well was imagining that he would soon leave the anti-aircraft fire zone and turn to his airfield. There he could expect a delicious dinner, cigarettes, a little alcohol (for relaxation), and then a stormy discussion with his comrades about the mission. And finally, a restful sleep in his relatively comfortable barracks. But in an instant, the whole life of the young pilot abruptly turned upside down. The parachute was rapidly lowering him into a huge, dark and gloomy city. At first, Oberleutnant Well saw only vague outlines of streets, canals and bright flashes of anti-aircraft guns in the darkness. Jumping out right over the 'Bolshevik stronghold'! Wow, what bad luck! If there had been a forest or a field under him, then he would have had at least a slim chance to reach German territory and return to his unit. However, underneath him was a city that Oberleutnant Well and his Staffel tried every day to force to surrender by their air attacks. There is nothing worse for a bomber pilot to land right where he recently dropped his bombs! What was waiting for Oberleutnant Well here, in a freezing and starving city?

With these bad thoughts, the German pilot landed in a snowdrift on one of the central streets of Leningrad. In any other situation, every pilot would be delighted with a successful jump and landing. But Oberleutnant Well was not up to joy! Somehow unhooking the parachute, he looked around and in the dim light saw approaching figures. These were the weakened and exhausted residents of Leningrad. The very ones whom Hitler wanted to starve to death. Each of them had already lost one or more close people and friends who had died from bombs and shells.

Oberleutnant Well knew that Leningrad was starving. He had also heard from Nazi propaganda about the complete inhumanity of the Bolsheviks. 'They'll tear you to pieces! They'll eat you!' – such were the pilot's first thoughts at the sight of the approaching crowd. There was only one thing left – to run. Fortunately, the residents, unlike the well-fed and well-dressed German pilot, simply did not have the strength to catch up with him.

So Oberleutnant Well ran through the streets of Leningrad until he was captured by a police patrol on Mayakovsky street. Considering the situation, it was the best ending for him! Oberleutnant Well was alive again. Although he had to forget about good cigarettes, schnapps and a soft bed for a very long time ...

Shortly after the interrogation of Oberleutnant Well at the Headquarters of the Air Defence Forces, 'Stalin's Falcon' Junior Lieutenant Alexey Sevastyanov, who had shot down a German bomber, arrived there. Oberleutnant Well was informed that this was the very pilot who had rammed his bomber. The German met him amiably and even gave Junior Lieutenant Sevastyanov his hand, as a sign of respect for his bravery. But 'Stalin's Falcon' did not give his hand in response! In Soviet Russia, shaking hands with a Nazi pilot could be interpreted as 'sympathy for the Nazis' and 'betrayal'.

Then there was an 'interview' with Oberleutnant Well by the newspaper *Leningradskaya Pravda*. Trying to ease his fate, the German pilot told the Russians the whole story about KG 4, his commander and the tactics of air attacks. He also publicly cursed the scoundrel Hitler, who viciously sent him to bomb peaceful Soviet cities.

From the point of view of Soviet propaganda, the first visual proof of the successful activity of its air defence, in the form of the fact of the downed German bomber in the centre of the city, had a huge psychological significance. Hundreds of hungry residents came to the Tauride Garden to admire the wreckage of 'Hitler's vulture'.

There remains one mystery in the story of the downing of He 111 H-5 '5J+DM'. According to Soviet information, two members of the German crew were captured. Two more corpses were found among the wreckage of the plane. But according to German information, the missing crew included five people: Oberleutnant Wilhelm Well, Unteroffizier Walter Striber, Unteroffizier Walter Heinson and Unteroffizier Walter Miksch, Oberleutnant Erich Meyer.[79] Where did the fifth crew member disappear to? Was he torn to pieces or eaten by evil inhabitants dying of hunger?

'Military fate' of a typical 'Stalin's Falcon'

Meanwhile, 7 November 1941 was approaching – the anniversary of the October Revolution of 1917, the main holiday in the USSR. In this regard, the Commander of Luftflotte 1, Generaloberst Alfred Keller, decided to present the residents with a 'gift' by delivering a massive bomb attack on the main

---

79. Gundelach, K., *Kampfgeschwader 'General Wever' 4*, Stuttgart: Motorbuch Verlag, 1978, p.359.

AERIAL WAR OF ATTRITION

'Bolshevik stronghold'. Moreover, the Germans did not hide the preparations for the bombing of the city. On the contrary, during 4–6 November, leaflets were dropped on the city, urging residents to 'wash up and lie down in coffins'. They even indicated the date of the upcoming air raid – 'the Revolution anniversary'.

Having learned about such preparations for the 'holiday', the command of the Red Army Air Force Leningrad Front decided to prevent the 'Nazi action'. A Soviet reconnaissance aircraft, which miraculously returned to its airfield unharmed, recorded that the largest number of German twin-engine bombers were concentrated at Siverskaya Air Base, 67km south of Leningrad. Aerial photography showed that there were about forty Ju 88s, thirty-one Bf 109s and four Ju 52s there. And this information was very close to reality.

To strike at the German air base, the Soviets collected literally everything that could fly. In addition to bombers and ground-attack aircraft, the attacking group included PVO (Air Defence) fighters and even flying boats. On 6 November, at 11.25, the first group of seven Pe-2 bombers from the 125th Short-range Bomber Aviation Regiment (125th BBAP), led by Major Vasily Sandalov, appeared over Siverskaya Air Base. Accompanied by ten MiG-3 fighters, they dropped bombs on the airfield from a height of 2,500m. Then six Il-2 ground-attack aircraft from the 174th Ground-attack Aviation Regiment (174th SHAP) led by Captain Sergei Polyakov and ten I-153 biplanes attacked Siverskaya from a low altitude. After that, at 14.30, the airfield was bombed by seven Pe-2 bombers, commanded by Captain Alexander Rezvykh.

According to Soviet data, eleven German planes were destroyed on the ground. Surprisingly, this time the Russians did not greatly overestimate their successes. According to German information, as a result of three air attacks on Siverskaya, seven Ju 88 A bombers from KG 77 and KGr. 806 were damaged. Most of the fuel reserves were also burned.

When repelling the attack, German fighters from JG 54 scored ten aerial victories. Among the downed aircraft was an Il-2 from 174th SHAP. Its pilot was 18-year-old Junior Lieutenant Anatoly Panfilov. The young pilot managed to jump out by parachute, after which he landed near Siverskaya Air Base. Junior Lieutenant Panfilov found himself on the territory of the enemy, whom Stalin's propaganda portrayed as beasts and monsters. Just as in the situation of Oberleutnant Wilhelm Well, this fact meant the sudden end of his combat career. The Soviet pilot, like the German pilot, no longer had a chance to return to his comrades and see his family in the near future. But there were also significant differences in the fate of Oberleutnant Well and Junior Lieutenant Panfilov. In the Wehrmacht, being captured was considered only an annoying nuisance. However, in the Red Army, soldiers who were captured were declared cowards and traitors in advance. The monstrously cruel Stalin believed that a soldier in enemy territory should prefer to commit suicide than surrender to the enemy. Junior Lieutenant Panfilov was one of those who believed Stalin's propaganda unconditionally. Therefore, he did not capitulate and give interviews to German newspapers. He took out a pistol and began shooting at the Germans running towards him. As a result, Junior Lieutenant Panfilov was killed in a shootout and thus did not become a 'traitor' to his country.

On the same evening, the Red Army Air Force attacked Krasnogvardeysk airfield. In addition to bombers and ground-attack aircraft, Beriev MBR-2 flying boats, taking off from the Gulf of Finland, participated in the raid. They dropped two 100kg bombs on the target.

Great Britain is to blame for all the troubles of the Soviet Union!

Meanwhile, residents of Leningrad turned on the radio and began to listen with excitement to the festive radio broadcast from Moscow. Joseph Stalin was speaking. In his speech, he solemnly announced that Hitler's Blitzkrieg had failed. Next, the 'Great Leader' for the first time tried to answer the question that had been bothering people for several months: what were the reasons for the grand defeats of the invincible Red Army? Stalin said that everything was to blame, including Great Britain. The lying 'Red Dictator' explained to his people:

> The main reason for the failures of the Red Army is the absence of a Western Front in Europe against German troops. Currently, there are no armies of Great Britain or the United States on the European continent that would wage war with German troops. Thanks to this, the Germans do not have to split their forces into two fronts, in the West and in the East.

Then Stalin began to scold the German army, which he described as a bunch of looters, crooks, rapists, lunatics and drunkards who drank buckets of vodka and robbed everyone. In addition, the 'Great Leader' accused Hitler of violating democratic freedoms and trampling on the rights of workers. Stalin even compared the Führer to the last Russian tsar Nicholas II, who also staged 'medieval Jewish pogroms'.

Stalin described the general situation at the front optimistically: the losses of the Wehrmacht were many times greater than the losses of the Red Army; all military factories had been evacuated to the east; the forces of the Red Army were growing, victory was near!

AERIAL WAR OF ATTRITION

The Luftwaffe's 'festive' psychological attack

While the residents of the city listened to this pathetically false speech of Stalin, air-raid sirens howled. Soon, German photoflash bombs ('chandeliers') slowly descending on parachutes hung over the centre of Leningrad. Huge 'chandeliers' filled the streets and avenues with streams of dead white light. It became as bright as day in the city centre. Then came the hum of the engines of German bombers.

In the combat report of the Headquarters of the Air Defence Forces of the Leningrad Front, it is reported:

> The bombing raid on Leningrad on November 6, 1941 began at 18.00 and continued intermittently until 19.55. The raid involved 19 enemy aircraft, which at altitudes of 5,000–6,000m, singly and in groups of 2–3 aircraft approached the city from the south-west, through the settlement of Srednyaya Rogatka and from the Gulf of Finland. Bombed: Vyborgsky, Frunzensky, Kuibyshev, Primorsky, Smolninsky, Dzerzhinsky, Oktyabrsky, Petrogradsky districts of the city. A total of 59 high-explosive bombs were dropped, of which 10 did not explode. Incendiary bombs were not used. 49 people were killed and 298 wounded. Of the important objects, the most damage was caused to woodworking plant No. 6 and Moskovskaya-Passajirskaya railway station. The use of time fuse bombs by the enemy is noted: one bomb exploded after 2 hours 17 minutes (Slucky street, 11), another bomb after 5 hours 05 minutes (Mohovaya street, 30). The 'Air alert' signal was announced twice in the city, with a total duration of 1 hour 22 minutes.[80]

In addition to high-explosive and fragmentation bombs, German planes dropped BM1000 parachute mines on Leningrad. These cylindrical objects, slowly descending on parachutes and with a blast area of over 50sqm, caused the most powerful explosions. The entire blast wave, formed by almost 700kg of TNT, went horizontally. A year before, the same mines fell on the streets of London. Even such a courageous man as British Prime Minister Winston Churchill was horrified by the force of their explosions and destruction. Some BM1000s had time fuses, so the explosions on the streets of Leningrad rattled

---

80. TSAMO RF. Foundation 217. Inventory 1221. Case 103. Sheets 326–327.

until morning. But the scale of the 'festive' Luftwaffe air attack was not much different from the usual strikes on the city on previous nights.

In the following days, the weather in the Leningrad and Lake Ladoga area deteriorated again. In this regard, only single Luftwaffe aircraft appeared in the air. According to the Headquarters of the Air Defence Forces of the Leningrad Front, on 9 November, two He 111s appeared over the city. They dropped bombs at random from behind the clouds, and also threw out bundles of propaganda leaflets in Russian, most of which landed at Kirov Factory No. 100.

It should be noted that after the failure of the Blitzkrieg, the Germans began to take very seriously various forms of psychological warfare on the Bolsheviks. In autumn, they scattered over Leningrad and its environs, as well as over the shores of Lake Ladoga, whole collections of carefully prepared and decorated propaganda leaflets. Some of them were really comics, compiled taking into account the psychology of most Russian soldiers, who had a very low level of education. Nurse Anna Lopatina recalled:

> In the first picture of such 'comics', a Nazi, smiling sweetly, takes a rifle from the hands of a Russian soldier, in the second picture the same the Hitlerite, smiling even sweeter, accepts a machine gun, in the third picture accepts a tank, in the fourth he is ready to accept an airplane. In the last picture, a Russian soldier who surrendered gets a 'well-deserved reward': he is sitting at a table with a busty, ruddy beauty, so well-fed that it seems that at any moment her dress will burst. The soldier smiles blissfully, and in front of him on the table is a bottle of vodka, boiling samovar (teakettle), there are mountains of pies, sausages, a gramophone sings 'At the samovar, me and my Masha'!

Shooting in the direction of sound and all-weather German bombers

Russian anti-aircraft artillery, unlike German bombers, always fired fairly randomly. According to the Headquarters of the Air Defence Forces of the Leningrad Front: 'Anti-aircraft artillery reflected the raids on Leningrad barrage firing and shooting in the direction of sound.'[81] At the same time, 1,980 shells of 85mm calibre and 330 shells of 76 mm calibre were used up. Barrage balloons

---

81. This means that Soviet anti-aircraft gunners used data obtained from the sound collector ZP-2 installation to aim anti-aircraft guns.

AERIAL WAR OF ATTRITION

rose to a height of 3,300m, then due to strong winds they were lowered to 1,500m. The Germans again demonstrated the wonders of accuracy, destroying one barrage balloon with a direct hit of a bomb.[82]

On 10 November 1941 at 12.30 another 'raid of attrition' on Leningrad began. Seven single German bombers flew over the city at intervals of fifteen to seventeen minutes. Each of them dropped one high-explosive bomb of large calibre, as well as regular portions of leaflets with 'comics'. This time, nine residents of Leningrad were killed, while thirty-four were wounded and shell-shocked.

If in September to early November 1941, air attacks were carried out mainly against military facilities, then in the second half of November they began to acquire a clear terrorist character.

Another raid occurred on the night of 12–13 November. The planes flew to the city on the route Krasnoye Selo–Uritsk–Gulf of Finland–Leningrad port of Torgovyi. The bombing was carried out from a height of 5–6km on Kirovsky, Leninsky, Krasnogvardeysky, Oktyabrsky, Petrogradsky, Moskovsky and Vasileostrovsky districts. At the same time, photoflash bombs were dropped over the target. Industrial facilities were practically not affected; most of the seventy high-explosive and over 400 small incendiary bombs dropped hit residential neighbourhoods and exploded in the streets. According to the Soviet Local Rescue Service (MPVO), sixty residents were killed and 266 people were injured.

Despite the constant air attacks, the 7th Fighter Aviation Corps Air Defence (7th IAC PVO) was still inactive. This was due to the Soviets' lack of fully fledged night fighters. Almost all fighter aviation regiments were focused on repelling daytime air attacks. Soviet commanders and pilots simply did not know how to deal with bombers in the dark and in difficult weather conditions.

The Headquarters of the Air Defence Forces of the Leningrad Front could not understand for a long time how the Germans manage to bomb the city in any weather. Blackout was observed everywhere in Leningrad, and visibility at night was close to zero. Nevertheless, the German bombers always moved to the target along the same route and dropped their 'cargo' exactly on Leningrad. There was an assumption that the main reference point was the volleys of Soviet anti-aircraft guns. But this explanation was a mistake. The technological lag of the Soviets was so strong that the Soviet military and engineers could not understand that the Germans had a special navigation system capable of bringing bombers to the target at any time of the day in any weather.

---

82. TSAMO RF. Foundation 217. Inventory 1221. Case 103. Sheet 331.

AIR BATTLE FOR LENINGRAD, 1941–1944

In fact, as was the case during the Battle of Britain, the Luftwaffe used a system of radio navigation specially developed for this purpose. The He 111s from I./KG 4 were equipped with highly sensitive X-Gerät radio navigation equipment, which allowed them to carry out missions at night or in bad weather using radio signals from the ground.

The interaction of the system of radio navigation components on the ground and on board the aircraft was carried out as follows. A radio transmitter was installed in the Luga area, which sent a directional radio signal through the towns of Krasnoye Selo and Uritsk to Leningrad. There was a second similar radio transmitter near Mga railway station. The two directional beams of radio navigation intersected exactly over the outskirts and the centre of Leningrad. The X-Gerät equipment made it possible to accurately record the intersection with the first beam, which was 20km from the target. After passing this point, the bomber's radio operator started a timer and started counting down the time. The next 10km was a measuring segment on which the exact value of the bomber's speed was set. After the end of the measuring segment, when 10km remained to the target, the radio operator pressed the timer again. The first arrow of the timer stopped, and the second began to move. Further, all complex navigation tasks were solved by precise automatic devices. The bomber pilots had only to maintain their course precisely, following the radio beam. Thus, the X-Gerät equipment was guaranteed to bring the bombers to the very middle of the intended object of attack.

Unlike in England, where scientists were able to quickly develop countermeasures, the Soviets were powerless to interfere with the work of X-Gerät. For this reason, the Germans on the Eastern Front used their system of radio navigation effectively until the very end of the war.

Chapter 6

The Schmidt's wasteland

'Now the "Bolshevik stronghold" will be forced to surrender without shedding the blood of German soldiers ...'

On the anniversary of the October Revolution of 1917, which could well have been the last for the Soviet government, the Germans presented Leningrad residents with a much more terrible 'gift' than the routine 'festive' bombing of the city.

On 5 November 1941, it was cold in the Leningrad Front area. The rivers and channels in the vast wasteland in the area of Tikhvin froze. After that, tanks and armoured personnel carriers of XXXIX Army Corps (mot.), commanded by General der Panzertruppen Rudolf Schmidt, finally entered the operational space. Three days later, they seized Tikhvin with a swift rush without a fight, cutting the last railway line leading from the depths of the USSR to Lake Ladoga.

On 9 November, Berlin radio broadcast a particularly important message every half hour about the capture of Tikhvin. It said: 'Now the "Bolshevik stronghold" will be forced to surrender without shedding the blood of German soldiers ...' And it wasn't an exaggeration. The capture of Tikhvin, which was a key point for organising the supply of the surrounded city, really meant an imminent catastrophe for Leningrad, the Soviet Baltic Fleet and the Leningrad Front troops. Now the cargoes sent from the depths of the country simply could not reach even Lake Ladoga. The nearest railway stations where the unloading of trains was possible were located in the wilderness 100–120km east of Tikhvin. Theoretically, food and supplies could be reloaded onto cars, and then delivered to Novaya Ladoga harbour by a winding route almost 250km long. However, in the swampy valley of the Pasha river there were only underdeveloped dirt roads, and besides winter was beginning.

The situation was complicated by the fact that the Germans did not stop there. Soon they crossed the Tikhvinka river and advanced another 20km up to the vicinity of Dubrovo. There was only a little more than 60km left before they connected with Finnish troops. But further to the north-east stretched impenetrable forests and swamps, where even bad roads were completely absent. The position of the advancing German units themselves was difficult. Because of the impassable mud, their supplies almost stopped. Chief of the General Staff of the Army High Command (OKH) Generaloberst Franz Halder wrote in his diary: 'The troops do not have any supplies and consume what they can get on the spot (potatoes, horse meat).' However, the morale of the German soldiers was still high, and it seemed to them that a couple more successes and the war would finally end.

The Germans were attacking in two directions at once: north-east to the river Svir and north to the town of Volkhov. It was only 25km from Volkhov and the Lenin hydroelectric plant there to Novaya Ladoga harbour, and in mid-November artillery cannonade could already be heard in the harbour, while at night a fiery glow could be seen in the south. The immediate threat of capture by the Germans hung over Novaya Ladoga, the new main base of the Ladoga Military Flotilla. Flotilla commander Captain 1st rank Vasily Cherokov had to call an emergency meeting of commanders and political commissars and order them to prepare the warehouses, buildings, wharves and bridges for destruction. The Flotilla ships that could not move independently due to damage were being prepared for scuttling. In the event of the Germans reaching Novaya Ladoga, the western shore of the lake near the settlements of Osinovets and Morier was chosen for the winter deployment of the ships.

In the event of the success of the German offensive, the same emergency measures were taken by the Soviets in Volkhov. By order of the Leningrad Front command, the equipment of the Lenin hydroelectric plant[83] was hastily dismantled, while the plant itself was prepared to be blown up.[84] This large energy facility, which supplied electricity to the Leningrad military factories, was one of the first industrial projects implemented by the Bolsheviks after the seizure of power in 1917. Thus, the threat of a German offensive stopped power generation there and left Leningrad without its necessary energy.

The hungry residents of Leningrad did not have the strength to descend into air-raid shelters

In the wake of the successes of XXXIX Army Corps (mot.), the Luftflotte 1 command considered that Leningrad was about to fall. In this regard, on the

---

83. The construction of the Lenin plant began in 1921 and ended in 1927.
84. Pavlov, D.V., *Leningrad is Under Siege*, Leningrad: Lenizdat, 1985, p.151.

night of 13–14 November 1941, five air attacks on the city were carried out in a row. The first 'air alert' was announced after dark, at 17.55. The second air raid lasted from 22.55 to 00.15, the third from 02.03 to 03.12, the fourth from 05.50 to 06.50. The next morning, at 10.31, when the work on dismantling the rubble, extinguishing fires and rescuing the victims was in full swing, forty German planes appeared over the city at once. During these attacks, about 350 high-explosive bombs of all calibres and several thousand small incendiary bombs (the Russians called them 'lighters') were dropped on the city. Thus, during the day, air alerts were announced in the city eight times – a record number! The most affected were the Vyborgsky and Primorsky districts, which were bombed four times and both industrial plants and residential buildings were severely affected. The No. 7 and No. 206, Russian Diesel and Mikoyan plants, and the electric substation No. 15 of the state-owned energy company Lenenergo, were partially destroyed. As of 18.00 on 14 November, ninety-five bodies had been found, and another 224 people were injured.

However, later, after clearing all the rubble of the destroyed buildings, it turned out that at least 176 people had been killed, and 365 people were wounded and shell-shocked. Several dozen more residents died from the explosions of 210mm and 240mm shells, which the German long-range artillery dropped on the city all night.

On the night of 14–15 November, another Luftwaffe raid on Leningrad took place. The bombing was much shorter in duration and consequences. German planes dropped fifteen high-explosive and about 150 incendiary bombs from a high altitude. Ten people were killed and fifty-seven were injured. The Soviet anti-aircraft artillery, as always, was not idle. In a report from Headquarters of the Air Defence Forces of the Leningrad Front, it was stated 'that anti-aircraft artillery conducted anti-aircraft fire in the direction of sound and chased away enemy aircraft from Leningrad'.[85]

Such a large number of victims, with a small number of bombs dropped, were caused by several reasons. Many residents of Leningrad had stopped paying attention to the mournful beeps of the 'air alert' and stayed at home. Hungry residents no longer had the strength to descend into air-raid shelters every time. This became especially noticeable during the next bombing of the city, which took place on the evening of 15 November. At 18.35, an 'air alert' was announced, and soon German planes appeared at an altitude of 6,000m. At this altitude, the bombers were outside the effective anti-aircraft fire zone so the German pilots did not need to be afraid of anti-aircraft guns and barrage

---

85. TSAMO RF. Foundation 217. Inventory 1221. Case 301. Sheets 357, 361.

balloons. However, at such an altitude, it was very difficult to achieve a targeted drop of bombs.

According to the Soviet Local Rescue Service (MPVO), out of thirty-three high-explosive bombs, twenty-seven exploded in vacant lots, in gardens, parks and in the water. The No. 2 car repair plant and 'C' plant, as well as residential buildings, were affected. Incendiary bombs caused fifteen fires, and the number of victims again turned out to be significant: twenty-four people were killed and 277 wounded. The Headquarters of the Air Defence Forces of the Leningrad Front summary reported:

> A large number of victims is the result of a weakening of discipline, since the population does not always go to air-raid shelters and earth bomb shelters from apartments and from the streets according to the 'air alert' signal. Out of a total of 277 victims, 155 were injured and killed in apartments (135 of them only in 5 houses), 101 on the streets, 21 in industrial plants and none in air-raid shelters.[86]

On 16 November, the Luftwaffe carried out two air attacks against Leningrad. Bombs were again dropped from a great height and from behind cloud. According to the Luftflotte 1 headquarters, such tactics were intended to exhaust the last forces of starving residents and air defence units, as well as force Russian anti-aircraft gunners to spend scarce supplies of shells aimlessly. The Headquarters of the Air Defence Forces of the Leningrad Front reported on 17 November at 18.00:

> In the second raid from 20.27 to 22.17, six single aircraft participated, which, according to radar stations, approached the city from the south-east of Lisino village, through Krasny Bor village, Kolpino town and further along the Neva river. After the bombing, the Germans went south through the Novaya Derevnya settlement and Vasilyevsky Island. The bombers were detected 22 minutes before the approach to the city. Under intense anti-aircraft artillery fire, bombs were dropped from a great height and randomly. In the city, only the Krasnogvardeysky district was bombed, and of the 23 high-explosive bombs, 20 fell on vacant lots, in courtyards and into the water, without causing any damage. Two bombs at the Vozrozhdenie factory caused a fire in a

---

86. TSAMO RF. Foundation 217. Inventory 1221. Case 301. Sheet 364.

cotton warehouse. One workshop was damaged, two people were injured, one person was killed. And two people were injured by one bomb on the street.[87]

Similar in scale and consequences, Luftwaffe raids took place on the evening of 17 November and on the night of 18 November 1941. Soviet air defence fighters and anti-aircraft artillery again did not achieve great success. The Headquarters of the Air Defence Forces of the Leningrad Front reported:

> During the raid on Leningrad, four night fighters flew out to intercept the enemy. There were no meetings with the Germans in the air. Anti-aircraft artillery intense barrage firing and firing in the direction of sound drove away enemy aircraft from Leningrad ...[88]

On the night of 19 November, German planes reappeared over Leningrad, dropping twenty-three high-explosive bombs. As a result, five people were killed and twelve people were injured in Kolomyaki and Shuvalovo (Vyborgsky district).

Soviet Local Rescue Service (MPVO) personnel excavated the rubble from the previous bombings around the clock. Only on 19 November, was it possible to extract all the bodies of those killed during a series of air attacks on 13 and 14 November. Sixty-nine corpses were dug up, and the previously announced death toll increased to 245 people. During the clean-up operation after the raids of 15 to 17 November, nine injured people and ninety-two corpses were recovered from the rubble.

The Luftwaffe's struggle with Leningrad's air bridge

In November 1941, the Germans launched several air strikes on Soviet airfields in the Leningrad area in order to interfere with the work of the air bridge organised by the Soviets. Every night, several Li-2 transport planes (a Soviet replica of the Douglas C-47 Skytrain) and Tupolev TB-3s delivered particularly important cargo to the city and took out Bolshevik officials. The main airfields that were used by the Soviets to connect the blockaded Leningrad with the central regions of the USSR were Uglovo and Levashovo Air Bases and Komendantsky airfield.

---

87. Ibid., Sheet 366.
88. Ibid., Sheet 385.

On the morning of 16 November, eight Ju 88 As appeared from the east over Uglovo Air Base, where 26th Fighter Aviation Regiment Air Defence (26th IAP PVO) night fighters were based, and dropped a series of bombs. Forty minutes later, at 10.10, German bombers attacked Levashovo Air Base, dropping twenty fragmentation bombs. Most of the bombs dropped hit the target, but did not explode.

On the night of 17–18 November, four high-explosive and over 200 incendiary bombs were dropped at the Uglovo Air Base. This combined mission was carried out by German bombers during the next raid on Leningrad. The accuracy of the bombing turned out to be extremely poor, and the bombs fell on the south-eastern outskirts of the air base. Neither aircraft nor airfield facilities were damaged.[89]

The Luftwaffe achieved much more success on the morning of 19 November. At 09.45, three Bf 109s from JG 54 suddenly appeared at low altitude over Komendantsky airfield, in the north-western suburb of Leningrad. They fired at ground targets, wounding six people, and then attacked and shot down a Li-2 passenger plane coming in to land. The crew of three and two passengers were killed.

German bombers over the marshes near Tikhvin town

Due to the lack of forces and bad weather, Luftwaffe aircraft provided only occasional support to their troops fighting in the area of towns of Tikhvin and Volkhov. Air attacks were carried out by single aircraft only against the most important targets.

For example, on 14 November, German Hs 126 and Bf 110 reconnaissance planes conducted aerial photography in the area of Novaya Ladoga town, Syasstroy settlement and Oyat, Novyi Byt and Pasha railway stations. After deciphering the received photographs, a pinpoint strike was inflicted on an important infrastructure facility. Fifteen high-explosive bombs were dropped on Volkhov, as a result of which the power line across the river Volkhov was destroyed.

The situation for the Soviet troops in the area of the German offensive remained critical. The lack of artillery to deter the German offensive forced the Soviets to use anti-aircraft guns for this purpose. For example, the 37th Separate Anti-aircraft Division (37th OZAD) defended the southern approaches to Volkhov. On 15 November, the division was forced to fire anti-aircraft guns

---

89. TSAMO RF. Foundation 217. Inventory 1221. Case 301. Sheet 385.

directly at the advancing German troops. After firing 297 shells, the Soviet gunners began relocating to an area 3 to 4km north of the city. At the same time, the anti-aircraft division was nearly surrounded, and a car searchlight was destroyed when the vehicle ran over a mine. One anti-aircraft gun and machine guns from the 37th OZAD were allocated for the anti-tank defence of the bridge over the river Volkhov.

On the afternoon of 17 November, several German bomber raids were recorded by the Soviets in the sector south and south-east of Lake Ladoga. Two high-explosive bombs were dropped on Kipuya village, 15km north-east of Volkhov. A truck was destroyed and two Red Army soldiers were wounded. The Germans also carried out air attacks against Soviet artillery batteries around Dymi and Bolshoi Dvor railway stations. A train was destroyed by Luftwaffe planes on the railway crossing Orensky. A single German plane dropped bombs on Soviet troops near the village of Obrino, east of Tikhvin.

The support of the advancing Wehrmacht divisions was also provided by the specialised Gruppe III./KG 4 of Major Wolfgang Buring. Earlier this Gruppe had been withdrawn from VIII. Fliegerkorps and from 15 November was based at Pleskau-Süd (city of Pskov). German bombers not only attacked the Soviet troops, but also supplied their own troops by dropping cargo containers with food and ammunition by parachute. Because of the poor condition of the roads, trucks and horse-drawn carts simply could not travel to many sections of the front in this swampy wasteland. The implementation of these missions was hampered by cloudy weather, which limited the visibility of the crews of German bombers. To ensure the guaranteed delivery of goods, the Germans had to fly at an altitude of 200–300m and below, putting their lives at considerable risk.

The crew of Leutnant Muller's He 111 H-6 '5J+DK' from 7./KG 4 got into a very unpleasant situation. On 17 November, at 09.50, it took off to bombard a village east of Tikhvin. There were Russian soldiers in the houses there, whom the Germans wanted to kill from the air. Apparently, they were near the village of Obrino mentioned above.

The pilot of the aircraft, Leutnant Rudolf, wrote in a report:

> We struck the village at 10.53, after which we observed the explosions of 12 SD50 bombs among the houses where Russian soldiers were. During the dropping of the bombs, we were under heavy anti-aircraft fire from three light anti-aircraft guns and several machine guns from the north-eastern part of the village. The first few rounds of anti-aircraft guns were very accurate. The right engine of our bomber was damaged, another shell hit the empennage. The number of bullets hitting the plane from machine guns could not be determined.

As a result of fragments of anti-aircraft shells hitting the right engine, the propeller spinner was torn off, the mechanism control to adjust the variable pitch of propeller and rpm was damaged, the cooler and engine oil tank were pierced. Engine oil and cooling liquid began to flow out of the tanks. The elevators were damaged by fragments of anti-aircraft shells that hit the empennage. The nose of the plane immediately began to lift up, we barely held it, adjusting the engine power ... Meanwhile, we were 12 kilometres behind the front line. I tried to fly the damaged bomber at least to my territory. However, it soon became clear that it would be very difficult to do this. When I increased the engine speed, the plane went up, as soon as I reduced the engine speed, at a speed of 180 kmh, it began to decline sharply. I reached the front line at an altitude of only 150 metres. But there was no free space ahead on which it would be possible to make an emergency landing. So we continued to fly in a westerly direction until the navigator found a large clearing in the middle of the forest. The right engine began to smoke more and more, which threatened to cause a fire. In addition, after engine failure, the plane would not be able to fly anymore. So I decided to land the plane on its belly. When I reduced the engine speed, the plane immediately lowered its nose. When we were already level with the forest, I instinctively gave the maximum engine speed again. As a result, the plane landed on the ground fairly smoothly.

During the emergency landing, I hit my head on the control column and lost consciousness for a moment. Other crew members also suffered minor injuries. At the site of the emergency landing, there was a layer of snow 20cm thick, as a result, the landing turned out to be quite soft. But due to the high landing speed, the brake track turned out to be about 300 metres long.

The He 111 landed just 10km from the front line at 11.03 Berlin time. The crew radioed a distress signal to the airfield while still in flight. After some time, He 111 H-5 '5J+EH' of commander 7./KG 4 Hauptmann Helmuth Boltze landed in the clearing. He evacuated the injured crew, as well as valuable equipment from the damaged bomber.[90]

---

90. Gundelach, K., *Kampfgeschwader 'General Wever' 4*, Stuttgart: Motorbuch Verlag, 1978, pp.161–162.

But not all flights ended so well for their German crews. On 17 November, Soviet anti-aircraft gunners claimed two Ju 88s shot down near Tikhvin and to the north of it. It was probably Ju 88 A-4 'V4+NP' commanded by Unteroffizierr H. Mertsching and Ju 88 A-5 'V4+AD' of Feldwebel O. Lendl from III./KG 1, who went missing along with their crews. One of these planes was found by the Russians lying in the middle of the forest a day later.

The Finns did not go to meet the Germans

On 18 November, when the Luftwaffe pilots who escaped death were still celebrating their rescue, and others were mourning their missing comrades, the advanced German units reached the outskirts of Volkhov. The town was only 6km away, and the German infantrymen could already clearly see the Volkhov hydroelectric plant, the Lenin dam and the bridges over the Volkhov river.

On this day, German aircraft intensified their raids on Soviet strongpoints and rear bases in this sector of the front. Thirty bombers accompanied by three Bf 109 F fighters attacked the Bolshoi Dvor railway station. Air attacks were also carried out against Volkhov and Novaya Ladoga, and Kolchanovo railway station. At the Georgievsky railway crossing, as a result of the bombing, a train carrying ammunition and the railway station building were smashed.

However, as so often happened when the Wehrmacht came close to its goal, its troops stopped! The offensive stalled both near to Volkhov and north of Tikhvin. The reason for this was that initially several difficult tasks were set at once for the small German ground forces in this sector of the front. The units of the XXXIX Army Corps (mot.) attacked separately in several directions at once, gradually moving away from each other.

At the same time, the right flank stretched for 150km, and there was no one to cover it. Instead of a solid front line, due to a lack of forces, the Germans organised only a chain of strongpoints. Despite the incompetent command and poor training of soldiers, the Red Army began to exert increasing pressure on the units of XXXIX Army Corps (mot.). In desperation, the German command turned to its Allies for help. The Chief of the General Staff of the Army High Command (OKH) Generaloberst Franz Halder, after a meeting with Hitler, wrote in his diary: 'We need to connect with the Finns. They have to come towards us (5th Division!).'

However, the Finns did not go to meet the Germans and instead of a reasonable tactical retreat in order to shorten the front line, the German troops received an idiotic order to hold the huge occupied wasteland. As a result, instead of the promised warm winter apartments, the soldiers remained in an open swampy area. But they still continued to hold Tikhvin for some time, which meant that Leningrad would continue to receive an insignificant amount of cargo, primarily food.

On the eve of a humanitarian catastrophe

The Soviets also had no reason to be optimistic. On 15 November 1941, shipping on Lake Ladoga ceased. From now on, even the cargoes available in the port of Novaya Ladoga became impossible to deliver to the western shore of the lake, and hence to Leningrad. As a result, the Military Council of Leningrad Front had to significantly reduce food distribution to troops and civilians. On 8 November, restrictions were imposed on the level of food supply to the army, and after another restrictions of food distribution began to apply to the already starving residents of the huge city. From 13 November, workers began to receive 300g of bread a day, and everyone else (women, children and the elderly) an insignificant 150g of bread a day. However, on 20 November, Andrei Zhdanov, the First Secretary of the Leningrad Regional Committee of the Communist Party, and also the main representative of Stalin in Leningrad, without hesitation signed an order to reduce the level of bread distribution to a virtually lethal 250g per day for workers and 125g for employees, dependants and children. The Commissar of the State Defence Committee for Food Supply of Leningrad Front Troops and Leningrad Population, Dmitry Pavlov, recalled: 'A difficult, painful time has come, and it is difficult for anyone who has not survived it to have an accurate idea of it. The besieged residents of Leningrad felt the breath of death more and more every day.'[91]

In addition to the almost complete lack of food, Leningrad also experienced the consequences of a shortage of electricity. The main supplier for the city was the Lenin hydroelectric plant in Volkhov. When the Germans reached the southern shore of Lake Ladoga, the power line from Volkhov to Leningrad was destroyed. After that, the supply of electricity to residential buildings and to most enterprises stopped. There were several thermal power stations in the city, but due to a lack of fuel, they worked at minimal power. Electric lighting remained only in the Smolny Institute (the office of the Bolshevik Party of Leningrad), the General Staff Building of the NKVD and police offices, headquarters of the anti-aircraft batteries, buildings of the central post office, telegraph, fire service, hospitals and bakery plants.

The deceitful Soviet government habitually shifted responsibility for the failure in the management of the city and defeats at the front to the residents

---

91. Pavlov, D.V., *Leningrad is Under Siege*, Leningrad: Lenizdat, 1985, p.58.

of Leningrad who were dying of hunger. By order of Stalin's servant Andrey Zhdanov, Leningrad issued special brochures on energy saving under the heading 'Economy is the law of war'. Information about additional ways to save electricity at enterprises was widely disseminated. 'Electricity wasters' were arrested and punished severely. Inspectors were constantly going to homes, factories and institutions, looking for violations of measures designed to save electricity.

Oleg Kobranov, an eyewitness of the events, said:

> The electrical network and water supply quickly failed, the apartments were illuminated with homemade lamps made of household soap: soap melts and burns, smokes, but does not go out. It turned out something like a long-burning candle. The rooms in the apartments were more like dark caves! It was also completely dark outside. In addition, because of the blackout, even lighting matches and cigarettes in an open area was strictly prohibited.

The Ice Road

From now on, all the hopes of the starving residents of Leningrad were connected with the ice, or more precisely with the road on the ice of Lake Ladoga. But the stormy lake did not want to freeze for a long time. Only on 20 November 1941 was the first Ice Road organised on the lake, along which a sledge wagon train that went to the eastern shore of Lake Ladoga. On 22 November, the first trucks ventured onto the still fragile ice. This meant that the long-awaited Ice Road, officially named Military Road No. 101 (VAD No. 101), began to function. It became the most dangerous section of Leningrad Military Road No. 102 (VAD No. 102), created at the end of November 1941 to supply the city dying of hunger. The Ice Road (VAD No. 101), which passed directly over the ice of Lake Ladoga, had such an important military significance that from the moment of its inception it was commanded by a general, Afanasy Shilov.

At first, the Ice Road functioned with great interruptions. Because of the brittle ice, only three or four bags of flour were put in each truck. Two or three more bags were put in the sledge attached to the truck from behind. In such an inefficient way, on 25 November 1941, only 70 tons of food were delivered to the west bank, on 26 November – 154 tons, and in the next three days 150 tons per day. On 30 November, a thaw came, which led to a decrease in daily supplies to 62 tons. In total, until 1 December 1941, Leningrad received only 800 tons of flour via the Ice Road, that is, less than the two-day needs of a multimillion population city.

During this period of time, due to the weakness of the ice, forty trucks sank and got stuck in the ice that broke under their weight. Difficulties also arose in other sections of VAD No. 102. For example, 350 trucks got stuck in the snow on the bypass road around Tikhvin in just three days and also on the Novaya Ladoga–Eremina Gora section. VAD No. 102 was hundreds of kilometres long. It started on the western shore of Lake Ladoga, then passed through the village of Lednevo, the town of Novaya Ladoga and the settlement of Syasstroy. Then it went around Tikhvin, through the villages of Karpino and Novinka, then through deserted forests and ended at the Zaborie and Podboreie railway stations. The infrastructure of VAD No. 102 consisted of many permanent and temporary warehouses. The road was served by a huge number of people.

Meanwhile, the situation with Leningrad's food supply was developing according to the worst-case scenario. In early December 1941, flour stocks in the city approached zero for the first time. Hitler's predictions came true, it was obvious that soon the whole Leningrad would simply die of hunger. The members of the Military Council of Leningrad Front had a choice: either to reduce the already insignificant ration again, or in six days the food in Leningrad would completely run out. A feverish search for a way out of the critical situation began. The inviolable stocks of flour and crackers for the Soviet Baltic Fleet were used. To increase the volume of 'food', completely unthinkable surrogates were created (ground tree bark, cake), which were added to 'bread'. These emergency measures should have at least temporarily postponed the imminent death of the majority of Leningrad residents from starvation.

Red Army Air Force planes are in the air again

The weather that worsened at the end of November provided a long-awaited respite for anti-aircraft gunners and Russian soldiers defending the area around Volkhov, Voibokalo settlement and in the Syas river floodplain. A cyclone formed south of Leningrad and German airfields were covered with 2m snowdrifts. In addition, due to constant snowfall, there was almost zero visibility. From 20 to 23 November 1941, the Luftwaffe was inactive due to cloud, and only in the evening of 24 November were several high-explosive bombs dropped on Leningrad. But the German long-range artillery, firing using coordinates, continued shelling the city. During 23 November, 234 large-calibre shells exploded on the territory of Leningrad, and as a result, the

No. 232 Bolshevik and MOPR plants, as well as several residential buildings, were damaged. Sixty-one people were killed and 155 were injured.[92]

In the area of the besieged city, the weather was somewhat better, which allowed Soviet aviation to briefly claim air supremacy. For example, on the night of 21–22 November and the next day the Leningrad Front Air Force carried out twenty-nine sorties. At night, seven Beriev MBR-2 flying boats made raids on Ivanovka and Sosnovskaya Polyana villages. One long-range Ilyushin DB-3 bomber from the Air Force Soviet Baltic Fleet (VVS KBF) and two high-speed SB bombers from the 44th Bomber Aviation Regiment (44th BAP) took off to strike the German airfields at Pleskau-Süd (city of Pskov), Siverskaya, Gorodec and Toroshkovichi. However, none of the bombers returned from the mission. Later, one SB was found burnt out on Soviet territory near Pargolovo settlement. The bodies of the pilot and navigator were found burned in the wreckage, but the gunner-radio operator survived and was sent to hospital with injuries.

The forces of 'Stalin's Falcons' were rapidly melting away, so it became increasingly difficult for the Soviets to resist the Luftwaffe. On 27 November 1941, the 7th Fighter Aviation Corps Air Defence (7th IAC PVO) had fifty-nine serviceable fighters, including nineteen I-16s, seventeen MiG-3s, five Yak-1s, five LaGG-3s and four I-153s. Only fifteen of them were formally considered night fighters.[93]

On 28 November, Soviet aviation carried out thirty-six sorties. Two planes attacked German artillery positions in the Figurnaya roscha settlement (on the front of the Soviet 55th Army). One Soviet aircraft fired at enemy firing points on the eastern outskirts of the Gorodok No. 1 settlement. Six fighters flew to the Volkhov area to support the counter-attacking Soviet troops. At the same time, two aircraft returned to their airfield without completing their mission as they did not find the target due to poor visibility.

Long-range DB-3 bombers and SB high-speed bombers carried out eleven sorties to attack German troops in the Gorodok No. 1 and Figurnaya roscha settlements. Another thirteen sorties were carried out by the Soviets to conduct aerial reconnaissance. The next day, the weather worsened again. The report of the Head of the Operational Department of the Leningrad Front Air Force Colonel Seleznev stated: 'The actual weather is solid cloud cover, cloud height from 30 metres, in places from 200 metres, light rain and drizzle, thick haze, fog in places, temperature +1° … +2° Celsius.' As already noted above, in conditions of continuous cloud, snowfall and zero visibility, Soviet aviation could not act.

---

92. TSAMO RF. Foundation 217. Inventory 1221. Case 191. Sheet 16.
93. TSAMO RF. Foundation 217. Inventory 1221. Case 189. Sheets 566–567.

AIR BATTLE FOR LENINGRAD, 1941–1944

The Luftwaffe bombs Leningrad again

Meanwhile, German aviation resumed air attacks against Leningrad. On 27 November, at 12.00, the 'air alert' signal was once again announced in the city. After that, twenty-two German planes flew over Leningrad at approximately equal intervals for five hours. From a great height, the bombers dropped fifty-five high-explosive bombs from behind the clouds, but the accuracy was unsatisfactory. Twenty-eight bombs fell on vacant lots, twelve on railway and tram tracks, six on streets, six on residential buildings and one on No. 363 plant. According to the Soviet Local Rescue Service (MPVO), six people were killed and fifty-eight people were injured. Some of the German bombs were equipped with time fuses. One of these bombs exploded twenty-two hours fifty-one minutes after it fell, while another went off after twenty-six hours fourteen minutes. As a result of the time fuse bomb explosions, three residential buildings were destroyed, one person was killed and five were injured.

The daytime air attack on 28 November proved to be much more severe in terms of the damage caused. Fifty-eight high-explosive bombs were dropped on Leningrad. Twenty-nine bombs fell on vacant lots and into the river, four on railway tracks, eleven on streets, eight on residential buildings and only two on industrial plants (workshops at the plants producing rubber technical products and at the tyre factory were destroyed). Twenty-four people were killed and 129 were injured. Of the total number of victims, at the time of the bombing, ninety-six were in their apartments, thirty-three were on the street and twenty-four were at industrial plants. Many residents of Leningrad, deprived of strength from hunger, still did not go to air-raid shelters, leaving their lives to the will of fate. In addition, thirty-two survivors and twenty-four corpses were recovered from the rubble from previous air attacks.[94]

The Germans clearly sought to harass the hungry residents by day and night. The next day was the third consecutive day of raids on Leningrad. The Headquarters of the Air Defence Forces of the Leningrad Front reported:

> The raid began at 12.00 and ended at 13.21. Radar stations detected the approach of German bombers from the south-west direction. The planes followed the direction from the villages of Lisino and Dyatlicy, through the settlements of Ropsha, Vysockoe, Volodarsky, Strelna and further over the Gulf of Finland – further to the city. The return of the German bombers

---

94. TSAMO RF. Foundation 217. Inventory 1221. Case 103. Sheet 414.

was carried out along the same route, with individual aircraft passing south through the settlement Ust-Izhora.

Enemy planes dropped 11 high-explosive bombs on the city from behind clouds from heights of 2,500–4,000 metres, of which 2 did not explode. The raid was accompanied by intense anti-aircraft fire. According to preliminary data: there are no casualties, the destruction is insignificant. Leaflets have been dropped in the area of the Voroshilov plant. The 'air alert' signal was announced twice, with a total duration of 2 hours and 19 minutes ... Anti-aircraft artillery repelled the raid on Leningrad by firing in the direction of sound and barrage firing. Projectile consumption: 85mm – 933, 76mm – 81. Barrage balloons did not rise into the air due to strong wind and snow.[95]

On 30 November, at 09.03, a Ju 88 reconnaissance aircraft appeared from the Gulf of Finland at an altitude of 3,000m. It flew over Kronstadt and Olgino village, then turned south. Most likely, the reconnaissance aircraft spotted a small convoy heading to Gogland island. The Soviet ships were soon attacked by Luftwaffe aircraft. The icebreaker ship *Oktyabr*, with a displacement of 663 tons, which was in front of the convoy, was severely damaged by German bombs. It soon sank, while seven people from its crew died in the icy waters. Also, as a result of a direct hit by German bombs, the transport ship *Scouts*, with a tonnage of 2,136brt, was destroyed. On the same day, the minesweeper *TSCH-67* (the former tugboat *Izhorets-71*) was also sunk in the Gulf of Finland in a Luftwaffe attack.

In the evening at 17.42, as soon as it got dark, air raids began on Leningrad. Within fifty minutes, German bombers dropped forty-one high-explosive bombs on the city. As a result, four residential buildings were destroyed and the water supply system was damaged in two places. Thirteen residents were killed and another sixty people were injured. More than half of the victims during the bombing did not descend into air-raid shelters, but were in their apartments. On this day, rescuers recovered twenty-five survivors and twenty bodies from the rubble.

Once again, the German long-range artillery caused much more damage to the city, firing 314 shells, including sixty-five shrapnel shells. One hundred and thirty-one shells exploded in the streets and vacant lots without causing much damage. But most of the shells hit residential buildings and industrial plants.

---

95. Ibid., Sheet 415.

Railways and tram tracks were also destroyed in many places. Forty people were killed and 176 people were injured.

On 30 November, the 7th Fighter Aviation Corps Air Defence (7th IAC PVO) carried out sixty-seven sorties and claimed one downed Bf 109 over Lake Ladoga. According to Soviet information, a German fighter crashed on Russian territory 5km south-east of Osinovets village. Three more Bf 109s were allegedly 'damaged'. The Soviets lost two fighters, while another was severely damaged but managed to return to base. According to German information, Bf 109 F-2 W.Nr. 2919 flown by Unteroffizier Karl Heinz Bornemann of 3./JG 54 went missing during an air battle. In a dogfight with Soviet fighters, Unteroffizierr Joachim Titzel from the same Staffel (3./JG 54) was wounded. His Bf 109 F-4, W.Nr. 8275, crash-landed on its fuselage on German territory near the Sinyavino settlement.

On 1 December 1941, at 14.41, a single Ju 88 reconnaissance aircraft flew from the Gulf of Finland. At an altitude of 5,000m, it followed the route Tolbukhin lighthouse–Gorskaya village–Novoye Devyatkino village. Then the reconnaissance aircraft turned around and flew back on the same course. Soon, to the west of Kronstadt, a single German bomber attacked the icebreaker ship *Tasuya*, which was clearing the fairway – the navigable route across the lake – of ice. The high-explosive bomb penetrated the deck and hit the cargo hold, but did not explode. After that, the captain took the damaged *Tasuya* to Kabotajnaya harbour in Kronstadt. Sappers were called to the ship but as soon as they started defusing the bomb, an explosion occurred and *Tasuya* quickly sank from the damage. Thirteen people were killed in the explosion.

Hunger is worse than German bombs

From the beginning of December 1941, Luftwaffe air attacks against Leningrad continued. On the night of 1–2 December, three bombings of the city were recorded., German planes dropped forty high-explosive bombs from 5,000m. Of these, ten fell into rivers, nine on streets and squares, fifteen on residential buildings and two on industrial plants. Seventeen people were killed and ninety-eight were injured.

'Stalin's Falcons' did not actively try to counter the Luftwaffe attacks. The rare encounters of Soviet fighters with German bombers in the sky over Leningrad were due to chance. For example, at 17.20, Senior Lieutenant Baklanov fighter from the 26th Fighter Aviation Regiment Air Defence (26th IAP PVO) was performing a patrol flight in his I-16. Suddenly, over the Uglovo Soviet Air Base, he saw a single He 111. According to the 'Stalin's Falcon' report, the enemy aircraft randomly dropped bombs in the area of the pilots'

THE SCHMIDT'S WASTELAND

barracks and then began to go south. Senior Lieutenant Baklanov pursued the bomber as far as Tosno railway station. However, 'Stalin's Falcon' was then forced to call off his attack as he began to run out of fuel.

On the afternoon of 2 December, the Luftwaffe carried out another air raid on Leningrad, dropping fifty-five high-explosive bombs. As a result of the bombing, twenty residential buildings were destroyed, the No. 13 research Institute building was damaged, and the water supply network, street lighting network and tram tracks were damaged in five places. However, the electric public transport (tram and trolleybus) no longer functioned due to the lack of electricity. Some broken and stuck tramcars were stranded right in the middle of the streets with open doors and covered with snow. Some of the German bombs were again equipped with time fuses. Three such bombs exploded three to five hours after the fall. Twenty-two people were killed and 123 people were injured. Most of the victims again did not go to air-raid shelters, waiting out the raid at home or moving around the streets.

The Head of the Air Defence of the troops of the Leningrad Front Major General Krylov wrote:

> Despite the extremely unfavourable meteorological conditions, the enemy still continues prolonged attrition air attacks against Leningrad. Obviously, he carries them out in order to reduce the productivity of industrial plants and cause transport downtime.[96]

On 3 December at 11.31 air-raid sirens sounded in Leningrad once again. The starving residents of the city were already so used to them that most perceived this signal as ordinary as the horns of cars on the streets or daily radio broadcasts. In three months Leningrad had changed beyond recognition. From a blooming and glowing city of palaces, parks and industrial plants, it had turned into a gloomy, dark and dying ghost town. During the September and October air attacks, people looked with amazement and horror at burning houses and bomb craters. Now they passed indifferently by the corpses of the dead, immersed in hungry indifference. The townspeople got used to the roar of anti-aircraft guns and were no longer afraid of the explosions of German bombs and shells. Therefore, this time, despite the air raid sirens, most continued to go about their business, stand in queues for bread and warm up in their still-surviving apartments. Residents were far more worried about where to get food and how to get a bread substitute for their food stamps. Hunger and cold permeated every apartment, institution and industrial plant. Thoughts about finding the

---

96. TSAMO RF. Foundation 217. Inventory 1221. Case 103. Sheet 428.

coveted black bread was constant and was the main leitmotif of the ongoing struggle for life.

The hum of German planes was heard from the south-west as usual. They were high in the sky over Krasnoye Selo, Uritsk and Torgovyi port. But there was something new in this raid that could not be overlooked. The hum of the bomber engines was audible due to the strong wind, but the residents of Leningrad did not hear the usual rumble of anti-aircraft guns. There were reasons for such an unusual silence.

Firstly, by the beginning of December 1941, the 2nd Leningrad Air Defence Corps had used up almost all of its ammunition. After the Germans captured Tikhvin, the supply of anti-aircraft shells was practically reduced to zero. The Soviet anti-aircraft gunners had only inviolable ammunition reserves, stored in case the Germans went on the offensive and the anti-aircraft guns would have to shoot directly at German tanks.

Secondly, the command of Leningrad Air Defence and the Military Council of Leningrad Front decided not to open fire during air raids. Wondering how the Germans always managed to find Leningrad and drop bombs in any weather and at any visibility, the narrow-minded Soviet commanders put forward a theory that German pilots were guided by the flashes of anti-aircraft guns. Unlike the residents of Leningrad, Stalin's commanders did not starve and tried in every possible way to prove their indispensability to the 'Red Tsar'. As a result, the 'wise' command of the city's defence allowed only anti-aircraft batteries installed in the so-called 'false Leningrad' to fire. It was a wasteland to the north of the city, where lights were specially lit at night in order to mislead the enemy. In the report of the Leningrad Air Defence Command dated 3 December it was reported: 'The anti-aircraft artillery of the 2nd Leningrad Air Defence Corps did not fire at enemy aircraft, with the exception of individual shots in the zone of "false Leningrad".'

The next air raid took place on the night of 4–5 December. The approach of German bombers was detected in advance by radar stations, and at 00.25 an 'air alert' was announced in Leningrad. The planes flew at an altitude of 4–5km along the usual route through Lisino village, Vysockoe settlement, the towns of Krasnoye Selo and Uritsk, the Gulf of Finland, Torgovyi port and Vasilyevsky Island. Forty-four high-explosive bombs were dropped on the city, of which twenty-four fell into reservoirs and on wasteland. Four bombs did not explode. As a result of the bombing, seven residential buildings were damaged. The warehouse, blacksmith shop, and the building where the shooting range was located were destroyed. The central heating system was damaged in one of the districts of the city. Twelve people were killed and forty-five were injured. The main part of the anti-aircraft artillery did not fire, and was conducted only from the 'false Leningrad'.

THE SCHMIDT'S WASTELAND

On the evening of 5 December, the Luftwaffe launched two consecutive air strikes on the city. In the first attack, from 17.23 to 19.05, eight German bombers participated, appearing over the city at intervals of two to four minutes. From an altitude of 3,200–4,000m, they dropped twenty-nine high-explosive and 1,800 small incendiary bombs. Four warehouses and a blacksmith shop were destroyed along with four residential buildings. The building of the Ethnographic Museum of Leningrad was damaged. Incendiary bombs caused nineteen fires. There were no fatalities, but forty-two people were injured. By the time of this raid, Soviet anti-aircraft gunners had replenished their ammunition reserves, which allowed them to resume barrage firing and 'shooting in the direction of sound'. However, they did not damage any Luftwaffe aircraft. After 21.30 two more German planes flew over Leningrad and dropped five high-explosive bombs of large calibre. As a result, three residential buildings were destroyed, eight people were killed and twenty-nine were injured.[97]

Who did the Germans want to influence with their incessant air attacks on a city dying of hunger? Did these bombing have any military significance? Apparently, the answer to this question is obvious. The command and pilots of Luftflotte 1 were simply following Hitler's inhuman order! The Nazi regime turned the educated and intellectually developed people who made up the majority of Luftwaffe airmen into soulless automatons, limp instruments of death.

'Piles of frozen corpses resembled blocks of marble'

The situation in Leningrad was deteriorating rapidly every day. In December 1941, a humanitarian catastrophe began in the besieged city. The Soviet regime did not take emergency measures to evacuate the civilians who had accumulated in the city. Leningrad's food supply had completely failed. Stalin, concerned about preserving his shattered power, in fact abandoned his citizens to the mercy of fate. Hunger had become a much more terrible and destructive weapon than German bombs and shells.

Dmitry Pavlov, a member of the State Defence Committee for Food Supply of Leningrad Front Troops and Leningrad Population, wrote:

> In December 1941, death mowed down people regardless of gender and age. Death overtook people everywhere: on the street, moving, a person fell and did not get up again; in an apartment, he

---

97. TSAMO RF. Foundation 217. Inventory 1221. Case 103. Sheet 429.

went to bed and fell asleep forever; often life ended at the machine. It was difficult to bury, transport did not work. On the streets there were icy trams, trolleybuses, buses, like a shroud covered with snow. Along the streets, broken wires hung in bizarre threads, dusted with a fluffy layer of frost. Along the streets covered with snow, a string of people trudged and, straining their last strength, pulled sledges on which the dead lay. The dead were buried without coffins – wrapped in a sheet or blanket, and later simply in the clothes in which the person died. Often, exhausted, people left the dead halfway to the cemetery.

Municipal infrastructure and healthcare workers, driving around streets and alleys daily, picked up corpses and took them away by trucks to Serafimovskoe, Bolsheohtinskoe, Smolenskoe and Bogoslovskoe cemeteries. But most of all, the dead were taken to the outskirts of the city, to a huge wasteland next to the old Piskarevskaya road. So the well-known Piskaryovskoye cemetery was formed. Cemeteries and entrances to them were littered with frozen, snow-covered bodies. There was not enough strength to dig deep frozen ground. Teams of soldiers blew up the ground and lowered dozens, and sometimes hundreds, of corpses into spacious graves, without knowing the names of the deceased.[98]

In such monstrous circumstances, Stalin was not afraid of an anti-Soviet uprising. The ordinary residents of Leningrad defended the city at the cost of their lives, while well-fed Stalin's servants wrote reports to Moscow under electric lighting and took idiotic measures to divert German bombers to false targets. For many years of the USSR's existence, Stalin's propaganda had tried to cover up all the failures of the leadership, who allowed the concentration of millions of civilians in a surrounded city without sufficient food supplies and openly abandoned them to mortal danger, with cheerful statements about the heroism of the Soviet people.

A resident of Leningrad Oleg Kobranov told one of the authors of this book:

> In December, so many people began to die that they did not have time to bury them. By the twentieth of December on our street (200 metres from Liteyny Avenue) there were five or six piles of the dead, 20 people in each. It was a terrible sight! The dead lay wrapped in sheets, in coats, fur coats, someone practically naked.

---

98. Pavlov, D.V., *Leningrad is Under Siege*, Leningrad: Lenizdat, 1985, pp.164–165.

They were mostly old people and teenagers! Piles of frozen corpses resembled blocks of marble ... There were 11 cemeteries and 109 gravediggers in the city, and by mid-December half of them had died. Municipal infrastructure in the city was abandoned. All the baths were closed and people never washed. The streets were littered with two-metres of thick snow, which no one cleared. Even trucks could not pass through most streets, and residents moved along narrow paths in the middle of the roadway. They were afraid to walk along the walls of the houses: the house could collapse at any moment and cover passers-by with debris. There was a catastrophic shortage of firewood in Leningrad; it was obtained in the forest north-east of the city. Getting to these logging sites was the dream of many residents! After all, the death rate there was 50% less, since the workers were fed tolerably well.

That's what kind of city the German bombers dropped their 'cargo' on. The city of the dead and dying, the city where cemeteries had signs with horrifying inscriptions: 'For digging up corpses for the purpose of eating – execution ...'

Bombing the Ice Road

Despite the bad weather, German reconnaissance planes soon discovered busy traffic on the Lake Ladoga ice. Chief of the General Staff of the Army High Command (OKH) Generaloberst Franz Halder wrote in his diary on 28 November: 'There is a path on the ice along Lake Ladoga, along which communication with Leningrad is carried out.'[99]

In early December, the commander of I./KG 4, Major Klaus Noske, received an order from Hitler's headquarters, which informed that from now on the main task of his Gruppe was to fight Russian cargo traffic on Lake Ladoga. At that time, the unit was based at Pleskau-Süd (city of Pskov) and had thirty-three He 111 H-5 bombers, of which twenty-three were in combat-ready condition. The first sortie against the new I./KG 4 target was carried out on 1 December and the operation against the Ice Road continued on the following days. Due to bad weather, low clouds and frequent snowfall, German aircraft operated at low altitude. In fact, in these missions, the bombers performed the functions of ground-attack aircraft. First they flew through the town of Shlisselburg to

---

99. Halder, F,. *From Brest to Stalingrad: A war diary. Daily records of the Chief of the General Staff of the Ground Forces 1941–1942*, Rusich, 2001, p.459.

the eastern shore of Lake Ladoga, then turned west and descended. Seeing the columns of Russian trucks, they performed several approaches to the target, dropping one high-explosive or fragmentation bomb. Along the way, the air gunners fired at trucks and horse-drawn carts with machine guns.

Chief of the General Staff of the Army High Command (OKH) Generaloberst Franz Halder wrote on 4 December 1941: 'Our aviation launched air attacks against transport going on the ice of Lake Ladoga.'[100]

The Soviets were alarmed by these attacks. The Headquarters of the Air Defence Forces of the Leningrad Front combat report dated 3 December 1941 reported:

> The enemy air forces were particularly active in the Lake Ladoga area, where from 12.35 to 14.50 they repeatedly bombarded and fired at transport columns on the Ice Road, Zelenec Island, Kobona village from dive and horizontal flight, and Kokorevo village. A total of 37 aircraft appeared over the lake, including 17 Ju 88s and up to 20 Bf 109s. Enemy aircraft operated as part of groups of 2–3 to 6 Ju 88 under the cover of fighters. Anti-aircraft artillery repelled the raids, Soviet Fighter Aviation conducted active air battles.[101]

Russian fighters completed twenty-two sorties and reported three enemy aircraft shot down (one Ju 88 and two Bf 109s). According to their data, one German fighter fell into the lake. The second German fighter was shot down over Kokorevo and crashed near settlement No. 16. This aircraft was soon discovered by Russian soldiers, who found the pilot's body in the cockpit.[102] It was Unteroffizierr Erwin Loffler from 1./JG 54. His Bf 109 F-1, W.Nr. 5684, went missing on 3 December. On the same day, another German pilot whose plane was shot down in a dogfight over Zelenec Island on 30 November was caught and captured near Kobona village. In all likelihood, it was the aforementioned Unteroffizierr Karl Heinz Bornemann from 3./JG 54.

The defence of the Ice Road from German attacks from the air presented a rather difficult problem. The placement of anti-aircraft artillery on the ice of the not yet completely frozen lake was limited by the weight of the gun. The ice could only support about 20mm and 37mm automatic anti-aircraft guns. Guns of a larger calibre could not be placed on the ice because of their strong recoil

---

100. Ibid., p.460.
101. TSAMO RF. Foundation 217. Inventory 1221. Case 103. Sheet 429.
102. TSAMO RF. Foundation 217. Inventory 1221. Case 103. Sheets 430–431.

when firing. Hence, 85mm anti-aircraft guns could only be installed on Zelenec Island, near the Ice Road.

Equipping permanent anti-aircraft artillery positions on the Lake Ladoga ice also brought great difficulties as the gunners had to build primitive shelters of snow and ice. Later they were replaced by simple bunkers made of logs with metal stoves for warming the soldiers.

Liberation of Tikhvin

On 5 and 6 December 1941, the Red Army launched a counteroffensive near Moscow. This meant that, despite all the efforts of the Wehrmacht, the main goal of Operation Barbarossa was never achieved. Hitler's dream that after the capture of the Soviet capital Leningrad would fall became much further from reality. The situation on the Eastern Front changed significantly and moved into a phase of permanent crisis. The Wehrmacht experienced significant difficulties in the south in the Rostov-on-Don area. In the Crimean Peninsula, the 11th Army under Generaloberst Erich von Manstein failed to master another 'Bolshevik stronghold' – Sevastopol.

On 9 December, taking advantage of the weakening of German troops, the troops of the Soviet Volkhov Front went on the offensive and managed to capture the town of Tikhvin. For the Soviets, this success had mainly a psychological effect because they could not immediately take advantage of its fruits. Tikhvin railway station and the extended section of the railway to the railway junction at Volkhovstroy had been damaged severely. The Germans blew up all the bridges and completely destroyed all the infrastructure for servicing steam locomotives and railway wagons. However, thanks to the liberation of Tikhvin, the length of the cargo delivery route to Lake Ladoga was significantly reduced.

Meanwhile, the Germans were retreating to Volkhov. The -30° frost had accelerated their pace and the days had become unusually short. At night, the roads between the marshes were illuminated by a bright moon, wolves howled from the forests, and the roar of artillery cannonade could be heard from behind. Despite the Soviets' efforts to continue the offensive, all their attacks were repulsed and soon the front in the area stabilised.

Hitler's new plans

At this time, the situation on many sections of the huge Eastern Front continued to deteriorate. In addition to Tikhvin, the Germans were forced to retreat from Rostov-on-Don. However, Hitler ignored the bad news from the front and still hoped for an early victory. After many hours of meetings with the military, the Führer finally found a place on the map where such a victory could be obtained without making much effort. A new offensive on Moscow was impossible, but the capture of the second most important city of the USSR seemed to Hitler quite an achievable goal.

The new plan of the offensive against Leningrad by the incompetent Führer looked very primitive, but at first glance impressive. Hitler proposed to create a shock fist from the 8th and 12th Panzer Divisions, providing them with the 93rd Infantry Division as a reserve. These forces were supposed to suddenly attack the positions of the Russian 55th Army defending the southern approaches to Leningrad. After the breakthrough of the Russian defence and the destruction of the 55th Army, the Wehrmacht should have reached the Neva river throughout its entire length. After that, according to Hitler, the city would be in a catastrophic situation and definitely had to fall. At the same time, the Führer seriously demanded the transfer of aircraft from the central sector of the front to carry out the planned operation! This 'brilliant' plan had one significant drawback: there were simply no troops to implement it. The 8th and 12th Panzer Divisions got bogged down in the fighting and lost a significant number of their tanks. Thus, in order to implement Hitler's plan, these divisions had not only to be quickly withdrawn from the front and replaced by some other German units, but also replenished with fresh forces. It is clear that all these 'projects' had nothing to do with reality and were not pursued any further.

However, the echoes of the 'brilliant' but unrealised operation still reached the Luftwaffe units in this sector of the front. After the capture of Tikhvin by the Russians, the commander of I./KG 4 was ordered to attack the railway line leading to Lake Ladoga. At the same time, individual I./KG 4 crews still flew out to bomb Leningrad. However, it is clear that the Germans simply did not have enough strength to carry out all these missions. Therefore, the air strikes were episodic and could not seriously hinder the work of the Road of Life. An additional obstacle to the actions of Luftwaffe aircraft was the bad weather. From 4 to 12 December, there was a blizzard over the lake; German airfields were also covered with snow. The Headquarters of the Air Defence Forces of the Leningrad Front reported: 'The almost complete inactivity of the enemy air force is caused by unfavourable meteorological conditions.' All this time, the Ice Road had been completely safe from air attacks. Soviet soldiers serving the road received a small eight-day respite.

By this time, the Soviets had fully formed the Ice Road air defence system. Batteries of 85mm anti-aircraft guns from the 25th Separate Anti-aircraft Division (25th OZAD) were located on the left (western) shore of Lake Ladoga

THE SCHMIDT'S WASTELAND

near Kokorevo village. Similarly, the positions of the 255th Separate Anti-aircraft Division (255th OZAD) were located on the right (eastern) shore of Lake Ladoga near Kobona village. Small-calibre 21st OZAD anti-aircraft guns were placed on the ice between them. In addition, the Soviets installed anti-aircraft machine guns along the entire length of the Ice Road.

On the other side of the front, the situation was diametrically opposite. Luftflotte 1 not only did not receive reinforcements, but also lost some of its units. Back in mid-December 1941, the specialised KGr. 806 flew to Germany for rest and replenishment. The formal reason for this was the coming of winter. Lake Ladoga and the Gulf of Finland had frozen by that time, so there were simply no targets left for the 'anti-ship' Gruppe. Simultaneously with KGr. 806, all bombers from Kampfgeschwader 77 (KG 77) flew to Germany. Later, these units were transferred to the Mediterranean theatre and did not appear on the Eastern Front anymore.

To compensate for the weakening of the Luftwaffe's capabilities for attacking Russian communications on Lake Ladoga, the German command had to look for an alternative to combat aircraft in a hurry. On 14 December, the German long-range artillery opened fire for the first time on the Ice Road and Cape Osinovets from the Shlisselburg area. The results of the shelling were negligible. One shell hit artillery battery No. 1 of the 21st Separate Anti-aircraft Division (21st OZAD) and destroyed a GAZ-AA truck with a direct hit.

On 17 December, taking advantage of a short-term improvement in weather conditions, Luftwaffe aircraft became active again. Enemy fighters and bombers bombed and shelled Military Road No. 101 (VAD No. 101), as well as Military Road No. 102 (VAD No. 102) near Sumskoye and Voibokalo settlements. From low level, Bf 109 fighters from JG 54 fired at a convoy of trucks moving across the ice. The consequences of this attack clearly showed that trucks were not only carrying food to Leningrad. The Bf 109 F-2 from 1./JG 54 flown by Unteroffizier Netle was damaged by debris from an exploding ammunition truck. However, the fighter was still able to return to Krasnogvardeysk airfield. The damage caused to the aircraft was estimated at 35 per cent on the German damage scale. Soviet anti-aircraft gunners from 21st OZAD claimed one downed German fighter, which allegedly crashed near Kobona village, broke through the ice of the lake and sank. However, according to German information, there were no irretrievable losses by JG 54 on this day.

In the following days, the weather worsened again. Only individual planes took to the air from both sides of the front, mainly for the purpose of reconnaissance. However, the Germans did not miss the opportunity to hinder the movement of Russian trucks with supplies on the ice of the lake. For example, on 21 December, a single Ju 88 A appeared over Lake Ladoga, which dropped eight bombs on the Ice Road.[103] On the same day, Luftwaffe planes dropped eleven high-explosive bombs on Leningrad. As it turned out, this was the last air raid on the city in 1941.

The cessation of the Leningrad bombing was due to the general deterioration of the strategic situation on the Eastern Front. In this regard, the task of forcing Leningrad to surrender had temporarily lost its relevance. The Luftwaffe had completely switched to supporting its troops and bombing the Ice Road. Only the German long-range artillery continued to shell the city.

Führer orders the ice is split

Meanwhile, the Road of Life was increasing its traffic. After the liberation of Tikhvin, the cargoes arriving by rail to this city were reloaded onto trucks. Commissar of the State Defence Committee for Food Supply of Leningrad Front Troops and Leningrad Population Dmitry Pavlov recalled:

> At the end of December, Tikhvin town resembled a giant anthill. Around the clock, thousands of workers and soldiers unloaded the arriving railway trains and continuously filled the trucks that arrived one after another with food.[104]

Next, trucks carried supplies along forest roads to the eastern shore of Lake Ladoga. This difficult route through wasteland and swamps was almost 200km long.

Soon the Soviets managed to somewhat reduce the length of the lines of communication to supply Leningrad. The Russian 54th Army pushed the Germans away from Voibokalo and Zhikharevo railway stations. This allowed trucks to deliver cargo from Tikhvin to Kolchanovo railway station and reload railcars from now on. After the arrival of trains at Voibokalo and Zhikharevo stations, the goods were again manually reloaded onto trucks. Such measures allowed the speeding up of cargo turnover, and the Ice Road began to work with increasing intensity. The lake ice had strengthened by that time, which made it possible to use the maximum load capacity of trucks. Soon the situation with Leningrad's food supply improved somewhat, but the exhausted residents of the city continued to die.

---

103. TSAMO RF. Foundation 217. Inventory 1221. Case 103. Sheets 475–476.
104. Pavlov, D.V., *Leningrad is Under Siege*, Leningrad.: Lenizdat, 1985, p.200.

THE SCHMIDT'S WASTELAND

Meanwhile, the incompetent commander Adolf Hitler was in a rage. His troops, contrary to his strict orders, faltered and retreated under the blows of the 'defeated' Red Army. In this shameful situation for the Wehrmacht, according to the Führer, it was not he who was to blame, but numerous cowards and weak-willed defeatists. The search for those responsible for Hitler's mistakes began. Clouds began to gather over the heads of the German military commanders, and soon a real personnel 'storm' broke out. Generals and Feldmarschalls, who had recently been at the peak of their military careers, were ignominiously expelled from the army. A milder version of the resignation of the German military leaders was the announcement of unexpected serious health problems. What can they do, they fought in Russia! Winter! It's cold! They caught a cold!

Every day, the psychopath Hitler signed formidable orders, gave 'valuable' advice to his military leaders and distributed all kinds of instructions on solving urgent problems of defence and fighting Russian frost. For example, on 20 December 1941, the Führer stated that 'any military bakery should be able to organise the defence of its facility', 'Richthofen should destroy settlements and small forest areas', and aviation should 'prevent any construction of railway lines by the enemy'.[105] Next, Hitler ordered the crews of aviation squadrons to be sent to the front lines, to the trenches, the troops to burn settlements (without specifying which ones), to take away all the clothes from the local population. And most importantly, according to Führer, it was necessary to introduce the will to resist into every German military unit. Among other things, Hitler forbade the use of the expression 'Russian winter'.[106] All these delusional statements clearly testified that the Führer of the German people was in a manic excitement caused by the unwillingness to come to terms with the total failures of his army in Russia.

And suddenly Hitler became aware that the Russians in Leningrad had not only not given up, but had organised mass transportation by trucks on the ice of Lake Ladoga. And this was happening right under the noses of the German troops! How was it allowed?! How dare they! Enraged, Hitler called the Commander of Luftflotte 1, Generaloberst Alfred Keller, by telephone and ordered him to immediately destroy the Ice Road. To the reasonable question of exactly how to do this, the 'brilliant' Führer suggested breaking the ice with large-calibre bombs!

---

105. Halder, F., *From Brest to Stalingrad: A war diary. Daily records of the Chief of the General Staff of the Ground Forces 1941–1942*, Rusich, 2001, p.463.
106. Ibid., p.463.

This mission was also assigned to I./KG 4 under the command of Klaus Noske. However, before carrying out such an idiotic operation, the sane Luftflotte 1 staff officers decided to first test the impact of high-explosive bombs on the ice cover. A long strip was marked on Lake Pskov, simulating the Ice Road. After that, He 111s consistently dropped SC500, SC1000, SC1800 and even SC2500 bombs on a conditional target. However, the effect of the bombs was insignificant. Heavy bombs pierced through the ice, after which they exploded under it or at the bottom of the lake. At the same time, small holes were formed in the ice cover, which were then quickly tightened with fresh ice. Thus, the holes from the bombs could not block the movement of Russian trucks for a long time. In addition, the gigantic area of the frozen lake allowed the Soviets to plot a new road on the ice at any time.

Thus, Hitler's 'brilliant' proposal failed and the crews of German bombers had to act on the basis of the previous tactics, which were also not the most successful. Up until Christmas, they made superhuman efforts to make daytime sorties over Lake Ladoga in terrible weather. In order to somehow prevent the busy traffic across the lake, Luftwaffe planes had to chase almost every Soviet truck. Based on the fact that the Russians used several thousand trucks for transportation along the Ice Road, such efforts of a few German bombers turned into a Sisyphean task.

The Luftwaffe's fight with the Ice Road continues

On 23 December 1941, during the time period from 11.55 to 15.35, the Ice Road was bombed and shelled from low level by fifteen He 111s and two Bf 109s. They dropped sixty-four high-explosive and fragmentation bombs, most of which missed their targets. The Soviets suffered four people injured and one truck damaged.

The next day, thanks to new combined tactics, the Germans were more fortunate. To suppress Russian anti-aircraft guns, He 111s from I./KG 4 dropped bombs on the Ice Road from a height of 1,000–1,200m. At this time, the Bf 109 fighters were descending to low level and shot at trucks and horse-drawn carts at point-blank range. Interestingly, the Russian anti-aircraft gunners identified the enemy planes they saw as 'He 113'[107] and 'Bristol Bulldog Mk. IVA'.

In the following days, the weather over Lake Ladoga deteriorated again, and there were continuous snowstorms. It is not surprising that for the whole day from 18.00 on 26 December to 18.00 on 27 December, only one Ju 88 was

---

107. The He 113 was a phantom, which never existed.

THE SCHMIDT'S WASTELAND

seen by the Russians over the entire territory from the Gulf of Finland to Lake Onega. It flew at an altitude of 4,000m near the settlement of Syasstroy.

On 27 December, air attacks against the Ice Road resumed. German planes bombed not only the road laid on the ice of Lake Ladoga, but also Kokorevo and Vaganovo villages. Several Soviet trucks were destroyed, thirty-eight people were killed and twenty-seven were injured. On this day, the long-awaited activity of 'Stalin's Falcons' was noted. Three I-16 fighters from the 13th Fighter Aviation Regiment Air Force Soviet Baltic Fleet (13th IAP VVS KBF) attacked a group of Bf 109s from JG 54 over the lake. Russian pilots reported one downed German fighter, which allegedly crashed on the ice. According to German information, there were no losses in the composition of JG 54 on that day.

The next day, the Germans again bombed the Ice Road and its forks on both shores of the lake. The village of Kobona suffered the most. German bombs destroyed several houses and five trucks. Thirty people were killed and wounded. The Soviet air defence positions were also seriously damaged. Several fragmentation bombs exploded at the positions of the 25th Separate Anti-aircraft Division (25th OZAD). One 37mm automatic anti-aircraft gun, a searchlight on the chassis of a car and three ZIS-5 trucks were destroyed. Five people were killed, including an officer for communication with aviation, Captain Kulikov. Three more people, including political commissar anti-aircraft battery Popenko, were injured. When repelling a raid by German bombers, anti-aircraft artillery fired intensively. Three anti-aircraft divisions expended 1,100 76mm and 85mm shells, as well as 786 37mm shells. Russian anti-aircraft gunners reported to the higher command about one downed He 111 and one Bf 109. In fact, the Luftwaffe did not suffer any losses in this raid.

Despite the opposition of the Soviet air defence, the crews of I./KG 4 avoided losses for a long time. However, the good time for this unit soon ended. On 31 December 1941, as a result of a direct hit by an anti-aircraft shell, He 111 H-5 '5J+KK' commanded by Feldwebel Nashann caught fire and crashed on Russian territory.[108]

Realising the low effectiveness of air attacks, the Germans tried to disrupt Soviet communications using various alternatives to aircraft. German long-range artillery periodically fired on the Ice Road from the Shlisselburg area. In early January 1942, a group of German infantrymen, dressed in white camouflage, made a sortie on skis into the area of Russian transport communications. Under the cover of the snow shroud, they managed to pass unnoticed on the ice of the

---

108. Gundelach, K., *Kampfgeschwader 'General Wever' 4*, Stuttgart: Motorbuch Verlag, 1978, p.162.

lake and get out on the Ice Road. There, the Germans fired at Soviet posts and destroyed several trucks, after which they retreated. But these were one-time actions that had only psychological significance.

Until 1 January 1942, 16,500 tons of various cargoes were delivered to the besieged Leningrad on ice. By the first day of the new year 1942, Soviet military engineering had completely restored the section of railway between Tikhvin and railway junction at Volkhovstroy. After a two-month break, on 1 January 1942 at 05.00, a train with cargo for Leningrad arrived directly at Voibokalo station. From now on, the need to send trucks in long, roundabout ways disappeared. As a result of this achievement, the number of cargoes delivered to the Leningrad increased significantly. However, for most residents of the city, these successes did not bring joy and relief. The meagre level of food distribution was slightly increased only by Christmas, 25 December 1941. By that time, hundreds of thousands of people had already died of starvation. Tens of thousands of survivors were so exhausted that they continued to die on a new increased food ration.

On 7 January 1942, the Red Army launched a large-scale offensive against Army Group North. All the meagre forces of the Luftwaffe were thrown into support of the German ground forces. Air attacks against the Ice Road, as well as against Leningrad itself, had completely stopped.

'Cemetery' of German aircraft

According to Soviet information, in the period from 8 September to 30 December, the Luftwaffe dropped 3,509 high-explosive bombs and over 66,000 small incendiary bombs on Leningrad. In turn, the German long-range artillery fired more than 13,000 shells at the 'Bolshevik stronghold'. As a result of air attacks and artillery shelling, 2,325 residential buildings, 673 administrative and plants buildings, twenty-two bridges and many other structures were completely or partially destroyed in the city. Some 4,483 people were killed, and another 15,543 were injured. In addition, Soviet Local Rescue Service (MPVO) units lost 117 people killed and 350 personnel were injured.

Russian air defence reported that in September–December 1941, 780 German aircraft were shot down in the Leningrad sector. Based on this optimistic information, the very limited area of the city and its suburbs should have become a real cemetery, completely littered with the wreckage of German aircraft. In fact, during the fourth quarter of 1941, the Luftwaffe lost 877 aircraft in all theatres of military operations (Western Europe, North Africa, the Mediterranean and the USSR).

THE SCHMIDT'S WASTELAND

The reality, which was very different from the optimistic reports, showed that the Russian air defence in the Leningrad area was completely useless. In conditions of bad weather and limited visibility, Russian fighters were almost always inactive, and anti-aircraft artillery fired 'in the direction of sound', that is, used data obtained from the ZP-2 sound collector installation. In conditions of strong winds and blizzards, the work of sound collectors, which transmitted data on the location of German aircraft to anti-aircraft batteries, was very inaccurate. In fact, Russian anti-aircraft gunners fired at random! Due to the shortage of ammunition, barrage firing was loose and less effective than in other major Soviet cities. But the most terrible truth about the effectiveness of Russian anti-aircraft fire was revealed later. At the beginning of 1942, Leningrad military engineers found that all the 2nd Leningrad Air Defence Corps Anti-aircraft artillery fire control devices (PUAZO) in service were defective and generated erroneous data. Thus, throughout the autumn of 1941, anti-aircraft gunners aimed at aircraft using erroneous calculation data! These blunders turned Russian anti-aircraft shells into useless fireworks.

The failure of Leningrad's air defence was so obvious that the Soviet leadership was forced to recognise it. By order of Stalin, on 9 December 1941, the Commander of the 2nd Leningrad Air Defence Corps, Major General Mikhail Procvetkin, was removed from office. 'For weak leadership' he was also demoted in military rank from major general to colonel. Only an acute shortage of commanders saved the incompetent Commander from execution. Mikhail Procvetkin's place as commander of the air defence in the Leningrad region was taken by Major General Gavriil Zashikhin. Changes in the organisation of air defence affected not only the command. Simultaneously with the personnel changes, the Leningrad Corps Air Defence Area was formed, where Major General Zashikhin took the post of Commander.

The city was captured by cannibals and bandits

The entire period of Stalin's power is characterised by the permanent half-starved existence of the Soviet people. In the case of any crisis, most often caused by the 'wise' foreign and domestic policy of the 'Red Tsar', local or total famine arose in the Soviet Union. The Leningrad Holodomor discussed in this book differed from other cases in that Stalin organised it in close cooperation with his old friend Hitler. In the city cut off by the land blockade from the main territory of the USSR, the famine had acquired terrible proportions.

One of the terrible consequences of this phenomenon was cannibalism. In December 1941, twenty-six people were arrested for eating human meat in Leningrad, and in January 1942, 366 people were arrested. In February

1942, which was the culmination of starvation deaths, there was a new large-scale outbreak of cannibalism. In the first fifteen days of February alone, the police arrested almost 500 cannibals in Leningrad. In the memo of the military prosecutor, Military lawyer of the 2nd rank Alexander Panfilenko, dated 21 February 1942, it was reported that 36 per cent of cannibals were men and 63.5 per cent were women. They were people of different ages from 14 to 80 years old. Among the cannibals caught there were even members of the Bolshevik Party![109]

This terrible phenomenon had become so widespread that whole gangs of cannibals appeared in the dying city.[110] Ominous rumours about the disappearance of children in the neighbourhoods and places where cannibals operated and about all sorts of creepy details of their activity spread throughout Leningrad. In reality, cannibals mostly ate the corpses of people who had died earlier or frozen in the street, and rarely committed murder for food. But, numerous facts of the sale of human meat on the Leningrad black market have become the most terrible sign of the scale of the spread of cannibalism!

From the point of view of the authorities' compliance with elementary formalities, the fight against cannibalism required legal grounds for punishing the perpetrators. But it soon became clear that there were no such grounds. Although this terrible phenomenon was not something new in the Stalinist USSR, there was no concept of 'cannibalism' in the false Soviet criminal code. Therefore, Soviet lawyers had a problem how to qualify such a crime. But the Bolshevik 'lawyers' quickly eliminated this problem. The Leningrad Prosecutor's Office decided to apply article 59-3 of the Criminal Code ('Banditry') to cannibals. In war conditions, such a measure allowed such 'bandits' to be shot at the scene of a crime or sentenced to death after a trial. Digging up buried corpses for the purpose of eating them was also punishable by immediate execution.

However, not all residents of the city were starving and looking for cadaverous meat. In Leningrad crime had increased massively. There were numerous criminal groups and gangs operating in the dying city, engaged in food theft, speculation and robberies. This destructive social phenomenon, widespread under the Bolsheviks, was not written about in Soviet newspapers. Stalin himself, being a former bank robber, claimed that banditry in the Soviet Union was long over.

---

109. The blockade of Leningrad in the documents of declassified archives, Moscow: AST, 2004, pp.679–680.
110. Ibid., p.679.

THE SCHMIDT'S WASTELAND

Gunfights between bandits and militia officers took place regularly in Leningrad. Moreover, sometimes the shootings turned into real street battles with the use of grenades and machine guns. A large arsenal of weapons was confiscated from the bandits destroyed during the year: 1,113 rifles, 820 hand grenades, 631 revolvers and pistols, thirteen machine guns and 70,000 rounds of ammunition. Half of the Soviet division could be armed with this number of small arms. Such high numbers of armed criminals was due to the gigantic loot that they had seized in the city and were ready to defend at the cost of their lives. During the two years of the Leningrad land blockade, NKVD officers confiscated 9.5 million rubles of cash from criminals, 41,215 rubles in the form of gold coins and 2.5 million rubles in government bonds, 70kg of gold, 500kg of silver, 1,537 diamonds, 1,295 gold watches, 36km of various fabrics and 483 tons of food![111] These impressive figures show that the standard of living in the besieged city was very different for different people!

By the spring of 1942 Leningrad was a sad sight. Many residential buildings were deserted, their residents either dead or evacuated from the city. City blocks were abandoned and lay in ruins. Due to the melting of snow on the streets and in the ruins of houses, a huge number of unburied corpses were exposed. To cope with this problem, the city authorities decided to create a crematorium at brick factory No. 1. The factory's tunnel kilns were used to burn the bodies. From 7 March to 1 December 1942, 117,300 corpses of Leningrad residents were cremated there.[112]

However, despite the incredible difficulties, Leningrad resisted. Military Road No. 101 (VAD No. 101) (the Ice Road) continued to operate until 24 April 1942. In 152 days, over 361,000 tons of various cargo were transported along it, including 262,000 tons of food. After Stalin allowed the evacuation of the starving population on 22 January 1942, more than 550,000 residents of the city were taken to the east along the Ice Road. Among them was 12-year-old Oleg Kobranov. He recalled: 'The blockade of the city changed us beyond recognition. When I looked in the mirror in April 1942, after the evacuation from Leningrad, I simply did not recognise myself!'

---

111. The blockade of Leningrad in the documents of declassified archives, Moscow: AST, 2004, p.698.
112. Ibid., p.705.

Chapter 7

Operation Eisstoss

Aerial attack on the lair of a mortally wounded beast

As already noted above, since January 1942, German aircraft located in the Leningrad area were mainly used to support ground forces and only occasionally flew out to strike Soviet communications. From time to time, small groups of German aircraft bombed the Ice Road through Lake Ladoga and railway stations in the rear of the Volkhov Front.

On 7 January 1942, the Red Army struck in the Valdai Hills area and broke into the deep rear of Army Group North and Army Group Centre. A month later, a 100,000 grouping of the German 16th Army was surrounded in the area of Demyansk. Hitler forbade a retreat and ordered the supply of the cut-off German divisions by air. Further, the Soviets surrounded the German garrison in the city of Holm, located on the Lovat river. To supply it, the Luftwaffe also had to urgently organise an air bridge.

In the Leningrad and river Volkhov area, Soviet troops also continuously attacked the Germans in order to break through the Army Group North front and lift the land blockade of the city. Despite the losses, the German defence was impenetrable. The Luftwaffe had also been embroiled in fierce attrition battles.

Under these conditions, the Commander of I. Fliegerkorps, General der Flieger Helmuth Förster, was very surprised to receive a directive from Commander of Luftflotte 1, Generaloberst Alfred Keller on 26 February 1942. It ordered:

> The I. Fliegerkorps command should prepare the reconnaissance and combat operations with the aim of destroying parts of the Russian fleet located in the Gulf of Finland. Shortly before the ice is opened in the Gulf of Finland, the heavy ships of the Russian fleet located there should be destroyed by a simultaneous concentrated strike of dive bombers, guarded by fighters. I. Fliegerkorps can count on the fact that another bomber Gruppe will be attached to it for this operation.

OPERATION EISSTOSS

Next, the general was ordered to submit to the Luftflotte 1 headquarters calculations on the expected composition of the forces and the plan for the attack. The deadline for the implementation of the received directive was clearly defined: 1 March 1942.

However, by the specified date, General Förster, of course, could not carry out such a large-scale operation. All of its aircraft were used to carry out more important missions to support ground troops.

In February 1942, I. Fliegerkorps bombers carried out 4,600 sorties and dropped 3,440 tons of bombs. In March, these figures more than doubled – 9,075 sorties and 8,170 tons of bombs. It seemed to General Förster stupid and impractical to use Ju 87 dive bombers to strike ships that were standing at the mouth of the Neva and did not pose a threat to German troops. In addition, by the spring of 1942 the remnants of the Soviet Baltic Fleet were of very dubious military value. General Förster hoped that 'the top' would change their minds, and there would be no need to execute this very strange directive.

At that time, the Luftwaffe faced the urgent task of supporting the operation to rescue the encircled group of German troops in Demyansk. Careful preparation for the blockade-breaking strike lasted a long time. The Germans managed to concentrate a strong strike group of the 8th Light Infantry Division and 122nd, 127th and 329th Infantry Divisions under the command of General der Artillerie Walther Kurt von Seydlitz-Kurzbach unnoticed by the Russians. On the morning of 20 March 1942, a large group of Ju 87s from II./StG 2 and III./StG 1 appeared in the sky. After a powerful air strike on the positions of Soviet troops south of the town of Staraya Russa, the German 16th Army launched a rapid offensive. With the massive support of the Luftwaffe, the German strike group forced the River Redya. By 25 March, the Germans had managed to drive a wedge 15km deep and about 13km wide into the Russian defence. There was only 16km left before the breakthrough of the Demyansk Pocket encirclement ring. In the current situation, the Soviets had no reserves to close the gap in the front line.

In the midst of these events, on 22 March 1942, for the second time General der Flieger Förster received a strange order to prepare his forces for the destruction of Soviet ships in Leningrad. The attacks should be carried out before the opening of the ice on the Neva, regardless of the scale of support for the units of the German 16th and 18th Army. At the same time, the order specifically emphasized that this 'most important operation' was planned by the Führer himself! Apparently, Hitler believed that the German garrison of Demyansk Pocket, which had been fighting in the encirclement for two months, could wait a little longer.

On 24 March, the Luftflotte 1 command received another order to prepare the operation as soon as possible with the involvement of all available aircraft.

AIR BATTLE FOR LENINGRAD, 1941–1944

All aviation actions in other sectors of the front should be completely stopped. The order again hinted that the Führer personally expected the destruction of the Soviet Baltic Fleet ships. It was impossible to ignore Hitler's direct orders, and General der Flieger Förster was forced to obey. In the absence of air support, Army Group North had to suspend the unblocking offensive in Demyansk. At this time, staff officers of I. Fliegerkorps began thorough preparations for a new operation to destroy Soviet ships.

By this time, Luftflotte 1 had the following forces:

Dno-Griwotschki airfield – Ju 88 A bombers from II./KG 1, III./KG 1 and I./KG 3, Ju 87 Ds from I./StG 2;

Gostkino airfield – Ju 87 Ds from the newly formed II./StG 2;

Gorodec airfield – Ju 87 Ds from III./StG 1;

Pleskau-Süd (city of Pskov) air base– Ju 88 A bombers from III./KG 3;

Korovye Selo air base – He 111 H bombers from I./KG 53 and II./KG 27;

Riga-Spilve airfield – He 111 H bombers from I./KG 4, II./KG 4 and 11./KG 100;

Siberskaya air base and Krasnogvardeysk airfield – Bf 109 F fighters from I./JG 54 and III./JG 54.

All these combat aircraft had to be used to destroy the target that, in Hitler's opinion, had the highest priority. Since the beginning of Operation Barbarossa, the destruction of Soviet Baltic Fleet ships had become Führer's obsession, to which he returned many times. With the same maniacal obsession, Stalin tried to save his ships. In 1941, the Fleet suffered catastrophic losses from Luftwaffe strikes. As already described above, in order to save the remnants of the Fleet, in autumn 1941 the Russians decided to transfer all its warships from Kronstadt to Leningrad. The main reason for this decision was the weakness of the Kronstadt air defences.

At the beginning of 1942, twelve large warships and ten different auxiliary vessels were stationed at the mouth of the Neva river on the territory of Leningrad at various berths. The battleship *Oktyabrskaya Revolutsiya* was located near the Vasilyevsky Island embankment (near the Gornyi Institute building). Opposite it, near the opposite bank of the Neva, stood the minelayer *Marti*. The cruiser *Kirov* was near the Sudomekh shipyard. The cruiser *Maxim Gorky* lay in the centre of Leningrad near the famous equestrian statue of tsar

Peter I, the Bronze Horseman. The destroyer leader *Leningrad* was located near the Voroshilov plant. Numerous submarines and other small ships were moored along the embankments of the Neva.

Leningrad's air defence at that time had strong enough forces to counter Luftwaffe attacks. It consisted of six anti-aircraft regiments, one anti-aircraft machine gun regiments, one anti-aircraft searchlight regiment and several battalions of the Soviet Air Surveillance and Communication Service (VNOS). In addition, Leningrad's airspace was controlled by seven RUS-2 'Redut' radar stations from the 72nd Separate Battalion VNOS. However, the fear of losing the last surviving Baltic Fleet ships was so great that the Soviets took additional measures to strengthen the air defence of this entire 'Great and Most Fortunate Navy'. In February 1942, the 9th Anti-aircraft Regiment (9th ZenAP) was formed, which consisted of three anti-aircraft divisions. Major Georgy Mukhamedov was appointed commander of this special unit. The 9th ZenAP had forty-six medium-calibre guns and eighteen 12.7mm DShK machine guns. The positions of the Soviet anti-aircraft gunners were located in Torgovyi port, on Vasilyevsky Island, at the Sudomekh shipyard and on different sections of the Neva embankment.

Also, Soviet Baltic Fleet ships were covered by two fighter aviation regiments of the Air Force Soviet Baltic Fleet (VVS KBF): 71st and 11th. The 71st Fighter Aviation Regiment Air Force Soviet Baltic Fleet (71st IAP VVS KBF) was based at Bychie Pole airfield (in the western part of Kotlin Island), while the 11th Fighter Aviation Regiment Air Force Soviet Baltic Fleet (11th IAP VVS KBF) was based at Gora Valdai airfield (near Oranienbaum).[113]

Thus, an attack from the air on such a well-protected target was associated with a great risk for Luftwaffe aircraft. The Soviets were ready for an air attack, so the destruction of such a complex target without significant losses of bombers seemed to the command and staff officers of Luftflotte 1 an extremely difficult task.

Preparation of the operation to destroy the remnants of the Soviet Baltic Fleet

The planning and preparation of the operation to destroy the remnants of the Soviet Baltic Fleet took place in compliance with all the rules of the art of war. After analysing the intelligence information, I. Fliegerkorps staff officers

---

113. *The air defence forces of the country in the Great Patriotic War*, Moscow: Voenizdat, 1968, p.119.

identified the highest-priority targets for an air strike. The main targets were identified as the battleship *Oktyabrskaya Revolutsiya*, cruiser *Kirov* and minelayer *Marti*. According to German intelligence, these ships were considered the most combat-ready.

On 26 March, the Commander of Luftflotte 1, Generaloberst Alfred Keller, ordered the organisation of exercises. The contours of Soviet Baltic Fleet warships were reproduced in full size on the ice of Lake Pskov. Their location exactly corresponded to the places where ships were moored on the Neva. Using these training targets, the German bomber crews practised dropping bombs. This was not the first time Lake Pskov had served as a training ground for Luftwaffe aircraft. In December 1941, it had been used to test the possibility of splitting the ice with heavy high-explosive bombs.

Practising in this way was not new in the Luftwaffe. For example, at the end of December 1940, the Ju 87 pilots from I./StG 1 and II./StG 2 who were ordered to destroy the British aircraft carrier *Illustrious* in the Mediterranean, trained on a contour layout of its flight deck installed off the coast of the island of Sicily. The exercises were beneficial, and on 10 January 1941, Stukas achieved six direct hits on the ship. Three more bombs exploded in the immediate vicinity of the sides of the ship. *Illustrious* suffered severe damage and was forced to leave for the USA for repairs that lasted almost a year.

In anticipation of the operation to destroy the ships of the Soviet Baltic Fleet, 3.(F)/Ob.d.L. (3rd Staffel of long-range reconnaissance at Oberbefehlshaber der Luftwaffe (Aufkl.Gr.Ob.d.L.) was assigned to conduct thorough aerial photography of the mouth of the Neva. It was necessary to establish the exact disposition of the ships and all the anti-aircraft batteries covering them. In order to shorten the flight time to the target, several Ju 88 D reconnaissance planes were transferred to Krasnogvardeysk airfield, just 25km south of Leningrad.

Shortly before receiving a new assignment, the crews from 3.(F)/Ob.d.L. returned to the Eastern Front after a short rest. From the beginning of Operation Barbarossa until the end of 1941, this aerial reconnaissance unit (3.(F)/Ob.d.L.) had operated on the southern flank of the Eastern Front. During this period, reconnaissance planes from 3.(F)/Ob.d.L. flew over the Black Sea, the Crimean Peninsula and the Caucasian coast of the Soviet Union. In the spring of 1942, crews from 3.(F)/Ob.d.L. were based at Gostkino airfield near Luga and supported Army Group North.

Due to the re-equipment with new aircraft models, the capabilities of crews from 3.(F)/Ob.d.L. increased significantly. Instead of the old Do 215 B-4 aircraft, this long-range reconnaissance unit received new Ju 88 D aircraft, which were specially equipped to perform reconnaissance missions. In March 1942, 3.(F)/Ob.d.L. also received several long-range reconnaissance Bf 109 F-4/R3s. This was a modification of the Bf 109 fighter, equipped with

OPERATION EISSTOSS

a Rb 50/30 high-altitude camera. Such reconnaissance aircraft had higher speed and manoeuvrability compared with twin-engine aircraft. Thus, the Bf 109 F-4/R3 had many advantages over enemy air defence fighters and could attack Soviet aircraft if necessary.

During March 1942, long-range Ju 88 D and Bf 109 F-4/R3 reconnaissance planes made many flights over Leningrad. The high activity of German aviation was recorded in combat reports of the 169th Anti-aircraft Regiment (169th ZenAP):

> March 6th. At 11.18 two Bf 109s at an altitude of 2,000 metres flew along the route Forovsky Bridge – Dom Sovetov – Avtovo district – Uritsk town.
>
> March 7. At 14.23 one Ju 88 at an altitude of 5,500 metres flew along the route Kirov Factory No. 100 – Uritsk town.
>
> March 28. At 10.54 one Ju 88 at an altitude of 6,000 metres flew on the course Uritsk town – Kirov Factory No. 100 – Gulf of Finland.
>
> March 29. From 13.52 to 15.14, one Ju 88 flew at an altitude of 6,000 metres along the route village Finskoe Koirovo – village Pulkovo – Baltiysky railway station – Isaakievskiy Sobor – Vasilyevsky Island – Leningrad Torgovyi port. Along this route, the enemy then made five more flights.[114]

In total, during March 1942, the Russians recorded 240 flights of German reconnaissance planes. As the result of such an intensive operation, the Luftflotte 1 command had a sufficient amount of important information in its hands. The location of all the targets of the future operation to destroy the remnants of the Soviet Baltic Fleet was established with maximum accuracy. All the efforts of the Soviets aimed at carefully disguising the warships stationed at the mouth of the Neva turned out to be completely useless.

The increased activity of Luftwaffe noticeably frightened Russian air defence commanders. Due to total incompetence, as well as outright stupidity, Soviet 'analysts' were completely unable to understand the true intentions of the Germans. They made the erroneous conclusion that they were studying the scheme of the city's air defence and were looking for the most profitable

---

114. *The Red Banner Soviet Baltic Fleet in the Battle for Leningrad. 1941–1944*, Moscow: Nauka, 1975, p.171.

directions for bombing Leningrad. No one from the Soviet command had any idea that the ships would be the target. Therefore, in response to the German preparations, the Russians limited themselves to a banal increase in attention to the sky over Leningrad. Anti-aircraft gunners were ordered to conduct daily training of artillery crews to practise combat techniques.

Meanwhile, the Germans were finishing their preparations for the operation. On 28 March, an order was issued for Luftflotte 1, which stated: 'Führer ordered that heavy Russian warships located in the port of Leningrad be destroyed by I. Fliegerkorps aircraft at the beginning of the ice drift.'[115] Operation Eisstoss (breaking ice) was scheduled for 4–5 April 1942. This name turned out to be very symbolic. Exactly 700 years before this event, a battle took place that in Russia is called Battle on the Ice. On 5 April, the German knights of the Livonian Order fought with troops of the Republic of Novgorod on the ice of Lake Peipus. According to Russian legend, during the battle, the German knights were pushed onto the thin ice of Lake Peipus. Under the weight of the armour, the ice split, and the German knights fell into the water and drowned. As a result, the Russians won a crushing victory. There are other versions of this event, where the circumstances and the scale of the Russian victory are presented more modestly.

'We are facing incredible anti-aircraft fire ...'

It was only at the end of March 1942 that the Soviets sensed the impending danger from the Luftwaffe and began to act. On 31 March, the Commander of the Leningrad Air Defence, Army Major General Gavriil Zashikhin, ordered all anti-aircraft batteries placed on high alert. Radar station operators had to monitor the airspace around Leningrad continuously. The anti-aircraft batteries of the 160th Anti-aircraft Regiment (160th ZenAP) and units of the 2nd Anti-aircraft Machine gun Regiment (2nd ZenPulP) were additionally transferred to the ships' docking areas, Lieutenant Schmidt Bridge and the Voroshilov plant.

On 4 April 1942, an operational group led by Colonel Aleksey Rysev was on duty at the Leningrad Corps Air Defence Area command post. Having started work, Colonel Rysev joked, telling his subordinates that the weather was clear and sunny, so an enemy raid was possible. However, most of the day passed quietly, and nothing foreshadowed the coming trouble.

---

115. Morozov, E., *The Failed Pearl Harbor, or why Operation Eisstoss Failed*, AviaMaster, Moscow, 2001. No. 3. p.24.

OPERATION EISSTOSS

The approach of German bombers was first recorded by the operators of RUS-2 'Redut' radar station No. 4, located near Volkhovo cemetery. At 18.05 (Moscow time) the radar station detected a large group of aircraft 115km south of the city. The station head, Lieutenant N.V. Shatalin, transmitted this information to the main post of the Soviet Air Surveillance and Communication Service (VNOS). Soon the approach of the 'aliens' was detected by RUS-2 'Redut' radar station No. 5. Then the radar stations detected two more groups of enemy aircraft, all moving in the direction of Leningrad.

After receiving information about the approach of Luftwaffe aircraft, concern arose at the headquarters of Leningrad Corps Air Defence Area, and an order was given for the urgent raising of barrage balloons. All the staff officers understood that for the first time since the terrible September 1941, the city was again waiting for a massive air raid. Army Major General Gavriil Zashikhin felt that his future fate depended on how the top leadership would perceive his actions in a crisis situation. Therefore, he immediately called the First Secretary of the Leningrad Regional Committee of the Communist Party, Andrei Zhdanov. In a telephone conversation, Major General Zashikhin promised Stalin's servant that the air defence forces would certainly repel an enemy air attack. Thus, he protected himself from accusations of indecision and confusion before an enemy attack.

Remembering the sad fate of his predecessor, Major General Zashikhin hesitated for a long time to declare an air alert in Leningrad. He understood that enemy bombs were unlikely to fall on his command post, but if the radar station operators made a mistake and there was no raid, then Stalin could accuse him of alarmism and deprive him of his position. Only at 18.52 did Major General Zashikhin finally give the order and air-raid sirens howled on the streets of the city. At that moment, German bombers were already approaching the target.

A total of 132 German aircraft participated in the first air attack: sixty-two Ju 87 D dive bombers, thirty-three Ju 88 As and thirty-seven He 111 Hs. They flew to Leningrad in three large groups, with the bombers covered by fifty-nine Bf 109 Fs from JG 54.[116]

The weather was good, and the sun was still shining over the Gulf of Finland. In the twilight of the setting sun, the German pilots clearly saw the grey city blocks, the chimneys of factories, the winding delta of the Neva and the clear silhouettes of numerous ships next to the embankments. Then flashes of flame and clouds of smoke appeared below. These were the bursts of shells from the German long-range artillery, which opened fire on the positions of Russian anti-

---

116. Gundelach, K., *Kampfgeschwader 'General Wever' 4*, Stuttgart: Motorbuch Verlag, 1978, p.171.

aircraft batteries and airfields where the fighters were based. Then numerous flashes of Soviet anti-aircraft guns flashed. Instantly, the pink-blue evening sky was painted with hundreds of clouds of anti-aircraft shell explosions.

The first German bombers, coming from the Gulf of Finland, turned sharply to the right and began to dive on the ships from out of the setting sun. Residents on the streets watched in horror as the Stukas, with sirens howling, dived to the ground. Then black dots separated from them, and a few seconds later columns of fire and smoke shot up into the sky. The area of the mouth of the Neva was filled with a terrible roar of explosions. Kontr Admiral Yuri Panteleyev recalled:

> The anti-aircraft guns were bursting, the sky was dotted with white clouds, between which, without changing course, German planes were flying. The planes dived on the depot ship 'Polyarnaya zvezda' and on submarines standing along the left bank of the river. Strong explosions, the ground is shaking underfoot, icicles flew from the roofs.[117]

German shells exploded at the positions of the anti-aircraft battery, which was located on the embankment near *Oktyabrskaya Revolutsiya*. Eight people were killed and seven others were wounded. However, the anti-aircraft gunners continued to fire at the Ju 87s. The anti-aircraft battery gunner Nikolai Kotienko recalled: 'It is not difficult to catch the Hunchback[118] in the sight, but it is much more difficult to keep it in the centre of the sight – it quickly dives and howls strongly. Skill and endurance are necessary for success.' Soon, a large-calibre, German high-explosive bomb landed in a warehouse next to the battery. The explosion lifted thousands of nuts, bolts and other pieces of iron into the air, which literally covered the anti-aircraft gunners, pounding frighteningly on their helmets.

During the first attack, the Germans managed to use the element of surprise. About 230 high-explosive and armour-piercing explosive bombs of all calibres were dropped on the ships' berths, of which seventy-two exploded in the immediate vicinity of the targets. Residential buildings on the embankments and the Admiralty Building were badly damaged. A total of 116 people were killed and 311 people were injured.

But the warships themselves somehow miraculously avoided direct hits! Within thirty-six minutes, *Oktyabrskaya Revolutsiya* was attacked by thirty German aircraft. All the bombs exploded in the river, on the embankment and

---

117. Panteleev, Y.A., *Sea Front*, Moscow: Voenizdat, 1965, p.119.
118. One of the Russian nicknames for the Ju 87.

in the adjacent blocks of houses. The German crews were never able to hit the battleship. Other targets, the cruiser *Maxim Gorky*, the destroyers *Svirepyi* and *Stoiky*, and submarines *P-2* and *M-79*, only received hits from fragments of bombs that exploded nearby.

Nine German bombs exploded near the cruiser *Kirov* and one hit the upper deck around frame No. 273. Breaking through two decks and the side of the warship, it flew out near the waterline and exploded under the ice. The bomb was armour-piercing but only had a small explosive charge and thanks to this the cruiser survived. Fragments of bombs that exploded next to the *Kirov* disabled rangefinding telemeters, and damaged one 45mm gun and one 100mm gun. The decks received significant dents and the outer skin was pierced in many places.

As a result of the attack, floating dock No. 508 received the greatest damage. It was behind *Oktyabrskaya Revolutsiya* and accidentally came under attack by German bombers. A bomb explosion completely destroyed the middle compartment of the docks fourth pontoon. In addition, a crane vessel with a payload of 200 tons was damaged by a nearby explosion.

Bombers from II./KG 27 appeared over Leningrad at the end of the attack. They had taken off from Korovye Selo Air Base at 17.00 (Berlin time) and reached their destination an hour later. Friedrich Bertch, of the 5th Staffel (5./KG 27), recalled:

> We carried out two attacks on Leningrad. We knew that several ships were still blockaded by the ice that had not melted, and we had to attack them. In the first sortie, we encountered incredible anti-aircraft fire, and this sortie did not have the desired success.[119]

The response from 'Stalin's Falcons'

Contrary to the plans prepared by the Soviets to protect ships from Luftwaffe attacks, 'Stalin's Falcons' appeared in the air after a long delay and acted extremely unprofessionally. The headquarters of the 7th Fighter Aviation Corps Air Defence (7th IAC PVO) simply did not know anything about the German air attack. The Russian fighters began to take off too late, twenty minutes after the bombing began. Over Torgovyi port four LaGG-3s from the 11th Fighter Aviation Regiment (11th IAP) attacked a pair of German aircraft identified

---

119. Waiss, W., *Chronic Kampfgeschwader Nr. 27 Boelcke. Part 3. 01.01.1942–31.12.1942*, Helios Verlag, Aachen, 2005, p.47.

by pilots as Do 215s. However, no sooner had the Russian fighters launched their attack than they themselves were attacked from behind by a pair of Bf 109s. As a result of a dogfight with German fighters, an LaGG-3 flown by Senior Lieutenant Gaponov was damaged. It tried an unsuccessful emergency landing at Komendantsky airfield but crashed into a fence and was completely destroyed.

Near the settlement of Strelna, four I-16 fighters from the 26th Fighter Aviation Regiment Air Defence (26th IAP PVO) attacked a group of German bombers and shot down two Ju 87s and one Ju 88. Aerial victories were won by Senior Lieutenants Oskalenko, Apollonin and Belikov.

At 19.08, a group of Soviet fighters consisting of four I-16s and two I-153s from the 26th IAP PVO took off from Gorskaya airfield. Squadron commander Captain Vasily Matsievich later wrote in his report:

> Over the south-western part of Leningrad at an altitude of 3000m, I met two He 111s, which I fired rocket-powered projectiles at. After that, I chased one He 111 that got away from my low-level flight attack. Then I lost sight of him. Returning to Leningrad, I entered into battle with a Ju 87. Then four more Ju 87s appeared. One Ju 87 tried to go to my tail and attack, but I turned around and went at him in a frontal attack. We flew only three or four metres apart. After that I was attacked by another Ju 87 and it hit me. The bullets pierced the engine, propeller and the canopy of the cab. I tried to reach Komendantsky airfield, but I couldn't do it and made an emergency landing on the fuselage in the Lakhta district.[120]

At 19.15–19.30, four I-16s from the 124th Fighter Aviation Regiment Air Defence (124th IAP PVO) conducted a dogfight with several German bombers identified as Bf 110s and Ju 88s. However, all the attacks of 'Stalin's Falcons' were unsuccessful.

At 19.30, a pair of Soviet Yak-1 fighters from the 123rd Fighter Aviation Regiment Air Defence (123rd IAP PVO) were patrolling at an altitude of 6,000m. The pilots saw a group of eight Ju 88s flying westward. Soviet fighters went in pursuit of them, but they could not catch up with the German planes.[121]

Despite the apparent fiasco that befell the Russian fighters, the Headquarters of the Air Defence Leningrad reported twenty-five downed and ten 'damaged'

---

120. TSAMO RF. Foundation 20506. Inventory 1. Case 129. Sheet 15.
121. Ibid., Sheets 16–17.

OPERATION EISSTOSS

German aircraft. As usual, these figures of German losses were the result of a great exaggeration of the success of 'Stalin's Falcons'. According to German information, on 4 April 1942, over Leningrad, the Luftwaffe suffered no irretrievable losses at all. Several bombers received various damage from anti-aircraft fire, but they all returned safely to their bases or made an emergency landing on German territory. For example, the bomber He 111 H-6 W.Nr. 4837 '1G+EN' from 5./KG 27 piloted by Oberleutnant Werner Kruger received a direct hit by an anti-aircraft shell in the left engine. On one engine, the plane was able to fly to the location of the German troops and landed safely near the city of Narva.

At 20.10, the air alert in Leningrad was cancelled. A few minutes after that, Major General Gavriil Zashikhin received a call from Andrei Zhdanov, one of Stalin's viceroys who very much valued his own safety. Zhdanov asked: 'Can the air raid be considered over?' In response, Zashikhin guaranteed Stalin's servant complete security. After that, the First Secretary of the Leningrad Regional Committee of the Communist Party arrived at the Air Defence Leningrad command post. Zhdanov was preparing a report to his powerful patron, Stalin, so he wished to hear Zashikhin's comments on the actions of the anti-aircraft artillery immediately.

Meanwhile, the German bombers returned to their bases at dusk but the mood of their crews was far from euphoria. The Luftwaffe pilots saw with their own eyes that the bombs they had dropped landed next to the Russian ships, but none of the ships exploded or sank. It became clear to the officers from the Luftflotte 1 headquarters that the mission had failed. The counteractions by the Soviet air defences turned out to be unexpectedly powerful. However, the Germans did not decide to end the operation.

Second air raid

According to the Operation Eisstoss plan, on the night of 5 April, bombers from I./KG 4 and II./KG 27 carried out a second air raid on the mouth of the Neva. At about 02.00, the leading aircraft, performing the role of pathfinder, dropped photoflash bombs over the ships' berths.[122] Machine guns of the 2nd Anti-aircraft Machine gun Regiment (2nd ZenPulP) and artillery batteries with 20mm and 37mm anti-aircraft guns immediately opened fire on the slowly

---

122. Gundelach, K., *Kampfgeschwader 'General Wever' 4*, Stuttgart: Motorbuch Verlag, 1978, p.171.

descending parachutes. Soon, the terrifying whistle of bombs dropped from a height of 1,000m was heard.

The main target of the bombing was again *Oktyabrskaya Revolutsiya*. However, its anti-aircraft guns were silent as its gunners had orders not to shoot, so as not to give away the location of the ship in the dark. At least nine PC1000 armour-piercing explosive bombs fell next to the battleship, and one at a distance of 20m from the side. All of them exploded at the bottom of the Neva without causing any damage. Many bombs fell on city blocks again, causing new casualties among the population. One PC1000 struck No. 2 Psychiatric hospital, while another bomb destroyed a hospital on Vasilyevsky Island. According to the Soviet Local Rescue Service (MPVO), fifty people were killed and about 100 were injured in the attack. Most of the dead were mentally ill people and the wounded, and all of them became the next unwitting victims of the senseless massacre.

During the raid, two I-153 and I-16 night fighters from the 26th Fighter Aviation Regiment Air Defence (26th IAP PVO) patrolled the sky over Leningrad. One of their pilots, Lieutenant Voevoda, saw how the searchlights illuminated one He 111. However, an attack was impossible, because the bomber disappeared in the dark with a sharp manoeuvre. Then Lieutenant Voevoda watched as a bomber performing the role of a pathfinder dropped photoflash bombs from an altitude of 7,000m, however he could not approach the German bomber and attack it as Soviet anti-aircraft artillery fired randomly in different directions. Anti-aircraft shells were constantly exploding at altitudes of 4 to 7km. The pilot of the second night fighter, Senior Lieutenant Maximov, also saw photoflash bombs descending on parachutes, but could not detect a single German aircraft.[123]

All the He 111s from KG 4 that participated in the raid returned safely to Riga-Spilve airfield. This fact was further evidence of the complete failure of Leningrad's air defence.

On the morning of 5 April, the whole city was covered with dense fog. The German long-range artillery opened fire on the mouth of the Neva again. Simultaneous to the artillery shelling, a German reconnaissance aircraft appeared over Leningrad and photographed the results of previous air attacks. The images obtained clearly showed that there were many craters and destroyed buildings on the Neva embankments near the Russian ships. Large-diameter ice holes gaped in the ice of the river. But no visible damage was observed on the battleship, cruisers and destroyers. It became finally clear that Operation

---

123. TSAMO RF. Foundation 20506. Inventory 1. Case 129. Sheet 21.

OPERATION EISSTOSS

Eisstoss did not achieve its goal and had literally turned into a simple breaking of the ice.

To achieve the result that Hitler demanded, repeated air attacks were required but the Commander of Army Group North, Generaloberst Georg von Küchler, intervened. He demanded the immediate postponement of any other missions and the resumption of bomber sorties to support the lifting of a blockade in the direction of Demyansk. The Führer eventually agreed to a pause in the implementation of his plans. In addition, bad weather with heavy fogs was established in the area of Leningrad, which in itself excluded the immediate continuation of air attacks against warships.

Pre-emptive Soviet air attacks against Luftwaffe air bases

Despite the change of priorities in the air war on the front line of Army Group North, German reconnaissance planes continued to appear regularly over Leningrad. The German long-range artillery also continued to shell the city and warships. All this gave the Soviets reason to think that this was only a temporary break in the air raids on Leningrad. Officers from the Headquarters of the Air Defence Leningrad were convinced that the Germans were conducting reconnaissance of targets and accumulating forces for new air attacks. For this reason, on 12 April 1942, the Military Council of Leningrad Front decided to launch preemptive strikes on enemy air bases.

To accomplish this task, the Soviet aviation command needed to obtain reliable information about the locations of German bombers. However, long-range aerial reconnaissance was the weakest point of Soviet aviation. Unlike the Luftwaffe, whose long-range reconnaissance planes flew up to 1,600km, Soviet aircraft could not penetrate far into enemy airspace. The range of Soviet reconnaissance planes was limited by the primitive design and poor quality of aircraft manufacturing at Soviet Aviation Industry factories. However, the public recognition of such shortcomings threatened the guilty with reprisals and executions. With the help of various kinds of misrepresentation and bureaucratic machinations, the leadership of the Air Force of the Red Army carefully concealed from Stalin the real characteristics of the reconnaissance planes. A chain of total lies permeated all state institutions of the USSR, including the Red Army. For this reason, 'groups of German bombers' were supposedly found on Pushkin and Krasnogvardeysk airfields, which were within the real range of Soviet reconnaissance planes. In fact, the main Luftflotte 1 air bases were Dno-Griwotschki, Pleskau-Süd, Korovye Selo and Riga-Spilve, that is 240–300km from Leningrad.

On the night of 14–15 April, Beriev MBR-2 flying boats from the Air Force Soviet Baltic Fleet (VVS KBF) raided Krasnogvardeysk airfield. Then at dawn, eleven fighters from the 26th Fighter Aviation Regiment Air Defence (26th IAP PVO) and 123rd Fighter Aviation Regiment Air Defence (123rd IAP PVO) attacked the same target. 'Stalin's Falcons' suffered losses even before the attack when, on the approach to Krasnogvardeysk airfield, the MiG-3 of the commander of the 26th IAP PVO, Lieutenant Colonel Boris Romanov, was shot down by anti-aircraft fire. The fighter crashed near the city of Krasnogvardeysk and exploded, with Lieutenant Colonel Romanov killed. Judging by the information from the reports of 'Stalin's Falcons', the Germans tried to repel the Soviet attack and two German fighters from 3./JG 54 tried to take off. Captain Georgy Zhidov got on the tail of one of them and fired his machine guns. Bf 109 F-2 W.Nr. 5694 was hit in the engine, then made an emergency landing. The second German fighter was able to take off and attacked the MiG-3 of Lieutenant Nikolai Shcherbina. The Soviet fighter was severely damaged, and later crashed while landing at its airfield, although Lieutenant Shcherbina was not injured. Upon returning to the base, the Russian pilots announced the destruction of ten aircraft (four Bf 109s, four Ju 87s and two Ju 88s). In fact, only one Bf 109 fighter received light damage.

On the morning of 18 April, twelve I-153s from the 71st Fighter Aviation Regiment Air Force Soviet Baltic Fleet (71st IAP VVS KBF) carried out another air attack on Krasnogvardeysk airfield. The Soviet fighters were again met with heavy fire from 20mm anti-aircraft guns. Two I-153 biplanes piloted by Senior Lieutenant Alexander Shitov and Lieutenant Yuri Spitsyn were shot down. At the same time, Senior Lieutenant Shitov did not leave the falling plane, but steered it directly into the parking area of the German aircraft. The pilot's comrades watched the burning fighter, like a meteorite, sweep over the runway and crash into one of the hangars. After that, a huge column of fire and smoke rose over Krasnogvardeysk airfield.

The self-sacrifice of Senior Lieutenant Shitov, performed in the spirit of a Japanese kamikaze, brought a significant result. Four Ju 88 D reconnaissance planes from 5.(F)/122 and 3.(F)/Ob.d.L. were destroyed. But was this damage, which could easily be made good by the Germans, worth the life of a 20-year-old man? In the following days, the Russian air force carried out several more air attacks against German airfields, but they did not cause serious damage to the aircraft.

Götz von Berlichingen over Leningrad

Meanwhile, the German 16th Army continued its blockade-relieving strike in the direction of the Demyansk Pocket and systematically drove a wedge into the Russian defence. On 20 April 1942, with the powerful support of Ju 87s,

OPERATION EISSTOSS

they managed to throw back the units of the Russian 397th Rifle Division, 41st Rifle Brigade and 44th Rifle Brigade. By the end of the day, German troops had captured the village of Ramushevo (a key point on the way to Demyansk) and reached the frozen Lovat river. This was the last water barrier in the way of the 16th Army. There were only a few kilometres left to the positions of the German II Army Corps and X Army Corps that had been cut off by the Russians. Simultaneous with the actions of the 16th Army units, the breakthrough of the blocked German troops from inside the Demyansk Pocket began. On 17 April, a shock group from SS Infanterie Division 'Totenkopf' (mot.) under the command of an ardent Nazi, Theodor Eicke, attacked the positions of Soviet troops blockading Demyansk. On the evening of 21 April, its soldiers broke through to the village of Ramushevo and met soldiers of the 8th Light Infantry Division. The Soviet blockade of Demyansk Pocket had been broken!

This success allowed I. Fliegerkorps to resume planning new air attacks against the Soviet Baltic Fleet. The new operation was code-named Operation Götz von Berlichingen. The failure of Operation Eisstoss forced the Commander of I. Fliegerkorps, General der Flieger Helmuth Förster, to think about changing the tactics of the attacks on the remnants of Soviet Baltic Fleet. Perhaps the name of the operation contains the answer to the question of the essence of the new tactics of using bombers against immobilised Russian ships. Von Berlichingen was a German knight who lived in the late fourteenth–early fifteenth century. He spent a long life in endless battles, winning victories and suffering defeats. After losing his right hand in battle, von Berlichingen used a very functional iron prosthesis, which is why he received the nickname Eiserne Hand (Iron Hand). He became for posterity a symbol of German military valour and indomitable will. For example, the Waffen-SS 17th SS Panzergrenadier Division was named after von Berlichingen, and the image of the Eiserne Hand (Iron Hand) became its emblem. Probably to finish off the remnants of Soviet Baltic Fleet, Command I. Fliegerkorps decided to conduct a series of air attacks by large groups of aircraft, using Ju 87s in the role of an all-destroying 'Iron Hand'.

Due to the rapid warming, by 23 April 1942, the Neva had already been completely cleared of ice. The next day, the Soviet Baltic Fleet command, in anticipation of new Luftwaffe raids, was going to transfer all the large ships to new berths. But suddenly it turned out that there was no fuel for the tugboats, and the Soviets had to postpone the relocation.

Since the morning of 24 April, low clouds had been hanging over Leningrad. It hindered the visual detection of aircraft and the targeted fire of anti-aircraft guns. I. Fliegerkorps staff officers decided that the right moment had come for a decisive blow on the remnants of the Soviet Baltic Fleet. The planes were supposed to dive on the warships and then immediately climb again to reach the protection of the clouds.

AIR BATTLE FOR LENINGRAD, 1941–1944

At 12.58 (Moscow time), the German long-range artillery opened fire on the positions of Russian anti-aircraft artillery and the warships' berths. Some 226 shells exploded in the Kirovsky district, and 154 shells exploded in the Torgovyi port area. Three 203mm shells hit the minelayer *Marti*, which was severely damaged. Also, the submarine *K-51* was seriously damaged by long-range shells.

Soon, RUS-2 'Redut' radar stations and posts of the Soviet Air Surveillance and Communication Service (VNOS) began reporting the detection of small groups of German aircraft. They were flying from the Gulf of Finland on the route Strelna settlement–Ugol'naya' harbour–Torgovyi port. These were forty-four Ju 87 Ds and eighteen Ju 88 As, and they were accompanied by twenty-eight Bf 109 Fs from I. and III./JG 54 led by Oberstleutnant Hannes Trautloft.

At 13.10, an air alert was announced in Leningrad. Twenty-five fighters from Air Force Soviet Baltic Fleet (VVS KBF) regiments and twenty-nine fighters from the 7th Fighter Aviation Corps Air Defence (7th IAC PVO) scrambled to intercept the German bombers. Soon, a lot of air battles took place in the sky over Leningrad. For example, four Curtiss P-40 Tomahawks from the 158th Fighter Aviation Regiment Air Defence (158th IAP PVO) attacked a group of nine Ju 88 bombers at an altitude of 4,000m. The Russian fighters went on to their opponents' tails and fired several machine gun bursts, but they were then suddenly attacked from above by several Bf 109s. German fighters shot down the P-40 of Lieutenant Vysotsky, who died during an emergency landing. The rest of the P-40s scattered in different directions and no longer tried to attack the German bombers.

Four LaGG-3s from the 11th Guards Fighter Aviation Regiment Air Defence (11th GIAP PVO) operated more successfully. Above Torgovyi port one of the pilots, Starshina (non-commissioned officer) Shah saw three Ju 87s flying at an altitude of 1,500m below him and the 'Stalin's Falcon' attacked the leading bomber and shot it down. After that, Starshina Shah saw another group of Stukas, but was unable to attack as he was driven away by German fighters. During this air battle, the Germans shot down the LaGG-3 of Sergeant Vasin. His burning plane crashed into the city and exploded, and the pilot was killed.

Five MiG-3s from the 123rd Fighter Aviation Regiment Air Defence (123rd IAP PVO) near the town of Oranienbaum intercepted a large group of German bombers, which were flying to Leningrad from the south-west. Senior Lieutenants Stychinsky and Tsisarenko and Junior Lieutenant Vasiliev shot down three Ju 87s. Senior Lieutenant Malyshev downed a Ju 88, and Lieutenant Barsov destroyed a Bf 109 fighter.

Lieutenant Shikunov and Senior Lieutenant Panirin, of the 26th Fighter Aviation Regiment Air Defence (26th IAP PVO), also claimed they had jointly shot down a Ju 87.

OPERATION EISSTOSS

Pilots from the 11th Fighter Aviation Regiment Air Force Soviet Baltic Fleet (11th IAP VVS KBF) reported five aerial victories, while losing three of their fighters.[124]

However, all the victory reports that 'Stalin's Falcons' provided to their commanders turned out to be lies. In fact, in a battle with LaGG-3 fighters, only one Ju 87 D from 3./StG 2 was damaged. Its pilot, Leutnant Herbert Bauer, was injured, but was able to land safely at Krasnoye Selo airfield. JG 54 suffered no losses that day.

From the ground and from warships, the attack of Luftwaffe bombers looked very intimidating. At 13.50, the anti-aircraft gunners of the 169th Anti-aircraft Regiment (169th ZenAP) noticed German planes flying over the clouds. The Soviets immediately opened barrage firing. However, despite the anti-aircraft fire, one by one the Stukas fell out of the clouds and dived onto the warships.

Twenty-five German bombs exploded near the battleship *Oktyabrskaya Revolutsiya* and flying fragments disabled two DShK 12.7mm anti-aircraft machine guns. One sailor was killed and eight were wounded. Fifteen bombs fell around the cruiser *Maxim Gorky*. As a result, the hull and superstructures of the ship received about 300 holes, that is, they were literally riddled with fragments. Four people were killed on the cruiser and eight more people were injured. The destroyers *Silnyi* and *Grozyashchiy*, two minesweepers, five patrol boats and the transport ship *Vakhur* also received damage from bomb fragments and artillery shells.

Kirov suffered more attacks than any other ship. Around 14.00, the pilots of the Ju 87s managed to achieve three direct hits on the cruiser. The bombs fell not far from each other, in the area of the aft smokestack. After the explosions on the cruiser, a fire started in the auxiliary boiler room and in rooms in the middle superstructure. The most terrible consequence of the fire was that it engulfed the ammunition stored there. The sailors began throwing shells overboard, and some of them exploded right in their hands. As the warship team later calculated, a total of 198 100mm and 376 37mm shells exploded, burned or were thrown into the river. When the flames began to spread down the ammunition lifts, *Kirov*'s commander mistakenly flooded the undamaged ammunition room No. 8.

The fire on the cruiser was only extinguished at 14.46. By this time, *Kirov* had already developed a roll of 2 degrees to port. Thus, as a result of the strikes by the German bombs and the fires that broke out after that, the ship was damaged severely. The ship's spare command post, aft bridge and signal bridge were destroyed, as were the middle superstructure on the upper deck

---

124. TSAMO RF. Foundation 20506. Inventory 1. Case 129. Sheet 24–26.

and the rooms below it on the lower (armoured) deck; the aft smokestack with chimneys, the mainmast supports, the aft aircraft catapult, davits, ship's galley, No. 9, 10 and 12 turbofan channels; the foundations of six 100mm guns and two 37mm automatic anti-aircraft guns, the bow bulkhead, as well as all the mechanism in the auxiliary boiler room. All the devices for torpedo firing were broken, and the right torpedo tubes were damaged. Eighty-six of the crew were killed and forty-six wounded. In addition, the battery of 85mm anti-aircraft guns, which was on the embankment next to the cruiser, was destroyed.[125]

Twenty high-explosive and fragmentation bombs exploded on anti-aircraft batteries from the 9th Anti-aircraft Regiment (9th ZenAP). Six high-explosive bombs hit the Naval Academy building, where the Soviet Baltic Fleet headquarters was located. As a result, nine people were killed and forty-seven were injured. In the yard of the Naval Academy, all the official cars were burnt out.

The residential areas of the city suffered from German attacks again. Bomb and shell explosions destroyed the Port of Leningrad headquarters building and thirty-nine residential buildings between 8th and 141st Streets on Vasilyevsky Island. The number of civilian casualties was 117 people killed and 340 wounded. Workshops at the Baltic and Admiralty Shipyards received significant damage.

After the raid was completed, Russian anti-aircraft gunners reported twenty German planes shot down. Of these, eleven destroyed aircraft were recorded on the combat account of the 169th ZenAP. Another downed German bomber was reported by sailors on board the destroyer *Silnyi*. However, according to German information, only three Ju 87s were damaged by anti-aircraft fire. One heavily damaged Stuka of 9./StG 1 fell on German territory. The pilot was killed but and the radio operator managed to take to his parachute.

Fake cruiser *Kirov*

The heavy damage sustained by the cruiser *Kirov* during the German air attack caused great concern to the Soviet Baltic Fleet command. The death of Joseph Stalin's beloved ship threatened unpredictable consequences of anger on the part of the 'Red Tsar'. But how to protect a cruiser at anchor on a river right in the middle of the city from the Luftwaffe? The last air raid showed that the German pilots, unlike the strikes at the beginning of the month, dropped bombs much more accurately. If the Germans continued to try, then the matter might

---

125. TSVMA. Foundation 704. Case 5016. Sheet 14.

end with the sinking of the warship. To save Stalin's beloved cruiser, the Soviets decided to sacrifice another ship.

In order for the Germans not to notice the substitution of the cruiser *Kirov*, the Russians had to conduct a special operation to move the ships. The fuel needed for this was soon found. On the night of 24–25 April, tugboats transferred the heavily damaged *Kirov* to Lieutenant Schmidt Bridge, located at the Red Fleet Embankment. The unfinished training ship *Svir*[126] was moored at the former cruiser's berth and covered with the same camouflage net.

Svir had similar dimensions and looked like a cruiser from above. Simultaneously with these manipulations, the Soviets moved the destroyers further apart, and some were moved to Malaya Nevka and Bolshaya Nevka – the arms of the Neva delta. The warships' relocation operation was conducted in strict secrecy. Patrols were on duty on the river embankments, which did not let any of the residents close to the shore. The Russians were afraid that German agents would see what was happening and inform the Luftwaffe command.

In parallel with the relocation to new berths, additional camouflage work was undertaken on the warships. For this purpose the foremast of the minelayer *Marti* was urgently cut off. Then, within a few days, all the major warships were painted in a protective grey colour.

On 25 April, the Luftwaffe launched another air attack on Soviet warships. At 11.53, a group of forty Ju 87 Ds at an altitude of 5,000–6,000m proceeded to the target along the usual south-western route through the Strelna settlement and Vasilyevsky Island. The Russians scrambled about sixty fighters to intercept the German bombers, but most of the 'Stalin's Falcons' could not detect the enemy in heavy cloud. In addition, German fighters were operating over the city and these protected the bombers from the Soviet fighters.

Of all the pilots of the 7th Fighter Aviation Corps Air Defence (7th IAC PVO) who took to the sky, only Lieutenant Zheltukhin in an I-16 was able to attack the Stukas. He later wrote in a report:

> I opened fire with machine guns from a distance of 150 metres. The Ju 87 plane smoked heavily. After that, I noticed another Ju 87 and attacked it too. The Ju 87 plane went south. After that, I saw a Ju 87 making a dive from behind the clouds and attacked it. The bomber evaded my attack and dropped bombs into the Neva.

---

126. The vessel with a tonnage of 9,686brt was built in the Netherlands in 1919. It was later bought by the Soviet Union, where it was given the name *Svir*. Before the war, it began to be converted into a training ship of the Baltic Fleet, but by June 1941 the volume of work performed was only 35 per cent.

> At that time, I saw another Ju 87 dive at me from behind and shoot at me at the same time. I was saved by another I-16 who distracted him.[127]

This was not the first time that Russian fighters were attacked by Stukas in the skies over Leningrad. After the battle with the German bombers, Lieutenant Zheltukhin's fighter began to run out of fuel and he returned to base. However, on his way back 'Stalin's Falcon' was attacked by German fighters. Lieutenant Zheltukhin was able to avoid a fight with the Bf 109s but then his luck changed. On landing at Kasimovo, both landing gear legs broke and his fighter crashed.

On 25 April, the main target of the air attack was *Oktyabrskaya Revolutsiya*, however, all the bombs just fell near the ship again. The Stukas also attacked the hulk (blockship) *Voroshilov*, which, due to its large size, looked similar to a cruiser. Ten bombs exploded around the ship and several underwater holes were blown in its hull. Fifteen hours later, the ship sank to the bottom. However, the depth of its berth was not enough for it to completely sink.

During the attack by the German bombers, the Soviets suffered other losses. Already damaged the day before, the transport ship *Vakhur*, with a tonnage of 900brt, received two direct hits from German bombs. As a result of these explosions, the hull was destroyed, and the bow deck and cargo hold were damaged. Despite a struggle to save the ship, it was not possible to keep it afloat.

Several high-explosive bombs fell on the positions of the artillery batteries of the 169th Anti-aircraft Regiment (169th ZenAP). One 85mm anti-aircraft gun and a rangefinding telemeter were smashed, and several people manning the guns were killed.

Anti-aircraft gunners reported eight enemy planes shot down, while seven more aerial victories were recorded on the combat account of the pilots of the 7th IAC PVO. The Russians' own losses amounted to two fighters. An LaGG-3 flown by Senior Lieutenant Derichev from the 11th Guards Fighter Aviation Regiment Air Defence (11th GIAP PVO) went missing. In a dogfight with German fighters, a MiG-3 piloted by Junior Lieutenant Vasilyev from the 124th Fighter Aviation Regiment Air Defence (124th IAP PVO) was shot down.

On 26 April, only German reconnaissance planes appeared over Leningrad. They produced aerial photography to clarify the results of the last two raids and determine the locations of new warship sites.

On the evening of 27 April, the German long-range artillery opened fire on Leningrad again. To adjust the firing results, the Germans used Hs 126

---

127. TSAMO RF. Foundation 20506. Inventory 1. Case 129. Sheet 67.

OPERATION EISSTOSS

artillery spotter planes. They circled over the outskirts of the city and radioed in real time the results of hits of artillery shells. German radio conversations were discovered by the radio operators of the cruiser *Maxim Gorky*, who tried to drown it out. According to some reports, German agents carried out artillery spotting directly from Leningrad. The effectiveness of the German artillery spotter can be judged by the accuracy of the shells falling. For example, at Senior Lieutenant Smolin's anti-aircraft artillery battery, located near the building of the Russian Academy of Arts, several powerful explosions thundered. German shells destroyed two anti-aircraft guns and killed fourteen gunners. More than eighty shells exploded at Leningrad port within twenty-four minutes. The fuel oil tanks were pierced by the flying fragments of German shells, and fuel leaking through the holes caught fire. The 169th ZenAP, whose anti-aircraft artillery batteries were located in the port, suffered serious losses.

Such activity of the German long-range artillery testified to the imminent beginning of a new air raid by Luftwaffe bombers. Soon, the main post of the Soviet Air Surveillance and Communication Service (VNOS) Leningrad Army of Air Defence[128] began receiving messages from RUS-2 'Redut' radar stations about the approach of several groups of enemy aircraft. The response of Leningrad's anti-air defence to this important message was very slow. Once again, one of the main drawbacks of the Soviet air defence system was revealed – the complete absence of radio communication. All communication between the command posts and anti-aircraft batteries was carried out via telephone wires. Moreover, ordinary city telephone lines were often used for communications. Their reliability in the conditions of bombing and artillery shelling was extremely low and communication was often disrupted. It took a lot of time to contact all the air defence units by phone. As a result, the 7th IAC PVO fighters again took off very late and could not interfere with the enemy's operations in any way.

Soon forty Ju 87 Ds appeared over Leningrad, accompanied by fifteen Bf 109 Fs. The Stukas fell out of the clouds and, with sirens howling, dived on the warships. Bursts of tracer shells fired from 37mm automatic anti-aircraft guns flew towards them. Black dots of anti-aircraft shell bursts multiplied against the background of clouds. Soon the explosions began again. Bombs were falling near warships, on the shore and in city blocks. Pieces of granite embankments of the Neva, fragments of buildings and tons of water flew into the air.

---

128. The Leningrad Army of Air Defence was formed on 5 April 1942 on the basis of the Leningrad Corps Air Defence Area.

AIR BATTLE FOR LENINGRAD, 1941–1944

On that day, the following entries were made in the logbook of the *Maxim Gorky*:

18.41 the enemy began artillery shelling. The work of artillery spotter aircraft was discovered. An order was received to shut down the work of the enemy radio station.

19.01. Attack of Ju 87, one of which was shot down at 19.03, the plane crashed in the port.

19.06. Another Ju 87 was shot down, fell astern of the ship.

19.21. Flight of three Bf 109.

19.30. On the starboard side five Bf 109.

19.44. Fifteen bombs were dropped from enemy aircraft.[129]

The main target of the air attack was the former berth of *Kirov* at the Sudomekh shipyard. But, there under the camouflage net was now the unfinished training ship *Svir*. The Germans did not notice the substitution of ships.

Well-trained Luftwaffe crews did not miss. *Svir* received a direct hit from bombs and water gushed into its hull. Soon the ship sank on to the bottom. Fragments of exploding bombs also damaged the nearby destroyer *Grozyashchiy* and the cruiser *Maxim Gorky*.

The German air raid ended around 20.00. The reports of the Soviet anti-aircraft gunners recorded fantastic figures of losses of German bombers and colourful descriptions of their deaths from anti-aircraft fire. They claimed that some of the downed bombers fell directly into the Neva and into the city. Russian anti-aircraft gunners claimed that on 27 April they shot down ten German planes. For example, six downed Stukas were recorded on the combat account of the 9th Anti-aircraft Regiment (9th ZenAP).

Three more aerial victories were claimed by pilots from 7th IAC PVO: Senior Lieutenants I. Shishkin, N. Tsisarenko and V. Malyshev. 'Stalin's Falcons' own losses amounted to one aircraft. MiG-3 Lieutenant Ivanchenko from 124th Fighter Aviation Regiment Air Defence (124th IAP PVO) was shot down in a dogfight with a Bf 109. The pilot escaped from the burning plane by parachute.

According to German data, on the evening of 27 April, during an air attack by Soviet warships, only one dive bomber was lost: Ju 87 D-1 W.Nr. 2033 of 1./StG 2. Both members of the crew – pilot Oberfeldwebel Bartsch and

---

129. TSVMA. Foundation 704. Case 5016. Sheets 29–31.

radio operator-shooter Unteroffizierr Stematscher – were killed. JG 54's only loss of that day was Bf 109 F-4/R1 W.Nr.13042 flown by Gefreiter Eduard Lengwenings of the 7th Staffel. During take-off from the Siverskaya Air Base, the inexperienced pilot made a mistake, and the plane turned over at high speed.

Night fell and, worried about the incessant air attacks, the Soviets decided to move their warships again. Tugboats approached the cruiser *Maxim Gorky*, picked up the tow and dragged it to a berth in the Sudomekh shipyard. *Maxim Gorky* turned out to be next to the place where *Kirov* had previously stood. After this relocation, the Soviets hastily disguised *Kirov* in the form of a bend of the embankment.

On 30 April, the Luftwaffe launched its last strike on the warships of the Soviet Baltic Fleet in Leningrad. 'Air alert' was announced at 13.20. There was heavy cloud cover over the city, which interfered with the targeted firing of Soviet anti-aircraft gunners. But the clouds also prevented the Stuka pilots from taking good aim. All the bombs dropped by German planes fell near the warships. Minor shrapnel damage was sustained by the *Oktyabrskaya Revolutsiya*, *Kirov* and *Maxim Gorky*, the destroyer *Silnyi* and submarine *M-90*.

Stalin is pleased

According to Soviet information, in April 1942, in order to fulfill Hitler's order to destroy the remnants of the Soviet Baltic Fleet, Luftwaffe aircraft expended 615 high-explosive bombs of all calibres with a total mass of 500 tons. During this mission, the Germans managed to severely damage the cruiser *Kirov* and sink three auxiliary vessels. As a result of the bombing, 233 people were killed and 661 were injured. Despite all the efforts made by dive bombers from I. Fliegerkorps, they failed to carry out Hitler's order. In the spring of 1942, the Germans were unable to sink the large warships of the Soviet Baltic Fleet that had survived the 1941 massacre. But, as already noted above, in fact, by the autumn of 1941, the Soviet Baltic Fleet had completely lost its combat capability. The large warships no longer had the ability to move independently, even over short distances. They posed some danger to the German troops blockading Leningrad but only as floating artillery batteries. But, even this very hypothetical threat could be realised only in the case of a new Wehrmacht offensive on Leningrad. However, changes to the Eastern Front made plans to storm the city in 1942 absolutely unrealistic.

In the spring of 1942, Hitler lost interest in Leningrad and changed his priorities. He decided to do away with another 'Bolshevik stronghold' – the city of Sevastopol. By order of the Führer, VIII. Fliegerkorps Generalmajor Wolfram von Richthofen was transferred to the Crimean Peninsula. He was assigned to paralyse Soviet transportation across the Black Sea, and then support the 11th Army's offensive on Kerch and Sevastopol. After this significant weakening of its forces, Luftflotte 1 had to be content with solving only limited tasks to deter Russian attacks in the area of Leningrad.

After such a significant weakening of Luftwaffe forces, there was a relative lull in the Leningrad sky. The Commander of the Leningrad Air Defence Army, Major General Gavriil Zashikhin, managed to convince Stalin's servant, Andrei Zhdanov, who was the 'party leader' of the Leningrad defence, that the decrease in Luftwaffe activity was caused by the effective actions of the city's air defence. Major General Zashikhin turned out to be much more capable than his predecessor, who was expelled from his post in disgrace. However, his competence lay not in the field of air defence management, but in the ability to compile reports for higher authorities. Misled, Zhdanov sent his patron in Moscow an optimistic report. The naive Stalin was pleased with the actions of Leningrad air defence. His beloved cruiser *Kirov* was saved, although it was seriously damaged. Soon Major General Gavriil Zashikhin was awarded the Order of Lenin.

Chapter 8

German air attacks against 'Ladoga battleships'

Lake bridge for Leningrad

By the end of the winter of 1941–42, a stalemate had developed around Leningrad. The Germans tightly blocked the city, but the Soviets continued to hold it firmly. Neither side had sufficient forces to radically change the situation. Almost simultaneously, Hitler and Stalin felt that the battle for Leningrad could last a very long time. However, the two bloody dictators did not give up hope of victory. Hitler and Stalin considered Leningrad their inalienable property and an important symbol of personal prestige. Despite many other important battles, they continued to closely monitor this secondary section of the huge Eastern Front.

Stalin's understanding of the impossibility of an early breakthrough of the Leningrad land blockade led him in the spring of 1942 to the decision to strengthen the supply of the city. The only free route by which cargoes from the interior of the USSR could get to Leningrad passed through Lake Ladoga. The Ice Road was going to literally melt soon; therefore, it was urgently necessary to prepare ships and port infrastructure to transport supplies for the city by water.

In the autumn of 1941, during the incessant disasters of the Red Army, Stalin was not confident in the ability of his troops to hold the city, so the freight traffic through Lake Ladoga was poorly equipped. The few lake piers could not cope with the reception of numerous cargoes. In the spring of 1942, Stalin ordered the immediate start of a large-scale arrangement of water communication on the lake. On 3 March, the Military Council of Leningrad Front adopted a resolution on the construction of several ports and intermediate warehouses on the shore.

Work began immediately and was carried out at a fantastic pace. The scope of the work on the arrangement of the port infrastructure was also enormous. For example, in harbour, located next to the village of Kobona on the eastern shore, extended piers were built almost from scratch, extending 270m into the lake. From Voibokalo railway station to the piers there was a specially built railway line, 30km long. In all the suitable bays on the western shore, berths and piers were built literally from scratch. Because of the shallow water, some of the berths extended 500m into the lake. At the new port infrastructure facilities, the Soviets took measures to mechanise loading and unloading operations, which had previously been carried out manually. Twenty cranes with a lifting capacity from 3 to 75 tons were installed. Warehouses, oil storage facilities and long sections of the narrow-gauge railway were built on the shore. By the beginning of navigation in 1942, Lake Ladoga's harbours could simultaneously accept twenty-two vessels for loading and unloading. Work on the arrangement of the port infrastructure continued during the opening of navigation on the lake.

In addition to waterways on the Leningrad supply route, there were also land sections that needed additional equipment. Overland communications were served by four transport battalions, as well as Moscow and Yaroslavl state transport companies, which had 1,110 trucks. Six fire stations were created to extinguish fires that could arise in the event of enemy opposition. Each of these fire stations served one of the six harbours on Lake Ladoga, designed to receive ships with cargo.[130]

In the area of lake communications intended to supply Leningrad, a fairly powerful air defence was created. Osinovets harbour, on the western shore, was covered by artillery batteries of the 20th Separate Anti-aircraft Division (20th OZAD), 25th Separate Anti-aircraft Division (25th OZAD) and 432nd Separate Anti-aircraft Division (432nd OZAD), as well as railway anti-aircraft batteries No. 1, 2 and 3. These units had forty-eight anti-aircraft guns of medium calibre, three anti-aircraft guns of small calibre and fifteen anti-aircraft machine guns. There were also six Projzvuk[131] anti-aircraft seeker stations and fifteen anti-aircraft searchlights. On the eastern shore, around Kobona village and Lednevo settlement 6km north of it, there were the 225th Separate Anti-aircraft Division (225th OZAD), 251st Separate Anti-aircraft Division (251st OZAD), 434th Separate Anti-aircraft Division (434th OZAD) and one anti-aircraft machine gun company. In these units there were thirty anti-aircraft guns of medium and six anti-aircraft guns of small calibre, nineteen anti-aircraft machine guns, seven Projzvuk stations and twelve anti-aircraft searchlights. Anti-aircraft guns were also located at Novaya Ladoga, Volkhovstroy, Gostinopolye, Voibokalo,

---

130. *On the Road of Life: memories of the front-line Ladoga*, Moscow, Voenizdat, 1980, pp.39–40.
131. The Projzvuk anti-aircraft seeker station included a ZP-2 sound collector, O-15-1 anti-aircraft searchlight and a control post.

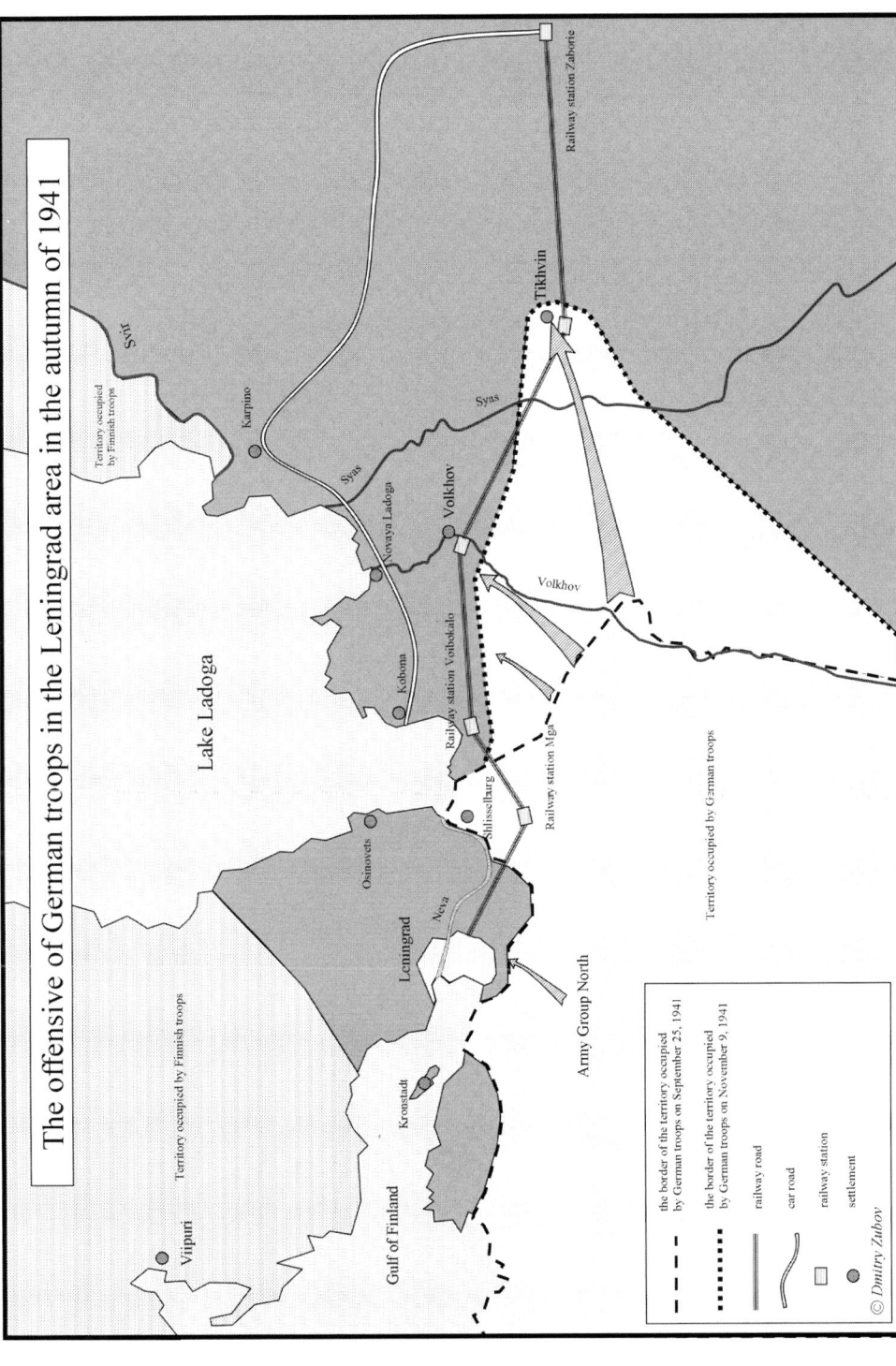

The offensive of German troops in the Leningrad area in the autumn of 1941

Above: People's Militia fighters march along one of the streets of Kronstadt. 1941.

Left: Aerial photograph Leningrad port Torgovyi, made by reconnaissance aircraft from 2./Aufkl.Gr.Ob.d.L. June 27, 1941

Below: One of the streets of Leningrad after the German bombing

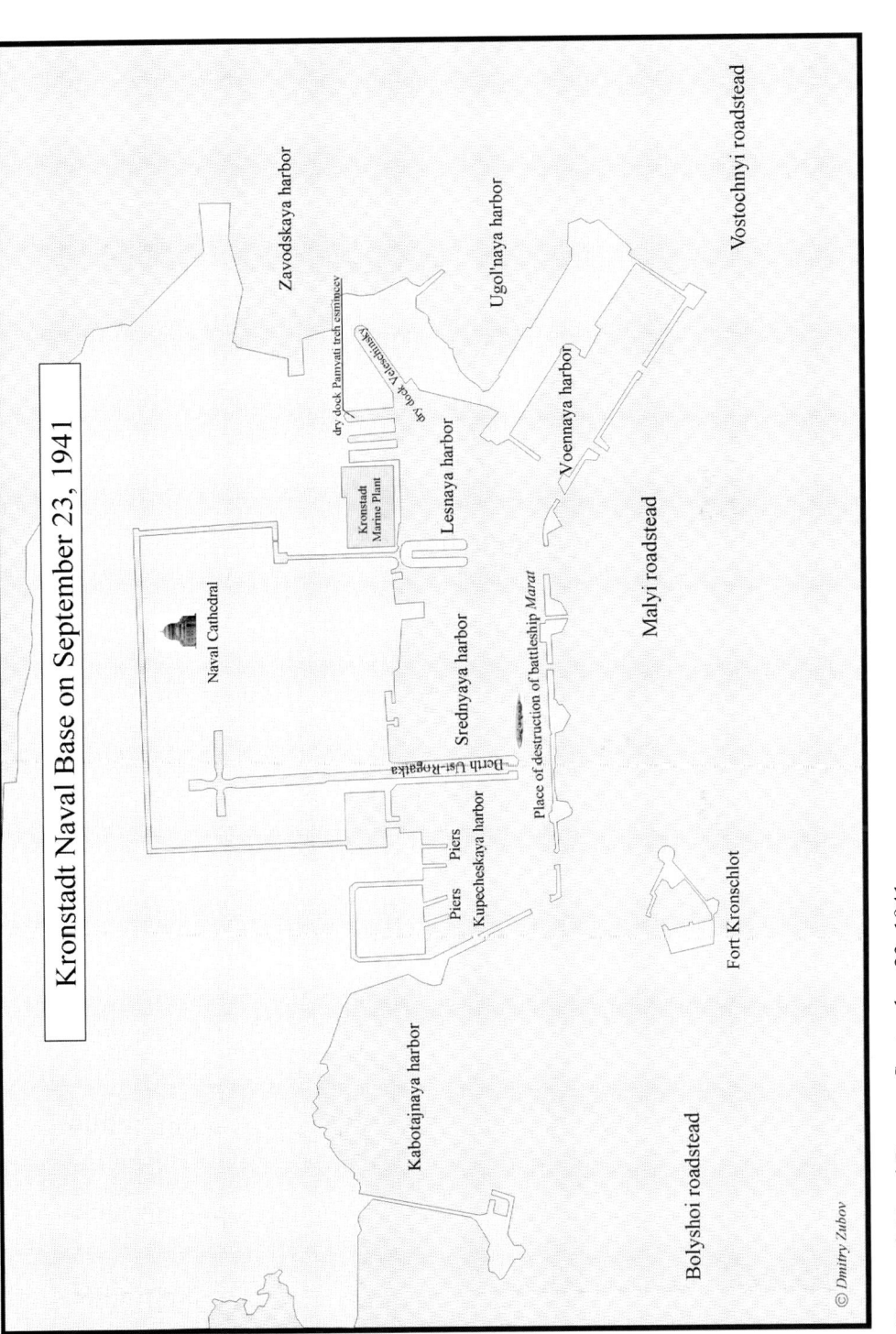

Kronstadt Naval Base on September 23, 1941

The explosion of battleship *Marat* in Kronstadt Bay. German aerial photography

Wooden barge towing by Lake Ladoga

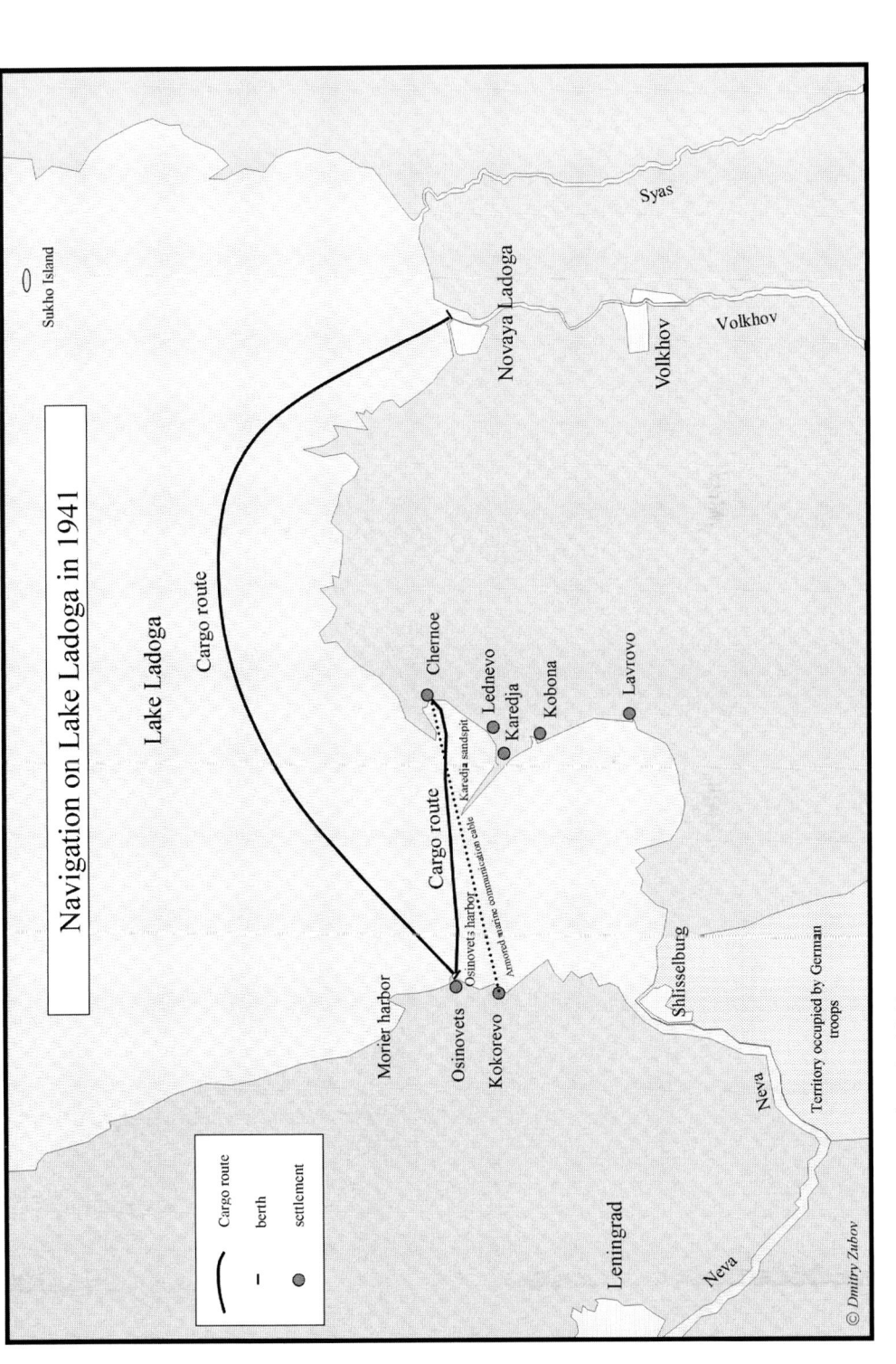

Navigation on Lake Ladoga in 1941

Left: Junior Lieutenant Alexei Sevastyanov, who shot down with the help of ram He 111 H-5 W.Nr. 3816 '5J+DM' over Leningrad on the night of November 4, 1941

Below: The wreckage of the downed Junior Lieutenant Sevastyanov He 111 bomber in Tauride Garden

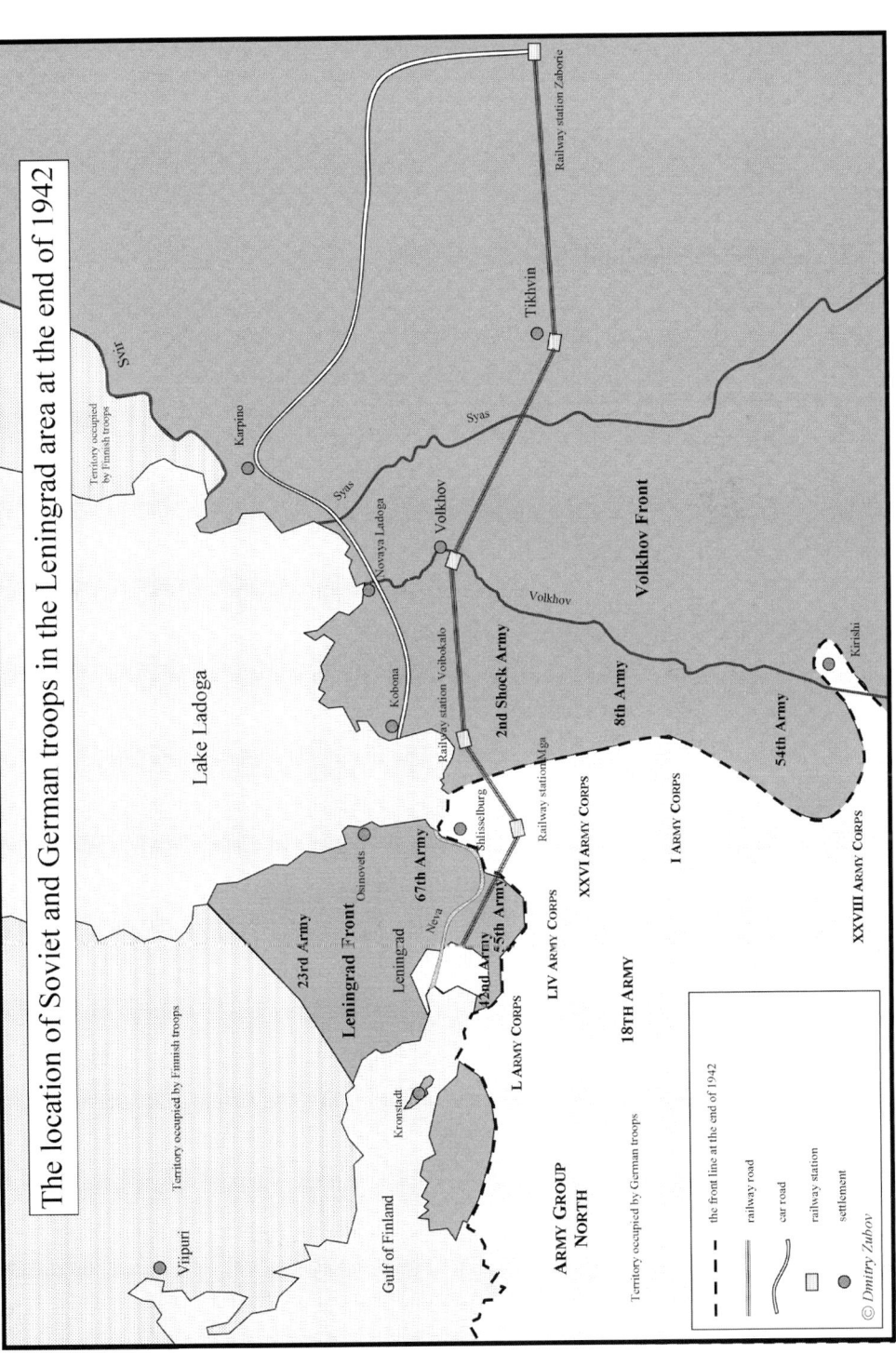

The location of Soviet and German troops in the Leningrad area at the end of 1942

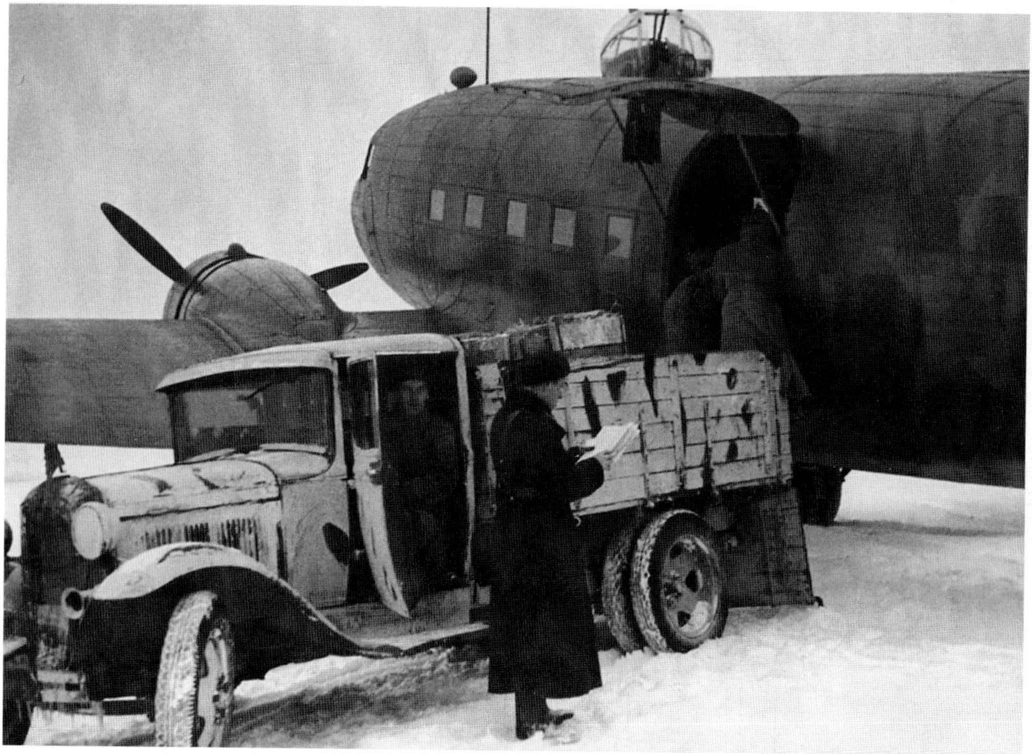

Loading supplies into the transport plane Li-2 (a Soviet replica of the Douglas C-47 Skytrain), which was used by the Soviets to supply the blockaded Leningrad

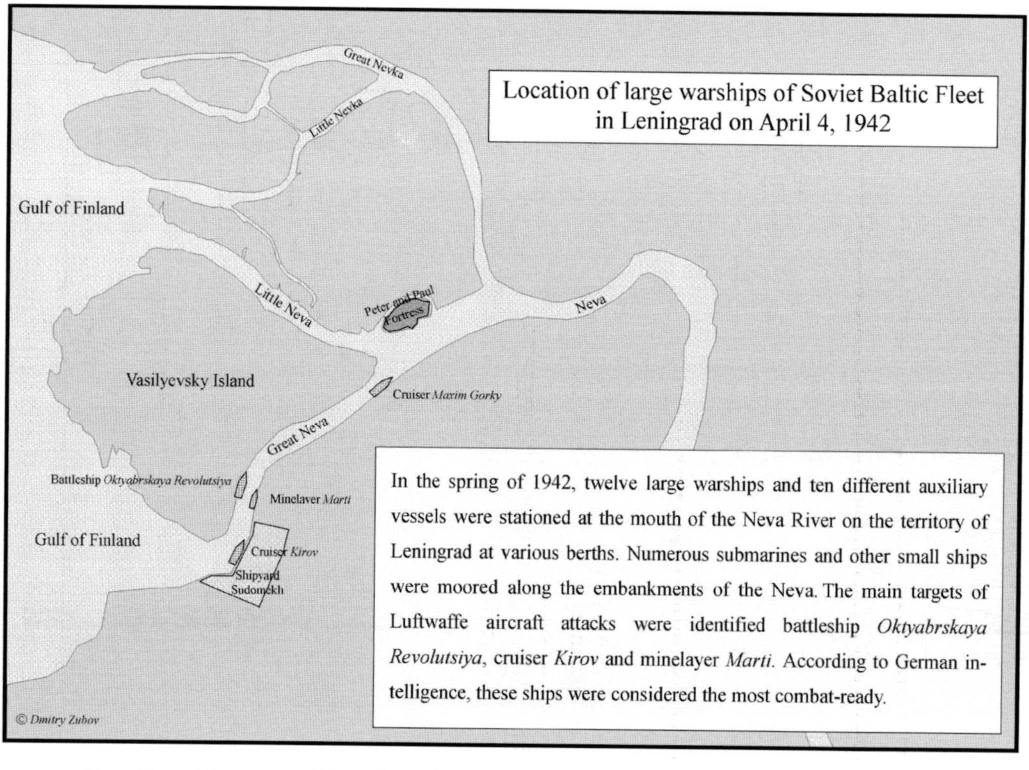
Location of large warships of Soviet Baltic Fleet in Leningrad on April 4, 1942
Great Nevka
Little Nevka
Gulf of Finland
Little Neva
Peter and Paul Fortress
Neva
Vasilyevsky Island
Cruiser *Maxim Gorky*
Great Neva
Battleship *Oktyabrskaya Revolutsiya*
Minelayer *Marti*
Gulf of Finland
Cruiser *Kirov*
Shipyard Sudomekh
In the spring of 1942, twelve large warships and ten different auxiliary vessels were stationed at the mouth of the Neva River on the territory of Leningrad at various berths. Numerous submarines and other small ships were moored along the embankments of the Neva. The main targets of Luftwaffe aircraft attacks were identified battleship *Oktyabrskaya Revolutsiya*, cruiser *Kirov* and minelayer *Marti*. According to German intelligence, these ships were considered the most combat-ready.
© Dmitry Zubov

Location of large warships of Soviet Baltic Fleet in Leningrad on April 4, 1942

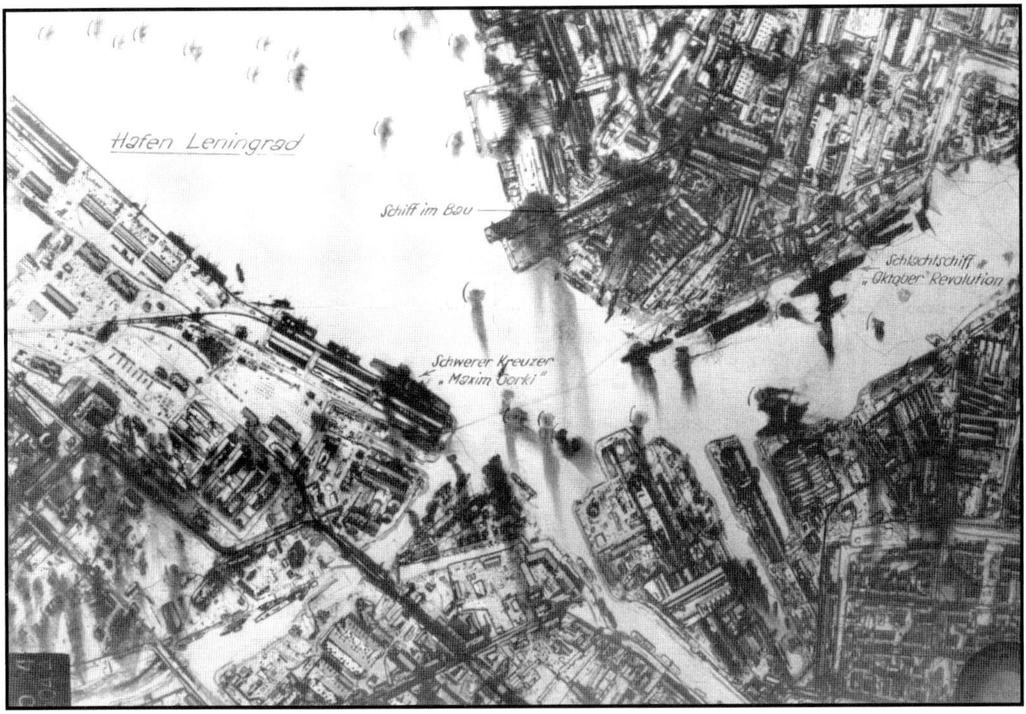

Aerial photography of the mouth of the Neva on April 6, 1942. The places of bomb hits in the ice of the river are clearly visible

Gunboat *Lakhta*

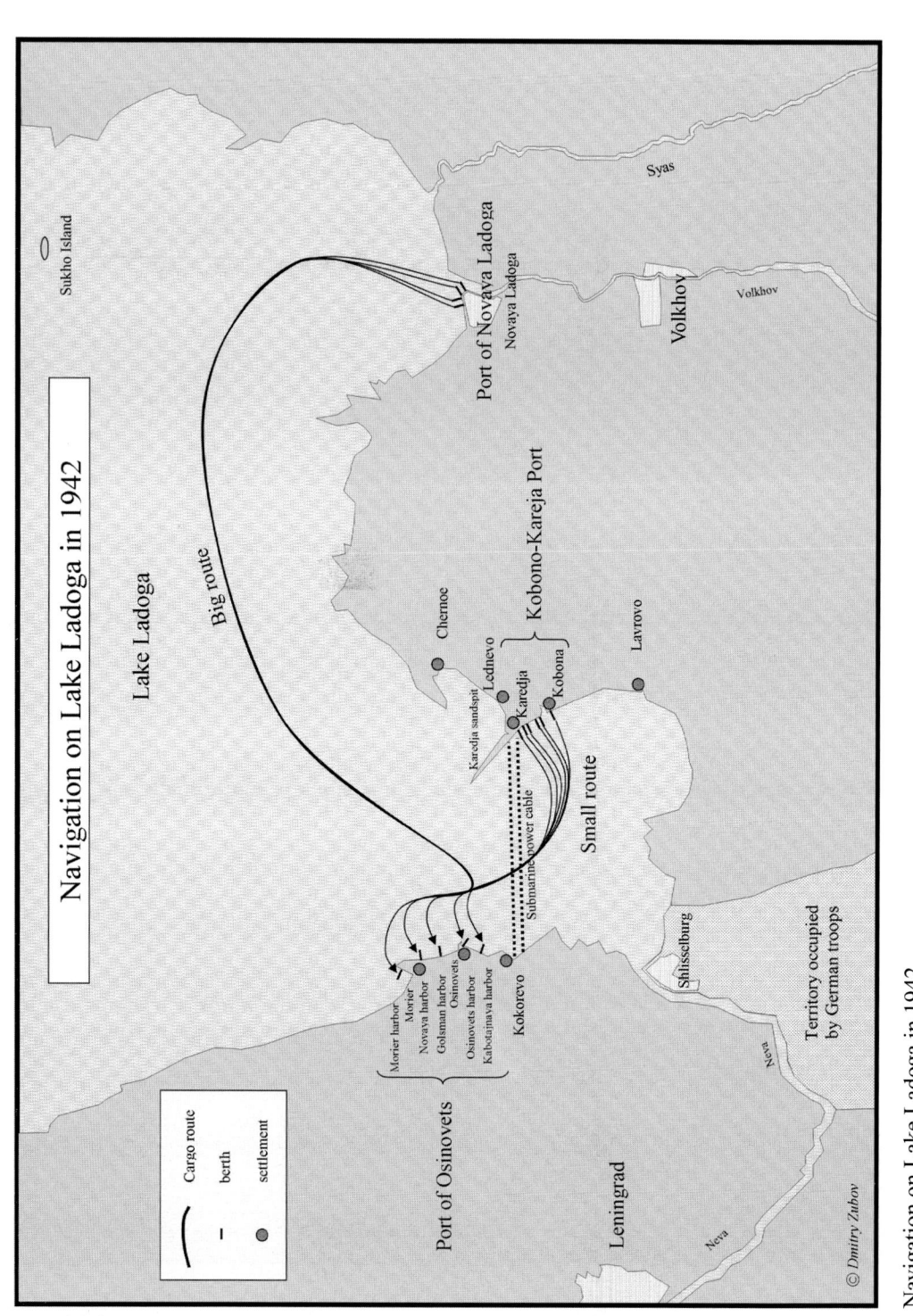

Navigation on Lake Ladoga in 1942

The wreckage of battleship *Marat*

Artillery piece on the background of the Naval Cathedral

Italian torpedo boat *MAS 528* on Lake Ladoga

Gunboat *Bira* sailing on Lake Ladoga on April 12, 1943

Red Army mans attack German positions in the settlement of Sinyavino

British infantry tanks Churchill in defense of Leningrad

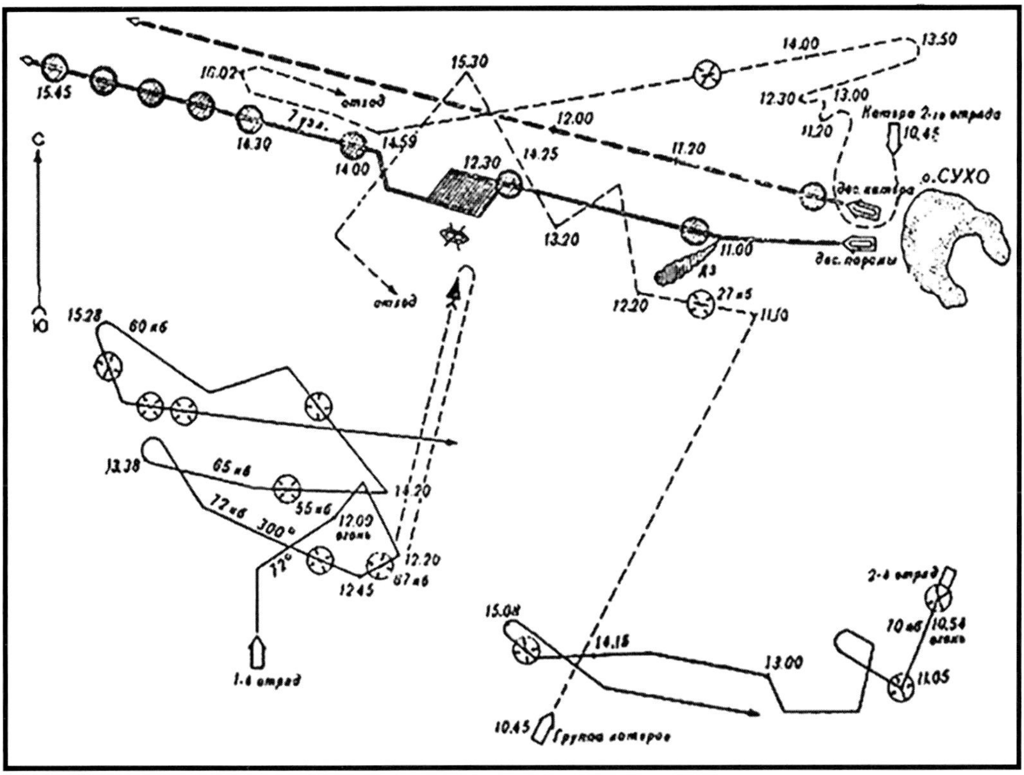

Soviet scheme of persecution of German Siebel ferries in the Sukho Island area

Abandoned by the Germans damaged Siebel ferries near Sukho Island

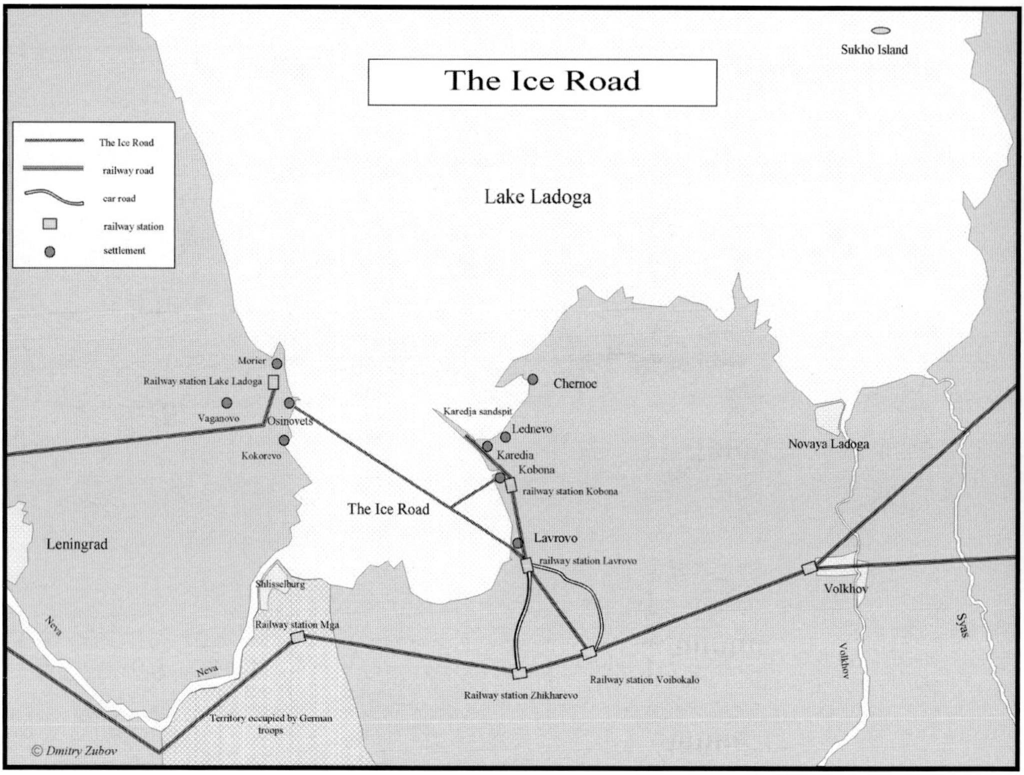

The Ice Road

A Soviet anti-aircraft machine gun is firing at the enemy on the Ice Road through Lake Ladoga. March 1942

Anti-aircraft seeker stations Projzvuk, 1942

Unexploded German large-caliber bomb

Construction of the Volkhov hydroelectric plant 'Lenin'. March 1926

Breakthrough of the land blockade of Leningrad. Meeting of Leningrad and Volkhov Fronts troops at settlement Ropsha, January 1944

Left: Cruiser *Kirov*

Below: Luftwaffe attacks on Leningrad, 1941-1943

Luftwaffe attacks on Leningrad, 1941-1943

Results of the Luftwaffe bombing attacks on Leningrad
(September 8, 1941 - September 1, 1943)

In total, during the entire period of the bombing of the city, approximately 73 air raids on Leningrad were recorded:

in 1941 – 38 air attacks	
September	2
October	9
November	22
December	5

in 1942 – 15 air attacks	
September	1
October	7
November	7

in 1943 – 20 air attacks	
January	6
February	2
March	2
April	3
May	3
July	1
August	2
September	1

© *Dmitry Zubov*

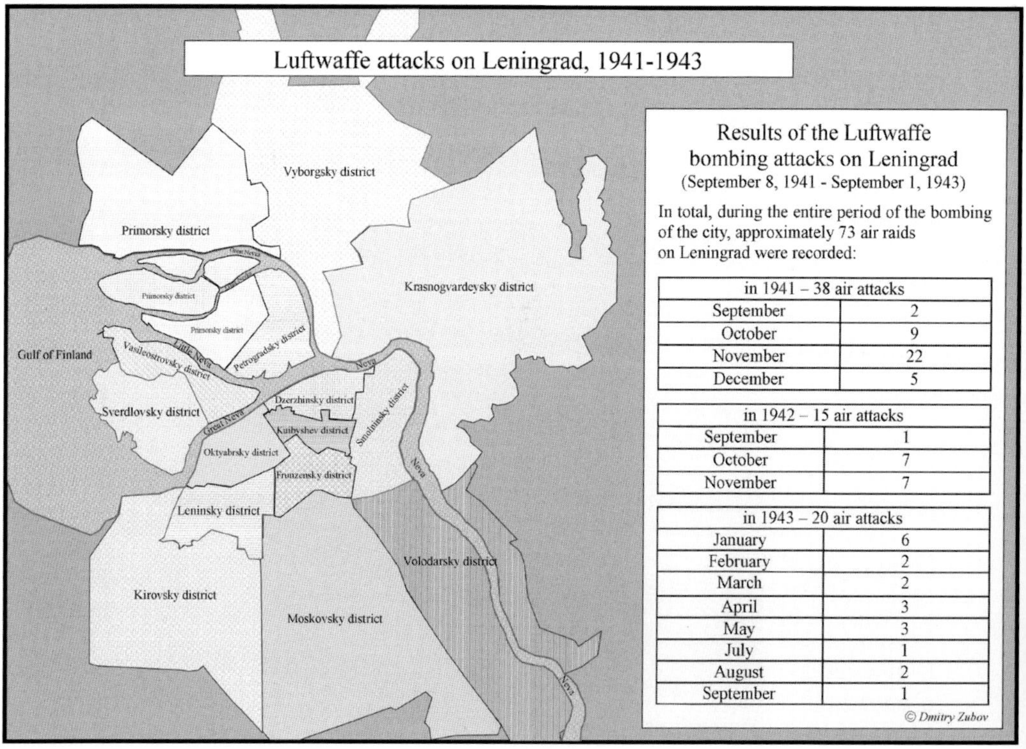

GERMAN AIR ATTACKS AGAINST 'LADOGA BATTLESHIPS'

Zhikharevo and Tikhvin railway stations. In total, 190 anti-aircraft guns, about seventy anti-aircraft machine guns, twenty-five Projzvuk stations and sixty-five anti-aircraft searchlights were allocated for the defence of Lake Ladoga communications.

To protect lake communications, in addition to ground-based air defence the Soviets also used fighter aviation. For this purpose, the 7th Fighter Aviation Corps Air Defence (7th IAC PVO) specifically allocated the 123rd Fighter Aviation Regiment Air Defence (123rd IAP PVO). The fighters from 123rd IAP PVO were supposed to protect warehouses and berths on the west bank. Fighters of the 3rd Fighter Aviation Regiment Air Force Soviet Baltic Fleet (3rd IAP VVS KBF) and 4th Guards Fighter Aviation Regiment Air Force Soviet Baltic Fleet (4th GIAP VVS KBF) were allocated to protect ships on the lake, as well as warehouses and berths around Lednevo, Kobona, Syasstroy and Kolchanovo settlements and Novaya Ladoga town. Lavrovo, Zhikhareva, Voibokalo, Pupyshevo, Volkhovstroy and Gostinopolye railway stations were included in the area of responsibility of the Leningrad Front Air Force fighters.[132]

At the same time, the Soviets took measures to arm cargo ships. On 9 April 1942, Stalin ordered Commander of the Soviet Baltic Fleet Vice Admiral Vladimir Tributs to provide river ships designed to transport cargo on Lake Ladoga anti-aircraft guns and machine guns. For this purpose, nine 45mm guns and 109 12.7 mm machine guns DShK were urgently allocated. All this arsenal was supposed to be installed on four tugboats and fifty-one barges. Usually one gun and one machine gun were placed on tugboats; two machine guns were placed on barges. As a result, by 28 May 1942, it was possible to arm twenty-five barges and five tugboats: *Morskoi lev*, *Orel*, *Nikulyasy*, *Buy* and *Gidrotechnik*.

By the beginning of the 1942 navigation, Commander of the Ladoga Military Flotilla Captain 1st rank Vasily Cherokov had 116 cargo ships at his disposal. These included five lake tugboats, sixty-three river tugboats, ten minesweepers, six gunboats, fifteen transport ships, twenty-six small motor vessels, fifty-eight river barges and eleven lake barges. All this 'Great and Most Fortunate Navy' was ordered to transport at least 4,200 tons of cargo, including 2,500 tons of food, to the western shore of Lake Ladoga every day.

---

132. *The Air Defence Forces of the Country in the Great Patriotic War*, Moscow: Voenizdat, 1968, p.121.

The beginning of lake sailing in 1942

During the 1941 lake navigation season there was a 115km-long waterway connecting the improvised ports of Novaya Ladoga and Osinovets, called the 'big route'. In addition, in 1942, the Soviets decided to organise a shorter way of transporting goods across Lake Ladoga. The new section of the waterway, only 29km long, connecting the ports of Kobona and Osinovets, became known as the 'small route'.

On 22 May 1942, the long-awaited navigation season on Lake Ladoga began for the Soviets. The first lake cargo sailings for Leningrad were carried out on the small route. On this day, the tugboat *Gidrotechnik* left Kobona harbour and delivered 40 tons of flour to the port of Osinovets. After that, regular lake transportation began between Osinovets and Kobona. The next day the transport ships *Sovet* and *Chapaev*, the minesweepers *No. 81*, *175*, *176* and the same tugboat *Gidrotechnik* transported another 37 tons of flour and 85 tons of ammunition along the small route.

The movement of vessels along the big route (a longer route passing away from the shore of Lake Ladoga) began later, as the ice did not melt for a long time at the mouth of the Volkhov. The first transport convoy consisting of two gunboats *Lakhta* and *Sheksna*, transport ships *Hansi* and *Stenso*, scow *Ligovo*, tugboat *Nikulyasy* with two barges and minesweeper *No. 65* with one barge managed to leave Novaya Ladoga for Osinovets only on 28 May 1942.[133]

German and Finnish reconnaissance planes regularly flew over the lake and its surroundings. Commander of Luftflotte 1 Generaloberst Alfred Keller and Commander of Army Group North Generaloberst Georg von Küchler quickly received shocking information about the huge port infrastructure built by the Russians. In response to an alarming report by Commander of Luftflotte 1, a strict instruction came from Hitler's bunker to disrupt the beginning of lake navigation and prevent the transportation of goods to Leningrad. The Luftflotte 1 headquarters urgently began planning a series of air attacks against warehouses, loading points and ship berths.

Dogfight between 'Stalin's Falcons' and 'Grunherz' aces

In the early morning of 28 May 1942, several German reconnaissance planes flew at high altitude over Kobona and Osinovets. Their mission was to collect

---

133. *On the Road of Life: memories of the front-line Ladoga*, Moscow, Voenizdat, 1980, pp.44–45.

GERMAN AIR ATTACKS AGAINST 'LADOGA BATTLESHIPS'

information about the movement of Soviet ships. Soon, after processing the received intelligence information, eighty German bombers took off from several airfields. On approach to the front line, they were met by twenty-four Bf 109 Fs from JG 54 led by Oberstleutnant Hannes Trautloft. German bombers came to Kobona and Lednevo harbours from different directions at an altitude of 2,000–2,500m with intervals between the groups of two to three minutes.

At 09.40, the Ladoga Divisional Air Defence Area command post received a message from radar stations that several groups of enemy aircraft had been detected south of Mga railway station, heading in the direction of Lake Ladoga. The information was immediately transmitted to the headquarters of the 4th Guards Fighter Aviation Regiment Air Force Soviet Baltic Fleet (4th GIAP VVS KBF). The Regiment was based at Vystav airfield (8km south-east of Kobona). Soviet fighters on alert began preparing to scramble. At 09.46, six I-16s from the 2nd Squadron of Senior Lieutenant Gennady Tsokolaev took off. A minute later, eight I-16s from the 3rd Squadron of Senior Lieutenant Vasily Golubev were airborne. At 09.55, eight I-16s from the 1st Squadron of Senior Lieutenant Mikhail Vasiliev scrambled. In total, twenty-two VVS KBF fighters took off to intercept the German bombers.

'Stalin's Falcon' Vasily Golubev later recalled:

> 09.45. The first group of six I-16s took off. Leading Tsokolaev, pilots: Suvorkin, Dmitriev, Rochev, Strelnikov and Bedukadze. Behind them is the second group of I-16s under my leadership, the pilots: Kozhanov, Baysultanov, Kuznetsov, Petrov, Kravtsov, Kulikov, Zakharov. Assuming the possibility of a 'star' raid, that is, from different directions and heights, Tsokolaev's group began patrolling over Kobona at an altitude of 2,500 metres, my group at an altitude of 3,000 metres. The regimental commander, having received information about the approach of a large number of German aircraft, lifted the last squadron into the air. Leader Vasiliev, pilots: Lagutkin, Filatov, Tvorogov, Dmitriev, Kirillov, Litvinenko and Pushkin. With the approach of the third group, in which there was no one from the leadership of the regiment, I, occupying the upper echelon, took command of all the fighters. Soon we saw enemy bombers and fighters. They approached Kobona from the south, south-west, west and from the north at high altitudes in groups of 6, 8, 10, 12 aircraft.[134]

---

134. Golubev, V.F., *Second Wind*, Leningrad: Lenizdat, 1988, pp.54–55.

AIR BATTLE FOR LENINGRAD, 1941–1944

In addition to the I-16s from the 4th GIAP VVS KBF, MiG-3s from the 159th Fighter Aviation Regiment (159th IAP) and I-16s from the 286th Fighter Aviation Regiment (286th IAP) took off to repel the enemy air attack. They were the first to attack the approaching German planes. Five MiG-3s led by Senior Lieutenant Pyotr Likholetov unexpectedly came upon the leading nine Ju 88 A bombers from III./KG 1 head-on. At the same time, another group of German bombers, also tackled head-on, was attacked by six I-16 fighters.

According to Soviet information, during the subsequent attacks, the pilots of the 159th IAP shot down five aircraft (three Ju 88s and two He 111 Hs), and the pilots of the 286th IAP shot down three German bombers. The remaining enemy bombers, according to the reports of 'Stalin's Falcons', 'randomly dropped bombs and turned to their airfields'. At the same time, one I-16 was severely damaged by the return fire from German bombers. The pilot, Sergeant Sergey Kotelnikov, received three bullet wounds but was able to fly to his airfield and land safely. During an inspection after landing, mechanics counted forty-six bullet holes in the fighter.

Meanwhile, the I-16 fighters from VVS KBF reached the air battle. According to Soviet information, six I-16s under Senior Lieutenant Tsokolaev attacked a group of fifteen Ju 88s and fired RS-82 rocket-powered projectiles at them. As a result, the formation of enemy bombers collapsed and randomly dropped bombs before reaching the target. Senior Lieutenant Golubev's group, repelling an attack by Bf 109s also with rocket-powered projectiles, broke the combat formation of another group of bombers, forcing them to randomly drop bombs. With the approach of Senior Lieutenant Vasiliev's group, the combat system of the German shock groups was completely disrupted. According to the results of the air battle, the pilots of the VVS KBF were credited with eleven aerial victories (seven Ju 88s, two He 111s and two Bf 109s).

In his memoirs, 'Stalin's Falcon' Senior Lieutenant Vasily Golubev colourfully described this aerial battle:

> We need to finish off the vultures! But I'm almost out of ammo?
> I gave the command to Vasily Zakharov:
> – Vasily, go ahead! Attack, I'll cover you.
>
> I expected that he still had ammunition, but Zakharov, without answering, continued to fly to my left. At that moment we were attacked from above by two Bf 109 F. I put the plane on the wing in a deep slide, and the machine gun bursts of the first Messer, to touch the right wing, passed by. It was too late to leave from under

GERMAN AIR ATTACKS AGAINST 'LADOGA BATTLESHIPS'

the fire of the second 'Messer'.[135] He was resolutely approaching, hoping to complete the attack from fifty metres. Vasily Zakharov turned out to be to the right and slightly lower than the Bf 109, he did not have time to attack him, and there probably were no more cartridges. And then he made the only right decision: he pulled his 'Ishak'[136] up to the left and rammed an enemy plane. In the blue sky over Lake Ladoga, a fireball flashed in place of two fighters, like a large land mine explosion.

So, saving the commander, the fearless pilot Vasily Zakharov gave his life. So a young combat friend died, with whom we flew for two months and fought together.[137]

Golubev described what happened as if he saw it all from the outside. But he was in the role of 'master', that is, he was ahead of Sergeant Zakharov, and all his attention was focused on the Bf 109 fighter attacking him. It is unlikely that Golubev had much time in the dogfight to look back and follow the actions of his wingman in detail. In addition, there was no radio communication between the Soviet aircraft.

The German version of events looks different. The pilots of the I-16s, with the help of rocket-powered projectiles, were able to upset the battle formations of two groups of German bombers. The pilots of the Ju 88 As were forced to manoeuvre vigorously. Moreover, several German planes narrowly avoided colliding with each other. Above the bombers were twenty-four Bf 109 Fs of JG 54. Seeing the attacking 'Rats',[138] Oberstleutnant Trautloft gave the order to his subordinates to attack them, upon which German fighters immediately dived. Oberstleutnant Trautloft recalled: 'I attacked three I-16s that were chasing a Ju 88s. I caught one "Rat" in my sight, but she managed to get out from under my fire with a sharp turn, and I couldn't follow her because of my high speed. Suddenly I saw tracers flash past my cabin.'[139] That was probably a machine gun burst fired by Sergeant Zakharov. But a second later Zakharov himself became a target for the Bf 109 fighter. Having received several direct hits from 20mm shells, Zakharov's I-16 exploded. Apparently, Senior Lieutenant Golubev saw

---

135. 'Messer' was the Russian nickname of the Bf 109.
136. 'Ishak' (donkey) was the Russian nickname of the I-16.
137. Golubev, V.F., *Wings Grow Stronger in Battle*, Leningrad: Lenizdat, 1984, p.143.
138. 'Rat' is the German nickname of the Soviet I-16 fighter.
139. Held, W., Trautloft, H., Bob, E., *JG 54. A Photographic History of the Grunherzgeschwader*, Schiffer Military History, USA, 1990, p.90.

this explosion and took it as the consequences of a collision between two fighters.

Oberfeldwebel Eugen-Ludwig Zweigert and Oberfeldwebel Wilhelm Schilling from 9./JG 54 stated that during the dogfight, each of them shot down one I-16 fighter. In fact, as a result of this air battle, only one I-16 was shot down. Its pilot, Zakharov, was killed. Eight more Soviet fighters were damaged. Three Soviet pilots were wounded, including one of the aces of the 4th GIAP VVS KBF, Senior Lieutenant Gennady Tsokolaev. There were no losses among the pilots from JG 54 and all the German fighters returned safely to Krasnogvardeysk airfield and Siverskaya Air Base.

Eight fighters from the 7th IAC PVO (four I-16s from the 123rd IAP PVO and four MiG-3s from the 124th IAP PVO) also took part in the air battle over Lake Ladoga. The first group of four I-16s from the 123rd Fighter Aviation Regiment Air Defence (123rd IAP PVO) were patrolling over the western shore of the lake. At 09.50, they received an order by radio: 'Fly to the eastern shore, there is a dogfight, the enemy is bombing.' When the fighters flew to the area, the Soviet pilots saw Ju 88s dive on the village of Lednevo and a train coming from the east. Lieutenant Gusev and Senior Lieutenant Andrianov attacked the enemy bombers closest to them. The Russian fighters first launched rocket-powered projectiles, then fired their machine guns. According to the reports of 'Stalin's Falcons', as a result of the Soviet attacks, two Ju 88s were damaged, and 'went south with smoking engines'.

A little later, the second group of four MiG-3s from the 124th Fighter Aviation Regiment Air Defence (124th IAP PVO) appeared over Lake Ladoga. However, they were immediately intercepted by German fighters. For eighteen minutes, an intense dogfight raged over the lake, which ended without aerial victories for either side.[140]

'There was nothing we could do ... thousands of people died'

What were the results of the German bombing raid? Around 10.00 the first groups of German bombers reached Kobona harbour. The approach of the German planes was observed by Commander of the Ladoga Military Flotilla Captain 1st rank Vasily Cherokov and Commander of the Soviet Baltic Fleet Vice Admiral Vladimir Tributs. Captain 1st rank Cherokov recalled: 'Soon we saw bombers and fighters. They approached Kobona harbour from the south,

---

140. TSAMO RF. Foundation 20506. Inventory 1. Case 132. Sheets 19–21.

south-west and west in groups of 12 to 24 aircraft. Our fighters took off to meet them. But there were few of them. Soon the anti-aircraft gunners opened fire.'[141]

Numerous transport vessels concentrated in Kobona harbour represented an excellent target for Luftwaffe aircraft. The Soviets did not have time to take any measures to disperse their ships. Soon, the first German bombs began to explode in the harbour and on the roadstead. At the beginning of the attack, the unloading of a large group of evacuated Leningrad residents ended. At the same time, food was being loaded and soldiers were preparing to land on gunboats. A huge number of people were concentrated in a small area – the coastal shoal and berths, and there was no organisation of the crowds. The hum of approaching German planes and the firing of anti-aircraft guns caused a terrible panic among the evacuated residents on the shoal. Frightened people began to make their way further into the shore, looking for salvation in the coastal bushes and boulders. However, the exits from the coastal shoal were so narrow that there was a deadly crush. In the terrible confusion, many people weakened by hunger fell and immediately went under the feet of the maddened crowd. Some of the evacuated residents were pushed by the crowd into the icy water, where many of them drowned. At that moment, German bombs began to fall on the shore and the coastal part of the lake. Some of them exploded right in the crowd, tearing people to shreds and throwing their remains tens of metres away. Severed arms and legs, logs from berths and pieces of coastal granite swept through the air. There was nowhere to hide from the German bombs. Frantic with fear, people rushed screaming along the shore in different directions, bumping into each other. Some German planes dropped bombs, then flew over Kobona harbour at a low altitude and shot at the crowd with machine guns. They flew so low that people could clearly see the faces of the pilots. Antonina Gorbacheva, a resident of Kobona, recalled: 'And again the Germans did what they wanted: they bombed from a low-level flight, fired ... Our anti-aircraft guns resisted, but there were very few of them. There was nothing we could do ... thousands of people died.'[142]

After the end of the enemy air raid, a terrible picture opened before the eyes of the survivors. The whole coast was pitted with craters and littered with fragments of berths. Burnt remnants of various foodstuffs mixed with blood and pieces of bodies lay everywhere. Huge columns of black smoke rose into the sky from the oil storage facilities burning nearby. Torn sacks, pieces of wood and corpses floated in the water. The waves washed this terrible evidence of the massacre on to the coastal rocks. A large number of the seriously wounded were

---

141. Cherokov, V.S., *For You, Leningrad!*, Leningrad: Leninzdat, 1988, p.75.
142. *Ladoga: Photo album*, Moscow: Planeta, 1989, p.34.

sent to a nearby hospital but it quickly overflowed and many people were laid on the street. Many died on the ground before they could be treated. Corpses and remains were collected nearby in a huge pile.

Official Soviet documents report that on 28 May 1942, German planes dropped about 300 high-explosive bombs of all calibres on Kobona harbour. The explosions destroyed two piers, warehouses and telephone lines. In addition to gunboats, several tugboats and barges were severely damaged. Seven railway wagons with food and eight railway wagons with ammunition burned on the railway tracks. Two stacks of bags with flour and cereals were broken. In repelling the raid, thirty-one German aircraft were claimed shot down.[143]

According to German information, Luftwaffe losses amounted to just two bombers: a Ju 88 A from KG 1 and a Ju 87 R from III./StG 1. The Ju 88 was shot down by anti-aircraft fire over Kobona harbour and crashed into a coastal shoal. The tail of the German aircraft remained sticking spectacularly out over the water not far from the berths. The Russians did not remove the wreckage of the bomber, leaving it as a symbol to raise morale.

The difficult repair of the gunboat *Bira*

The main objective of the Kobona harbour air attack on the morning of 28 May was the Soviet gunboats, which formed the basis of Ladoga Military Flotilla and played a major role in providing transport communications on the lake. The bombing proved to be quite effective and one bomb hit the gunboat *Bira*. A powerful explosion destroyed the entire bow of the ship along with the bridge. The commander of the gunboat division, Captain 1st rank Nikolai Ozarovsky, wrote in his diary:

> May 28, 1942. We came to Kobona harbour at night. At about 9:30 a.m., the gunboats *Nora* and *Bira*, which were part of the formation I commanded, stood on both sides of one of the piers waiting for food supplies and troops to be transferred to the west bank. Gunboats *Selemdzha* and *Bureya* stood on the roadstead ... Enemy planes suddenly appeared and began bombing the harbour. The ships opened anti-aircraft fire. The first bombs fell to the right of the gunboat *Nora*. One bomb fell on the pier. *Nora* backed up and quickly retreated to the roadstead. It was surrounded by columns of splashes and the smoke of explosions.

---

143. TSVMA. Foundation 399. Case 32. Sheet 60.

GERMAN AIR ATTACKS AGAINST 'LADOGA BATTLESHIPS'

> The stabilisers of the next series of bombs howled. Something hit my leg. The way was blocked by an explosion that destroyed the berth. At this time, the bomb hit the bow of the gunboat *Bira* ahead of the bridge. The anti-aircraft guns on the forecastle of the ship opened intense fire. The commander of the anti-aircraft battery Lieutenant Popov, with a bloody face loudly and energetically commanded ... German Ju 88s aircraft made a new approach to ships, piers and warehouses on the shore. They dropped bombs from a dive or from horizontal flight at an altitude of 200–300 metres ...[144]

Fourteen crew members of the gunboat Bira were killed, while thirty-seven more crew members were injured. Among the wounded was the commander of the ship, Captain-lieutenant Alexander Dudnik. Soon, the heavily damaged ship ran aft into a shoal and ran aground in shallow water.

Other gunboats in Kobona harbour also received various damage from German bombs. Thirteen bombers dived on *Nora* one after another. As a result of numerous explosions near the ship, about 170 holes were blown in its hull and superstructures, and thirty crew members were injured. Artillery pieces and auxiliary mechanisms were damaged, and a fire broke out in the boiler room. The struggle to save *Nora* began immediately, as sailors repaired the holes and pumped out the water. A group of machinists led by the chief technician of the ship, Engineer-Captain Vladimir Pyryalov, also managed to extinguish the fire inside the ship.

The gunboat *Selemdzha* was also damaged, while two of the crew were wounded by shrapnel. Thus, three of the four gunboats in Kobona harbour received various damage.

As it turned out, the Germans chose a very difficult target for an air attack. It was very hard to sink gunboats converted into warships from scows built in Germany. Even direct bomb hits did not guarantee the imminent death of the ship. German shipbuilders, unaware of the future purpose of the vessels, made the scows almost unsinkable. They were designed and built with a huge margin of safety. On the sides around the self-unloading cargo hold were compartments separated by waterproof bulkheads. To ensure the rigidity of the hull, the cargo hold and compartments were connected by longitudinal and transverse steel beams. To destroy such a target, it was necessary to hit the ship with at least three 250kg or 500kg high-explosive bombs or one bomb of a larger calibre.

---

144. Rusakov, Z.G., *Our Sea was Ladoga*, Leningrad: Lenizdat, 1980, p.91.

After a quick inspection of the heavily damaged *Bira*, it turned out that four aft compartments, including the powder chamber, were flooded as a result of the explosion of the enemy bombs. The system of pipes was also damaged and the steering gear was destroyed. However, before repairing *Bira*, it was necessary to remove the damaged ship from the shoal and take it to open water. To free the ship took the joint efforts of three minesweepers and two tugboats. On the evening of 29 May, this heavily damaged 'Ladoga battleship' was towed to a small bay on the southern shore of the lake and anchored.

It was only possible to repair *Bira* in a floating dock, and with great difficulty, the Soviets managed to find such a wooden dock in the lower reaches of the river Volkhov. Previously, it had been used to transport ships along the White Sea–Baltic Canal. However, due to the large draught, the gunboat could not enter the mouth of the Volkhov. For this reason, the Russians had to withdraw the floating dock to Lake Ladoga. After that, with great difficulty, it was possible to deliver the floating dock containing *Bira* to the river Volkhov and start repairs there. The difficult repair of the ship lasted four months. Only at the end of September 1942 was *Bira* able to return to Lake Ladoga.

'Coming out of earth houses, we saw destroyed buildings, twisted rails'

On the evening of 28 May 1942, Russian radar stations again spotted groups of German aircraft heading for Lake Ladoga. It turned out that ninety German bombers were flying under the protection of sixty-one Bf 109 Fs. The Soviet pilots, not having had time to celebrate the morning victories, again ran to the dispersal areas of their planes. In total, twenty-six fighters from the 4th Guards Fighter Aviation Regiment Air Force Soviet Baltic Fleet (4th GIAP VVS KBF), 158th Fighter Aviation Regiment (158th IAP) and 159th Fighter Aviation Regiment (159th IAP) were scrambled. They flew to the eastern shore of the lake, which turned out to be a serious mistake. This time, the targets of the German bombers were Osinovets harbour and Lake Ladoga railway station, located on the western shore. As a result, the Russian fighters in the Kobona harbour sector could not prevent the Germans from attacking Osinovets.

At 20.05, seven I-16s from the 123rd Fighter Aviation Regiment Air Defence (123rd IAP PVO) took off from Uglovo on alert. Arriving at Cape Osinovets, the pilots saw Ju 88 bombers circling over Osinovets harbour. 'Stalin's Falcons' immediately began to attack the enemy planes. Junior Lieutenant Potapov, piloting one of the I-16s, dived on the nearest German bomber and opened fire. 'Stalin's Falcon' reported after returning to the air base that an enemy plane had

GERMAN AIR ATTACKS AGAINST 'LADOGA BATTLESHIPS'

crashed near Cape Mar'in Nos. Senior Lieutenant Kharitonov first shot down a Ju 88, which fell into the water, and then attacked and shot down a Ju 87. The I-16 pilots claimed they had shot down three more Ju 88s, two Ju 87s and one Bf 109. Aerial victories were won by Lieutenants Gusev and Kharitonov, Senior Lieutenant Zheltukhin and Senior Sergeants Andrianov and Bachin.[145] German sources do not confirm these kills.

Leonid Ivanov, the captain of Osinovets harbour roadstead, recalled:

> An armada of Ju 88s and Ju 87s appeared in the sky. We ran to earth-houses. In earth-houses there were evacuated children from Leningrad, who did not have time to be transported to the other side of Lake Ladoga overnight. It's hard to tell what started after that ... Bombers appeared wave after wave above us, with a roar and howl of dive on a narrow strip of land and dropped their deadly cargo. The ground was shaking. We were deafened by the roar of explosions, suffocated by dust and burning. But the scariest thing was not even that. In our earth-houses, children who had already experienced a lot of grief in their short lives snuggled up to us. They didn't cry or scream. Only the children snuggled closer to us and shuddered with their very thin bodies from prolonged starvation. The bombing lasted several hours in a row. Coming out of earth-houses, we saw destroyed buildings, twisted rails.[146]

As a result of the German bombing of Osinovets harbour, a lot of damage was done to the port infrastructure. Most of the warehouses containing food burned down. Eight railway wagons were destroyed at the railway station near Osinovets harbour. The transport ship *Vilsandi*, which was making the passage along Lake Ladoga to Osinovets harbour, was damaged.

From a great height, the picture of the destruction caused by the German bombing was especially impressive. The commander of JG 54 Oberstleutnant Trautloft wrote in his diary: 'The giant flame rising into the dark, cloudy sky was a terrifying picture.'[147]

---

145. TSAMO RF. Foundation 20506. Inventory 1. Case 132. Sheets 34, 38–39.
146. *On the Road of Life: memories of the front-line Ladoga*, Moscow: Voenizdat, 1980, p.58.
147. Held, W., Trautloft, H., Bob, E., *JG 54. A Photographic History of the Grunherzgeschwader*, Schiffer Military History, USA, 1990, p.97.

AIR BATTLE FOR LENINGRAD, 1941–1944

The culmination of Luftwaffe air attacks against Russian communications at Lake Ladoga

On the morning of 29 May, Soviet radar stations again detected the approach of several groups of German aircraft from the south-west. This time the Luftwaffe carried out air attacks against Voibokalo railway station and the Volkhovstroy junction. Some of the enemy planes also attacked transport ships sailing along Lake Ladoga.

Four LaGG-3s from the 11th Guards Fighter Aviation Regiment Air Defence (11th GIAP PVO) took off to intercept German bombers from Smolino airfield. However, they did not reach Osinovets harbour. Over the village of Novaya Dubrovka (25km east of Leningrad), the group was suddenly attacked from behind by four Bf 109s. In a swift dogfight, the Germans shot down three Soviet fighters. They were piloted by Junior Lieutenant Ermakov, Sergeant Vakin and Junior Lieutenant Rybin. Two LaGG-3s made crash landings and were completely destroyed. Junior Lieutenant Rybin escaped by parachute.

Thirty-five P-40s from the 158th Fighter Aviation Regiment (158th IAP) and 159th Fighter Aviation Regiment (159th IAP) also flew to intercept German bombers. Five P-40s led by Captain A. Lyubimov tried to attack a group of fifteen Ju 88 As. However, when entering firing range, the Soviet fighters encountered eight German Bf 109s and a fierce dogfight began. Captain Lyubimov and Captain Senkevich recorded two aerial victories on their combat account. In fact, on 29 May, the fighters from JG 54 did not suffer any losses.

'Stalin's Falcons' from the 159th IAP reported four downed Ju 87s, while one P-40 fighter went missing. According to German data, it was shot down by Leutnant Friedrich Rupp from 7./JG 54. Another Soviet fighter was seriously damaged during this dogfight, but was able to return to its airfield.

On the evening of 29 May 1942, I. Fliegerkorps carried out the fourth air attack against Soviet communications at Lake Ladoga. Soviet radar stations detected the enemy in time. Soviet data recorded one large group of German aircraft south of Leningrad was divided into two parts. German information confirms the Russian data. Ju 87 Ds from Stab./StG 1 and III./StG 1 headed for Kobona harbour, and Ju 88 As from KG 1 flew to Osinovets harbour. Both groups of German bombers were covered by fighters from JG 54.

'Stalin's Falcons' tried to counteract the enemy attack. Nineteen I-16s from the 4th Guards Fighter Aviation Regiment Air Force Soviet Baltic Fleet (4th GIAP VVS KBF) took off from Vystav airfield. However, in the rapidly gathering dusk, some inexperienced pilots lost their bearings and were forced to return to their airfield. The remaining 'Stalin's Falcons' discovered Stukas at the moment when they crossed the front line near the town of Shlisselburg and approached Kobona harbour from the south-west. I-16s attacked the German bombers head-on. After returning to their airfields, 'Stalin's Falcons' from VVS KBF announced seven dive bombers shot down. The Luftwaffe reported the loss of only one Ju 87.

Meanwhile, eight LaGG-3 fighters from the 11th GIAP PVO were approaching Lake Ladoga. Soon they split into two groups of four. The first four LaGG-3s attacked a single Ju 88 near Shlisselburg. Russian pilots claimed that after the attack, a German bomber crashed on the southern shore of Lake Ladoga. Lieutenant Deev and Senior Lieutenant Yuryev claimed the victory. Then a large group of Bf 109 fighters appeared in the sky and a fleeting dogfight ensued, which ended with losses on both sides. Lieutenant Deev shot down one Bf 109, while the Germans shot down the LaGG-3 of Sergeant Shvets. The pilot of the downed Soviet fighter was recorded missing.

The second four Russian fighters from the 11th GIAP PVO in the Osinovets harbour area attacked a group of eighteen German bombers. 'Stalin's Falcons' recorded in their report:

> Senior Lieutenant Smirnov attacked one Ju 88 bomber and quickly shot it down. The enemy plane caught fire and fell into the lake. Senior Lieutenant Titovets and Lieutenant Danilov in a pair attacked a Do 215 bomber. After the attack, he caught fire and dived into the lake. After the attack, the enemy bombers dispersed and began to head south one by one. They were covered by Bf 109 fighters. Our planes flew to their airfield after the air battle. The Bf 109 group began to chase our fighters, but could not catch up with them.[148]

Contrary to the colourful description given in the 'Stalin's Falcons' report, in fact, the Germans lost only one Ju 87 in this area, and it was shot down by anti-aircraft fire from the ground.

The last dogfight over Lake Ladoga on 29 May occurred at 21.25. Four MiG-3s from the 26th Fighter Aviation Regiment Air Defence (26th IAP PVO) and several P-40s from the 158th IAP fought with a group of Bf 109s. The dogfight lasted until dark, after which the parties flew home.[149] That evening, two from 3./JG 54, Oberfeldwebel Rudolf Rademacher and Unteroffizier Gerhard Beutin, recorded one aerial victory each on their combat account. They identified the

---

148. TSAMO RF. Foundation 20506. Inventory 1. Case 132. Sheet 40.
149. Ibid., Sheets 41–43.

downed Soviet planes as Yak-1s. Oberstleutnant Trautloft wrote in his diary that he saw four Russian fighters that fell into Lake Ladoga 'like burning torches'.

Why was Hitler's order not carried out?

As a result of the series of attacks by the Luftwaffe, significant damage was caused to the port infrastructure of the cargo communications passing through Lake Ladoga. Berths and warehouses in Kobona and Osinovets harbours, access roads at Lake Ladoga and Voibokalo railway stations and Volkhovstroy junction were seriously damaged. The Germans also managed to heavily damage the gunboat *Bira*, damage sister ship *Nora* and several transport ships and sink several barges. The consequence of the air attacks was a temporary decrease in the volume of cargo delivered through Lake Ladoga to Leningrad. On 27 May 1,743 tons of cargo passed through Osinovets harbour, but on 29 May it was only 1,309 tons. However, on 30 May, the Russians transported 4,079 tons of cargo across the lake, and the next day this figure exceeded 5,000 tons. Thus, the German bombing carried out at the end of May 1942 not only did not stop the flow of cargo for Leningrad, but it was not even able to significantly reduce it. There were many serious reasons for such a disappointing result for the Luftwaffe.

Firstly, the main feature of the communications at Lake Ladoga was the extreme archaism of the port infrastructure and the predominant use of manual labour for all loading and unloading operations. Primitive piers and berths, built of wood and stones, could be restored very quickly. The demolished temporary warehouses, built of rough wooden planks, could easily have been built elsewhere. The destruction of several port cranes or warehouses could not significantly affect the speed of cargo movement. The Russians learned to restore damaged railway tracks literally within a day. Moreover, the Soviets could attract an almost unlimited number of workers, including young women, to the restoration work. Thus, the primitive port infrastructure on Lake Ladoga could be completely restored after the air strikes in a few days or even faster.

Secondly, the Russians had a huge number of transport vessels on Lake Ladoga. Most of them were small, primitive lake tugboats and barges. To sink all this mass of ships dispersed over a huge lake, a huge number of aircraft and experienced crews were required. In addition, the losses of lake tugboats and barges were also compensated for by the Soviets fairly quickly.

However, the main reason for the failure of this Luftflotte 1 operation was an erroneous idea of the situation on this section of the Eastern Front coming from the top political leadership of Germany. It must be admitted that the task set by Hitler for Luftflotte 1 was impossible. Even if the hypothetical possibility

GERMAN AIR ATTACKS AGAINST 'LADOGA BATTLESHIPS'

of transferring additional Luftwaffe forces to this section of the Eastern Front was realised, this could not significantly change the situation. The dispersion of objects, primitive mechanisation and the unlimited human resources of the Soviets did not allow the hope for a long-term effect from air attacks. Only German ground forces in cooperation with aviation could stop cargo traffic on Lake Ladoga. However, Hitler's incompetent actions deprived the Wehrmacht of offensive potential and forced the German soldiers to switch to the defensive in the Leningrad area.

Chapter 9

Operation Froschlaich

The Luftwaffe should lock up Soviet warships and submarines at the naval base

On the eve of the 1942 summer military campaign, Hitler continued to be disturbed by the ghost of the Soviet Baltic Fleet. He was haunted by the several damaged and blockaded warships at the mouth of the Neva. In addition, the psychopath Hitler feared the intensification of the actions of Russian submarines in the Baltic Sea. Despite the heavy losses suffered in 1941, the Russians still had three dozen submarines on this section of the Eastern Front. The Führer believed that a possible threat to shipping coming from Russian submarines could have serious economic and political consequences for Germany and its allies. Hitler's favourite miracle weapon, the naval bottom mine, was supposed to prevent the realisation of this hypothetical threat. Fulfilling the wish of the Führer, Oberkommando der Luftwaffe (OKL) ordered the command of the Luftflotte 1 to carry out a new operation to mine fairways in the area of Kronstadt and Leningrad. It was the numerous bottom mines that were supposed to finally lock up the large ships of the Soviet fleet at the mouth of the Neva and prevent submarines from entering the Baltic Sea.

The new fairways mining operation was code-named Froschlaich (Frog Spawn) and was scheduled for 10 May 1942. The crews of the bombers from KG 4 'General Wever' were assigned to the task of laying bottom mines from the air.

However, by the specified date, the ice in the eastern part of the Gulf of Finland and in the Kotlin Island area had not yet melted. In addition, it was not possible to deliver a sufficient number of parachute mines to Luftwaffe airbases in a timely manner. The prolonged spring Rasputitsa (season of bad roads) also interfered with the mission. The planes had to take off with two BM1000 parachute mines under the fuselage, weighing a ton each. The poor quality of the ground at Luftflotte 1 airfields, including Riga-Spilve where bombers from KG 4 were based, did not allow for a safe take-off with such a heavy

OPERATION FROSCHLAICH

load. As a result, Operation Froschlaich was postponed several times and was eventually put off to the end of May 1942. By this time, all three Gruppen Kampfgeschwader 4 had relocated to Prowehren airfield in East Prussia, where there was a long runway with a concrete surface.[150] In addition, the Prowehren base was well known to the crews. It was from this air base in 1941 that KG 4 began its protracted combat 'business trip' to the Eastern Front. And now almost a year had passed and the crews of this Kampfgeschwader again had to carry out the same mission – to drop parachute mines in Russian waters.

The previous winter had been very difficult for the crews of KG 4 under Oberst Hans Joachim Rath. After the encirclement of German troops in the Demyansk and Holm area, the bombers were used mainly in the role of transport planes. Their dangerous mission was to drop cargo containers by parachute. In addition, the bombers acted as tugs for Go 242 and DFS 230 cargo gliders. The flights took place in conditions of severe frosts and blizzards. Due to the bad weather conditions, the engines consumed an extremely large amount of fuel, which significantly reduced the flight range. Aircraft wings were often covered with ice in the air. Long low-level flights caused by poor visibility due to fogs significantly increased the likelihood of aircraft coming under fire from the ground. All these circumstances led to the losses of German bombers. From 1 February to 11 March 1942, KG 4 lost nine aircraft and sixteen crew members. By the end of May 1942, there were seventy-eight He 111 H-5s and H-6s in this Luftwaffe subdivision, of which just forty-nine were in airworthy condition. Thus, by the beginning of the summer military campaign of 1942, KG 4 was in a rather shabby state.

Executing the order of the Oberkommando der Luftwaffe (OKL), the officers of the Kampfgeschwader, together with the Luftflotte 1 headquarters, began thorough preparations for the implementation of the operation to mine the Soviet fairways. All minelaying missions were planned to be performed only at night. In order to complicate the work of the Soviet air defences, a complex route of aircraft approach to the target was developed. After taking off from Prowehren, the bombers had to fly to the north-east. In the area of Koporye Bay, they crossed the southern coast of the Gulf of Finland and, without changing course, flew over the Gulf of Finland. Having reached the northern shore near the Finnish town of Terijoki, the He 111s turned to the south-east and then flew along the coast occupied by Finnish troops. Once opposite Kotlin Island, the bombers lay down on a 180 degree course and

---

150. Gundelach, K., *Kampfgeschwader 'General Wever' 4*, Stuttgart: Motorbuch Verlag, 1978, p.181.

went straight to Kronstadt. Having reached the planned fairways sector, they dropped parachute mines from a height of 500–600m. The bombers then descended to the water and headed south-west, towards the dark part of the horizon. Such a complex route made it possible to reduce the time spent by German aircraft in the Soviet air defence zone and, accordingly, reduce the likelihood of losses.

Exploding 'paratroopers'

The evening of 28 May over the Gulf of Finland was clear and windless. The sea was calm, only small waves quietly rolled on the piers and wharves of Kronstadt riddled with fragments. The navy base was no longer the same as it was a year ago. All the major warships had left Kronstadt long ago and gone to Leningrad. For a long time, the debris of the battleship *Marat* became a kind of 'decoration' of the naval base. Its mangled skeleton rested on the very spot where, on 23 September 1941, it was hit by a bomb dropped by Oberleutnant Hans-Ulrich Rudel. Only minesweepers, minelayers, submarine chasers, patrol ships and torpedo boats were on the roadsteads. Only these small ships waged their 'small war' with the enemy among the skerries and islands of the Gulf of Finland. There were many destroyed and burned buildings in the harbour and the city, but the symbol of Kronstadt – the huge Naval Cathedral – still stood out against their background with its grey bulk.

Only battered submarines reminded of the former power of Stalin's Baltic Fleet, but the Soviets had few of them left. Twenty-seven submarines were destroyed by the explosion of sea mines, air attacks and by other causes. Thus, by May 1942, the Soviet Baltic Fleet had lost half of the submarines available at the beginning of the war.

On the night of 28–29 May, an 'air alert' signal was heard in all air defence divisions of Kronstadt Naval Defence Area under the command of Lieutenant Colonel Dorofei Osipchuk. Operators of the RUS-2 'Redut' radar station, located in a camouflaged position on Fort Shanc (in the western part of Kotlin Island), discovered a group of aircraft heading for Kronstadt. All air defence units were put on alert.

The first German planes were approaching from the north from Finland. They flew in pairs and singly with an interval of one to two minutes, skirting the Kronstadt Naval Base from the west. The altitude of the bombers was 800–1,200m.

The midnight sun period significantly hampered the actions of the Soviet air defence. The search for aircraft and the aiming of guns with the help of optics were complicated by insufficient illumination. The effectiveness of highlighting searchlight targets was also low, since their rays were scattered in the semi-darkness of the midnight sun. As a result, Soviet anti-aircraft gunners saw only vague silhouettes of indeterminate shape in their binoculars' eyepieces. Nevertheless, the anti-aircraft guns of the 1st Anti-aircraft Regiment (1st ZenAP) and the 49th Anti-aircraft Regiment (49th ZenAP), as well as coastal batteries, opened fire on the detected targets. The anti-aircraft guns of the ships anchored in the harbours at Kronstadt also began firing at the German planes.

For the first mission, the Germans chose the waters around the northern forts of the Kronstadt Fortress, where the Northern Reserve Fairway was located. Soon, black cylinders began to separate from the fuselages of German bombers and these slowly parachuted into the water. At the same time, some of the mines were dropped without parachutes from a very low level. These actions increased the likelihood of the BM1000 mine falling on land or in shallow water. Such mines could easily fall into the hands of the Soviets, who sought to seize high military technology. Anticipating such a situation, German military designers created an effective mechanism for preserving the secret of their miracle weapons. Luftminen were equipped with a special device for self-destruction when they came down on land. The explosion was supposed to occur twenty-two seconds after hitting a solid surface.

Meanwhile, Lieutenant Colonel Osipchuk's command post continued to receive information about the rapidly changing situation in the air. Some artillery batteries reported the start of firing, others the fall of mines, and others the transfer of fire from one target to another. The command post of the 71st Fighter Aviation Regiment Air Force Soviet Baltic Fleet (71st IAP VVS KBF) reported the scramble of fighters. However, not all air defence units acted professionally. Separate posts of the Soviet Air Surveillance and Communication Service (VNOS) reported the landing of enemy troops from the air. At dusk, they mistook cylindrical objects descending on parachutes for paratroopers. After the fall of each such 'paratrooper' a terrible explosion followed on the ground.

Many Soviet anti-aircraft gunners demonstrated confusion and a lack of understanding of the essence of the events that were happening around them. Some observers, confused by the powerful explosions, reported to the command post that a ground battle had begun on the island! Soon there was visual evidence that something extraordinary was happening in the Kronstadt Naval Base area. A huge piece of metal, which was a fragment of a bottom mine, flew with an ominous buzz near the observation tower at Lieutenant Colonel Osipchuk's command post and fell into the swamp.

AIR BATTLE FOR LENINGRAD, 1941–1944

Soon the German planes flew away, and the collection of reports on the events began in the Soviet headquarters. Posts of the Soviet Air Surveillance and Communication Service (VNOS) reported that twenty-one German aircraft had flown over the Kronstadt area. The headquarters of anti-aircraft regulations reported four downed German bombers.

After learning about the drops of bottom mines, the Soviet Baltic Fleet command immediately suspended the entry into the sea of all submarines.[151] Thus, Operation Froschlaich had a positive result at the initial stage of its implementation.

On the night of 29–30 May, bombers from KG 4 reappeared over Kronstadt. Within two hours they dropped about sixty Luftminen. Strong anti–aircraft fire forced the He 111 pilots to increase their altitude over the target by 200–300m. Therefore, this time the Germans dropped bottom mines only by parachutes.

On the following night of 30–31 May, posts of the Soviet Air Surveillance and Communication Service (VNOS) recorded the flight of nineteen German aircraft. Each He 111 dropped two BM1000 in fairways around Kronstadt Naval Base. For the first time, Ju 88 A bombers from KG 1 'Hindenburg' participated in the mission, taking off from Pleskau-Süd (city of Pskov). In addition to carrying out the main mission of minelaying fairways, Ju 88 As dropped fragmentation bombs on the positions of anti-aircraft artillery batteries on Kotlin Island. Additional difficulties for the Soviets were created by the German long-range artillery, which began shelling Kronstadt Naval Base from the Petergof area simultaneously with the minelaying operation from the air. Thus, the Germans again applied the effective tactics of combined artillery and bombing strikes, already tested during Operation Eisstoss.

Impotence of Soviet night fighters

Only after the third raid on Kronstadt did the Soviet Baltic Fleet and air defence divisions of the Kronstadt Naval Defence Area decide to take serious measures to counter the attacks. First of all, the Russians wanted to know from which air bases the German mine-setting planes operated. At first, they tried to track the flight route of the bombers using radar stations, but their primitive radio intelligence provided very chaotic information. Allegedly, mine-setting planes had taken off from Veimarn, Glubokoye and Luga, and landed at five airfields: Gorlovo, Peipin, Koporie, Gorki and Pskov. Realising the complete futility of such information, the Russians decided to abandon solving the problem with

---

151. Ladinsky, Y.V., *Military Watchstanding*, Moscow: Voenizdat. 1983, p.71.

the help of complex but useless radar stations. As an alternative, the Soviets chose the simplest 'device' for obtaining intelligence data – the eyes of Russian pilots. Night fighters were sent in pursuit of enemy planes. On one night of the midnight sun, a pair of I-153 biplanes flown by Captain Konstantin Solovyov and Senior Lieutenant Alexei Baturin from the 71st Fighter Aviation Regiment Air Force Soviet Baltic Fleet (71st IAP VVS KBF) were sent to perform this dangerous mission. They flew behind one of the He 111s and followed it at a distance of visual contact. However, after a while, the Soviets' fuel supply began to run out when they were close to Koporye Bay. Realising that their reconnaissance mission could not be completed, the pilots remembered that they were flying fighters and decided to attack the enemy bomber. After closing to about 400m, the I-153s simultaneously fired RS-82 rocket-powered projectiles at their target. Returning to their airfield, Captain Solovyov and Senior Lieutenant Baturin reported that they had shot down the enemy bomber.[152]

German information does not confirm this aerial victory. The probability of a hit with rocket-powered projectiles at night from a distance of 500m was negligible. Thus, 'Stalin's Falcons' simultaneously failed two missions: reconnaissance and fighter. However, remember that the bombers from KG 4 came from Prowehren airfield in East Prussia; the Soviets simply did not have fighters capable of flying such a long distance and returning back.

All these events once again showed the total impotence of Soviet night fighters. By the end of May 1942, there were only four pilots trained for night flights in the 71st IAP VVS KBF under Lieutenant Colonel Vladimir Koreshkov. Later, in just a few days, five more night fighter pilots were supposedly 'trained'. It is clear that such 'training' was useful only for compiling false bureaucratic reports for the authorities. In the Luftwaffe and the RAF, it took at least one year to train a fully-fledged night fighter pilot.

In addition to the shortage of pilots, the Soviets also had technical problems that were not eliminated until the end of the war. The fact is that the Soviet planes that played the role of 'night fighters' were prepared for night missions as 'carefully' as their pilots. Usually, for these purposes, the Soviets resorted to all sorts of risky improvisations, which worsened the already poor flight characteristics of Soviet aircraft. For example, several obsolete I-16 and I-153 fighters were equipped with large-calibre machine guns and RS-82 rocket-powered projectile launchers instead of standard weapons. A rarer phenomenon was the equipping of improvised night fighters with radio equipment for targeting from the ground. The Soviets simply did not have specially designed and adequately equipped and armed night fighters during the war.

---

152. TSVMA. Foundation 57681. Case 4. Sheets 41–43.

AIR BATTLE FOR LENINGRAD, 1941–1944

On the night of 31 May–1 June 1942, the Luftwaffe carried out the fourth mission to mine Soviet fairways. In response to the increased opposition of the Soviets, the tactics of using German mine-setting planes were changed slightly. The bombers crossed the front line in small groups at high altitude, while performing a flak-evasion manoeuvre. Then they moved from different directions to Kronstadt Naval Base. All stages of the mission were calculated to the minute. Exactly one to two minutes before the first planes appeared over the target, German long-range artillery opened fire on the locations of Russian anti-aircraft guns and searchlights. The probability of German shells hitting directly into the positions of Soviet anti-aircraft guns from a distance of 15–20km was quite low. However, the powerful explosions of 170mm and 280mm shells had a strong psychological effect on Soviet anti-aircraft gunners. Then the German bombers started minelaying bottom mines. If it was not possible to aim accurately at the fairway the first time, the bombers made a second and sometimes third approach to the target.

As expected, the actions of the Soviet night fighters proved ineffective. In addition to the unsatisfactory training of pilots and the use of outdated aircraft, another important factor complicated the situation: there was a complete lack of collaboration between night fighters and anti-aircraft batteries. As a result, anti-aircraft gunners and night fighter pilots simply interfered with each other. The pilots of the I-16s and I-153s, going to attack the German bombers, did not give any signal to the gunners of the anti-aircraft guns. As a result, anti-aircraft firing continued and night fighters 'stumbled' on the explosions of friendly anti-aircraft shells. Sometimes the opposite situation occurred in the sky. The anti-aircraft gunners stopped firing, seeing their planes in the air, but the night fighters did not attack the enemy since they could not see the target.

Stupid attempts by the Soviets to collaborate night fighters and anti-aircraft artillery

The next day, the command of the Russian air defence, copying the Germans, once again hastily tried to establish a collaboration of its limited forces. The 71st Fighter Aviation Regiment Air Force Soviet Baltic Fleet (71st IAP VVS KBF) held a briefing on the topic of aviation and anti-aircraft artillery collaboration. The commander of the 1st Anti-aircraft Regiment (1st ZenAP), Major Nikolai Kotov, listened attentively to the claims and wishes of the night fighter pilots. As a result, special signals were developed for the collaboration of night fighters in the air and anti-aircraft gunners. The parties agreed that special observers would be assigned to each artillery battery in order to monitor the aircraft and the signals they sent. A special table was compiled that determined the order of action of anti-aircraft artillery and night fighters. This document was immediately given to all commanders and staff officers to study. The collaboration of night fighters and anti-aircraft artillery was based on the principle of zone distribution. Anti-aircraft batteries were supposed to fire within the firing radius of their guns. Night fighters had the right to attack bombers on approach and departure from the target, that is, outside the zone of fire of anti-aircraft guns. At the same time, if night fighters when attacking air targets entered the area of responsibility of anti-aircraft artillery, anti-aircraft gunners had to cease fire. Only after the fighters left the firing zone could the anti-aircraft guns resume firing at enemy aircraft.

The command of the 71st IAP VVS KBF found that the Germans practically did not change their routes and flight times when performing minelaying fairway missions around Kronstadt. Based on this, approximate 'waiting areas' were calculated for night fighters, through which German bombers were supposed to fly. In addition, coastal artillery batteries equipped with large-calibre artillery pieces were allowed to shoot at German aircraft.

Anti-aircraft fire control was to be carried out from the tower of the commander of the air defence division Kronstadt Naval Defence Area by radio and wired telephone. Fighter aircraft control was to be carried out from the command post of the commander of the 71st IAP VVS KBF. A telephone cable was laid between these points for the constant exchange of information.

However, the Soviets never managed to put into practice all these beautiful collaboration plans, completely borrowed from the Germans. The level of education and military training of commanders and privates was extremely low, and the technical equipment of anti-aircraft batteries and night fighters was very primitive. Under these conditions, it was impossible to organise a long-term effective collaboration between anti-aircraft artillery and night fighters.

Clear the fairways of German bottom mines!

Meanwhile, the Soviet Baltic Fleet leadership faced the problem of clearing the fairways, at the bottom of which lay a lot of mines equipped with magnetic fuses. To solve this problem, the commander of the Protection of the water area (OVR),[153] Captain 1st Rank Yuri Ladinsky, ordered the formation of a special minesweeper division. The division had nine ships converted from former fishing seiners: *Sig*, *Povodec*, *Piksha*, *Voronin*, *GS-1*, *GS-2*, *Svir*,

---

153. Protection of the water area (OVR) was a unit within a naval base designed to protect the main forces of the fleet in its home areas from enemy actions from the sea.

Kasatka and *Yastreb*. The main advantage of such improvised minesweepers was their wooden hulls, which meant they were not in danger of being blown up on bottom mines equipped with magnetic fuses. However, only a third of these 'ultra-modern' ships were able to achieve effective mine clearance using a towed minesweeping barge. The rest of the minesweepers had only a tail distance sweep and could only perform auxiliary functions.

The flagship of the division was the wooden minesweeper *Sig* with a displacement of 208 tons, while the rest of the wooden vessels had a displacement of 40 to 80 tons. The commander of the special minesweeper division was Captain-Lieutenant Mikhail Bezborodov.

Preparation for mine clearance was complicated by the fact that the Soviets did not know exactly what types of mines the Germans had used. Unlike primitive Russian mines, which had hardly changed since the First World War, the enemy had hi-tech mine weapons with several types of sensors. Consequently, the Soviet command did not understand how to conduct minesweeping. As a result, the Russians again resorted to the most crude and ineffective method of mine clearance. The 'technology' of such mine clearance was extremely risky: high-speed submarine chasers manoeuvred at full speed in a narrow fairway randomly dropping depth charges. According to the plan of the incompetent Russian commanders, in the event of a successful underwater explosion next to a German mine lying at the bottom, it was supposed to be detonated. However, in a whole day of such risky manoeuvres, the submarine chaser managed to destroy only one bottom mine. Such a 'success' clearly disappointed the Soviet command, because according to their information more than a hundred German bottom mines were lying at the bottom of the fairway around the Kronstadt Naval Base. It soon became clear to the Soviets that it was necessary to use a more effective clearance tool. On 2 June, wooden minesweepers towing a minesweeping barge came out to clean up the fairways. The first two days of work did not bring any results as the German mines did not react in any way to the repeated passage of wooden minesweepers with their towed barges. The next few days were more successful and through titanic efforts they were able to neutralise eleven German bottom mines. However, even such 'impressive' results of mine clearance could not guarantee the safe passage of ships along numerous fairways around Kronstadt.

Further, the Soviets, finally realising the prospect of the Germans continuing to mine fairways, attempted to create a system for localising the bottom mine laying sites based on observing where they fell. Such measures made it possible to focus mine clearance on areas that represented a real danger, rather than spending resources on checking all the fairways. For this purpose, a detachment of mobile water observation posts was organised under the command of Captain-Lieutenant Nikanor Shklyarsky. Twenty motor boats and twenty-six ships' boats were allocated to carry out this work. Observation posts were set up in the period from 22.00 to 04.00 near the Kronstadt lighthouses and in the fairways that led to Oranienbaum and the Karelian Isthmus coast. Observers were provided with direction finders and binoculars. Their mission was to fix the approximate location of the German bottom mines falling into the water. The collected data was transmitted to the Protection of the water area (OVR) headquarters.[154]

It is strange, but the 'brilliant' idea of organising the observation of the places where mines fell only came to the mind of Soviet commanders only in the second year of the war. There is no doubt that the application of such a simple measure in 1941 could have greatly simplified the work of clearing fairways and saved several ships from destruction.

On one of the June nights of 1942, important information was received from the observation posts. The Soviets recorded the fall of two bottom mines on the shore of Kotlin Island, near Bychiy Pole airfield. For some reason, the self-destruct mechanism did not work and the German mines did not explode. The Soviet command decided to neutralise the mines and study their internal structure. This extremely dangerous task was performed by sappers led by engineer Captain 2nd Rank Mikhail Mironov. Fortunately, Soviet specialists had received detailed information about the devices and how to disarm them from the British. Thanks to the help of their ally and a certain amount of luck, the operation to neutralise the German mines was successful. Having examined the internal structure, Russian specialists were once again able to observe the huge technological gap between the Soviets and Germany.

Night 'Seagulls'[155]

On the night of 1–2 June 1942, Operation Froschlaich resumed after a short pause. First, Ju 88 A dive bombers from KG 1 appeared over Kronstadt. They attacked the positions of the 1st Anti-aircraft Regiment (1st ZenAP) and 6th Anti-aircraft Regiment (6th ZenAP) artillery batteries. Ju 88 As dropped thirty-eight high-explosive and fragmentation bombs on Soviet anti-aircraft guns. Then He 111 H-6 bombers from KG 4 appeared in the sky and these began mining Soviet fairways. In total, about forty German bombers participated in the raid.

---

154. Ladinsky, Y.V., *On the Fairways of the Baltic*, Moscow: Voenizdat, 1973, p.44.
155. 'Seagull' (Chaika) is the nickname of the Soviet Polikarpov I-153 biplane fighter, on account of its characteristic bend in the upper wing.

AIR BATTLE FOR LENINGRAD, 1941–1944

After receiving information about the approach of German aircraft from Bychie Pole airfield, located in the western part of Kotlin Island, I-153 night fighters took off. The mission was attended by the commander of the 71st Fighter Aviation Regiment Air Force Soviet Baltic Fleet (71st IAP VVS KBF), Lieutenant Colonel Vasily Koreshkov, and the political commissar of the 71st IAP VVS KBF, Ivan Serbin. They sent their planes towards the Tolbukhin lighthouse and began to patrol there, waiting for German bombers.

However, Major Bisin, who had also begun a patrol mission over Kronstadt Naval Base in his I-153, was the first to discover the enemy. In the faint light of searchlights, the pilot saw the silhouette of a twin-engine aircraft. He began to approach it, deciding to attack head-on. When the Seagull approached a distance of about 500m, Major Bisin pressed the start button and six fiery RS-82 rocket-powered projectiles rushed towards the German bomber. The pilot then opened fire with his four 7.62mm ShKAS machine guns. After that, according to Major Bisin, the He 111 attacked by him 'fell on the wing, entered a steep dive and crashed into the water near the Northern forts of the Kronstadt Fortress'.[156]

According to German information, after completing this mission, He 111 H-6 W.Nr. 4714 of 6./KG 4, piloted by Leutnant Horst Finke, did not return to its base. In addition, 9th Staffel (9./KG 4) radio operator Wilhelm Grahl was wounded that night as a result of shelling from the ground. These losses were evidence that, despite the measures taken by the Germans to increase the safety of combat missions, the Kronstadt air defences had not been completely neutralised.

Attempts by Ju 88 A bombers from KG 1 to suppress anti-aircraft batteries by bombing also proved ineffective. At dawn on 2 June 1942, the commander of the 1st ZenAP, Major Kotov, together with the commander of the 2nd Artillery Division (2nd ZAD), Timofey Gorokhov, arrived at the position of Anti-aircraft Battery No. 42. There they saw the walls of the fort riddled with fragments, dents on the guns and a broken rangefinding telemeter. But the anti-aircraft gunners themselves did not suffer losses, and they felt cheerful and confident, believing that they had shot down a couple of German planes. The powerful stone walls of the fort reliably protected the anti-aircraft artillery positions.

The very fact of the presence of Soviet night fighters in the sky also unnerved the bomber crews. One of the German pilots recalled: 'In addition to very powerful anti-aircraft fire and searchlights, night fighters appeared, and

---

156. TSVMA. Foundation 57681. Case 4. Sheets 48–50.

OPERATION FROSCHLAICH

therefore the missions did not bring the desired success.' Such opposition from the Soviets forced the bomber crews to drop bottom mines from a height that was higher than optimal. As a result, the accuracy of the installation of bottom mines significantly decreased and only individual Luftminen fell directly into fairways.[157]

The following night, from 2 to 3 June, the Luftwaffe carried out the sixth mission to mine the Kronstadt fairways. Soviet night fighters again participated in repelling the air attack. Political commissar 71st IAP VVS KBF Ivan Serbin and pilot-inspector Alekseev took off on patrol. At the time when German planes usually appeared, I-153s were in the sector between the Tolbukhin and Shepelev lighthouses at an altitude of about 1,000m. Soon the pilots found a single He 111 flying south. After a brief pursuit, the Seagulls got close to it, after which they attacked with RS-82 rocket-powered projectiles. According to the 'Stalin's Falcons' report, as a result of the shelling, the German plane 'abruptly went into a steep dive, crashed into the shore and exploded'.

Returning to his patrol area, political commissar Serbin saw another He 111 flying at an altitude of 1,500m towards Kotlin Island. The German bomber was illuminated by searchlights, so its crew did not notice the night fighters flying behind. According to the reports of 'Stalin's Falcons', they got on the enemy's tail and opened fire with machine guns from a distance of about 100m. After the attack, the German plane caught fire and fell into the waters of the Gulf of Finland.

Another dogfight was conducted by a pair of night fighters of Commander 71st IAP VVS KBF flown by Lieutenant Colonel Koreshkov and squadron commander Major Ivan Gorbachev. After reaching the patrol area, the I-153 fighters began circling over the water. From a height of 1,000m Kotlin Island with its navy base, forts, jetties and harbours, was very distinct. Soon, in the crosshairs of searchlights, the pilots clearly saw the silhouette of a twin-engine aircraft, and the Seagulls immediately headed towards the enemy. A few minutes later, the night fighter pilots saw the He 111 flying over the water at an altitude of 1,600m. According to the report of Lieutenant Colonel Koreshkov and Major Gorbachev, they attacked the enemy bomber, after which it 'fell into the water at Cape Ino'.[158]

Another downed German bomber was claimed by searchlights maintenance personnel. They claimed that several beams of their searchlights captured a

---

157. Gundelach, K., *Kampfgeschwader 'General Wever, 4*, Stuttgart: Motorbuch Verlag, 1978, p.183.
158. Cape Ino situated on the northern shore of Neva Bay in the Gulf of Finland.

He 111 flying at low altitude. The German crew, trying to escape from the light field, lost orientation and the bomber crashed into the water.[159]

In total, in their reports for the night of 2–3 June 1942, the units of the Russian air defence announced four downed German aircraft. In fact, KG 4 lost only one He 111 H-6, W.Nr. 4894, from the 3rd Staffel (3./KG 4), piloted by Leutnant Gustav Burger. The deceased crew consisted of young inexperienced pilots who had been transferred from the training unit IV./KG 4 a few days earlier. This was their first and last combat mission. After this loss, the Germans took a time out for a day.

On the night of 5 June, posts of the Soviet Air Surveillance and Communication Service (VNOS) again received a message about the approach of German aircraft. At 00.30, air-raid sirens sounded in Kronstadt and Major Gorbachev's I-153 night fighter took off from Bychie Pole airfield. Patrolling at an altitude of 2,000m, the pilot observed the explosions of anti-aircraft shells, and then saw searchlights illuminate an He 111. Major Gorbachev radioed the anti-aircraft gunners to stop firing and began to approach the target. He decided to attack the bomber from the front. However, the German pilot noticed the Soviet biplane rushing towards him and abruptly turned aside. Major Gorbachev claimed in his report that he did not lose sight of the enemy and chased him all the way to Finland, where he shot him down.

The Seagull piloted by pilot-inspector Alekseev also patrolled over the sea. Peering intently into the sky, he noticed a single Ju 88 bomber preparing to drop bottom mines. The enemy aircraft was about 1,000m away and pilot-inspector Alekseev began to approach it. Soon he saw two bottom mines detach from the Ju 88 and their parachutes open. The Seagull carefully flew around the bottom mines that were slowly descending on parachutes and attacked the Ju 88. Six rocket-powered RS-82 projectiles raced towards the German bomber. However, they all passed well below the target. After such an impressive fireworks display, arranged by a Russian pilot, the Germans noticed their pursuer. The Ju 88 bomber dived sharply and flew away at a low level towards Fort Ino.

Further actions to intercept German bombers were described as follows by pilot-inspector Alekseev:

> I returned to my patrol zone. Political commissar Ivan Serbin joined me here. At an altitude of 2000 metres, we found a He 111 bomber and decided to attack it. We went to his tail and opened fire from a distance of 200 metres. The bomber's air

---

159. TSVMA. Foundation 57681. Case 4. Sheet 54.

OPERATION FROSCHLAICH

> gunner fiercely fired at us in long bursts, but soon fell silent. Then the He 111 had a smoke trail and the bomber began to lose altitude. VNOS posts confirmed the fall of an enemy bomber.[160]

After that, pilot-inspector Alekseev discovered another He 111 at an altitude of 2,500m. The pilot fired at it with machine guns and loosened off two rocket-powered projectiles, upon which he later claimed the damaged bomber crashed near the Tolbukhin lighthouse. Upon returning to the airfield, Alekseev then found a Ju 88. However, the pilot of the German bomber also noticed the enemy and escaped by climbing.

Despite the colourful details of the enemy's attacks recorded in the reports of 'Stalin's Falcons', in fact, all the German planes returned safely to their air bases that night.

On the night of 5–6 June, the Luftwaffe departed on another mission to lay mines in the Soviet fairways. At 00.15 (Moscow time) an air alert was announced in Kronstadt. Posts of the Soviet Air Surveillance and Communication Service (VNOS) recorded twenty-four enemy aircraft parachuting twenty bottom mines. Several Ju 88 As again attacked the positions of anti-aircraft batteries on Kotlin Island.

Already reputed to be a night ace, pilot-inspector Alekseev flew to intercept the enemy bombers in his I-16. The weather had deteriorated sharply, and layered clouds hung over the eastern part of the Gulf of Finland. Such weather conditions made it difficult for night fighters to detect the German aircraft. At 01.15, the I-16 broke through the upper cloud layer and continued flying at an altitude of 3,500m. The blunt-nosed little fighter was cutting through the cold air, its engine roaring furiously. Soon 'Stalin's Falcon' spotted the enemy. Pilot-inspector Alekseev recalled:

> Here, on the turn, I found the Ju 88. I managed to go on the attack from behind and give a burst of machine guns from above on the fuselage and on the right engine. The enemy increased his speed and tried to hide in the clouds. I released two rocket-powered projectiles on it. One of them exploded near the right wing of the Ju 88, and the German crashed into the water between Kotlin Island and Fort Krasnoflotsky.[161]

---

160. TSVMA. Foundation 57681. Case 4. Sheet 55.
161. Ibid., Sheet 56.

On the same night, pilot-inspector Alekseev made another flight, which ended in vain.

The continuation of the German raids forced the commander of the 71st IAP VVS KBF, Lieutenant Colonel Koreshkov, to increase the intensity of night fighter sorties. Deceived by the pilots' repeatedly exaggerated reports about the effectiveness of their activities, Koreshkov decided that the key to success lay in simply increasing the number of night fighters. But, since the Soviets had a chronic shortage of pilots, it was decided to have two combat-ready aircraft at the airfield for each night pilot. This measure made it possible to avoid wasting time on refuelling and rearming the fighter. On the following nights, the most experienced pilots, after returning from the first departure, transferred to pre-prepared fighters and took to the air again. Thus, 'Stalin's Falcons' Lieutenant Colonel Koreshkov, political commissar Serbin, Captain Sharov, Senior Lieutenant Baturin and pilot-inspector Alekseev managed to make two sorties in one night.[162]

The next minelaying mission was carried out on the night of 7–8 June. According to posts of the Soviet Air Surveillance and Communication Service (VNOS), German planes dropped forty-five bottom mines and twenty-one fragmentation bombs on Soviet anti-aircraft artillery and searchlights positions.

Another Soviet mine clearance operation around Kronstadt Naval Base

Meanwhile, Soviet Baltic Fleet minesweepers tried to neutralise the bottom mines installed by the Germans. As a result of the work of the observation posts, it turned out that since 5 June 1942, the Germans had focused their efforts on mining the main fairway and the Bolshoi roadstead of Kronstadt. This forced the commander of the Protection of the water area (OVR), Captain 1st Rank Yuri Ladinsky, to expand the minesweeping zone. On the morning of 8 June, submarine chaser *MO-201* and boat *ZK-38* passed through the main fairway, dropping thirty-eight depth charges at short intervals. As a result of using such a crude technique, none of the hi-tech German mines that lay at the bottom of the fairway exploded. In fact, the whole risky minesweeping operation turned out to be completely useless. Nevertheless, this did not prevent the sailors from informing the command about the mine clearance of the main route of the ships – the Morskoy channel of Kronstadt. Irresponsible and incompetent

---

162. Ibid., Sheets 57–58.

OPERATION FROSCHLAICH

Soviet commanders believed that if German mines did not explode, then they simply did not exist.

Despite the obvious danger from mines, the Soviets did not abandon their decision to send the first submarines to the Baltic Sea. For additional verification of the proposed route of the submarines, they decided to send minesweepers. On the night of 9–10 June, *TSCH-304* and *TSCH-317* set off for the open sea. While following the fairways along the Kronstadt lighthouses, the sailors saw German planes dropping another portion of bottom mines. The sailors watched as the terrifying huge cylinders fell into the water with a small splash and sank. At the same time, explosions of bombs dropped by the Germans on Soviet anti-aircraft batteries were heard from Kotlin Island. From the escort boats accompanying the minesweepers, the sailors opened fire on the enemy bombers with anti-aircraft machine guns. After the minesweepers safely passed through the fairways, the Soviet command finally decided that submarines were absolutely safe to enter the Baltic Sea.

The Germans discovered Russian attempts to conduct mine clearance and immediately reacted. On the afternoon of 10 June, six Ju 87 Ds and four Ju 88 As suddenly appeared over Kronstadt. The target of the German bombers was the Russian minesweepers stationed in Battery Bay. However, all thirty-three bombs they dropped exploded in the water. VVS KBF fighters flew out to intercept the raiders. After returning to the airfields, Senior Lieutenant K. Prisyazhnyuk and Junior Lieutenant V. Tkachev claimed one downed Stuka and one downed Bf 109. The Germans shot down one Soviet LaGG-3 fighter with return fire.

On the night of 10–11 June, German aircraft made their eleventh mission to mine the fairways, dropping thirty-five Luftminen. At 11.35, four Ju 87s appeared in the sky over Kronstadt. This was another attempt by the Germans to prevent the Russians from carrying out mine clearance. Coming from the direction of the sun, the bombers dived into the berths of the submarine chasers in Battery Bay. Three powerful explosions thundered astern of the submarine chaser *MO-103*. Its stern was completely destroyed, and it soon sank. Russian anti-aircraft batteries expended about 1,700 shells on repelling the enemy and claimed two downed Stukas.

Adventures of the crew of a German bomber

During the German Operation Froschlaich, Soviet pilots and anti-aircraft gunners regularly reported German planes shot down in the Kronstadt area. However, in reality, on its many successful missions KG 4 lost only two bombers. After ten days of Froschlaich, this Luftwaffe unit suffered a third loss. On the night of 13–14 June, He 111 H-6 '5J+FT' from 9./KG 4, under the command of Hauptmann Hesse, did not return to base. However, the reason for the loss was not down to Soviet night fighters or anti-aircraft fire from the ground.

On that day, He 111 H-6 '5J+FT' took off from Prowehren at 21.18 (Berlin time). However, the bomber crew could not carry out its mission as there was low cloud cover over Kronstadt Naval Base. Hauptmann Hesse decided instead to dump mines on a back-up target, Leningrad, and at 00.11 he got rid of his dangerous cargo.

According to Soviet information, four Luftminen on parachutes were dropped on the city on the night of 13–14 June. One mine landed on Jeleznodorojnaya street and did not explode. The second mine fell on the burnt-out Univermag (department store) building on Vasilyevsky Island. A powerful blast wave broke all the windows in houses within a 500m radius. Seventeen people were injured. The third mine BM1000 exploded on Digonalnaya street (north of Finlyandsky railway station), the blast wave destroying two wooden houses. Six people were killed and twenty-one were injured. The fourth mine landed on the roof of an apartment building, but did not explode.[163]

After dropping the Luftminen, the German bomber turned to the southwest. However, after thirty minutes of flight, the left engine began to work intermittently, and then completely caught fire. It became clear to the crew that they could not even reach the nearest German airfield in Riga city.

Hauptmann Hesse later described this crisis situation in his report:

> The engine started to burn badly. The flame stretched above and below the wing. The height was already 600 metres. The time had come for the decision to evacuate. I called all the crew members by name. When they responded, I said: We jump at the same time, I take a signal pistol and rockets. After landing, I release flares, and we get together. Everyone should take guns and flashlights ... The height is 400 metres, the engine burns even more, it's not normal. I'm going back. The hatch is open. Flight engineer looks at me, I nodded, he jumps and the parachute opens. The radio operator is also jumping; his parachute is also in perfect order.

---

163. TSAMO RF. Foundation 217. Inventory1221. Case 1594. Sheets 161–163.

OPERATION FROSCHLAICH

> And then I see that the pilot is still in his place. I go back to the cockpit and ask: Bergmann, what's going on? He shouts: 'I can't let go of the controls, the plane immediately starts falling ...[164]

As a result of a short conversation with Hauptmann Hesse, the pilot, Leutnant Bergmann, decided to make an emergency landing. At 00.50, the He 111 successfully landed on its fuselage 75km north of Pskov city. It was German territory, but in the conditions of Russia, this fact did not guarantee the pilots' safety at all! Many German pilots, having jumped out with parachutes or made emergency landings in the German rear, then disappeared without a trace. Some died of hunger, being in a deserted area, some became a victim of wild animals, some drowned in a swamp. Even more Germans became victims of local partisans.

Having rested, examined the terrain and waited for dawn, at 03.30 Hauptmann Hesse and Leutnant Bergmann went in search of German units. Hauptmann Hesse continued his story:

> After an hour of walking over rough terrain, we saw a settlement. We decided to eat there and, if necessary, grab a horse by force and drive on in the direction of the nearest town. Everything turned out great. The population was peaceful and friendly. We received fresh milk, a horse, a hay cart and a cab. Leutnant Bergmann knew Czech, thanks to which we learned the name of this place – Shtechegei and the nearest German post (Novoselie), as well as the direction and distance to it. We had to drive 20 kilometres to Novoselie. This trip lasted three hours. All this time we were smoking cigarettes and drinking cognac from an emergency container. In case the guerrillas appeared, we kept MP 40 submachine guns on our knees.[165]

The pilots managed to reach the German occupation authorities quickly enough. Then the mounted police and Estonian volunteers promptly went in search of two other crew members of the He 111. At 11.30 on 14 June, radio operator Brodatzki was discovered, and two hours later flight engineer Scholz was found.[166] Thus, the dangerous adventures of the crew of the German bomber, caused by a banal technical malfunction, ended with a safe return to their unit.

---

164. Gundelach, K., *Kampfgeschwader 'General Wever' 4*, Stuttgart: Motorbuch Verlag, 1978, pp.183–185.
165. Ibid., p.186.
166. Ibid., p.187.

Results of Operation Froschlaich

In total, from 29 May to 14 June 1942, bombers from KG 4 carried out twelve missions to mine Russian fairways around Kronstadt Naval Base. In total, the German aircraft carried out 316 sorties.

Soviet posts of the Soviet Air Surveillance and Communication Service (VNOS) recorded a drop of 413 Luftminen. However, given the number of missions carried out, the Germans actually installed at least 600 mines with different types of sensors. At the same time, Soviet anti-aircraft batteries claimed fifty-one downed aircraft. The 71st Fighter Aviation Regiment Air Force Soviet Baltic Fleet (71st IAP VVS KBF) claimed twenty-four aerial victories. Following this false information, the USSR Air Defence Command assessed the actions of the anti-aircraft gunners as extremely successful. As a result, awards were showered on anti-aircraft gunners. On 18 June 1942, the 6th Anti-aircraft Regiment (6th ZenAP) Lieutenant Colonel Ermolaev was renamed the 22nd Guards Anti-aircraft Regiment (22nd GZenAP). Thus, this subdivision of anti-air defence became the second artillery regiment to receive the honorary title of 'Guards'. Officers commanding anti-aircraft units also received awards. For example, the commander of the 42nd artillery battery 1st Anti-aircraft Regiment (1st ZenAP), Lieutenant Konstantin Trifonov, was awarded the Order of Lenin.

In fact, the losses of KG 4 during Operation Froschlaich amounted to three bombers. The circumstances of the loss of these He 111s have been described above.

For Kampfgeschwader KG 4, Froschlaich was the last combat work that it carried out as an entire unit. After that, Stab./KG 4, I./KG 4 and II./KG 4 were transferred to Seshchinskaya Air Base (in the central section of the Eastern Front), where the bombers were used to carry out various missions. Only III./KG 4 retained the status of a specialised aviation Gruppe. Soon the bombers from III./KG 4 went to Germany to Fassberg airfield to train cargo glider towing crews, and from there they were transferred to eastern Ukraine. He 111s from KG 4 no longer appeared over Leningrad.

After the completion of Froschlaich, there was a lull in the skies of Kronstadt and Leningrad for four months. The sweeping of mines placed by the Germans during the twelve nights of Froschlaich lasted until the end of 1942. However, the successes of the Soviet minesweepers turned out to be modest. All sorts of sweeps and depth charge explosions managed to neutralise only fifty-nine Luftminen, that is, 10 per cent of those laid. During the operation, two minesweepers, *Voronin* and *Piksha*, were blown up. Thus, the wooden minesweepers division lost a third of the ships from its original composition.

OPERATION FROSCHLAICH

Despite the deadly threat from German bottom mines, Russian submarines, minesweepers, gunboats and submarine chasers continued to be based at Kronstadt. They had to leave almost daily through mined fairways in Gulf of Finland and return back the dame way. Their small size saved them from destruction, but the threat of detonation on the German bottom mines was ever present for the surviving Soviet Baltic Fleet warships even after the end of the war.

Chapter 10

'Natural coffee' by Generaloberst Alfred Keller

Disturbing raids by small groups of bombers

Despite undertaking many other important missions, German bombers continued to carry out attacks against Soviet harbours and ships on Lake Ladoga. For example, on 2 June 1942, the Germans bombed Kobona harbour. The Luftwaffe operated in small groups of two to four aircraft, trying to use the effect of surprise. Usually such raids were carried out by single bombers during the midnight sun or at dawn. Planes always attacked from Lake Ladoga with muted engines, appearing over the target suddenly. These actions were often coordinated by German agents who operated on the shores of the lake. Secret agents radioed Luftflotte 1 headquarters with information about the movement of ships and the time of unloading in harbours on the lake coast.

The same tactics, designed to maximise the element of surprise, were used by German bombers during attacks against single ships and caravans on the lake. During the daytime, bombers suddenly attacked transport ships from the direction of the sun or from the clouds. Night attacks were carried out during the midnight sun period, when sufficient lighting allowed bomber crews to search and attack targets in the waters of Lake Ladoga.

For example, on 3 June, the transport ship *Kuzneck* was attacked while it had several barges in tow. Fragments of German bombs and machine gun fire literally riddled the ship. Almost the entire crew was injured and concussed. The captain, Ivan Alexandrov, despite three injuries, steered the ship standing at the helm and managed to bring it and the barges to the harbour. When on the shore, Captain Alexandrov soon died from his injuries.

On 10 June, eighteen German bombers under the cover of Bf 109 F fighters from JG 54 made another raid on Kobona harbour. As a result of the bombing, two piers were destroyed and five barges containing food were sunk. Two more vessels were damaged.[167]

---

167. Cherokov, V.S., *For You, Leningrad!*, Leningrad: Leninzdat, 1988, p.80.

As already noted above, German bombers carried out searches and attacks on Soviet ships carrying cargo across the lake to Leningrad. The transport ship *Hansi*, while sailing on Lake Ladoga from Kobona to Morier, was attacked by five German aircraft. The bombers attacked from the direction of the sun and dropped four high-explosive bombs from a height of about 400m. Ten metres from the starboard side of the ship, huge water columns rose. Having received serious damage, *Hansi* began to list to port. The electric lights went out and the engine room was filled with clouds of black dust thrown out by the concussion from coal bunkers. Due to damage to the steering gear, the crew lost control of the ship. Smoke grenades exploded on the forecastle from bomb fragments, filling the decks with acrid grey smoke. This circumstance saved *Hansi* from destruction. Seeing that the ship had lost its course and was enveloped in clouds of smoke, the German pilots decided that they were done with it and flew away. Despite the disappearance of the air threat, the position of the vessel continued to remain critical. In the forward room of the transport ship, the wooden skin and the uniforms folded there caught fire. The starboard side of *Hansi* received many holes, through which the cargo hold began to gradually fill with water. There were numerous casualties among the ship's crew. The commander of the ship, Lieutenant Grigory Korkin, his chief mate Alexey Sporyshev and boatswain Philip Okhapkin were killed. Political commissar Ivan Bogdanov was seriously wounded. The struggle for the rescue of *Hansi* was taken over by the helmsman Starshina (non-commissioned officer) Alexander Sedov. The sailors who remained in the ranks managed to patch up the holes, extinguish the fire and call for help. As a result, the heavily damaged transport ship was towed to the port of Morier.

Ladoga flotilla of the Axis powers

In the spring of 1942, Hitler realised that it was impossible to paralyse Russian transportation along Lake Ladoga by air attacks alone. For the officers from the Luftflotte 1 headquarters, this simple truth had been obvious from the beginning, but they did not dare to criticise their incompetent Führer. The Soviets continued to supply Leningrad and Red Army divisions, which, thanks to the supply of ammunition, constantly attacked the ring of the German land blockade from the inside. This state of affairs drove the hysterical Hitler into an indescribable rage. Soon someone from the Führer's entourage suggested to him a 'brilliant' idea to solve this complex problem. The way out of the impasse was for Germany to create its own Ladoga flotilla on the lake. Its ships would then attack Soviet vessels and lay mines on their routes. The Italian allies agreed to participate in this adventurous venture, offering to send their torpedo boats to Lake Ladoga. Hitler, fascinated by such a simple solution to a complex problem, ignored the fact that in 1942 there was not a single German ship on Lake Ladoga, or even a boat, and a flotilla had to be created literally from zero.

In May 1942, the Germans announced their plans to create a Ladoga flotilla to their Finnish allies. The help of the Finns was needed to create a navy base on the northern shore of Lake Ladoga, which was controlled by Finland. The Axis powers responded to the German proposal by agreeing on the condition that the future Ladoga flotilla of the Axis powers should be headed by a Finnish commander. The Germans agreed, but put forward a counter-demand. They believed that the Finnish commander should coordinate all his actions with representatives of the Wehrmacht. This was a typical case when the lying Third Reich tried to portray partnerships with its allies. In reality, despite the formal transfer of command to Axis powers representatives, all important decisions were made exclusively by the Germans.

Finnish Colonel Jorvinen became the commander of the future Ladoga flotilla of the Axis powers. He had to coordinate his actions with the Commander of Luftflotte 1, Generaloberst Alfred Keller. The main base of the Axis flotilla was Lahdenpohja harbour, located in one of the deep fjords on the northern shore of the lake. Thus, on paper, Hitler's 'brilliant' idea was successfully implemented, but in reality that was far from the truth. The Germans and their allies still did not have any ships on Lake Ladoga. To get them to the lake, it was necessary to organise and carry out a difficult transport operation. It took a lot of time and effort to implement Hitler's 'brilliant' plan.

Adventures of Italians in Russia

On 22 June 1942, the first ships of the future Ladoga flotilla of the Axis powers arrived at Lahdenpohja harbour. These were the Italian torpedo boats *MAS 526*, *MAS 527*, *MAS 528* and *MAS 529* from the 12th Torpedo Boat Division led by capitano di corvetta G. Bianchini. Their journey from warm Italy to cold Russia turned out to be very difficult and tedious. First, torpedo boats were loaded onto flat railway wagons at the port of La Spezia (on the coast of the Ligurian Sea) and delivered to the German port of Stettin on the Baltic Sea coast. There they were reloaded on board the transport ship *Tilbeck*, which arrived in Helsinki on 9 June. Then torpedo boats were launched and towed along the northern shore of the Gulf of Finland to the Finnish town of Viipuri (now Vyborg). From there they were towed via the Saimaa Canal to Lake Saimaa. Then the Italian torpedo boats were loaded onto flat railway wagons again. On 22 June, they arrived at Lahdenpohja harbour. There the torpedo boats were launched again, and the long journey of 3,100km was finally completed.

'NATURAL COFFEE' BY GENERALOBERST ALFRED KELLER

By the beginning of July 1942, the Italian sailors were ready to begin active operations, but their German allies were still missing. Nevertheless, the Italians began to make voyages on Lake Ladoga as they needed time to gradually master the unfamiliar theatre of military operations. On 24 July, capitano di corvetta Bianchini defined the mission of the Italian torpedo boats: 'To attack the Soviet lake communication extending from the town of Uusi-Laatokka (Novaya Ladoga) to the settlement of Morier.' However, the debut of the Italians was unsuccessful, although the Soviet Ladoga Military Flotilla had nothing to do with their troubles. On 27 July, during one of the exits to Lake Ladoga, torpedo boat *MAS 526* ran into rocks near Myokerikyo island. The damage turned out to be serious, and the torpedo boat was under repair at Lahdenpohja harbour until 10 August.

Luftwaffe warships prepare for battle

The Kriegsmarine allocated six mine boats from the 31st Minesweeping Flotilla to carry out minelaying on Lake Ladoga. However, by 27 June 1942, only four mine boats had arrived in Helsinki – *KM 3*, *KM 4*, *KM 8* and *KM 22* – under the overall command of Oberleutnant Reymann. Having made the same journey as the Italians, they reached Lahdenpohja harbour on 7 July. There it turned out that all the German mine boats were manned by inexperienced crews and also needed repairs. They had to be sent to Sortavala, where there was a suitable dry dock. The German boats only returned to their base in Lahdenpohja harbour on 10 August.

The insignificant resources allocated by the naval forces of Germany and Italy looked completely ridiculous on the vast expanses of Lake Ladoga. It would be dangerous to report to Hitler, full of stupid hopes for the cessation of Russian shipping on the lake, about such a paltry composition of the Ladoga flotilla. The situation, as always, was saved by the faithful Führer leadership of the Luftwaffe! Unexpectedly, the greatest forces for action on Lake Ladoga were allocated by Reichsmarschall Hermann Göring!

As part of Luftflotte 1, the 'Eastern Ferry Operations Staff' (Einsatzstab Fähre Ost) was created, headed by Oberstleutnant Wachtel. He had twenty-two Siebel ferries at his disposal. These unique vessels were designed by the owner and executive director of the Siebel Aircraft Factory, Dr Fritz Siebel. On the eve of the planned landing in England (Operation Sea Lion), he proposed to build a simple landing ferry. It was supposed to consist of two army pontoons connected by a platform. Such an improvised vessel could accommodate troops, cargo and weapons. Early examples of Siebel ferries were powered by three BMW VI 750hp aircraft engines. After the cancellation of Operation Sea Lion, Siebel continued to improve his ferries. The latest Siebel ferries with several modifications had been delivered to Lake Ladoga.

Seven Siebel ferries with the numbers 11, 13, 15, 17, 21, 23 and 25 were armed with three 8.8cm Flak and two 2.0cm Flak guns. Five Siebel ferries with numbers 12, 14, 16, 22 and 26 were armed one 3.7cm Flak and ten 2.0cm Flak. The remaining nine ferries were cargo ferries (they had the letter 'T' in the designation) and did not have weapons.

Siebel ferries in disassembled form were delivered by rail to Lahdenpohja harbour. The first of them arrived at their destination on 12 July 1942. The ferries teams did not consist of sailors, but were manned by infantrymen from Luftwaffe Field Divisions and gunners from the 144th Anti-aircraft Division (Flakabteilung.144), also part of the Luftwaffe.[168] It was a unique case in military history. Usually the fleet had its own aircraft. In this paradoxical case, due to the boundless ambitions of Göring, aviation had its own fleet. Such a strange situation was possible only in the Third Reich, where several military groups (Luftwaffe, Kriegsmarine, Heer and Waffen-SS) competed for Hitler's attention!

The assembly of Siebel ferries was carried out by specialists of the 128th Ship Repair Battalion (Werft-Bataillon 128), 22nd Detachment of the 2nd Construction Battalion Luftwaffe (LW-Baubataillon 22/II). All the hard work was done by numerous Russian prisoners of war.

As noted above, Lahdenpohja harbour had become the main naval base for the Ladoga flotilla of the Axis powers. Temporary bases were located closer to the front: in Sortanlahti, Saunaniemi and other bays on the winding rocky coast of Lake Ladoga.

Although some ships appeared on the flotilla, it must be admitted that it was impossible to defeat the Soviet lake shipping with such modest forces. Nevertheless, in the summer of 1942, the Axis flotilla was given large-scale tasks: 'to destroy the Russian strongholds on land and drive the ships into Shlisselburg Bay'. In addition, the Germans wanted to disable the 'especially dangerous' enemy ships. The number one target for them was the flagship of the Soviet Ladoga Military Flotilla, the patrol ship *Purga*. To increase the chances of performing such large-scale missions, the Luftflotte 1 headquarters planned to periodically strengthen the Ladoga flotilla with Ju 87s from III./StG 1 and Ju 88s from KG 1.

---

168. Keskinen, K., Stenman, K., *German Aircraft in Finland 1939–1945*, Apali Oy, Finland, 1998, p.107.

The command of the Russian Ladoga Military Flotilla learned about the arrival of German ships at the end of July 1942. This happened largely randomly when a Pe-2 reconnaissance aircraft flew over Lahdenpohja harbour with muffled engines and took photographs from a low altitude. The images clearly showed landing ferries moving along the coast with a characteristic double wake. This information fully corresponded to the Allied intelligence warning about the likely transfer of German Siebel ferries to Lake Ladoga. Further, the Soviets, imitating the actions of the Germans, planned and carried out a series of air attacks on the ships and infrastructure of the Ladoga flotilla. Soviet bombers and flying boats began to regularly bomb German naval bases on the north-western shore of the lake. In addition, on the night of 26–27, Soviet gunboats fired the first bombardment of the Saunaniemi harbour from a distance of 13km.[169] However, this combination of air attacks and artillery shelling did not cause any significant damage to the Axis ships and infrastructure.

Kommando I./JG 54 in action

The German command was well aware that for the Ladoga flotilla to be successful, reliable air cover would be required. However, in the conditions of interaction between Germany and its Finnish ally, the solution of this problem resulted in lengthy negotiations with the observance of many bureaucratic formalities. As a result, the two allies divided Lake Ladoga into the 'Finnish' and 'German' areas of responsibility, the border between which ran along the line of latitude at 60° 30′ north. Each of the parties had to provide aviation support for its zone. The Luftflotte 1 headquarters formed a special unit, Kommando I./JG 54, to operate directly over Lake Ladoga. It consisted of a very modest force, fifteen Bf 109 Fs from the 1st and 2nd Staffeln (1./JG 54 and 2./JG 54). Kommando I./JG 54 was headed by Commander I./JG 54 Hauptmann Hans Philipp. The main mission of this unit was to protect the Axis flotilla from Soviet aviation.[170]

On 15 July 1942, Bf 109s from Kommando I./JG 54 flew to Petäjärvi. It was a small, well-camouflaged airfield near Viipuri. Later, the Germans also used an airfield near Lahdenpohja harbour to carry out sorties over the lake. In addition to the main mission, German fighters from Kommando I./JG 54

---

169. Cherokov, V.S., *For You, Leningrad!*, Leningrad: Leninzdat, 1988, pp.106–107.
170. Keskinen, K., Stenman, K., *German Aircraft in Finland 1939–1945*, Apali Oy, Finland, 1998, pp.123–126.

independently searched and attacked Soviet vessels, for which one 250kg bomb was suspended under their fuselages.[171]

In addition to the Bf 109 fighters, four Ar 196 seaplanes arrived at Kakisalmi Harbour on the west coast of Lake Ladoga. They could be used both for aerial reconnaissance and as rescue aircraft. The Ar 196 flew at speeds up to 310kmh and had quite powerful weapons – two 20mm aircraft autocannon MG FF mounted in the wings and one 7.92mm machine gun MG 17 in the fuselage above the engine. Thanks to the defensive armament, the crew could successfully fend off attacks by Russian fighters, and on occasion attack single vessels. As history has shown, Ar 196s often engaged in battle over Lake Ladoga with Russian Beriev MBR-2 flying boats from the 58th Separate Squadron Air Force Soviet Baltic Fleet.

While the Luftwaffe was building up its lake fleet, and a special aviation unit to support it from the air, German bombers continued to create problems for the Soviets on Lake Ladoga. A new success in the fight against lake shipping was the air attack against Novaya Ladoga harbour on 30 July 1942. As a result of the German bombing, nine barges and three tugboats were destroyed. The infrastructure of this important port, on the eastern shore of the lake, was also seriously damaged. The berth's wooden flooring was completely destroyed, while all nearby wooden buildings were burned down. The losses amounted to hundreds of dead and wounded. The next day, the damage suffered by the Soviets from German attacks was increased by bad weather. On 31 July, a Force 10 storm broke out on Lake Ladoga. In Osinovets harbour, a fuel oil barge was thrown onto the rocks and 350 tons of fuel oil poured into the lake. Powerful waves stranded the transport ship *Stenso*, four barges and the minesweeper *TSCH-175*.

Despite the very modest forces, fighters from Kommando I./JG 54 also tried to join the fight against transport communications passing through Lake Ladoga in the summer of 1942. For example, on 24 August at 09.40 four Bf 109s dropped four bombs on Morier harbour, on the western shore of Lake Ladoga. All the bombs fell into the water without causing damage. At 12.05 the same four German fighters dropped bombs on the same target. As a result, a fire truck was destroyed, two people were killed and eight people were injured. At 15.55, two Bf 109 fighters appeared over Morier harbour. They entered the target from the side of the lake and dropped two bombs on the harbour. A truck was destroyed, three workers were killed and three people were injured.

---

171. Weal, J., *Jagdgeschwader 54 'Grunherz'*, Osprey Aviation, 2001, p.241.

'NATURAL COFFEE' BY GENERALOBERST ALFRED KELLER

On 25 August, German fighters carried out four air attacks against Morier harbour. Bomb explosions damaged one tractor and killed six Russian sailors swimming in the water.

On 28 August, Bf 109s from Kommando I./JG 54 carried out three more bombing raids on Morier. They used their usual air attack tactics in which Bf 109s approached the harbour at a high altitude and then descended sharply and attacked the target from the direction of the sun. This tactic made it possible to avoid losses from anti-aircraft fire, since the Soviet gunners did not have time to start shooting. However, the damage from such rapid, but not targeted, attacks was insignificant. For example, on 28 August, all eighteen German bombs exploded in the water or in a coastal forest.

During July–August 1942, Bf 109 fighters from Kommando I./JG 54 made 104 sorties from Finnish airfields against communications on Lake Ladoga. However, as expected, they failed to achieve serious success. Fighters, as a rule, could not sink even a small vessel. However, the fire from aviation cannon and machine guns was fatal for the people on board. A large number of sailors and passengers were killed and injured by bomb fragments and shells and bullets. At the same time, there was no time to take many of the wounded to hospital, and they died from elementary blood loss. Heavy losses among the lake ship crews forced the Russians to organise special emergency rooms on all six berths in Osinovets harbour. There, the wounded were given first aid and then sent to hospital.

Minor damage from attacks by fighters from Kommando I./JG 54 did not affect the ability of Soviet tugs and barges to deliver cargo to Leningrad, which was still blockaded on land. The bullet-riddled vessels were quickly repaired and sent back to the lake. Air attacks against Soviet harbours on the shores of Lake Ladoga caused even less damage. As already noted above, even after massive bomb attacks, primitive port facilities, as a rule, were restored to working condition within two to three days. Thus, the Luftwaffe attacks in the summer of 1942 were like disturbing pinpricks.

Russian fighters could not provide serious opposition to Bf 109s from Kommando I./JG 54. The Chief of Staff of the 4th Guards Fighter Aviation Regiment, Air Force Soviet Baltic Fleet (4th GIAP VVS KBF) Major Peter Roitberg recalled:

> The enemy has perfectly studied the technical capabilities of our aircraft. They usually knew in which area our fighters were patrolling. Since we were patrolling at an altitude of 2–3 thousand metres, the enemy flew to the water route with an advantage in altitude, from the direction of the sun and, finding

our planes, made an attack at high speed, and then left with a climb. Having taken a position to attack, the enemy repeated it again.[172]

In order to reduce losses from air attacks, the Ladoga Military Flotilla command began to send most ships as part of convoys. This facilitated air defence and assistance to damaged transport vessels. The typical convoy consisted of two or three tugboats with one or two barges in tow. They were accompanied by one gunboat. Sometimes a submarine chaser or minesweeper was also included in the convoy. At the same time, the warships protecting the convoy also transported cargo and towed barges. To reduce the likelihood of a German attack, the convoys were leaving the harbours of Lake Ladoga in the evening and arriving at their final destination at dawn.

In June 1942, Soviet transport vessels, including Ladoga Military Flotilla ships, delivered 105,000 tons of cargo to the western shore of the lake. In July 1942, over 121,000 tons were delivered. Despite the growth in traffic volumes, these cargoes were not enough to supply the surviving residents of Leningrad and the soldiers of the Leningrad Front. Stalin's directives and the task of the Military Council of the Leningrad Front to increase the volume of transportation were chronically unfulfilled. Despite a minimum transportation plan of 6,000 tons per day, it was only possible to transport 3,500–3,900 tons of cargo to the western shore of Lake Ladoga. However, the main reason for such a failure of Leningrad's supply plans was not the opposition of the Luftwaffe, but the total inefficiency of the Soviet management system.

Russians increase their transport 'fleet'

The insufficient number of transport vessels forced the command of the Soviet Ladoga Military Flotilla to begin the construction of new wooden barges. In the Syasstroy settlement, an improvised Syas shipyard was hastily organised at a sawmill. At the end of May 1942, the first three wooden barges, created according to the technologies of the eighteenth century, were launched at this 'shipyard'. The new barges had a length of 40m, a width of 8m, an inside height of 3.2m and a draft of 1.8m. They held more than 380 tons of cargo.

---

172. *Ladoga Native (Memoirs of veterans of the Red Banner Ladoga Flotilla)*, Leningrad: Lenizdat, 1984, p.66.

'NATURAL COFFEE' BY GENERALOBERST ALFRED KELLER

These were extremely primitive vessels, which, however, fully corresponded to the technological level of communications organised by the Soviets on Lake Ladoga. The Russians rightly believed that any vessel capable of staying on the water was suitable for supplying Leningrad. Thanks to the heroic efforts of the Syas shipyard workers, twenty-seven more wooden barges were launched before 31 September.

In addition, the construction of simplified metal barges also unfolded on the shores of the lake. By 23 July 1942, it was possible to build eleven of such vessels, then the Soviets built three more. These vessels, with a length of about 51m and a width of 9m, could carry up to 900 tons of cargo. In fact, these 'barges', built in just ten to twenty days, were just large rectangular boxes. Nobody thought about streamlining the hull, and therefore their speed was minimal. The sides bent from the blows of the waves and rivets flew out, but with great difficulty tugboats still dragged them through the troubled waters of the lake.[173]

Later, the Soviets introduced more know-how – the train barge-ferry. This vessel could accommodate three steam locomotives with tenders or ten two-axle railway wagons. In total, in the summer of 1942, the Russians managed to build three train barge-ferries. From 12 August, two such 'wonder vessels' started sailing on Lake Ladoga.

On the first flight, train barge-ferry *No. 4530* was attacked by German planes, but still managed to reach the harbour on the western shore of the lake. Train barge-ferries trips then became regular. The Soviets tried to use these clumsy and bulky vessels only in good weather. The freeboard of the train barge-ferries was so low that to an outside observer it seemed as if the steam locomotives or railway wagons that were on deck were travelling directly on the surface of the water! These vessels, requiring skilled workers and scarce materials for their construction, were considered especially valuable by the Soviets. The loss of each train barge-ferry was considered irreparable by them, so such vessels crossed the lake only as part of a guarded convoy.

Simultaneously with the construction of wooden and metal barges at the dilapidated Leningrad factories, the production of a self-propelled tender[174] of a simplified type began. The work was carried out by hungry workers almost manually. After the completion of construction, the tenders were delivered by rail to the shore of Lake Ladoga. The self-propelled tender was a small steel vessel with the simplest rectilinear contours of the hull.

---

173. TSVMA. Foundation 1003. Case 546. Sheets 288–301.
174. The self-propelled tender was a flat-bottomed motor vessel. It had a small draft, a load capacity of up to 30 tons and a crew of two or three people.

Depending on the modification, from 15 to 25 tons of various cargoes could be placed in one or two cargo holds. Small dimensions – length 15m, width 4m – contributed to great manoeuvrability and at the same time made the ship a very difficult target for aircraft. The flat bottom and a draft of only 50–60cm allowed the self-propelled tender to literally get ashore, which facilitated unloading even on an unequipped beach. The ZIS-5 truck engine installed on the vessel allowed it to travel at up to 6 knots. A total of 118 self-propelled tenders were built during the navigation of 1942! Thus, while Luftflotte 1 was trying to attack transport communications on Lake Ladoga from the air and was preparing to use its Siebel ferries, the Soviets made great efforts to increase its number of transport vessels on the lake.

In parallel with the increase in the transport fleet, the Soviets constantly expanded the port infrastructure on the shores of Lake Ladoga. Osinovets included five harbours: Morier, Novaya, Golsman and Kabotajnaya. By August 1942, there were already fourteen piers with a total length of more than 2,200m. If by the beginning of navigation in 1942, the port of Osinovets could simultaneously receive only eight barges, then by August it was already twenty, and by September 1942 it was twenty-two. As already noted above, the Soviets did not experience a shortage in people. Almost all loading and unloading operations at Lake Ladoga were carried out manually. For these purposes, seventeen separate working battalions were additionally transferred to the lake ports. Eight working battalions were located on the eastern shore, and nine on the western. By 1 November 1942, there were about 7,000 people in separate working battalions. As a result, the total number of Lake Ladoga Transportation Department personnel in the last phase of navigation in 1942 was 12,000 people.[175] If necessary, this number could be quickly doubled or even tripled.

The Axis flotilla begins active combat operations

By early August 1942, the Luftwaffe was finally able to assemble a more or less complete Ladoga flotilla of the Axis powers. To enhance the 'power' of the flotilla, the Finns 'generously' included in its composition the old torpedo boat *Sisu*, as well as several tugboats and boats.

On 14 August, the Axis flotilla began active combat operations. The first combat mission on the lake was carried out by the Italians, whose torpedo boats had already studied the conditions of sailing quite well. On the night

---

175. TSVMA. Foundation 1003. Case 546. Sheets 304, 318–320.

'NATURAL COFFEE' BY GENERALOBERST ALFRED KELLER

of 15 August, near the western shore of Lake Ladoga, three Italian torpedo boats engaged in battle with three Russian gunboats. According to the Italians, a torpedo sunk one of the Russian ships. The successful torpedo attack was carried out by torpedo boat *MAS 527* under the command of sottonente[176] Bechi. In fact, the Italian torpedo passed along the left side of the gunboat *Selemdzha* and exploded, hitting the shoal.

On the night of 27–28 August, torpedo boats *MAS 527* and *MAS 528* intercepted a Russian convoy heading from Novaya Ladoga harbour to the port of Osinovets. A torpedo from the *MAS 528* sottotenente Benvenutto boat sank a large barge with ammunition, which was pulled by three tugboats at once. However, this 'success' of the Italians was not confirmed by Soviet information.

On the night of 24–25 August, the Italians were finally joined by combat Siebel ferries. The first operation by Einsatzstab Fahre Ost was named 'Bohnenkaffee' (natural coffee). In addition to artillery Siebel ferries, three light Siebel ferries, three landing boats and two KM mine boats took part in the raid. The first exit of Siebel ferries into the lake immediately revealed the difficulties of managing so many vessels at night. In the dark, almost all ships lost visual contact with each other, and several ferries collided. The Ladoga flotilla's air cover during daylight hours was provided by four Bf 109s from Kommando I./JG 54. The Axis flotilla spent ten hours sailing on Lake Ladoga. However, it was not possible to meet the enemy on such a huge expanse. At the same time, German fighters covering the actions of the Axis flotilla reported two downed 'I-180s'. Also, one destroyed aircraft of the same type was claimed by anti-aircraft gunners on Siebel ferries. The authors of this book cannot confirm or dismiss this data on the losses of Russian fighters.

The fighter 'I-180' was the same phantom, or non-existent type, for the Germans as the 'He 113' was to the Russians. In both cases, the confusion arose due to incorrect intelligence information. The 'I-180'[177] was a prototype of the Soviet fighters of the 'New Type'. Although this aircraft was not mass-produced and never entered service with the Soviet Red Army Air Force, the Germans periodically claimed to have shot it down in different sectors of the Eastern Front. Most likely, the Germans mistook the I-16s fighters from the 4th Guards Fighter Aviation Regiment Air Force Soviet Baltic Fleet (4th GIAP

---

176. Sottonente the rank in the Italian army, aviation and navy roughly corresponds to the rank of lieutenant.
177. Details about its development and the failure of the I-180 'super Rat' can be read in the book by Zubov, D., *Stalin's Falcons: Exposing the Myth of Soviet Aerial Superiority over the Luftwaffe in WW2*, Barnsley, UK: Air World/Pen & Sword, 2023.

VVS KBF) patrolling over the lake for the 'I-180'. It was easy to make such a mistake, since the I-180 was a development of the I-16 and, with an almost identical appearance, differed from its predecessor only with a new, more powerful engine.

On 30 August, the Axis flotilla again sailed on the lake. On this day, Siebel ferries reached the big route (the Germans called it the 'external navigation route'), along which Soviet ships sailed from the port of Novaya Ladoga to the port of Osinovets. However, they failed to find a single Soviet vessel, and the Ladoga flotilla of the Axis ships returned to their base in Lahdenpohja harbour having achieved nothing.

Chapter 11

Third Sinyavino meat grinder

Operation Nordlicht

On 12 August 1942, Generalfeldmarschall Erich von Manstein returned to the Crimean Peninsula from a holiday after the successful assault on Sevastopol. On that day, he received Hitler's instructions to immediately go north to Leningrad with the headquarters of the 11th Army and prepare an operation to capture another 'Bolshevik stronghold'.

The summer campaign of 1942 developed very successfully for the Wehrmacht. In August, Army Group A troops were rapidly advancing into the Caucasus, and Army Group B was moving irresistibly towards the Volga. The Red Army was on the verge of collapse again. It seemed to Hitler that victory was close and it was necessary to take advantage of Stalin's weakness. In this regard, the Führer's attention turned again to Leningrad, which was bothering him. He believed that things were going so well that the Wehrmacht was able to allocate twelve divisions to capture 'the cradle of Bolshevism'. The prudent Hitler even took care of good air support for the upcoming operation. According to the plan, immediately after the capture of Stalingrad, the Führer promised to transfer the legendary VIII Fliegerkorps to the Leningrad area for the second time.

On 17 August, Generalfeldmarschall Erich von Manstein arrived in the Leningrad area and began planning the upcoming operation. He later wrote in his memoirs:

> During the reconnaissance of the area on the front south of Leningrad, we saw a city protected by a deeply echeloned system of field fortifications, but located, as it seemed, very close to the positions of the German troops. A large factory in the town of Kolpino on the Neva was visible, still producing tanks. The Pulkovo shipyards were visible off the Gulf of Finland. In the distance, the silhouette of Isaakievskiy Sobor (Saint Isaac's

Cathedral) and the spire of the Admiralty Building, as well as Peter and Paul Fortress loomed ... I was sad to see that the victims of the war were the royal palaces known to me in 1931: the beautiful Catherine Palace in Tsarskoye Selo (town of Pushkin), as well as another smaller palace here, in which the last tsar lived, and the delightful Peterhof Palace ('Peter's Court') on the shore of the Gulf of Finland. They were burned by Russian artillery.[178]

Soon, the experienced military professional determined an offensive plan, tentatively called Operation Nordlicht (Northern Light). According to von Manstein, German aircraft and artillery were to deliver a massive blow to the Russian fortifications south of Leningrad. Then three army corps from the Pushkin area, with the support of assault guns, were to break through to the southern outskirts of the city. After that, two or three German divisions would occupy the defence. The main forces were to cross the Neva to the southeast of Leningrad and advance to the east – in the direction of Lake Ladoga railway station and the port of Osinovets. Thus, if the von Manstein plan were implemented, Leningrad would be completely cut off from its supply routes. It was assumed that in this stalemate, the defending Soviets would be forced to surrender without street fighting. The implementation of Operation Nordlicht was tentatively scheduled for mid-September 1942.

The Third Sinyavino meat grinder

However, the plans of the conqueror of Sevastopol were not destined to come true. Having learned from intelligence about the arrival of German large-calibre artillery and numerous trains carrying soldiers in the Leningrad area, the Soviet command guessed that the Germans were preparing to storm the city. As a result, Stalin decided to forestall Hitler. He ordered the next offensive of the troops of the Volkhov Front under General of the Army Kirill Meretskov to immediately begin in order to break the blockade of the city. The place of the offensive was obvious to both the Soviets and the Germans – the so-called 'Shlisselburg-Sinyavino ledge'. It was formed by the beginning of October 1941, when the Germans managed to completely cut off Leningrad from the main territory of the USSR. This was the third attempt by the Soviets to attack well-fortified German positions head-on. Only a few tens of kilometres separated the Soviets from their cherished goal – the breakthrough of the Leningrad land blockade,

---

178. Manstein, E., *Lost Victories*, Smolensk: Rusich, 1999, p.316.

THIRD SINYAVINO MEAT GRINDER

but the Germans repulsed the attacks every time. Such persistence turned into huge sacrifices for the Red Army, but incompetent Soviet generals stubbornly drove their soldiers to death.

On 27 August, the offensive of the Soviet 8th Army began in the village of Gaytolovo and north of this settlement. After two hours of softening up by artillery, the 6th Guards Rifle Corps was able to break through the German defences at the 223rd and 227th Infantry Divisions. After that, Red Army soldiers crossed the Chyornaya River and began to advance to the settlement of Sinyavino. The greatest success was achieved by the units of the Soviet 265th Rifle Division, which quickly captured the strongholds of Tortolovo and 1st Estonian settlement. At the same time, the 19th Guards Rifle Division advanced 6km to the west and reached the vicinity of the settlement of Sinyavino on 29 August. In order to break through the ring of the land blockade around Leningrad, the Russians had only a few kilometres to overcome. At the same time, the Soviet 128th Rifle Division attacked the Germans on the southern shore of Lake Ladoga and advanced west for several kilometres.

Sinyavino was located on a large limestone hill that towered over the entire surrounding area. In the north, these Sinyavino Hills descended steeply to the low-lying shores of Lake Ladoga. In the south, the Sinyavino Hills turned into a swampy plateau overgrown with ancient coniferous forest. In places, it was cut by narrow riverbeds with high (up to 5–6m) banks. Around these hills there were numerous peatlands, which were a treeless, rugged terrain with drainage channels and recesses. This gloomy swampy wasteland was ideal for defence, but it was very difficult for any offensive.

In response to the attacks of the Red Army divisions, German troops entrenched themselves in several strongholds and took up a circular defence. Especially fierce battles unfolded for the Kruglaya roscha stronghold, through which the only paved road in this area, the Arkhangelsk Tract, passed.

End of the patrol ship *Purga*

At this crucial moment of the Russian offensive, Ladoga Military Flotilla was ordered to provide maximum support to the Red Army units attacking the Sinyavino Hills. The patrol ship *Purga* and the gunboats *Selemdzha*, *Bureya*, *Nora* and *Lakhta* went to the southern shore of the lake to fire at German troops from the water. In response to these actions, bombers from I. Fliegerkorps attacked the Russian ships several times. For example, *Bureya* was subjected to air attacks on sixteen occasions over the course of four days. However, the accuracy of the bombing was low and not a single German bomb hit the warship.

AIR BATTLE FOR LENINGRAD, 1941–1944

On 31 August at 06.30 *Purga* and *Nora* once again sailed to Shlisselburg Bay and opened fire on ground targets. At 15.41 the ships were attacked by three German Ju 88 A bombers, which dropped eighteen bombs. However, again there were no hits on the ships. From 19.00 to 20.25 *Purga* fired two volleys from its 102mm guns at German artillery batteries in the area of settlement No. 2. As soon as it got dark, at 21.40 the patrol ship left the firing position and anchored in the area of Jeleznica bank.

The next day at 09.20 *Purga* weighed anchor for the passage to Osinovets harbour. The ship was heading north-west at a speed of 12 knots. At 09.48, German planes appeared in the sky, attacking the ship from the direction of the sun. The captain of *Purga*, Ivan Gorovoy, ordered an increase in speed and opened fire from four 45mm anti-aircraft guns and four machine guns. However, these protective measures did not save the ship. Soon three Ju 88s flew low over *Purga*, and after that the ship was shaken by a powerful explosion.

A high-explosive bomb had pierced the deck and bottom in boiler room No. 1 and exploded in the water. The patrol ship had received a big hole. The water quickly flooded boiler room No. 1, the interior and engine room No. 1. Several more bombs exploded near the sides of the patrol ship. Their fragments pierced the fuel tanks, after which a fire started. The surviving sailors, led by the wounded Military technician of the 1st Rank Nikolai Solntsev, began the struggle to save *Purga*. In order to avoid an explosion, the bow powder chamber had to be flooded. Soon the ship began to list to port.

Soon *Nora* approached *Purga* and its crew joined the rescue efforts. The fire was extinguished, but the position of *Purga* still remained critical. The deck began to sink into the water because the pumps could not cope with the volume of water coming inside. It became clear to everyone that the ship could not be saved. Under these conditions, the crew was forced to abandon ship. At 10.13 *Purga* capsized over the port side and floated upside down for a while. The ship sank 4.6km east of Cape Osinovets at a depth of 9m. Thirteen sailors were killed and more than thirty crew members were injured.

The sinking of *Purga*, the flagship of the Ladoga Military Flotilla, was a major success of the Luftwaffe. The ship became a victim of the pilots of the Ju 88 bombers from KG 1. Also, during the attack, *Selemdzha* was severely damaged, and the gunboat was sent to the floating dock on the Volkhov for repairs.

However, the Germans, in attacking the Soviet ships suffered quite painful losses. On 3 September, during a flight over Lake Ladoga, the commander of KG 1, Major Hans Keppler, was killed. Just two weeks before his death, Major Keppler was awarded the Knight's Cross. The second loss was even more painful for Luftflotte 1. During a flight over the lake, Ju 88 A-4 W.Nr. 4037 collided with Bf 109 G-2 W.Nr. 10430 'Weisse 6' of 7./JG 54 for an unknown reason. The fighter was being flown by Gefreiter Eduard Langwenings. Both planes crashed and all those on board were killed. Like Major Keppler, Gefreiter Langwenings was quite an experienced pilot. He had fought on the Eastern Front since March 1942 and had won two aerial victories in Russia.

The advancing Russian troops are completely defeated by the Luftwaffe

By the beginning of September 1942, the Soviet 8th Army, at the cost of heavy losses, managed to wedge itself quite deeply into the German defence. The Soviets reached the northern approaches of the Mga settlement, a key defence point of the German 18th Army. At the same time, from the west – from Leningrad – the Nevsky Group of Troops, which included the 86th, 46th and 70th Rifle Divisions and the 11th Rifle Brigade, went on the attack.

An important contribution to the outcome of this battle in the Third Sinyavino meat grinder, as usual, was made by the Luftwaffe. However, the limited forces of I. Fliegerkorps were clearly not enough to fully support the German troops. He 111s from Stab./KG 53 commanded by Oberst Paul Weitkus, II./KG 53, under Major Schulz-Müllensiefen, and III./KG 53, under Major Hubert Mönch, were transferred from the central sector of the Eastern Front. These Gruppen from Kampfgeschwader 53 'Legion Condor' not only promptly joined the air attacks on the advancing Soviet troops, but also settled for what would become a long time in the area of operations of Army Group North.

The reinforcements that arrived allowed the Luftwaffe to significantly increase the pressure on the Red Army units. Bombers and Stukas struck the battle formations of the advancing Soviet rifle divisions from morning to night. Supply lines, through which reinforcements and ammunition for the Soviet strike group were delivered, were destroyed from the air. For example, on 2 September 1942, the Soviet 140th Rifle Brigade suffered heavy losses from air attacks by Ju 87s. German dive bombers, in the complete absence of counteraction from the ground, systematically bombed the positions of this unit. The Soviet 4th Guards Rifle Corps, advancing south of Sinyavino, was also constantly subjected to German bombing and shelling from the air.

The Soviet troops suffered huge losses from the Luftwaffe strikes. For example, the 3rd Guards Rifle Division lost 5,344 men from 27 August to 8 September 1942, after which only 379 soldiers remained in it. The 191st Rifle Division lost 2,307 troops, and only 1,835 soldiers remained in it. The 53rd Separate Rifle Brigade lost 2,379 men in ten days, as well as most of the horses and trucks. The 259th Rifle Division lost 4,444 soldiers (including 295 officers), and only 24 per cent of its personnel survived. In the 137th Separate Rifle Brigade, after heavy fighting, there were only seventy-nine Red Army troops! Soviet tank units also suffered heavy losses, and just fifteen remained in the 16th Tank Brigade, and there were only two T-70 light tanks left in the 98th Tank Brigade.[179] Most of these losses were related to air attacks. As a result, on 3 September, due to the constant threat of Luftwaffe bombing, Soviet divisions were forced to carry out all movements only at night.

After such fatal losses, no reasonable commander could think of a further offensive. However, as will be described below, Stalin held the opposite point of view.

'The operation to force the Neva river to be temporarily stopped!'

Bloody Stalin did not want to accept the obvious defeat. On his instructions, the Leningrad Front and Volkhov Front ordered a new 'general' offensive for 9 September 1942. During the regrouping of thoroughly battered divisions, much attention was paid to the psychological treatment of soldiers. Streams of false propaganda had descended on the Red Army survivors. Rallies and party meetings were held in Soviet combat units. Pretentious appeals were spreading for troops to gather the courage and finally break the ring of the Leningrad land blockade. In the encircled city, Soviet soldiers were also addressed with an appeal: 'Comrades Red Army men! The hour of decisive action has come to liberate Leningrad from the enemy blockade. The battle we are going up to today should bring us victory and serve as the beginning of the defeat of the hated Hitler's hordes near Leningrad.'[180]

Reinforcements were urgently delivered to reinforce the divisions storming Sinyavino Hills. By order of Stalin, the Soviet 2nd Shock Army was introduced into the battle. Regardless of the losses, Red Army men attacked the German positions again. However, by this point, the German troops in Mga and Sinyavino areas had also strengthened significantly. Russians met fierce resistance everywhere. German heavy artillery began a systematic shelling of the forest captured by the enemy. The Luftwaffe also constantly attacked the advancing Soviet troops. On 12 September, the headquarters of the Volkhov Front reported: 'The advancing Red Army units were under the continuous influence of enemy aircraft.' The next day, the 2nd Shock Army headquarters complained to the higher command: 'Army units were subjected to massive

---

179. TSAMO RF. Foundation 344. Inventory 5554. Case 402. Sheets 302–303.
180. *The blockade of Leningrad in the documents of declassified archives*, Moscow: AST, 2004, p.536.

artillery and mortar attacks, as well as constant air attacks by bombers and ground-attack aircraft.' The critical situation was complicated by the traditional criminally inadequate supply of materiel Red Army troops. Many Russian units were left without ammunition at the crucial moment. Rifle regiments borrowed boxes of ammunition and shells from 'neighbours'! The shortage of supplies forced Soviet aircraft to drop bags of ammunition to its troops from the air.[181]

In the dark, the advanced units of the 2nd Shock Army clearly saw the glow over the horizon and heard the roar of artillery cannonade on the Neva from Leningrad. The Nevsky Group of Troops tried to attack there. However, the 2nd Shock Army units were not able to overcome the small area of swampy terrain that separated them from the city blockaded by the Germans.

The same situation was found to the west of Leningrad. On 9 September, at 16.00, two rifle divisions from the Nevsky Group of Troops began another ferrying attempt across the Neva. The Germans responded by opening a hurricane of mortar and artillery fire on the Russian crossings. As a result, only fifty men reached the eastern bank. The second attempt, made early in the morning on 10 September, also failed. All the landing boats and rafts were sunk by the Germans along with the Red Army fighters. However, Stalin's commanders continued to drive soldiers to their slaughter.

On 11 September, at 04.30, the troops of the Nevsky Group of Troops again tried to cross the river. This time, separate groups of Red Army soldiers managed to cross the river around the villages of Annenskoe and Moskovskaya Dubrovka. However, at 08.00, the Germans counter-attacked the positions of the surviving Soviet soldiers and forced them to flee across the river again. Only thirty-five men reached the west bank of the Neva. In these three days alone, two hundred pontoons and thirty boats had gone to the bottom of the Neva! The banks of the river were littered with the corpses of Red Army soldiers in several layers.

On the morning of 12 September, angered by the failure of the offensive, Stalin signed a directive:

> Since Leningrad Front proved unable to intelligently organise the crossing of the Neva River and stupidly ruined a large number of commanders and Red Army men with its inept actions, Headquarters of the Supreme High Command ordered the operation to force the Neva River to be temporarily terminated.[182]

---

181. TSAMO RF. Foundation 204. Inventory 89. Case 181. Sheets 16–18.
182. TSAMO RF. Foundation 3. Inventory 11556. Case 10. Sheet 23.

The response of Generalfeldmarschall Erich von Manstein

After the Soviets halted their offensive, it was the turn of Generalfeldmarschall Erich von Manstein and his 11th Army to show their might. Heavy artillery was delivered to the battle area (Sinyavino and Mga settlements) that had been previously intended for the Leningrad assault (about 500 large-calibre artillery guns in total). When heavy artillery was deployed, the Germans began an incredible bombardment of Soviet positions. Hs 126 tactical reconnaissance aircraft circled above the forest at high altitude. The aerial observers radioed the German gunners the coordinates of the targets and the results of hits. To protect against Russian fighters, Bf 109 fighter pairs constantly circled the slow-moving Hs 126s. Thanks to the activity of the artillery spotting planes, the shells hit their targets with great accuracy.

Along with the massive shelling of heavy artillery, Luftwaffe units were again involved in the destruction of Soviet troops. During this period, bombers and Stukas from I. Fliegerkorps carried out four hundred sorties a day. They attacked both the advanced positions of the Soviets and the rear areas near the bulge formed as a result of Soviet attacks. The actions of Luftwaffe aircraft significantly hampered the transfer of reserves and the regrouping of Soviet troops. Generalfeldmarschall Erich von Manstein recalled:

> After the concentration of the remaining divisions of the army that had arrived by this time, we could launch a decisive offensive. The counteroffensive was organised from the north and from the south, from the strongholds of the surviving front, in order to cut off the enemy's wedged troops right at the base of the wedge.[183]

Then the Germans carried out a classic operation to encircle the Soviet troops who broke through the front. As a result of these actions, on 21 September 1942, most of the troops of the Soviet 2nd Shock Army were cut off from the main forces. The resulting pocket was located between Sinyavino and Gaitolovo settlements. The Commander of the Volkhov Front, General of the Army Kirill Meretskov hid from Stalin the true state of affairs in this sector of the front. He well knew what NKVD executioners were doing to the generals who had angered the Red Tsar. Therefore, General Meretskov, in correspondence with Stalin, tried to create the appearance that the operation to break the blockade of Leningrad was still going according to plan. Keeping silent about the position

---

183. Manstein, E., *Lost Victories*, Smolensk: Rusich, 1999, p.314.

THIRD SINYAVINO MEAT GRINDER

of the 2nd Shock Army, he complained to the Red Tsar about the lack of tanks and the inability to use bombers due to the lack of fighters.

During this period, the Luftwaffe completely dominated the air, inflicting continuous blows on the resulting pocket. On 25 September, the 2nd Shock Army headquarters reported: 'Enemy aircraft bomb artillery firing positions, command posts, combat positions and army communications all day.' On 26 September, Germany dropped airborne troops from Ju 52 aircraft in the forest west of Gaitolovo village.

Additional problems for the Soviets were created by the German heavy artillery, which fired day and night. Generalfeldmarschall von Manstein wrote: 'Thanks to this shooting, the forest area in a few days was turned into a field pitted with craters, on which only the remains of the trunks of once proud giant trees were visible.'[184]

On 28 September, from the east, the Red Army launched an attack on German positions with the forces of two rifle divisions and nine tanks in order to unlock the pocket. A combined group of soldiers from the 19th Guards Rifle Division, 294th Rifle Division and 33rd Separate Rifle Brigade attacked the German troops from the west. However, almost all the Soviet tanks were immediately destroyed. Then the German heavy artillery opened a powerful fire on the attacking troops. The total defeat of the Soviets was completed by the Stukas that appeared over the battlefield in the afternoon. It was only due to the fact that the German forces were limited and there was no solid front line that on 29–30 September some of the soldiers from the 2nd Shock Army and the 8th Army were able to get out of the encirclement. Separate scattered groups of Red Army troops continued to seep out of the encirclement through the swamps and peatlands for another two days.

On 2 October 1942, the Third Sinyavino meat grinder ended. In the area between Mga settlement and Gaitolovo village, the Germans destroyed seven Soviet rifle divisions, six separate rifle brigades and four tank brigades. Twelve thousand Red Army troops were captured by the Germans. This meant that Stalin's plans to break through the Leningrad land blockade had once again failed. The Red Army had paid a very high price for the incompetence of its command. On 10 September 1942, the 2nd Shock Army consisted of 55,000 men, 7,332 horses, 1,205 vehicles, 574 artillery pieces and 128 tanks. By October 1, 1942, these figures had decreased to 34,000 men, 6,785 horses, 511 vehicles, 321 artillery pieces and 12 tanks.[185]

---

184. Ibid., p.318.
185. TSAMO RF. Foundation 204. Inventory 89. Case 181. Sheets 51, 54.

AIR BATTLE FOR LENINGRAD, 1941–1944

By 5 October, the Soviet troops who were trying to break through the corridor from Leningrad and join the main forces were in a similar state of complete defeat. Despite the steadfastness and self-sacrifice, the Nevsky Group of Troops units repeated all the mistakes of their comrades from the Volkhov Front divisions. On 26 September 1942, after a two-week lull and after receiving reinforcements, the Russians launched another offensive from Leningrad. Separate units of Red Army troops managed to get ferried to the eastern bank of the Neva. However, their further progress was hampered by continuous Luftwaffe air attacks. As a result, the units of the Nevsky Group of Troops suffered heavy losses and fought in separate groups. Red Army soldiers managed to hold a small bridgehead on the eastern bank of the Neva for almost ten days, waiting for reinforcements. However, after the final defeat of the 2nd Shock Army, this heroism lost all meaning. On 5 October 1942, permission was given to evacuate the remnants of the Soviet troops from the eastern bank.

After the failure of the Leningrad plan to break the blockade, the search for those responsible for the failure in the management of the troops began in Moscow. Stalin believed that incompetent fools, the commanders of the Soviet fronts (General of the Army Kirill Meretskov and Colonel General Leonid Govorov) were to blame for the collapse of the offensive. Naturally, he himself did not take responsibility for the heavy defeat in the autumn of 1942.

Soviet aviation losses

In the battles of the autumn of 1942, the Red Army Air Force also suffered a heavy defeat. As an example, the combat path of the 279th Fighter Aviation Division (279th IAD) under Colonel Fyodor Dementiev can be cited. This aviation division was formed at the end of August 1942. The 279th IAD included the 283rd Fighter Aviation Regiment (283rd IAP) and the 845th Fighter Aviation Regiment (845th IAP). Despite this externally impressive composition, there were only thirteen Yak-7 fighters in the aviation division. In 1942, after the defeat of Soviet aviation in the first year of the war, the regular number of aircraft in fighter aviation regiments was reduced by more than half and amounted to twenty aircraft and twenty pilots. But due to the high losses and the insufficient production volumes of fighters, even such greatly reduced complements could not be staffed. Often at that time there were only two or three combat-ready fighters in an aviation regiment.

On 27 August 1942, on the first day of aerial combat over the Third Sinyavino meat grinder, the 279th IAD lost four fighters. One plane was accidentally shot down by Russian anti-aircraft artillery. Two fighters collided in the air and crashed. One fighter was missing. The next day, on 28 August, fighters from the

THIRD SINYAVINO MEAT GRINDER

279th IAD covered their troops in the Sinyavino settlement area. To implement this mission, they carried out thirty sorties and suffered one loss. In a dogfight with German fighters, Lieutenant Eliseev's Yak-7 No. 1631 was shot down and was killed.[186]

On 29 August at 11.24 three Yak-7 fighters from the 283rd IAP flew to intercept German Ju 88 bombers. However, this mission ended in a complete fiasco, and because of friendly fire. Two of the three fighters were immediately shot down by Russian anti-aircraft artillery. Their pilots, political commissar Fedulov and Senior Sergeant Lukyanenko, took to their parachutes but received severe injuries. Frightened by the Luftwaffe strikes and poorly trained, Soviet anti-aircraft gunners fired at all air targets they spotted. Another Yak-7 was shot down in a dogfight and its pilot Senior Lieutenant Ryabenko was killed. On the same day, the 279th IAD suffered another loss. After carrying out a combat mission to intercept German bombers, Yak-7 No. 1901 flown by Senior Lieutenant Prokofiev went missing.[187]

The next three days passed safely for the 279th IAD. However, on 2 September 1942, this unit suffered losses again. On their way to escort Il-2 ground-attack aircraft to the Mga settlement area, Yak-7 No. 1856 flown by Senior Sergeant Suvorov went missing. Yak-7 No. 82401 of Captain Bendyug was also heavily damaged (the rudder was broken and there were large holes in the wings). The pilot made an emergency wheels-up landing. On the same day, the battered 845th IAP received six new fighters to make up for losses.[188]

On 3 September, the 845th IAP carried out twenty-nine sorties and lost three aircraft. German fighters shot down Yak-7 No. 82324 flown by political commissar Kolesnikov, Yak-7 No. 2788 of Sergeant Rumyantsev and Yak-7 No. 1930 of Sergeant Krasnoperov. Their pilots survived.[189]

On 6 September, after an air battle in the area of Sinyavino settlement, Yak-7 No. 1914 flown by Sergeant Korolev was damaged on landing. 'Stalin's Falcon' Sergeant Korolev was not injured.[190]

The reason for such large losses of Soviet aircraft was the dominance of German fighters in the sky over the battle area. As already described above, German bombers constantly attacked the positions of the 2nd Shock Army. German fighters covering them stopped any attempts by Russian fighters to prevent the bombing.

---

186. TSAMO RF. Foundation 20249. Inventory 1. Case 5. Sheet 6.
187. Ibid., Sheet 8.
188. Ibid., Sheet 11.
189. Ibid., Sheet 11.
190. Ibid., Sheet 13.

AIR BATTLE FOR LENINGRAD, 1941–1944

With each passing day, the losses of Russian fighters continued to increase. On 8 September, during a dogfight with Bf 109s from JG 54, Yak-7 No. 3188 piloted by Lieutenant Grishchenko and Yak-7 No. 1688 of Sergeant Rumyantsev were shot down. Lieutenant Grishchenko escaped by parachute but Sergeant Rumyantsev died.[191]

On 9 September, fighters from the 279th IAD carried out only thirteen sorties and again lost three aircraft. Two pilots were missing: Captain Bendyug, in a Yak-7, and Senior Sergeant Moskaleva from the 283rd IAP. The Yak-7 of Lieutenant Chebotarev from the 845th IAP made an emergency landing on Russian territory. On the same day, the 845th IAP received several American Bell P-39 Airacobra fighters as replenishments, which immediately took part in air battles.[192]

On 10 September, fighters from the 279th IAD carried out thirty-one sorties and lost two aircraft. P-39 'AN-715' of Junior Lieutenant Yeremeyev was shot down in a dogfight and the pilot was killed. On the same day, Yak-7 No. 2536 flown by Junior Lieutenant Usenko went missing.

The next day on 11 September, Yak-7 No. 3557 of Senior Sergeant Ivanova and a Yak-7 piloted by Senior Sergeant Ratnikova went missing. The Yak-7 of Senior Sergeant Khovaev was shot down in a dogfight with German fighters; the pilot survived by parachute.[193]

On 12 September, the 279th IAD suffered heavy losses. Despite having completed only six sorties, it lost four Yak-7s. Two fighters were shot down in dogfights, one was destroyed by German anti-aircraft artillery and another was missing. After such losses, the drained 279th IAD was able to carry out only a minimal number of sorties. However, 'Stalin's Falcons' continued to suffer losses.[194]

On 14 September, Yak-7 No. 2006 flown by Sergeant Zhuravlev was shot down; the pilot survived by parachute.[195]

Just two days later, Sergeant Zhuravlev was again shot down, in Yak-7 No. 2540, in combat with a Bf 109. This time he was unable to leave the burning plane and died. The fighter of his comrade, Lieutenant Zaitsev, was also damaged in a dogfight with German fighters and made an emergency landing on Soviet territory.[196]

On 20 September, 'Stalin's Falcons' from the 279th IAD again suffered heavy losses. In air battles, Yak-7 No. 2138 piloted by Senior Sergeant Khovaev

---

191. Ibid., Sheet 13.
192. Ibid., Sheet 14.
193. Ibid., Sheet 15.
194. Ibid., Sheet 17.
195. Ibid., Sheet 18.
196. Ibid., Sheet 19.

THIRD SINYAVINO MEAT GRINDER

and P-39 'AN-301' flown by Junior Lieutenant Khlevny were shot down. Khovaev survived again but Khlevny died. Another P-39 from the 279th IAD went missing.[197]

On 22 September, pilots from the 279th IAD completed only five sorties, but again suffered losses. In a dogfight with Bf 109s, Captain Varlashin's Yak-7 from the 845th IAP was shot down and the pilot was killed. On that day, the almost completely destroyed 279th IAD was suspended from participating in the battle for Sinyavino.[198]

The 279th Fighter Aviation Division (279th IAD), which had thirteen fighters at the beginning of the battle, lost thirty-six aircraft during twenty-seven days of participation in combat operations. Thus, the losses were three times higher than the initial number of fighters in the division. The losses of pilots from the 279th IAD also turned out to be very significant. Seventeen pilots were killed and missing in dogfights with German fighters, while several more were seriously injured.

A similar sad fate befell fighter pilots from the 524th Fighter Aviation Regiment (524th IAP) under Major Ivan Lakeev. Until August 1942, this regiment was based on the southern bank of the River Svir and for a long time fought with the Finnish aviation. The Finnish front was a kind of 'resort' for 'Stalin's Falcons'. The qualifications of Finnish pilots and the combat qualities of Finnish fighters were significantly inferior to the Germans, so the Russian pilots felt relatively safe there. However, the transfer of the regiment to support the Russian offensive in the Sinyavino area meant the end of their relatively safe life.

On 8 September, the 524th IAP relocated to Vyachkovo airfield. At that time, the 524th IAP had eleven combat-ready fighters (six LaGG-3s and five Yak-1s). The next day, the regiment carried out the first missions to escort Pe-2 bombers to the Sinyavino area. In air battles the next day, LaGG-3 No. 3121874 of Lieutenant Soshin and LaGG-3 No. 31211079 of Senior Lieutenant Reshetikhin were shot down. Both pilots were missing. The first losses of fighters from the 524th IAP were more convincing proof of German air supremacy over the battle area.[199]

On 10 September, pilots from the 524th IAP reported two aerial victories over Bf 109s. Its own losses amounted to one LaGG-3, No. 3121819 flown by Captain Shumilov. The pilot survived by parachute.[200]

---

197. Ibid., Sheet 20.
198. Ibid., Sheet 21.
199. TSAMO RF. Foundation 22753. Inventory 0105884s. Case 0004. Sheet 51.
200. Ibid., Sheet 52.

On 11 September, while escorting Il-2s, Yak-1 No. 3834 flown by Senior political commissar Pomkov went missing. On 14 and 16 September, the 524th IAP lost two more aircraft. Also, several fighters were unable to fly for technical reasons. As a result, by 17 September, only two combat-ready fighters remained in the 524th Fighter Aviation Regiment. After that, the 524th IAP began to operate in conjunction with the 92nd Fighter Aviation Regiment (92nd IAP), which also had two fighters left. Despite such a small number of surviving pilots and combat-ready fighters, losses continued to mount up.[201]

On 21 September 1942, LaGG-3 No. 312186 of Lieutenant Colonel Oleinichenko was shot down in an air battle; the pilot was reported missing.[202]

On 25 September, two fighters from the 524th IAP covered their troops and attacked German Ju 88 bombers, shooting down one of them. After that, Captain Remizov's Yak-1 was attacked by Bf 109s and was shot down; the pilot survived by parachute.[203]

After the complete exhaustion of forces, the 524th IAP was withdrawn from the battle. In total, from 9 to 25 September 1942, the pilots of the 524th IAP carried out 115 sorties. During this period, the losses of the regiment amounted to eight aircraft and four pilots.

Russian ground-attack aviation regulations also suffered heavy losses. For example, the 872nd Ground-attack Aviation Regiment (872nd SHAP) numbered thirteen Il-2 ground-attack aircraft by 27 August 1942. During three weeks of fighting in the Sinyavino settlement area, eleven planes were shot down. Nine ground-attack aircraft were victims of German fighters from JG 54. Eight Soviet pilots from the 872nd SHAP were killed and posted missing. As a result, by 18 September, the 872nd SHAP had completely lost its combat capability. These facts clearly show the scale of the disaster that befell the Soviet Air Force during this brutal battle.

Luftwaffe losses in the third Sinyavino meat grinder

The losses of the opposing side during the battle in the Sinyavino and Mga area are easy to analyse using the example of Jagdgeschwader 54 'Grünherz' (JG 54).

On 3 September Bf 109 G-2 W.Nr. 10444 'Gelbe 8' flown by Feldwebel Karl Klopp of 6./JG 54 was shot down in a dogfight over the Neva; the pilot was

---

201. Ibid., Sheet 53.
202. Ibid., Sheet 68.
203. Ibid., Sheet 72.

reported missing. On the same day, Bf 109 G-2 W.Nr. 10430 'Weisse 6', flown by Gefreiter Eduard Langwenings over Lake Ladoga, collided with a Ju 88 A-4 from KG 1 (this was covered in detail above).

On 4 September, Bf 109 G-2 W.Nr. 10455 'Weisse 7' was shot down in a dogfight near Sinyavino. Unteroffizier Heinz Joneleit of 4./JG 54 was killed.

On 5 September, Bf 109 G-2 W.Nr. 10432 'Schwarze 4' was shot down in an dogfight near the village of Moskovskaya Dubrovka (south-east of Leningrad). Unteroffizier Johannes Schubert from 8./JG 54 was captured by the Russians.

The remaining losses of JG 54 were directly caused by pilot error and were only indirectly related to the performance of combat missions. On 21 September during a dogfight over Sinyavino Bf 109 G-2 W.Nr. 10405 'Schwarze' of Oberfeldwebel Erwin Siegert from 8./JG 54 collided with a Pe-2 bomber flown by Senior Lieutenant Alexei Lynchevsky from the 4th Guards Bomber Aviation Regiment (4th GBAP). Oberfeldwebel Siegert made an emergency landing on German territory, but died in the resulting fire. Only one person escaped from the crew of the Soviet bomber.

On 25 September, at the German Relbicy airfield (near Novgorod), Bf 109 G-2 W.Nr. 10454 'Weisse' piloted by 'master' Oberleutnant Berndt Schulten from Stab/JG 54 collided with the Bf 109 of his wingman, Feldwebel Heinrich Wefers. Oberleutnant Schulten was killed in the crash.

In total, in September 1942, JG 54 lost just six fighters. Moreover, only three of them were shot down in aerial battles on the outskirts of Leningrad. Thus, the losses of professionals from the Luftwaffe turned out to be several times less than those of incompetent and inexperienced 'Stalin's Falcons'.

Chapter 12

Operation Brazil

New Luftwaffe attacks against Soviet communications at Lake Ladoga

In addition to supporting German troops in the battle for Sinyavino, Luftflotte 1 bombers continued to strike at infrastructure facilities and ships transporting cargo across Lake Ladoga for the blockaded Leningrad and Leningrad Front troops. During September 1942, the Luftwaffe bombed Voibokalo railway station twenty-two times and attacked Volkhovstroy railway junction ten times. In addition, German aircraft carried out five bombing attacks on Kobona harbour, Gostinopolye station and harbour and one air attack on Tikhvin station. As a result of the German bombing, large traffic jams occurred on many sections of the railway. A significant part of the military cargo and troops did not reach the front during the decisive battles.

The Germans also carried out seven air attacks against Russian convoys on Lake Ladoga. The greatest success was the sinking of the tugboat *Uzbekistan* on 6 September 1942 in which Captain Mikhail Pashiev and ten others from the crew died. The tugboat's valuable towed railway ferry also sank and its skipper, Popov, was killed. On the same day, Luftwaffe planes severely damaged the tugboat *Podolsk*.[204]

On 30 September, the minesweeper *TSCH-126*, which was on patrol, was attacked by four Bf 109 Fs, during which the bridge was riddled with bullets. The commander of the ship, Senior Lieutenant Vasily Oreshko, and chief mate Senior Lieutenant Boris Petrovsky were killed. The surviving Soviet sailors fired desperately from machine guns and a single 45mm anti-aircraft gun. The rate of fire and accuracy of firing from this weapon was very low. The shells exploded far away from the German planes, causing them no harm. German fighters repeated their attacks several times with impunity, shooting *TSCH-126*

---

204. The blockade of Leningrad in the documents of declassified archives, Moscow: AST, 2004, p.309.

with cannon and machine guns. As a result, the ship received numerous holes and a fire broke out in the interior. However, the surviving sailors managed to extinguish the fire and took the heavily damaged vessel to its base. In total, four people were killed on the ship and nine others were injured.[205]

As already noted above, without the support of the German land forces, the Luftwaffe could not interrupt or even significantly disrupt Soviet communications passing through Lake Ladoga. However, the active actions of Luftflotte 1 still brought some results. In September 1942, the total volume of cargo transported to the western shore of Lake Ladoga amounted to 137,000 tons. Thus, in comparison with August 1942, the volume of goods delivered to Leningrad decreased somewhat. The Soviets finally felt the power of the Luftwaffe and took a number of organisational measures to reduce the damage from enemy attacks from the air. The unwieldy Stalinist bureaucratic apparatus finally began to act. On 19 September, the Military Council of the Leningrad Front demanded that the Head of the Transportation Department, the Commander of the Ladoga Military Flotilla and the Head of the North-Western Shipping Company do everything to ensure the smooth operation of movement of cargoes on Lake Ladoga. This formidable order of the authorities was carried out very slowly. It was only by the end of the 1942 navigation that the accumulation of transport vessels on the western shore of the lake was finally prohibited. Traffic along the small route (Kobona–Osinovets) was organised in such a way that it arrived in Osinovets harbour at night.

The first battle of the Siebel ferries

In contrast to the effective actions of the bombers, the successes of the Axis flotilla turned out to be much more modest. In September 1942, Italian torpedo boats completed seventeen patrol missions. They attacked Soviet convoys moving across Lake Ladoga several times, but were unable to achieve any significant results. For example, on 29 September, in the Severnaya Goloveshka bank area, two torpedo boats attacked a Russian convoy that consisted of several tugboats pulling barges. However, the torpedo fired by the Italians did not hit the target. The reason for such a failure was very banal: Russian vessels moved mainly in shallow water, while Italian torpedoes could only be used at depths of at least 20m.

The actions of the German mine boats were also not very effective. On 20 August 1942, the first mines were loaded onto them and tests began on

---

205. Cherokov, V.S., *For You, Leningrad!*, Leningrad: Leninzdat, 1988, pp.111–112.

minelaying Russian transport routes. The tests ended in a crushing failure, after which all four mine boats had to be sent back to dry dock for repairs. After a long repair, the German vessels again began to prepare for missions on minelaying the lake. On 9 September, three mine boats – *KM 3*, *KM 4* and *KM 22* – were ready to leave for Lake Ladoga. However, only on 29 September, were they able to install the first twelve bottom mines north of Kobona harbour. Four more minelaying missions were planned, but all of them were cancelled due to technical malfunctions of mine boats or bad weather conditions.

Siebel ferries made two missions after a one-month break (on the nights of 26–27 September and 28–29 September). Both voyages on Lake Ladoga ended in failure for the Germans.

On the evening of 30 September, Siebel ferries set off again to carry out a mission to search for and destroy Soviet ships. After leaving different bases, separate groups of ferries joined into a single formation and headed to the southern part of the lake. There they first encountered the ships of the Russian Ladoga Military Flotilla.

The German combat report reported:

> On October 1 at 02.10 flotilla Siebel ferries found enemy ships in the 1167M square. Our position at that moment was 1164M square. At 02.25 we opened fire from a distance of 4,500 metres at a ship identified as a gunboat, which was 10° ahead on the starboard side and was heading south-west. A short time later, gunboat responded by firing about 40 large-calibre shells. One ship with guns of about 76mm calibre entered the battle from the enemy from the south-eastern and south-western directions, and then about ten more patrol boats with 45mm anti-aircraft guns. Russian patrol boats moved around flotilla from the south-east and fired from the dark horizon (the moon was in the south-east at that time).

In the description of Commander of the Ladoga Military Flotilla Captain 1st rank Vasily Cherokov, the battle looked like this:

> On the night of October 1, the sailors of the gunboat *Nora*, following as part of the convoy, heard the noise of engines in the area of Severnaya Goloveshka bank. A combat alert was declared. Soon seventeen silhouettes of some ships appeared. We made a request, but there was no response. Gunboat opened fire on the ships. The enemy responded with volleys of guns and bursts of automatic anti-aircraft guns. A German plane appeared over the

gunboat *Nora* and dropped photoflash bombs. Enemy ships also spotted the submarine chaser *MO-262* under the command of Senior Lieutenant Mikhail Kudryavtsev. At this point, *MO-262* was north of the big route (Novaya Ladoga–Osinovets). The submarine chaser followed a parallel course, and the commander reported: 'Found four landing barges and thirteen torpedo boats of the enemy.' For five minutes, the submarine chaser *MO-262* fired at the enemy, but then returned to the patrol area.[206]

If the opposing sides' descriptions of the beginning of the lake battle looks almost identical, the endings are very different. According to the Commander of the Ladoga Military Flotilla, Captain 1st rank Vasily Cherokov, he sent Beriev MBR-2 flying boats and torpedo boats into action. However, the flying boats turned out to be too slow, and the torpedo boats organised the search for the enemy poorly. Cherokov did not mention the further actions of the gunboat *Nora* at all. The reason for such modesty in the description of the battle is obvious when studying the records of the German side.

According to German data, at 02.50 *Nora* withdrew from the battle, hiding behind a smokescreen. After that, the Ladoga flotilla of the Axis powers, having made a sharp turn to starboard, began searching for other Soviet ships. A German report reports:

> Attempts to locate the enemy by firing lighting projectiles led to the conclusion that the entire enemy group in the west disappeared behind a smokescreen. At 03.30 flotilla set a course of 250° and at 04.00 turned to the base. From the fact that the enemy withdrew from the battle under the protection of a smokescreen, it can be concluded that the flotilla artillery fire was accurate. There were no losses on our side.

The first battle involving Siebel ferries showed that German ships armed with long-range artillery could successfully fight the largest ships of the Ladoga Military Flotilla – gunboats which the Russians proudly called 'Ladoga battleships'. However, the Germans clearly did not have sufficient time to get enough experience for fighting in Lake Ladoga conditions. The deployment of the flotilla was so delayed that Siebel ferries were only ready for combat operations in September 1942, when the most favourable period for sailing on the lake was nearing the end.

---

206. Cherokov, V.S., For You, Leningrad!, Leningrad: Leninzdat, 1988, p.120.

AIR BATTLE FOR LENINGRAD, 1941–1944

The first attempts to implement Operation Brazil

The fact that the Ladoga flotilla of the Axis powers had not yet achieved any success worried the German command. Soon 'Eastern Ferry Operations Staff' (Einsatzstab Fähre Ost) received an order to activate operations on the lake. In early October 1942, the Luftwaffe decided to conduct a major operation on the lake under the code name Brazil. Its goal was to destroy the Soviet three-gun 100mm coastal artillery battery and lighthouse on Sukho Island. There was a garrison of ninety Soviet sailors on the island under the command of Senior Lieutenant Ivan Gusev. Sukho Island was located 35km north-west of Novaya Ladoga harbour and was important for the operation of the big route (transport route between ports Novaya Ladoga and Osinovets).

Sukho Island was of artificial origin and was a tiny piece of land measuring 90 by 60m. In the eighteenth century, the Russians brought stony soil to a small shoal. Gradually, the shoal turned into an island sticking out in the middle of the lake. Later, a lighthouse was built on it, which facilitated navigation in the southern part of Lake Ladoga.

On 9 October, the Axis flotilla sailed to Sukho Island as part of an attack force of twenty Siebel ferries (twelve artillery ferries, six transport ferries, one staff ferry and one hospital ferry), three Italian torpedo boats MAS, two mine boats KM and three landing boats. A total of twenty-eight warships took part. However, bad weather and errors in navigation led to the situation that by dawn the flotilla was still far from the island. The element of surprise was lost, and the Ladoga flotilla decided to return to its base.[207] However, on the way back the Germans and Italians unexpectedly encountered Soviet submarine chasers.

On the evening of 8 October, on the eve of the events described above, three groups of Soviet submarine chasers left Morier harbour and entered Lake Ladoga. Their mission was to search for and destroy Italian torpedo boats. Throughout the night, a group consisting of submarine chasers *MO-175*, commanded by Lieutenant Pustynnikov, and *MO-214*, under Lieutenant Bogdanov, patrolled off the southern part of Konevec island. This island is located on the western shore of the lake opposite Sortanlahti Bay. The Soviet command assumed that the Italian torpedo boats were based there. At dawn, having found no one, the Russian submarine chasers left the Konevec island area and headed east at low speed into the open part of the lake. There they planned to be on patrol until nightfall.

---

207. Keskinen, K., Stenman, K., *German Aircraft in Finland 1939–1945*, Apali Oy, Finland, 1998, p.109.

OPERATION BRAZIL

At 06.45, on the right, the silhouettes of two boats suddenly appeared out of the fog, coming towards them at high speed. Having decided that the Italians were in front of them, the Soviet sailors presumptuously decided to give them a fight and rushed to the attack. How big was the surprise of the crews of the Soviet submarine chasers when the fog cleared and they saw a whole enemy flotilla in front of them!

The commander of the submarine chasers detachment, Senior Lieutenant Alexander Miklashevsky, gave the command to open fire. At the same time, a message was sent over the radio to the headquarters in plain text: 'We have engaged in battle with superior enemy forces!' After that, *MO-214* began to put up a smokescreen, and *MO-175* began firing at the enemy from two 45mm guns. Miklashevsky later recalled:

> The first large-calibre shell from the head Siebel ferry hit the chart room. The blast wave threw me off the bridge. Overcoming the pain of bleeding wounds, I struggled back up to the bridge. I saw that the commander of the submarine chaser Lieutenant Pustynnikov was lying dead by the broken main compass. He was the favourite of the entire division.
>
> From the bridge, I saw how the sailors, despite the shells bursting around, fired from cannon and machine guns. One of the German shells hit the aft compartment. A fire broke out. The steering of the submarine chaser had failed. Mechanic Alexander Radostnev and helmsman Skalsky tried to do something to preserve the survivability of the ship, but all to no avail. The submarine chaser abruptly slowed down and began to dive into the water.[208]

MO-175 soon sank. The Germans rescued nine Soviet sailors from the water, including Senior Lieutenant Miklashevsky. Since radio communication with the ship was interrupted after the announcement of the engagement, the crew of the submarine chaser was considered dead at the headquarters of Ladoga Military Flotilla.

On 12 October, a second attempt was made to implement Operation Brazil. However, this time, due to bad weather, fog and navigation errors, the Ladoga flotilla attack on Sukho Island was postponed again. The Germans began to prepare the third attempt of Operation Brazil.

---

208. Rusakov, Z.G., *Our Sea was Ladoga*, Leningrad.: Lenizdat, 1980, p.97.

The battle of Sukho Island

On the evening of 21 October 1942, nineteen Siebel ferries left the ports of Kakisalmi and Taivallahti, on the western shore of Lake Ladoga. This was the Siebel ferries' ninth combat trip to the southern part of the lake. The flotilla consisted of twenty-seven ships:

- seven Siebel ferries with 88mm guns;
- four Siebel ferries with light anti-aircraft artillery (Nos. *12*, *14*, *22* and *26*);
- three Siebel ferries (*T2*, *T4* and *T6*) with seventy infantrymen on board;
- one Siebel ferry headquarters (Oberstleutnant Wachtel was on it);
- one hospital Siebel ferry;
- seven landing boats, five of which were intended for landing;
- one Italian torpedo boat, *MAS-526*.

This time, thanks to the rain, which sometimes turned into snow, the Ladoga flotilla approached Sukho Island unnoticed at the scheduled time. On the island, the Soviets did not expect an attack. Due to the thick fog and snow, visibility around Sukho Island did not exceed tens of metres. After waking up, the garrison was preparing for breakfast. Navigation on the lake was coming to an end, winter was approaching.

Suddenly, the distant noise of engines was heard and the lookout on duty reported this to the commander of the Soviet artillery battery. At the command post, it was decided that the noise had come from a friendly transport caravan that was heading to Novaya Ladoga. But after a few minutes there was an ominous whistle of a flying projectile. At 06.15 (Moscow time), the 88mm Siebel ferries guns opened fire on the island from a distance of 7,500m. A few metres from the shore, a column of water rose. Soon the Luftwaffe gunners adjusted their aiming and shells began to explode among the rocks of the island. A direct hit destroyed the coastal artillery battery command post and soon the lighthouse was ablaze. The first Soviet victim was the head of the observation and communication post, Starshina (non-commissioned officer) Lysov, whose head was torn off by a shell fragment. The shells accurately aimed by the German gunners smashed the rangefinding telemeter and destroyed the radio station and the radio antenna of the surveillance and communications service. Telephone communication with combat posts in different parts of the island was interrupted.[209] However, the most terrible consequence of the accurate shooting of the Luftwaffe gunners was to deprive the Soviet garrison on Sukho Island with radio communication with the coast and ships.

It seemed to the Germans that the operation was developing successfully. However, soon the first problems began to appear. Siebel ferry *No. 11*, which was on the left flank of the battle formation of the German ships, touched bottom and had to change course. By this time, the Soviet gunners were coping with the confusion caused by the sudden appearance of the Germans. Soon, the Russian 100mm coastal artillery battery returned fire. Now water columns began to rise among the Siebel ferries.

Sometime later, two ships were spotted by observers from Siebel ferries in the south, and a little later four more ships. The Germans identified them as two Russian gunboats and four patrol boats and opened fire on them. However, the observers on the Siebel ferries were wrong. In reality, the ships were the minesweeper *TSCH-100*, commanded by Senior Lieutenant P.K. Kargin, and submarine chaser *MO-171*, under Senior Lieutenant V. Kovalevsky. A message was transmitted in clear text by a minesweeper to the Ladoga Military Flotilla headquarters over the radio about the battle taking place around the island: 'Attention! There is an enemy fleet operating near Sukho Island!'

At 06.48, according to the Operation Brazil plan, German planes appeared in the sky. These were nine Ju 88 A dive bombers from KG 1 and they struck at Sukho Island. The island was covered with smoke from bomb explosions, and the surviving Soviet gunners were disorientated. For the Germans, it was a favourable time for the planned landing on the island.

At 06.50 Siebel ferries with light anti-aircraft artillery (*Nos 12, 14, 22* and *26*) approached the island and launched landing boats. During these actions, Siebel ferry *No. 12* ran aground near the western shore of the island. Siebel ferry *No. 13* tried to help it, but also struck rocks and ran aground.

At 06.55, the Germans landed three assault groups of infantrymen and one group of sappers. The paratroopers quickly destroyed two Soviet coastal guns at the northern and western ends of the island. However, the 100mm cannon on the east bank continued to fire. At 07.04, Siebel ferry *No. 22* was hit by a 100mm shell fired by Soviet weapons from the eastern tip of the island. As a result of the explosion, the control bridge, both engines and one gun on the port side were seriously damaged. Siebel ferry *No. 22*, which had lost its course and control, began to be carried to the shore. Siebel ferries *No. 14* and *No. 26*, which

---

209. Ibid., p.167.

went to its aid, ran onto the rocks. As practice showed, shoals had become the main 'enemy' of the Axis flotilla in this battle!

At 07.10, when a group of German sappers approached the burning lighthouse, a red and white signal rocket suddenly flew into the air. This was the signal for the immediate return of the landing party to the ships. Oberstleutnant Wachtel ordered the rocket to be fired after radio communication with the landing party was interrupted for some reason. As a result, all the German assault groups hastily returned to the Siebel ferries, taking with them five Russian prisoners.

At this time, the Siebel ferries with 88mm guns on board provided cover for the actions of the paratroopers. They were moving in a column heading south-south-east, firing at Soviet ships visible in the south. At 07.49, the Germans noted a direct hit on one of them, after which the enemy disappeared behind a smokescreen.

By 08.00, Oberstleutnant Wachtel decided that Operation Brazil had achieved all its goals and it was time to get off the island. However, it turned out that it was impossible to do this quickly. Almost all the vessels that had approached Sukho Island were stranded. For more than an hour, the Germans made unsuccessful attempts to refloat Siebel ferries Nos *12*, *13* and *26*. In order not to put the remaining vessels at risk, the flotilla commander Oberstleutnant Wachtel decided to destroy the immobilised ferries. The crews of the stranded vessels were hastily evacuated to other flotilla ships. Between 09.00 and 09.11 Nos *12*, *13* and *26* were sunk by German artillery fire.

At 09.14, flotilla Commander Oberstleutnant Wachtel gave the signal for a general withdrawal to the base. As it turned out, it was a very timely decision. By this time, the Soviets had already learned about the events on Sukho Island and had hurriedly tried to organise a rebuff to the actions of the Axis flotilla. The Commander of the Ladoga Military Flotilla, Captain 1st rank Vasily Cherokov, immediately sent everything he had at hand to the battlefield: the gunboats *Nora*, *Bira* and *Selemdzha*, three minesweepers and several submarine chasers. At 09.20 from the north-east direction, the ships of the Axis flotilla were attacked by three Russian submarine chasers. The attack was unsuccessful, but the number of Russian ships rushing to Sukho Island was constantly increasing. At 09.45 gunners on *Bira* began firing on the Siebel ferries from the south from a long distance.

However, the troubles of the Germans did not end there. It turned out that their ships could not get away quickly to their base as the weather conditions deteriorated sharply. As a result of the storm, the speed of Siebel ferries decreased to 5 knots. The column of numerous flotilla vessels stretched for several kilometres. If the vessels at the head of the column had already gone far enough to safety, then the Siebel ferries at the back of the column were still in the waves near the Russian island. This was taken advantage of by the

OPERATION BRAZIL

gunners of the only surviving 100mm gun on Sukho Island, which the Germans considered defused. Suddenly, the gun began to fire at the German ships. Flotilla commander Oberstleutnant Wachtel ordered Siebel ferries with 88mm guns to suppress the Russian cannon. However, it turned out to be useless to conduct aimed fire from guns from a long distance in the stormy conditions on the lake. At 10.13 Siebel ferry *No. 21* had to return to the island and suppress the surviving Russian cannon with the fire of its 88mm guns. However, before the Russian gun fell silent, several shells fired during the return fire managed to damage *No. 21*'s hull. Water began to flow into the pontoons through many shrapnel holes and at the same time the drainage pumps failed. As a result, the damaged ferry began to sink. Oberstleutnant Wachtel ordered the ferries *Nos 11* and *23* to remove the crew from the sinking ship, and then sink *No. 21* with artillery fire.[210]

All this activity further delayed the escape of the Axis flotilla in dangerous proximity to Sukho Island and the Russian ships rushing to the aid of the garrison on the island. At 10.30 the gunboats *Nora* and *Selemdzha* appeared in the south, as well as several other boats. However, in the conditions of the storm, the slow-moving Russian ships were unable to damage the ships of the Axis flotilla, which not only had great speed, but also numerous long-range 88mm anti-aircraft guns.

The last attempt to delay the Axis ships leaving for their bases was an attack by the Russian torpedo boats. At 11.32, 11.35 and 11.40, *TKA-61* and *TKA-81*, under the cover of a smokescreen, tried to attack the Siebel ferries, which were behind the main forces. Transport Siebel ferries *T6*, which had engine problems, and *T4*, which was towing the damaged hospital ferry, lagged behind the main group of German vessels. However, all three attacks by Russian torpedo boats ended in vain.

The Soviet ships continued to pursue the enemy until 15.18. However, the Russians could not catch up with Siebel ferries. The speed of the 'Ladoga battleships' was too low. The only high-speed ship in the Ladoga Military Flotilla – the patrol ship *Purga* – had long been lying at the bottom of the lake.

Thus, despite the many obstacles and outright bad luck that accompanied the Siebel ferries during the implementation of Operation Brazil, their bold actions went unpunished by the superior forces of the Ladoga Military Flotilla. The Soviets failed to attack the Germans with all their might, because Russian ships approached the battlefield at different times and from different directions, and there was no unified command of numerous ships.

---

210. Keskinen, K., Stenman, K., *German Aircraft in Finland 1939–1945*, Apali Oy, Finland, 1998, p.207.

AIR BATTLE FOR LENINGRAD, 1941–1944

A threat from the sky

However, the troubles for the Axis flotilla in this campaign were not limited to bad weather, Lake Ladoga shoals and Russian ships. During the last phase of the battle at Sukho Island and throughout the return route, the flotilla was subjected to continuous air attacks by Soviet aircraft. The Soviet command threw almost everything that could fly against the Axis ships. The Siebel ferries were alternately attacked by twin-engine bombers, I-15 biplanes, Il-2 ground-attack aircraft and LaGG-3 fighters.

These air raids are described in detail in the German combat report. The first aerial bombardment was recorded at 08.25, followed by nineteen more air attacks until 11.10. From 11.20 to 13.35 the bombing stopped, and the Germans were already hoping that they had gone far enough from the Russian air bases. But at 13.35 seven I-15s appeared. These clumsy biplanes bombed and shelled German ships from different directions for fifteen minutes. In response, the Siebel ferries fired from all available guns. Unlike the Russian anti-aircraft gunners, the personnel of the Luftwaffe anti-aircraft units had excellent weapons and high-quality training. Soon the slow Soviet aircraft began to suffer noticeable losses. At 13.41 one of the I-15 biplanes disintegrated from a close explosion of a German anti-aircraft shell. Then a second Soviet fighter was shot down. German sailors watched as the pilot of the burning I-15 jumped out and descended into the lake under his parachute.

This was followed by a new, and as it turned out later, biggest air attack by the Soviets. At 14.06, twenty-six Il-2s appeared flying low over the water, accompanied by eight I-15 fighters. German anti-aircraft gunners noticed them in time and opened fire in advance. The whole sky above the Axis flotilla was painted with the black clouds of anti-aircraft shell explosions. Dozens of shell casings crashed onto the deck of the Siebel ferries. Falling bombs whistled and many columns of water rose 50–70m from the sides of the ships. The Siebel ferries abruptly changed course, dodging bomb hits. Manoeuvring and intense anti-aircraft fire nullified the effect of the Soviet attack. The attackers themselves suffered significant losses. A German anti-aircraft shell tore the tail off one Il-2, while another fatally damaged Il-2 disintegrated and crashed into the water.

Despite the losses, the Soviets continued to fanatically attack the enemy flotilla and the last raid on the Siebel ferries was recorded at 19.56.

In total on 21 October, the Red Army Air Force carried out about two hundred sorties to attack the Axis ships. Siebel ferries' anti-aircraft gunners claimed six downed Russian planes, which was almost accurate. The real Soviet losses were five aircraft (Il-2s and two I-15bis). The Axis ships were undamaged by air attacks.

Results of Operation Brazil

On 23 October, at 03.15, the Axis ships returned to their bases. The lake raid lasted thirty-five hours. Its result was the destruction of the Soviet 100mm coastal artillery battery and the disabling of the lighthouse on Sukho Island. During the battle, the Soviet garrison lost six people killed, five people were captured and twenty-three more were wounded. During an artillery duel with the Ladoga Military Flotilla ships, the Germans noted four hits and an explosion in the stern of one of the Russian gunboats. According to Soviet information, the gunboat *Selemdzha* was damaged, while two sailors were wounded.

Despite the implementation of all the planned Operation Brazil goals, it is impossible to conclude it was a complete success. The losses of the Axis Ladoga flotilla turned out to be significant and amounted to four Siebel ferries, eighteen people killed and fifty-seven wounded, with four more people were missing. At the same time, it should be noted that four Siebel ferries were lost by the Germans due to a lack of experience sailing on Lake Ladoga and technical problems. It must be admitted that Siebel ferries were not only not inferior in firepower to much larger Russian ships, but they were superior in their speed and accuracy of fire. There is no doubt that with more experience the Axis flotilla could create significant problems for Soviet communications passing through Lake Ladoga in 1943. However, the situation changed and a new opportunity for the Siebel ferries to prove themselves did not present itself.

Chapter 13

'Hydra'[211] of Ladoga against 'mosquitoes' and 'bedbugs'

Hold your positions!

In October 1942, Hitler was still considering the possibility of seizing Leningrad. When Generalfeldmarschall von Manstein informed him that most of the ammunition intended for firing at the Russian defence had been used up during the battle around Sinyavino and Mga, the Führer offered a compromise option. The fanatically minded Hitler believed that it was still necessary to conduct an offensive, but with limited goals. For example, German troops could advance to the Neva, straightening the front line. Or it was necessary to take a Soviet bridgehead in the Oranienbaum area with an unexpected blow. The Führer invited von Manstein to his the Führerhauptquartier Werwolf (werewolf) Eastern Front headquarters to discuss the details of this upcoming limited offensive.

On 25 October 1942, von Manstein flew to the meeting. Shortly before that, he buried his adjutant, who tragically had died in a plane crash, whom he treated like a son. The Generalfeldmarschall was in a depressed state and was tormented by bad forebodings. Just four days later, on 29 October, his eldest son would die on the Eastern Front. The death of two sons (native and adopted) would be a terrible reckoning for von Manstein's cooperation with Hitler and would torment him until the end of his days.

In contrast to von Manstein's depression, at that moment Hitler was experiencing another manic mood lift. At the end of October 1942, it seemed to the Führer that his business was going well. Good news was flowing from the huge Eastern Front. On the eve of the meeting with the Generalfeldmarschall, Hitler was informed that the German 1st Panzer Army had broken through the front and launched an offensive on the city of Ordzhonikidze, and German

---

211. Hydra is a serpentine water monster in Greek and Roman mythology. Later versions of the Hydra story add a regeneration feature to the monster: for every head chopped off, the Hydra would regrow two in its place.

bombers had attacked Soviet tankers in the Caspian Sea. On the Führer's desk were spectacular photographs of the completely destroyed Stalingrad, brought ten days ago by Generaloberst Wolfram von Richthofen. Hitler believed that, despite the fact that the Wehrmacht failed to achieve all the goals of the 1942 summer campaign, the German troops had advanced far ahead.

At the meeting, Hitler informed von Manstein that he had decided to 'abandon' the Leningrad assault for the time being. The Führer decided to send the headquarters of the 11th Army to the Vitebsk area, where a major Russian offensive was expected. Thus, Hitler made it clear to the conqueror of Sevastopol that this was the end of his mission in Army Group North.[212] This meant that Hitler's hopes of capturing Leningrad, the main 'Bolshevik stronghold', were finally buried. Just a month after this significant meeting, von Manstein was used by the Führer to mount a new mission – to lead the rescue of the German 6th Army, surrounded in Stalingrad.

In the autumn of 1942, according to Hitler's order, Army Group North was to continue to hold all occupied lines. Luftflotte 1, in turn, was to re-strengthen air attacks against Russian communications on Lake Ladoga. However, a lot had changed in the year since the German troops reached the shores of the lake, and the scale of Hitler's plans were noticeably reduced. Now the purpose of the bombing was not to force Leningrad to surrender, but to create problems when transferring Soviet troops across the lake. A year earlier, the fighting in this sector of the huge Eastern Front was conducted in order to achieve victory and capture a huge city. In the autumn of 1942, the Germans themselves turned the Leningrad neighbourhood into an impregnable citadel, in which they repelled countless Soviet attacks. Slowly, but inexorably, the troops of the German 18th Army turned from besiegers into besieged.

End of minesweeper *TSCH-82*

The Luftwaffe carried out Hitler's orders in a disciplined manner, intensifying its air attacks. On 30 October, twenty-six He 111 Hs from KG 53, accompanied by Bf 109 F fighters, raided Kobona harbour. On the way to the target, the German crews noticed a ship pulling a large barge. It was the minesweeper *TSCH-82*, towing a train barge-ferry with ten railway wagons. Inside the railway wagons were wounded soldiers and factory equipment exported from Leningrad. The goal seemed to the German pilots important enough to allocate forces for an immediate attack. Soon, the sailors on *TSCH-82* watched with

---

212. Manstein, E., *Lost Victories*, Smolensk: Rusich, 1999, pp.320–322.

horror as seven He 111s and five Bf 109s separated from the main group of bombers and headed for the Soviet ship.

The Russians had negligible chances of repelling an enemy attack as *TSCH-82* was armed with only one 45mm cannon and two machine guns. The Soviet gunners immediately began firing at the attacking aircraft. The commander of the ship, Senior Lieutenant Ivan Tyunkov, began to manoeuvre, trying to avoid direct hits from German bombs. The manoeuvre turned out to be successful, but several bombs still exploded right at the side. Damage to the steering gear limited the minesweeper's ability to perform evasive manoeuvres from air attacks. Then the Bf 109 fighters attacked after the bombers. With roaring engines, they swept several times directly over the deck, pouring machine gun fire into the minesweeper. *TSCH-82* received very heavy damage. The blast wave and large fragments of bombs cut masts, broke the trawl winch and damaged the bridge and the radio station. Considering the position of the minesweeper hopeless, the Luftwaffe aircraft stopped their attacks and rejoined the main formation.

TSCH-82 was in a critical situation. During a cursory inspection, the sailors counted more than twenty-five holes, through which water began to flow rapidly into the engine room and other rooms. There were numerous casualties among the crew. Six people were killed, including both machine gunners, and sixteen more were seriously injured. Among the wounded were the commander of the ship, Tyunkov, boatswain Starshina (non-commissioned officer) Nikolay Arkhipov and the whole mechanics and firemen's team.

In this difficult situation, chief mate Senior Lieutenant Pavel Averin took command of *TSCH-82* and under his leadership, a desperate struggle began to save the minesweeper. The situation was complicated by the fact that some underwater holes were near the coalbunkers and it was impossible to seal them from inside the hull. The chief technician, Lieutenant Alexey Valkov tied himself with a rope and went overboard into the icy water. Freezing, he managed to hammer wooden corks into the holes with a sledgehammer. At the same time, it was possible to restore control of the ship and secure the rope on the towed train barge-ferry. After that, the heavily damaged minesweeper headed for Kobona harbour. Fortunately, the ship had to travel only a very short distance to the shore. Soon *TSCH-82* brought the towed train barge-ferry to the port roadstead. However, the minesweeper itself could not be saved, and it sank in shallow water.[213]

---

213. Cherokov, V.S., *For You, Leningrad!*, Leningrad: Leninzdat, 1988, pp.136–137.

'HYDRA' OF LADOGA AGAINST 'MOSQUITOES'

Endless air attacks by small Luftwaffe forces

On 31 October 1942, the Russian Ladoga transport infrastructure experienced one of the most powerful Luftwaffe air attacks it ever faced. At 09.30, nine German bombers, accompanied by fighters, attacked Kobona harbour. Twenty minutes later, another group of German planes struck Pier No. 3 at Kobona port and the village of Kobona itself. At 10.09, the tugboat *Forel*, approaching the port, was attacked by Luftwaffe aircraft. Then at 10.20 the Germans bombed tugboat *No. 7*, which was standing on the roadstead of Kobona with a barge in tow. The barge was severely damaged, and eventually sank. At 11.20, after an hour break, six Ju 88 As attacked tugboat *No. 82* and achieved a direct hit. The ship was severely damaged, but remained afloat.

At 11.50 German planes attacked tugboat *No. 8*, which was pulling several barges. Eight high-explosive bombs were dropped on the Russian ship. At 12.02, *No. 8* was attacked again and twenty-one bombs exploded near its barges. *No. 8* and its barges were holed in numerous places and reached Kobona with great difficulty in a half-sunken state.

At 13.55 on the approach to Kobona harbour, Luftwaffe aircraft attacked another tugboat with barges in tow. One of the barges caught fire and a tugboat, *Pojarnyi*, was sent from Kobona to help. At 14.55, the Germans bombed tugboat *No. 81* in Kobona, however, none of the fifteen bombs dropped hit their target.

At 16.05, the tugboat *Gidrotechnik*, which was loading at Kobona harbour, was attacked and many Red Army personnel were killed and wounded.

At 19.40 forty German bombers again attacked Kobona's piers, and a large fire broke out at pier No. 3.

The last raid took place at dusk when, at 21.11, twenty-two He 111s bombed Kobona port again.[214]

In total, in October 1942, the Luftwaffe managed to disable five tugboats and eight barges. However, despite the loss of these transport ships, the Soviet lake communication worked very intensively. The maximum monthly amount of cargo for the entire navigation period – about 192,000 tons – was transported to the western shore of Lake Ladoga. On average, about 6,200 tons of supplies were delivered to Leningrad via the lake per day.

In early November, the German air attacks continued. On 1 November, a convoy of two tugboats with barges loaded with fuel oil left the port of Novaya Ladoga. The transport vessels were escorted by a gunboat. Almost the whole journey was quiet. However, on the approach to the port of Osinovets, Bf 109 Fs

---

214. TSAMO RF. Foundation 13642. Inventory 0020244. Case 0037. Sheet 34.

appeared in the sky and attacked the Soviet vessels. The captain of the tugboat *Nikulyasy*, Ivan Mishenkin, recalled:

> Our tugboat was badly damaged, the left engine was disabled, the hull, steam lines and superstructures were damaged. Machine gunner Tolya Plahotkin and the favourite of the team, radio operator Valya Petukhova, were killed. Everyone who could, quickly provided assistance to the wounded. Technicians repaired the damage. The friendly crew of the vessel withstood the tests. Two barges with fuel oil were delivered to their destination in Morier harbour.

On 5 November, the German pilots achieved serious success. A particularly valuable train barge-ferry *No. 4529* with ten loaded railway wagons was sunk in an open lake. Thus, by the end of the 1942 navigation, two train barge-ferries out of four vessels of this type that were operated on Lake Ladoga had been lost.

On 6 November, as a result of an air attack, the tugboat *Arzamas* was severely damaged.

On 8 November, at 15.20, fourteen He 111s from KG 53, accompanied by four Bf 109s, raided the harbour of the Spit of Lednevo. This harbour was located on the eastern shore of Lake Ladoga and was also used to send supplies to Leningrad. One hundred and twenty high-explosive bombs were dropped on the target. As a result, pier No. 5's loading platform and access to the railway tracks were destroyed, and eight railway wagons with coal were wrecked. During the attack, fifteen people were killed and nineteen were injured. Several German bombs exploded at the positions of artillery battery No. 3 of the 434th Separate Anti-aircraft Division (434th OZAD). As a result, two anti-aircraft guns, a rangefinding telemeter and a car were destroyed. Five gunners were killed, including the commander of the battery, Senior Lieutenant Porosenkov.[215]

On 11 November at 10.35 seven Ju 87s carried out an attack on Lavrovo railway station (7km south of Kobona). The main objectives of the Stukas were the railway bridge over the Ladoga Canal[216] and the unloading station. As a result, three steam locomotives, two railway wagons and stacks of bags with food were damaged. At 14.05 Ju 87s repeatedly attacked this target.

---

215. Ibid., Sheet 37.
216. Ladoga Canal is a 117km transport route along the shore of Lake Ladoga, connecting the Volkhov and Neva Rivers, which was built at the beginning of the eighteenth century. It was intended to supply St Petersburg but it was abandoned after the construction of a new canal in 1866.

'HYDRA' OF LADOGA AGAINST 'MOSQUITOES'

On 21 November at 10.30 seven He 111s again raided the harbour at the Spit of Lednevo. However, due to poor visibility (heavy clouds), all their bombs fell 250–300m from the target.

The next day, the Stukas bombed Spit of Lednevo harbour again, dropping twenty-eight bombs. As a result, 10m of railway tracks were destroyed and two railway wagons were damaged.

During 23 November, He 111s and Ju 87s bombed the Spit of Lednevo and Kobona harbours, and Lavrovo railway station, several times. As a result, one pier was damaged and four railway wagons and two warehouses containing food were destroyed. Due to heavy anti-aircraft fire from the Soviet side and poor visibility, most of the German bombs fell past their targets. This was the last Luftwaffe air attack against Russian harbours and bases at Lake Ladoga in 1942.[217]

In November 1942, the main enemy of the Russian transport fleet was bad weather.[218] The Commander of the Ladoga Military Flotilla, Captain 1st rank Vasily Cherokov, recalled:

> The worst thing for us was storms and ice again. The waves broke the tow ropes, the hulls of even lake tugboats and barges could not withstand the pressure of the elements. The low-power engines could not cope with the strong waves and wind, and the ships were carried out into the lake. We had to organise their search and rescue. So, at the end of October, a self-propelled tender was blown away by a storm from the small route (Kobona–Osinovets). The tender spent the whole night tossed around the lake until it was nailed to the edge of the broken ice at Cape Shuryagsky. The gunboat *Bira*, sent out to search, found the stricken vessel with difficulty.[219]

On the night of 4–5 November, waves stranded fourteen barges and a train barge-ferry at once. Five railway wagons fell into the water from another train barge-ferry and sank. On the same day, a barge with ammunition, previously damaged by a storm, sank on Morier roadstead. On 15 November, a storm broke the tow rope connecting a barge carrying coal and a tugboat. The waves carried the uncontrollable barge in an unknown direction. Five days later,

---

217. TSAMO RF. Foundation 13642. Inventory 0020244. Case 0037. Sheets 39–40.
218. In the western part of Russia, the actual winter weather usually begins in November.
219. Cherokov, V.S., *For You, Leningrad!*, Leningrad: Leninzdat, 1988, pp.146–147.

another empty barge went missing. Minesweepers were sent to search for the barges, but they could not be found among the raging expanses of Lake Ladoga.

On 7 November 1942, the first ice floes of the winter appeared on the lake. The frost intensified, the lake began to gradually become covered with ice, and the navigation of ships became more and more dangerous. After 25 November, cargo delivery to Leningrad was carried out only by gunboats. Some of them managed to break through the ice until 8 January 1943! However, the volume of traffic on the lake routes decreased significantly. In November 1942, only 67,500 tons of cargo were delivered to the western shore, and in December only about 7,000 tons. Of the cargo transported at the end of the 1942 navigation, a significant amount was wood. By the end of 1942, almost all the trees in the vicinity of Leningrad had already been cut down. Wood was used as fuel and material for the construction of defensive structures.

In total, during the second military navigation of Lake Ladoga, 1.1 million tons of various cargo and over 850,000 people were transported in both directions. A total of 202 tanks and 631 artillery pieces were delivered to the western shore. For example, the gunboat *Selemdzha* transported 2,890 tons of food, 580 tons of other cargo and towed nineteen barges.

Due to Luftwaffe air attacks and natural storms, the Soviets lost fifty ships of various types during the navigation of 1942. This was about 45 per cent of all ships available at the beginning of the period. However, these losses were made up quickly. During the summer and autumn, the Russians managed to commission 172 new vessels. Almost all of them were of poor quality and of low load capacity. Examples of similar transport vessels have already been given above; most were rectangular boxes made of wood or metal. In addition, the Soviets were constantly expanding their port infrastructure, which was also extremely primitive, but allowed a huge number of workers to manually move an increasing volume of cargo for Leningrad. All these measures allowed the Soviets to significantly increase their transport fleet and expand the port infrastructure on the lake. Three new barges appeared on the site of one sunken barge, two new piers grew on the site of one destroyed pier. Thus, as often happened on the Eastern Front, the Germans waged an endless battle on Lake Ladoga with a kind of 'Hydra'.

Luftwaffe pinpricks

From July to early autumn 1942, the limited forces of Luftflotte 1 were busy attacking communications on Lake Ladoga and supporting ground forces, so Leningrad was not bombed. The air attacks on the city resumed only in the evening of 28 September, when one German bomber carried out a raid on

No. 232 Bolshevik plant, which was firing artillery shells. Of the seven bombs dropped, five hit exactly on target, damaging two workshops. Seven people were killed and twenty-one were injured.[220]

The next air attack took place exactly a month later. On the afternoon of 28 October, three German planes dropped bombs on the Elektrosila plant. The Russian air defences had lost their combat capability during the lull and were caught off guard. Although the German bombers were detected by radar stations, Russian fighters did not take to the air and anti-aircraft artillery fire turned out to be inaccurate and erratic.

On the night of 30–31 October, a single German bomber flew unhindered at an altitude of about 5,000m over the positions of the 115th and 189th Anti-aircraft Regiments. He dropped bombs on the Malaya Ohta microdistrict, part of the Krasnogvardeysky district. Russian searchlights 'partially' illuminated the German bomber, but mistook it for a friendly aircraft. On 31 October, the Commander of the Leningrad Front, Colonel General Leonid Govorov, angered by such inefficiency of anti-air defence, wrote to the Commander of the Leningrad Air Defence, Army Major General Gavriil Zashikhin:

> For the period from October 21 to October 30, Leningrad Air Defence Army units, having spent 3279 shells, did not shoot down or damage a single enemy aircraft, giving him the opportunity to carry out reconnaissance and bombing on the objects of the city with impunity.[221]

However, Major General Zashikhin, awarded the Order of Lenin for his ability to qualitatively misinform his superiors, was once again able to justify the inefficiency of the anti-aircraft units subordinate to him.

On 3 November, at 15.43, six high-explosive bombs were dropped on Leningrad. All of them exploded in vacant lots and caused no damage. On the night of 8–9 November, ten high-explosive and one hundred small incendiary bombs were dropped on the city. As a result, a six-storey residential building in the central district (Borovaya street, 26) was destroyed. While extinguishing the fire, a huge brick wall collapsed directly on the fire brigade. Several people tackling the fire were killed.

On the night of 10 November, three German bombers attacked the Krasnyi neftyanik plant, in the south-eastern part of Leningrad. The plant was the main fuel storage facility in the city. As a result of a direct hit by a high-explosive

---

220. TSAMO RF. Foundation 217. Inventory 1221. Case 1594. Sheets 181–184.
221. Ibid., Inventory 1258. Case 125. Sheet 148.

bomb on tank No. 28, where diesel fuel was stored, a huge fire broke out. Then a nearby fuel oil tank burst into flames. Huge columns of flame rose into the sky and burning fuel spread through the streets and ditches. The fire continued until the morning and more than 2,000 tons of fuel oil was lost.[222] This was the Luftwaffe's only real success in Leningrad but it could not influence the situation in this sector of the front in any way.

Bombing the Ice Road

December 1942 was characterised by abnormally warm weather, and Lake Ladoga did not freeze for a long time. Due to these weather anomalies, the Russians were only able to organise vehicle traffic on the ice of the lake at Christmas. On 26 December, the thickness of the ice on the lake reached 30cm. Such ice allowed Soviet trucks to move along the Ice Road with a cargo weighing 1 ton.

The next day, the German long-range artillery from the Shlisselburg area began shelling the Ice Road. However, the Germans did not know the exact coordinates of their target and fired almost at random. In addition, the distance to the road was at the limit of the firing range of German guns. As a result, all the shells fell away from the road.

On 29 December 1942, the Luftwaffe launched its first air attacks against the new Ice Road. The Germans used a special tactic of searching for and destroying Soviet vehicles moving on the ice. Pairs of German fighters appeared over the lake at an altitude of 2,000m. Such a flight altitude was optimal for detecting and mounting rapid attacks on trucks and horse-drawn convoys moving along the Ice Road. Following a course across the road, Bf 109s dropped to a low level and dropped bombs. Then they gained altitude, turned around and attacked the road again, shooting trucks and horse-drawn wagons with cannon and machine guns. The fighter attacks continued until the ammunition was used up. However, even these specially developed tactics did not bring the Germans much success.

The next day, the air attacks continued. The first pair of Bf 109s appeared over the lake at 10.00. Then the bombing and shelling continued intermittently until 15.00. In addition to the Ice Road attacks, the pilots of JG 54 shot down a Russian Pe-2 reconnaissance aircraft that had flown over the western shore of the lake. The burning Soviet plane crashed on the ice, broke through it and sank.

---

222. Ibid., Inventory 1221. Case 1594. Sheets 190–193.

'HYDRA' OF LADOGA AGAINST 'MOSQUITOES'

In two days, the Bf 109 dropped eighty bombs on the Ice Road and fired at many targets. All these efforts yielded negligible results – three trucks and one tent were destroyed. In addition, eight people were killed and thirty wounded.[223] It was impossible to achieve great results with small forces in the conditions of the endless ice expanses of the lake. Trucks easily drove around areas of broken ice caused by falling bombs. In addition, if necessary, the Soviets quickly changed the route of movement on the lake.

The Russians also took care of the air defence of the Ice Road. By 30 December 1942, the thickness of the ice reached 40cm. This was enough to place light anti-aircraft guns on it. The next day, the Soviets installed seventeen 37mm automatic anti-aircraft guns and fifty-three anti-aircraft machine guns along the Ice Road.

The electric cable of life

By the end of 1942, the Soviets had achieved another success. They were able to break through the energy blockade of the city! In the autumn, after eliminating the threat of the Germans capturing the town of Volkhov, the Russians reactivated the Lenin hydroelectric plant there, which had been deactivated at the end of 1941. In 1942, they managed to put into operation three hydroelectric units with a capacity of 8 MW each. Simultaneously with the partial restoration of the plant, they began laying a secret electrical cable along the bottom of Lake Ladoga for the Leningrad power supply. The submarine power cable, with a length of 100km, was manufactured at the Sevkabel plant in Leningrad. The power cable had three conductors with an area of 120 sq mm, and could transmit electricity with a voltage of 10 kilowatts (kW). Due to the lack of a special material for the insulation coating of the submarine power cable, watermarked paper of the type used to make money was used. The ready-to-install power cable was delivered to Morier harbour on forty coils, where laying it on the bottom of Lake Ladoga began. The equipment for laying the coils was placed on a barge hidden in the harbour. Work on laying the cable to a depth of 18–20m was carried out only at night. Electricity began to flow to Leningrad on the first branch of the cable on 23 September 1942.

After the lake was covered with ice, the 'Ice electric power transmission line' was built in addition to the submarine power cable. Electrical wires were strung on support poles frozen in ice. Stretching for 30km (from the eastern shore of Lake Ladoga to the substation in Kokorevo village), the electric

---

223. TSAMO RF. Foundation 13642. Inventory 0020244. Case 0037. Sheets 56–59.

power transmission line was put into operation on 13 January 1943. After the creation of new electric lines, Leningrad's power supply improved significantly. A significant increase in electricity supplies allowed the Soviets to gradually restore production at factories and restart tram services in the city. Electric lighting reappeared in the homes of Leningrad residents, although it was limited to only two hours a day. The 'Ice electric power transmission line' lasted for sixty-eight days and was dismantled in the spring of 1943.

As expected, at the end of 1942, air strikes could not seriously interfere with supplies to Leningrad. In fact, the Luftwaffe's actions now resembled bedbugs and mosquitoes, which periodically bit their 'victim', prevented her from sleeping, but could not cause her serious damage. Meanwhile, the 'victim' was methodically preparing for a crushing blow to her 'bloodsuckers'.

Chapter 14

Operation Iskra

Attack through metal beds

By the beginning of 1943, the situation in the Leningrad sector remained almost the same as it was a year earlier. Infantry divisions of the German 18th Army still held the positions they had captured in September 1941. From Lake Ladoga, the front line went south, and then curved in an ornate protrusion in the area of Kirishi railway station. It was this railway station, located on the eastern bank of the River Volkhov, that Hitler ordered to be considered one of his 'fortresses', where Soviet attacks were to be repelled to the last German soldier.

After the defeat of the 2nd Shock Army in the fall of 1942, the Soviets were accumulating forces for a new strike in order to break through the land blockade of Leningrad. By order of Stalin, Operation Iskra (Spark) was developed. The scheme as a whole repeated the plan of the previous attacks. The Red Army was going to simultaneously attack German positions from Leningrad and Volkhov. After breaking through the ring of the Leningrad land blockade, the Russians were going to attack Mga and Tosno railway stations. The ultimate goal of Iskra was the complete defeat of the German 18th Army.

The time for the decisive offensive, as it seemed to Stalin, was well chosen. In the conditions of the Stalingrad crisis, the German command had no reserves. Almost all its He 111s had been commandeered for the air bridge service to support the 6th Army. At the same time, the Soviets attacked the Germans all over the long Eastern Front: in the Voronezh sector, in the Rzhev sector, in the town Velikiye Luki sector (at the end of December 1942, the city was surrounded by the Red Army) and other places.

However, the retention of Wehrmacht positions under Leningrad was of particular importance to Hitler. He believed that if it was not possible to starve and storm the 'Bolshevik stronghold', then it was necessary to at least maintain the status quo in this sector of the Eastern Front. It must be admitted that the Wehrmacht had every chance to fulfill Hitler's wish. The 18th Army was reinforced by the former 11th Army Generalfeldmarschall Erich von Manstein. Most of the infantry and artillery units of the 11th Army, after the October 1942 battles for Sinyavino Hills, were left near Leningrad. The German defence in this sector of the Eastern Front had been brought up to perfection. Most of the settlements captured from the Russians in 1941 were turned by the Germans into well-equipped strongholds. The front line of defence and positions in depth were protected by numerous minefields, wire obstacles and wood-earth blockhouses. On the banks of the Neva River, the main nodes of the German defence were the structures of Power Plant No. 8, Gorodok settlements Nos 1 and 2 and the town of Shlisselburg. The second line of German defence passed through urban-type settlements No. 1 and No. 5, Podgornaya and Sinyavino railway stations, urban-type settlement No. 6 and Mikhailovsky settlement. Leningrad Front headquarters described the defensive line of the German 18th Army as follows:

> The houses in settlements and railway embankments were adapted by the enemy for defence. The trenches system in settlements made it possible to keep a circular defence and manoeuvre quickly. As obstacles, the enemy used minefields, rubble, Dragons' teeth, ditches, wire obstacles, cheval de frise, fences and snow shafts. In some areas, metal beds placed at a distance of 10 metres were used to create defensive obstacles. These beds were braided with wire obstacles, and the gaps between them were sealed with wire obstacles and cheval de frise. On the front line of defence, the enemy installed an alarm system to warn of an approach to the front edge (bells, cans, flares).[224]

Weather conditions also contributed to the stability of the German defences. Due to the abnormally warm weather in December 1942, the marshes and streams in the area between the rivers Neva and Volkhov did not have time to be covered with sufficiently strong ice. The entire area of the planned Russian offensive was covered with loose snow half a metre deep. These conditions hindered the movement of Soviet infantry and armoured vehicles.

Breakthrough of the Leningrad land blockade

The Soviets prepared for the offensive very carefully. To overcome the cratered river ice, the troops were equipped with special ladders, poles and bridges that

---

224. TSAMO RF. Foundation 5678. Inventory 19877. Case 13. Sheets 5–7.

OPERATION ISKRA

were thrown over the areas of open water within the ice. To storm the high banks of the rivers, the soldiers were given hooks, hooks, assault ladders and boots with a sole covered with spikes. To overcome the swamps, long corduroy roads were made from logs and numerous other devices.

All movements of Soviet troops in the areas of concentration of forces for the upcoming offensive were carried out only in the dark and in cloudy weather. The railway transportation of troops, military equipment and ammunition across the River Volkhov was carried out only at night and during snowfalls. By the evening of 11 January 1943, Red Army soldiers had secretly taken up their starting positions on both planned sections of the breakthrough of the German defences. Imitating the Germans, the Soviets anticipated the offensive of the troops with a powerful bomb and artillery strike on German positions. On the night of 12 January, Russian bombers carried out raids on German strongholds. At 09.30, a hurricane artillery bombardment began, which lasted more than two hours. After that, Soviet troops launched an offensive against German positions simultaneously from the west and east.

Soon, an incredibly intense battle unfolded in the vicinity of Sinyavino settlement, battles that continued day and night. Often the encounters turned into brutal hand-to-hand fights between German and Russian soldiers. By the evening of 15 January, the Russians managed to capture the northern neighbourhoods of Sinyavino, the urban-type settlements No. 4 and No. 8. From the west, Soviet troops advancing from Leningrad were also able to deeply wedge themselves into German positions. On 16 January, Russian assault groups reached the vicinity of Shlisselburg. The advanced units of Leningrad Front and Volkhov Front were now separated by only a couple of kilometres.

On 18 January, at 12.00, Red Army soldiers from the 136th Rifle Division met with units of the 2nd Shock Army. In the evening of the same day, the battalion armoured cars of the Soviet 61st Tank Brigade broke into the town of Shlisselburg. Thus, the Leningrad land blockade was broken.

In this critical situation, the German command reasonably allowed the units of the 227th Infantry Division, 96th Infantry Division and 5th Mountain Division cut off near Shlisselburg to make their way south to join their troops. There was no solid front line at that time, so there were sufficiently favourable conditions for the rescue of the trapped German troops. Most of the encircled German group (about 8,000 men) dispersed and broke past urban-type settlement No. 5 to the south. By 20 January 1943, all units of the 227th Infantry Division, 96th Infantry Division and 5th Mountain Division escaped death and captivity and joined their own troops. Then the Germans took a pre-prepared position along the line of urban-type settlement No. 6 – Sinyavino – the western part of Kruglaya roscha settlement. At this line, 2½km from the southern shore of Lake

Ladoga, the 18th Army managed to hold on. Despite the subsequent furious attacks of the Red Army, the Soviets were unable to advance any significant distance.

Formally, Operation Iskra ended in success. However, the result achieved by the Soviets at the cost of heavy losses turned out to be very modest. The width of the corridor connecting the city with the central regions of the USSR was only 8–11km. Much more important for the Soviets was the psychological effect of understanding the slow but steady progress towards victory over the Germans. Meanwhile, when the Soviet command began to count the losses, they again turned out to be very heavy. By 30 January 1942, about 34,000 Soviet troops participating in the offensive had been killed or were missing. German losses were five and a half times fewer – about 6,000 killed and wounded.

All quiet on the Leningrad Front

Despite the initial successes of the Red Army, by the spring of 1943, the general military situation in the Leningrad sector had hardly changed. The only difference from the situation on this section of the Eastern Front in 1942 was that the Soviets had established a strong land connection with the city. In February 1943, they even built a single-track railway through Shlisselburg. This allowed the Soviets to improve the food supply of the surviving residents of the city. On 22 February, the norms for issuing food to residents were increased. From now on, workers and engineers of military factories received 700g of bread a day, the rest of the workers 600g a day. Consumption rates of other products also increased slightly. As a result of such 'generosity' by Stalin the standard of living of the starving population of Leningrad approached that of the half-starved existence of residents of other Russian cities located far from the front line.

But the Germans were still at the outskirts of Leningrad, and could look at the Isaakievskiy Sobor (Saint Isaac's Cathedral) and the spire of the Admiralty Building with the naked eye. They stood firmly on the Neva and held the front along the River Volkhov. This success of the German defence was primarily due to the relative freedom of action possessed by the command of Army Group North. Hitler trusted Generalfeldmarschall Georg von Küchler implicitly and believed that he would undoubtedly be able to hold the front. The commander of Army Group North took full advantage of this trust to save his troops from certain death during the Russian offensive (Operation Iskra). At a crucial moment, von Küchler delayed sending a message to Hitler that the town of Shlisselburg had been cut off from the main German forces and the situation of the troops in the area was critical. Führer found out about this only when German troops were already breaking out of the pocket, and there was no way to declare Shlisselburg a fortress. Otherwise, the 18th Army could have repeated the terrible fate of the German troops in the Stalingrad and Velikiye Luki pockets.[225] The troops encircled there were sacrificed to Hitler's boundless ambitions. If not for the determination of von Küchler, who was not afraid to deceive Hitler, then further events would probably have developed according to the already well-known tragic scenario. Von Küchler at least temporarily saved German soldiers from the terrible death that the bloodthirsty Führer had prepared for them. Thus, it was much more difficult to defeat the Wehrmacht when it was commanded not by the megalomaniac Hitler but by professional commanders.

On the Soviet side of the front, another incompetent commander was also eager to realise his boundless ambitions. On 16 February 1943, Joseph Stalin set grandiose tasks for the troops. The Red Tsar ordered his troops to 'cut off the communications of the enemy group in the Leningrad-Volkhov area', 'capture and hold the city of Pskov', 'capture the area of the towns of Kingisepp and Narva, cutting off the enemy's escape routes to Estonia' and so on. At the same time, reports on the deterioration of the psychological state of the German troops were distributed among the Soviet troops and the population of the USSR.[226] Red Army soldiers were again thrown into senseless carnage, trying to attack well-fortified German positions head-on. But eleven days later, Stalin was forced to admit that the attacks 'did not give the expected results' and had led to 'aimless large casualties in manpower and equipment'. Nevertheless, in the following months, until the beginning of April 1943, the Soviets continuously attacked the positions of the 18th Army along their entire length. However, neither flanking attacks nor desperate frontal assaults gave the expected effect. The approaches to the hills near Mga railway station, littered with corpses and damaged armoured vehicles, seemed to be a cursed place for the Russians. After the failure of the suicidal Russian attacks, the war in this sector of the Eastern Front again assumed a positional character.

Actions of Soviet aviation in Operation Iskra

By the beginning of 1943, there were quite large forces of Soviet aviation in the Leningrad area, which the Soviets planned to use to support Operation Iskra.

---

225. A detailed review of the events that took place in the Stalingrad and Velikiye Luki pockets can be found in: Degtev, D., and Zubov, D., *Hitler's Air Bridges: The Luftwaffe's Supply Operations of the Second World War*, Barnsley, UK: Air World/Pen & Sword Books, 2022.
226. TSAMO RF. Foundation 148a. Inventory 3763. Case 103. Sheets 253–254.

AIR BATTLE FOR LENINGRAD, 1941–1944

The 13th Air Army (13th VA) and 7th Fighter Aviation Corps Air Defence (7th IAC PVO) had 287 aircraft (26 bombers, 40 ground-attack aircraft, 171 fighters, 50 reconnaissance planes and liaison aircraft). The 14th Air Army (14th VA) had 374 combat-ready aircraft.

Due to bad weather in the early days of the Soviet offensive, the actions of the Red Army Air Force were limited. For example, on 12 January, the 13th VA and its subordinate 7th IAC PVO carried out a total of 159 sorties. Of these, only thirty-one were designed to attack ground targets. Losses amounted to seven aircraft. The next day, these aviation units carried out 102 sorties, including twenty to attack ground targets.

On 14 January 1943, on the western flank of the offensive, Soviet aircraft carried out 191 sorties, including thirty-four to attack ground targets. Ten aerial battles took place on this day, after which 'Stalin's Falcons' claimed four aerial victories (two Bf 109s, one Fw 190 and one Ju 88). The Russians' own losses amounted to eight aircraft (two P-40s, one Hawker Hurricane and five Il-2s).

On 15 January, aircraft from the 13th VA and 7th IAC PVO flew 181 sorties, including twenty-seven to attack ground targets.

On 16 January, aircraft from the 13th VA performed a total of twenty-seven sorties, on 17 January twenty-nine, on 18 January twenty, and on 19 January four. The reason for the latter reduction was snowfall and heavy cloud.

Despite obvious inefficiency, the Soviet pilots reported fantastic successes to Stalin. According to the Red Army Air Force report for January 1943, 'Stalin's Falcons' destroyed 208 German aircraft in the Leningrad area: seventy-four aerial victories were won by the 13th VA, ninety by the 14th VA and forty-four by the Air Force Soviet Baltic Fleet (VVS KBF).[227]

In fact, Luftflotte 1 lost a total of twenty-six aircraft in January 1943, including eleven He 111s, eight Bf 109s, four Ju 87s and three Fw 190s. Another seven aircraft were lost due to non-combat reasons. However, specifically in the Leningrad sector, the Luftwaffe losses were even fewer. For example, JG 54 lost only two pilots. On 16 January, during an air attack against Russian trucks on Lake Ladoga, Fw 190 A-4 W.Nr. 142310 'Schwarze 2' flown by Unteroffizier Helmut Brandt from 2./JG 54 accidentally shot off the blades of his own propeller. This was due to a technical malfunction of the synchronisation gear for the machine guns. Unteroffizier Brandt made an emergency landing on the ice south-east of the town of Shlisselburg and was captured by the Russians. On 23 January, Bf 109 G-2 W.Nr. 10389 'Weisse 11' piloted by Unteroffizier Otto Durkop from 1./JG 54 went missing near Shlisselburg.

---

227. TSAMO RF. Foundation 362. Inventory 0006169. Case 0106. Sheets 300–304, 318–340.

The losses of the Soviet Red Army Air Force in the Leningrad sector during a month of air battles amounted to 181 aircraft. For example, the 13th VA lost 137 aircraft (seventy-seven Il-2s, twenty-seven La-5s, nineteen Yak-7s, four Yak-1s, three Pe-2s, two P-40s, two I-16s, two U-2s and one I-153). It is known that approximately seventy of the 181 aircraft lost by the Soviets were shot down by the Germans in aerial battles. The reasons for the losses of the remaining Soviet aircraft have not yet been established by the authors. However, despite the huge losses, Soviet aviation did not have a serious impact on the course of Operation Iskra.

Bombing out of habit

If we exclude from the analysis the operation to support the defending units of the Wehrmacht, then the actions of the Luftwaffe in the area of the Ice Road and over Leningrad in January 1943 were not very effective. The main reason for this was the extremely small number of aviation units operating in this section of the Eastern Front. It was rather bombing out of habit, carried out with the formal purpose of filling out reports on the activities of Luftflotte 1. Such reports, sent from various secondary sectors of the front, were pleasing to Hitler and created for him the illusion of a successful course of a lost war.

According to Soviet information, during January 1943, the Germans carried out thirty-six air attacks against the Ice Road. They mainly involved He 111s from KG 53 and Fw 190s and Bf 109s from JG 54. To attack ice communications on Lake Ladoga, bombers used conventional high-explosive and fragmentation bombs. German fighters attacked the Ice Road with AB 500 cluster bombs, filled with sub-munition – small SD 2 fragmentation bombs. To increase the effectiveness of the impact, cluster bombs were dropped on the target from a great height. During the fall, the shell of the bomb was automatically opened, and numerous sub-munitions scattered over a large area. Some of the SD 2 sub-munitions exploded upon contact with ice; some penetrated into snow and ice and did not explode. After that, the sub-munitions became improvised mines that exploded when Soviet trucks accidentally hit them. However, the damage from these raids again turned out to be minimal for the Soviets. Six GAZ-AA trucks were damaged, three people were killed and six were injured.

Another typical method of using Luftflotte 1 single bombers was in attacks on Soviet railways in the Leningrad area. Because of their regularity, these missions became a kind of routine for German crews. However, due to bad weather and increased Russian air defences, these bombings usually did not cause serious damage.[228]

Equally ineffective were the air raids on Leningrad. For example, on the evening of 6 January 1943, a German plane dropped two high-explosive and seventy small incendiary bombs on the city. However, the bombs did not hit the planned target, but accidentally severely damaged the Palace Bridge – one of the main historical attractions of the city. The bridge is located in the central part of the city near the former residence of the Russian tsars, the Winter Palace. So, the effect of this air attack was more psychological than military.

On the night of 10–11 January, two German bombers made another air attack against Leningrad. The operational summary of the Soviet Local Rescue Service (MPVO) describes its consequences:

> Two combined incendiary bombs with an incendiary mixture[229] fell on Zvenigorodskaya Street. The walls were sprayed with a combustible mixture. Windows are broken in the houses. The tram wire at house No. 12 is torn. There was an ignition of the spilled mixture. There are no casualties ...
>
> One high-explosive bomb weighing 500kg hit the chimney of the furnace of house No. 11 on Borovaya street and did not explode. The furnace split in half. There are no casualties ...
>
> One incendiary bomb with a combustible mixture broke through the attic ceiling and exploded in the stairwell of the house No. 75 on Marat Street. There was a fire. There are no casualties ...
>
> One high-explosive bomb weighing 500kg fell on empty three-storey house No. 10 on Borovaya Street, broke through the foundation of the house and did not explode.[230]

On the evening of 12 January, twelve small incendiary bombs were dropped on Leningrad. They did not cause any damage. As already noted above, all these actions of Luftwaffe were more like bug bites and mosquitoes than serious military actions.

---

228. TSAMO RF. Foundation 13642. Inventory 0020244. Case 0061. Sheet 13.
229. A canister of flammable liquid with an incendiary bomb tied to it.
230. TSAMO RF. Foundation 217. Inventory 1221. Case 3141. Sheets 7–11.

OPERATION ISKRA

'To break the morale of the Russians and weaken the military potential of the city!'

In the midst of the battle on the southern shore of Lake Ladoga (Operation Iskra), Luftflotte 1 received an unexpected instruction from Hitler's Führerhauptquartier. When the Commander of Luftflotte 1 Generaloberst Alfred Keller read it, he could not believe his eyes! Hitler ordered the immediate resumption of massive bombing raids on Leningrad 'to break the morale of the Russians and weaken the military potential of the city'. All this was proposed to be done during the deepest military crisis of the Wehrmacht, when the bombers were trying their best to support their troops. In addition, Generaloberst Keller was informed that from now on the Führer would personally direct air attacks and determine the targets for bombing. Once again, the Luftflotte 1 headquarters was faced with the need to carry out the senseless orders of an incompetent Nazi leader. It is worth noting that the suicidal nature of Hitler's orders grew as the situation at the front worsened.

On 19 January, Generaloberst Keller arrived at Pleskau-Süd air base, where He 111s from KG 53 were based. He read out Hitler's order to the pilots lined up in a row about the beginning of the massive bombing of Leningrad. The discouraged crews heard that this operation is 'of crucial political importance' and 'the Bolsheviks will realise that the Luftwaffe is still strong'.

On the same day, at 20.07, an air alert was announced in Leningrad, which lasted six hours. During this time, the Germans dropped sixteen high-explosive bombs on the city. As a result, the Rabotnica weaving plant, six residential buildings and a soldiers' barracks were destroyed. Twenty-three people were killed, with 108 injured and concussed.

On the evening of 20 January, eighteen high-explosive bombs were dropped on Leningrad. The Sudomekh shipyard, the office at Torgovyi port and three residential buildings were damaged. Four people were killed and forty-two injured. Simultaneously with bombing by the Luftwaffe, the German long-range artillery also fired on the city.

After a long break, the air attacks on the city resumed. On the evening of 29 January, twelve high-explosive bombs were dropped on Leningrad. Electric substation No. 20 and four residential buildings were damaged. One person was killed and eight were injured.

Such illusory activity of bombers over Leningrad formally gave the basis for Generaloberst Keller to report regularly to the Wolfsschanze (Wolf's Lair) on the implementation of the Führer order. This trick allowed the Luftwaffe to focus on the really important missions to support the Wehrmacht and not to risk their crews over Leningrad in vain. The naive Hitler enthusiastically joined the game started by Generaloberst Keller. A phone call was made daily to Luftflotte 1 headquarters from OKL headquarters in Berlin. From there, the adjutants reported on the next goal chosen by Hitler and demanded a report on the results of previous missions. However, in February 1943, this 'fun game' was put on pause. In the Leningrad sector, the weather was so terrible that any air attacks on the city had to be stopped. Airfields were littered with a thick layer of snow and there were constant blizzards, creating almost zero visibility. To carry out urgent missions, the Germans used the system of radio navigation. The main equipment of this system was installed at Pleskau-Süd (city of Pskov) air base. Additional elements of the German system of radio navigation used to clarify the course and location of the bombers were located at airfields in Krasnogvardeysk, Kingisepp and Lyuban.

Hitler's idiotic operation to break the morale of Russians by bombing Leningrad resumed only at the end of winter. On the night of 22 February 1943, two single German bombers dropped thirty-two bombs on Leningrad. Plant No. 323 was damaged (two workshops were destroyed and Varshavskaya-Passajirskaya railway station, the Skorohod plant and the tram depot were hit. Three people were killed and ten were injured.[231]

On the night of 22–23 February, an 'air alert' signal was announced in Leningrad for the 488th time. Luftwaffe planes dropped twelve high-explosive bombs on the city, which caused minor damage. The He 111 H-11 W.Nr. 8089 'A1+NT' of 9./KG 53 was probably lost during this raid. The bomber went missing along with the crew (pilot Oberfeldwebel Hans Nowak). Much greater casualties and destruction were caused by artillery shelling, which took place simultaneously with the bombing from the air. A total of 350 shells of the German long-range artillery fell on the city, explosions of which thundered throughout its territory. Several residential buildings were destroyed, thirteen people were killed and fifty-five were injured.[232]

On the night of 5–6 March, a single German plane dropped ten high-explosive bombs on the western part of Leningrad. As a result, the Radischev leather factory, located on Vasilyevsky Island (on the shore of the Gulf of Finland), was damaged. None of the factory workers was injured.[233]

On the afternoon of 25 March, another Leningrad bombing raid was carried out and seventeen high-explosive bombs were dropped on the city. The Luftwaffe's main target was plant No. 232, which produced artillery shells. As a result of the explosions of five German bombs, three workshops were

---

231. Ibid., Sheets 13–27.
232. Ibid., Sheets 32–39.
233. Ibid., Sheet 40.

damaged, an oil pump was disabled and a 10-ton bridge crane collapsed from the blast wave. Power plant No. 5 was also seriously damaged, on the territory of which ten German bombs fell. Two electric substations, railway tracks and an overpass with a fuel elevator were destroyed.[234]

On the morning of 30 March, German bombers dropped seven high-explosive bombs on the Kirov weaving plant in the centre of the city. Two workshops and a warehouse were destroyed. One person was killed and three were injured. In the evening of the same day, the Germans conducted a powerful artillery bombardment of the central part of Leningrad. Some 476 shells of the German long-range artillery fell on the city. The Primus plant, the Krasni treugolnik plant (producing rubber products) and Leningrad-Baltiiskaya 'Leningrad-Baltic' and Leningrad-Varshavskaya railway stations were destroyed. In addition to industrial plants, the buildings of two hospitals and several dozen residential buildings were badly damaged. Thirty-nine people were killed and eighty-four were injured.[235]

The bomber crews understood the utter futility of the Leningrad raids and perceived these missions as a routine and dangerous duty. Leutnant Gilbert Geisendorfer, who served in 6./KG 53, later wrote:

> For a while we raided Leningrad, and our target was plants and power plants on the Neva. Russian air defence has always been extremely strong. However, the air defence in the Leningrad area was unsurpassed. Some of my comrades talked about 120 heavy anti-aircraft batteries, and each of them, as a rule, had eight guns ...
>
> We dropped bombs from a height of between 6,000 and 8,000 metres, as high as our heavy bomb load allowed. The intervals between individual planes led to the fact that all the anti-aircraft guns fired at you alone. But the raids had to last all night, and each crew carried out two sorties one after the other. Every time it was an impressive sight. Searchlights flashed, trying to capture us in the crosshairs of their beams, which in most cases succeeded, followed by explosions of anti-aircraft shells, shock waves from which sometimes made the plane shudder. Using all sorts of tricks to get away from the fire, we groped our way to the goal. A map with a scale of 1:25,000 was used for orientation. The well-recognised numerous bends of the Neva River were of

---

234. Ibid., Sheets 42–43.
235. Ibid., Sheets 43–46.

great help in detecting the target. But what was to be done when the anti-aircraft explosions were approaching, and when a black cloud the size of an aeroplane suddenly appeared almost in front of the cockpit, and you flew through it with the feeling that the next salvo should inevitably hit your plane.

But what, however, to do if you are flying at night over Leningrad, and the pilot is experiencing a natural human need, and the tension is increasing until, finally, it can no longer be tolerated? We had special rubber containers for this, but we never used them, because the whole procedure of using them was too inconvenient and hardly suitable for use. Did anyone think that we were wearing a uniform, a flight suit, and also tied with parachute straps. The rest of the crew solved this problem very simply. They were just heading to the bomb bay and urinating through it.[236]

The efforts of the He 111 crews, of course, did not bring any 'political' let alone military results on the front line around Leningrad. In fact, the operation was reduced to time-stretched air attacks, in which from one to five German bombers participated. In the conditions of endless Red Army attacks across the vast Eastern Front from the Baltic Sea to the Valdai Hills, Luftflotte 1 simply did not have the strength to actually carry out the Führer's order.

And again bottom mines ...

In early April 1943, German reconnaissance planes began to fly regularly over the Gulf of Finland and the Russian Navy base in Kronstadt. They photographed the ice situation, the anchorages of ships and the positions of anti-aircraft artillery. All this activity was sparked by the fact that Luftflotte 1 staff officers were preparing a new operation to mine fairways.

On the night of 20–21 April, twenty-six Ju 88 A-4 bombers from III./KG 1 took off from Dno-Griwotschki airfield. Approaching the southern shore of the Gulf of Finland, the planes dropped to an extremely low level, after which they headed for Kronstadt Naval Base. Due to their low altitude, the bombers were not detected by the Russian radar stations. This allowed the Germans to achieve the effect of surprise. Their approach was visually noticed only by posts of the Soviet Air Surveillance and Communication Service (VNOS), located at

---

236. Kiehl, H., *Kampfgeschwader 'Legion Condor' 53*, Stuttgart: Motorbuch Verlag, 1996, p.388.

the southern forts of the Kronstadt Fortress. As in the previous summer, the first Ju 88s struck the positions of anti-aircraft batteries, dropping twenty-eight fragmentation bombs on them. The remaining bombers parachuted forty bottom mines with acoustic and magnetic fuses. Some of the mines, as had often happened before, exploded when falling on the shallows. This was the beginning of the third fairways air mining operation since the beginning of the war in the Kronstadt area.

By this time, the air defence of Kronstadt Navy Base had increased significantly. It included three anti-aircraft regiments, four batteries of 45mm anti-aircraft guns operated by the Air Defence Sector of the Kronstadt Naval Base and several Projzvuk stations. The 1st Anti-aircraft Regiment (1st ZenAP) under Major Nikolai Kotov was stationed in Kronstadt town. Artillery batteries of the 6th Anti-aircraft Regiment (6th ZenAP) Lieutenant Colonel Viktor Ermolaev were scattered throughout the rest of Kotlin Island. The anti-aircraft guns of the 49th Anti-aircraft Regiment (49th ZenAP), commanded by Major Nikolai Polunin, stood on the southern shore of the Gulf of Finland, on the Oranienbaum Bridgehead.[237] The 71st Fighter Aviation Regiment Air Force Soviet Baltic Fleet (71st IAP VVS KBF), armed with I-153, I-16 and I-15bis fighters, was still based at Bychie Pole airfield (in the western part of Kotlin Island). It consisted of twenty aircraft, more than half of which were obsolete biplanes. Such a dominance of outdated aircraft models is explained by the fact that the command of the VVS KBF did not have the necessary skills in compiling false reports to prove its importance to Stalin. Therefore, new fighter models only arrived in the VVS KBF aviation regiment after a long delay. On the night of 20–21 April, not a single Russian fighter managed to fly out to intercept the German bombers.[238]

On 21 April, at 22.23, sixteen German bombers carried out a second minelaying mission near Kronstadt Naval Base.

On 22 April, at 03.40, the third mission took place, in which twenty-three to twenty-eight aircraft participated. This time forty-five bottom mines were dropped in fairways and thirty-five fragmentation bombs were released on the positions of anti-aircraft gunners. The effect of surprise was lost and strong

---

237. Oranienbaum Bridgehead was territory isolated from Leningrad, formed on 7 September 1941 when the Germans reached the Gulf of Finland during the offensive on the city, cutting off an area 65km long and up to 25km deep along the Baltic coast from the main forces of the Red Army. This area was heavily fortified and defended by Red Army soldiers and Soviet Baltic Fleet sailors until 14 January 1944, when the 2nd Shock Army successfully attacked from the bridgehead, joining with Soviet troops advancing from Leningrad.
238. TSVMA. Foundation 219. Case 134567. Sheets 77–79.

barrage firing prevented the German crews from dropping bottom mines with the necessary accuracy. For this reason, some of the Luftminen again fell on the shore and shallows, producing powerful explosions.

The next night, the Luftwaffe carried out the fourth mission to mine the Kronstadt fairways, after which they considered the operation completed. This time, Russian night fighters claimed three aerial victories. In turn, the Soviet anti-aircraft gunners claimed two downed German bombers. According to German information, no losses were registered by III./KG 1 on these days.

Over the course of four nights, posts of the Soviet Air Surveillance and Communication Service (VNOS) recorded the dumping of 112 bottom mines in various fairway areas around Kronstadt Naval Base. Several dozen bottom mines fell into shallow water and exploded.

The danger posed by the German bottom mines forced the Soviet Baltic Fleet command to close the fairways for sailing and carry out minesweeping. As a year earlier, first of all the Soviets used the roughest method of mine clearance by dropping depth charges from high-speed submarine chasers. After that, minesweepers passed through the fairways with minesweeping barges in tow to carry out distance minesweeping. However, despite all this effort, only five bottom mines were neutralised. After that, the Russians decided that there were no more German bottom mines, and sailing resumed in the fairways.

The doomed crew of the Russian submarine

Stalin could not accept the fact that his Baltic Fleet was completely blockaded in Leningrad. The Commander of the Soviet Baltic Fleet, Vice Admiral Vladimir Tributs, who tried to please his cruel 'Red Lord', periodically ordered the surviving submarines to attempt a suicidal breakthrough into the Baltic Sea. The first stage of such a deadly campaign was the transition from Leningrad to Kronstadt. On the night of 30 April to 1 May 1943, another group of Russian submarines went to meet their death.

The famous Soviet submariner Captain 1st Rank Pyotr Grishchenko recalled:

> The transfer of ships from Leningrad to Kronstadt was a difficult operation. It was carried out, as a rule, at night, but often the night turned out to be a bad ally. Under enemy fire from the settlement of Strelna – a town of in the Petergof area – our ships had to pass through a narrow fairway, no more than ten metres deep. The submarines group left Leningrad. Lighted beacons and lighthouses were extinguished on the entire route of the

OPERATION ISKRA

water crossing for the purpose of camouflage. Only one buoy at the exit of the fenced part of the Morskoy channel indicated the beginning of the fairway axis. On the submarine *Shch-406* sailing ahead was the commander of the submarines Captain 2nd rank group V. Poleshchuk, the commander on it was my former pupil, Hero of the Soviet Union Evgeny Osipov. I was also on the same submarine as a representative of the Soviet Baltic Fleet Headquarters.[239]

On the submarine *Shch-406*, which was the first in the group, when leaving the fenced part of the Morskoy channel, there was a technical malfunction, specifically the gyrocompass broke. In order not to delay the transition of the entire group of submarines, Captain 2nd rank Poleshchuk ordered the commander of *Shch-323* to take its place at the head of the column. This was a very responsible job that required a lot of experience and exceptional attention from the crew and, above all, the navigator and commander of the submarine. In conditions of poor visibility, due to an error in determining its position, the submarine missed the turning point by almost half a mile, went beyond the safe fairway and eventually blew up on a German bottom mine.

Captain 1st Rank Grishchenko continued his story:

> At about 01.00, when the submarines were opposite the Strelna settlement, we heard a strong explosion. At the place where the submarine *Shch-406* was supposed to sail, I saw a huge water column, and when it disappeared, the submarine also disappeared.[240]

Shch-323 sank at a shallow depth and its periscope pedestal remained on the surface. The submarine chaser, following alongside the submarine, picked up three seriously injured sailors from the water. Five more sailors who were on the bridge at the time of the explosion, including the commander, Andronov, were killed.

The crippled *Shch-323* lay on the bottom. As a result of severe damage, the hull of the submarine was flooded with water from the first to the fifth compartments. However, in the sixth and seventh compartments the bulkheads withstood the blow, although their seals were broken. The surviving crew

---

239. Grishchenko, P.D., *Fight Under Water*, Moscow: Molodaya Gvardiya, 1983, pp.163–164.
240. Ibid., p.165.

members managed to move to the seventh, aft, compartment. A total of sixteen people gathered there. In total darkness, they began to prepare for evacuation through the aft torpedo tube. Since the depth at the site of the flooding of *Shch-323* did not exceed a few metres, the survivors had a good chance of salvation. Chief Starshina (non-commissioned officer) Dmitry Trubin, who was a scuba diver athlete, was the first to leave the hull of the sunken submarine. He managed to surface without difficulty and reconnoitre the situation. After finding out that this path was relatively safe, he returned back to the submarine. Starshina Trubin informed the survivors that part of the periscope's pedestal and radio antenna were sticking out of the water, and suggested that they hold on to them after surfacing. After that, the crew members began to leave the damaged hull one by one.

However, it was too early to think about a miraculous rescue. All the Russian ships had long gone, and the Soviet Baltic Fleet command, confident in the death of the crew, refused to carry out a rescue operation. As a result, sixteen surviving crew members ended up in cold water in the middle of the Gulf of Finland. To prevent the current from carrying them into the sea, they held on to the antenna and the periscope's pedestal. Meanwhile, dawn broke, and the weather, unfortunately, improved.

On the shore near the sunken submarine, German observers spotted the periscope pedestal and the surviving Soviet sailors, upon which the nearest artillery battery opened fire. Captain 1st Rank Grishchenko wrote:

> It was necessary to urgently go back to the submarine and wait for nightfall. But no one guessed to do this, apparently not imagining all the danger of their situation. Perhaps this is explained purely psychologically: not everyone will dare to climb back into the sunken submarine.[241]

As a result, the sailors spent sixteen hours in cold water under fire. It was almost impossible to survive in such conditions. Only after dark did two Soviet submarine chasers arrive at the submarine. By that time, only two people remained alive. Moreover, these were not crew members of *Shch-323*, but Alexander Nazarov, a seaman from the depot ship *Aegna*, and Ivan Kharchenko, an electrician from submarine *L-55*, who were on board the submarine as passengers. Taking into account the three seriously injured sailors who were pulled out of the water immediately after the explosion, the

---

241. Ibid., p.165.

total number of those rescued was only five people. Thirty-nine crew members were killed.[242]

The Luftwaffe bombs Leningrad again

During April 1943, the Luftwaffe carried out several air attacks against Leningrad, during which a total of 112 high-explosive and eighty-six small incendiary bombs were dropped on the city. As a result, seventeen people were killed and another hundred were injured.

In May 1943, Jabo (fighter-bomber) Fw 190 As from I./JG 54 were first used for daytime raids on the city. As a rule, they dropped one 500kg high-explosive or fragmentation bomb from a great height. After completing the mission, the Fw 190 As immediately retreated to their territory. For example, on the morning of 9 May, German planes twice appeared suddenly over the city, dropping four high-explosive bombs. As a result, the Jelyabov plant, the No. 4 Kalinin plant and power plant No. 2 were damaged.

Rare raids by German twin-engine bombers also continued. On the night of 10 May, eleven bombs were dropped from them on Leningrad but they fell on unbuilt-up areas and did not cause any damage. On the afternoon of 17 May and on the night of 17–18 May, single bombers from KG 53 carried out five raids on Leningrad. A total of thirty-seven high-explosive bombs were dropped on the city. As a result, nine residential buildings were destroyed and the water supply system and tram tracks were damaged. Five people were killed and ninety-eight were injured.[243]

The Red Army Air Force responded to the German bombing with the usual templated method; that is, it carried out attacks against enemy airfields. This tactic, as a rule, did not produce any results and led to large losses of the attackers themselves.

Unexpected success in the fight against Luftwaffe air bases was achieved by Russian artillery. The Soviet Baltic Fleet included the 101st Naval Railway Artillery Brigade under the command of Major General Ivan Dmitriev. The most powerful and long-range artillery guns in its composition were three Soviet 180mm TM-1-180 railway gun batteries and one Soviet 356mm TM-1-14 railway gun battery. The main task of the 101st Naval Railway Artillery Brigade was a counter-battery fight against the German siege artillery shelling Leningrad. In

---

242. In the summer of 1944, the remains of *Shch-323*'s hull were lifted from the bottom and delivered to Leningrad. The bodies of the dead were buried at the Smolensk cemetery.
243. *The blockade of Leningrad in the documents of declassified archives*, Moscow: AST, 2004, pp.720 –721.

addition, the Soviet railway artillery periodically fired at other targets, including German airfields. This was possible due to the long firing range of these guns. For example, the 180mm TM-1-180 railway gun had a range of 37km.

On 9 April, after careful preparation, Soviet railway guns fired at Krasnogvardeysk airfield. All the 180mm shells hit their target, causing serious damage. At Krasnogvardeysk airfield, eight He 46s were destroyed (W.Nr. 0261, 0306, 0323, 0327, 0404, 0755, 1154 and 1227) and four Ar 66s (W.Nr. 0279, 1005, 1223 and 1227) from Stoergruppe L.Fl.1. These outdated biplanes played the role of light night bombers, copying the actions of the Russian Polikarpov U-2 night bombers. At night they flew over the Russian rear, dropping bombs on railway stations, main roads, warehouses, bridges and other targets. Like annoying mosquitoes, these slow-moving biplanes did not allow Red Army soldiers to sleep peacefully. After the loss of almost all the aircraft, Stoergruppe L.Fl.1 was disbanded.

Navigation on Lake Ladoga in 1943

Since the Soviets had failed to move the German 18th Army a considerable distance from Lake Ladoga, Leningrad's normal level of supply was still not restored. The single-track railway laid through the liberated town of Shlisselburg could not fully meet all the needs of the city. In the spring of 1943 it became clear to the city's leadership that it would be necessary to reactivate the water supply route across Lake Ladoga.

By the beginning of the 1943 navigation, the Ladoga Military Flotilla had received significant replenishment and now included four more armoured boats and two minesweepers. On 13 April, the repaired patrol ship *Constructor* entered service. Later, in June 1943, two midget submarines, *M-77* and *M-79*, sailed to Lake Ladoga. For what purpose the Russians transferred these midget submarines to the lake is not entirely clear. One can only assume that they intended to threaten the Siebel ferries of the Axis Ladoga flotilla with them.

In addition, all the gunboats, pathetically called 'Ladoga battleships' by the Russians, had been upgraded. A third 100mm gun was installed on the gunboat *Bira*. On the gunboat *Selemdzha*, similarly worn-out guns were replaced with more powerful 130mm weapons. On the gunboats *Bureya* and *Nora*, the outdated 76mm guns were also replaced with 130mm guns. Their anti-aircraft armament was also strengthened. On most gunboats, more efficient 37mm automatic anti-aircraft guns were installed instead of the outdated 45mm type.[244]

---

244. Cherokov, V.S., *For You, Leningrad!*, Leningrad: Leninzdat, 1988, p.154.

OPERATION ISKRA

The Soviets did not forget about protecting the ships travelling across Lake Ladoga from air attack. In order to strengthen air defences, the 240th Fighter Aviation Division (240th IAD) under Colonel Georgy Zimin was transferred to the Leningrad Front, and this unit included the 156th Fighter Aviation Regiment (156th IAP), 630th Fighter Aviation Regiment (630th IAP) and 744th Fighter Aviation Regiment (744th IAP). It was tasked with protecting railway bridges across the River Volkhov, the Lenin hydroelectric plant, Volkhovstroy railway junction and Ladoga water communication facilities from the Luftwaffe. Soviet fighters were based at Valdoma, Kipuya and Volkhov. At the disposal of the 240th IAD was one RUS-2 'Redut' radar station, capable of detecting enemy aircraft at a distance of up to 150km. It was located in a forest clearing north-west of Volkhov.[245]

On 29 March 1943, pushing the ice floes, the first cargo ships passed along Lake Ladoga. Due to the large amount of ice, initially only the small route (Kobona–Osinovets) functioned. The main volume of transportation was initially carried out by gunboats, which had a very solid construction. Attempts to use other less-resistant vessels turned into tragedy. On 6 April, the transport ship *Vilsandi*, with a tonnage of 350brt, was trapped by ice and sank. Due to poor ice conditions on the lake, passage along the big route (Novaya Ladoga–Osinovets) became possible only on 22 April. On this day, the first large convoy passed along that route. From that moment on, loads poured into Leningrad and its surroundings in an endless stream.

---

245. *The air defence forces of the country in the Great Patriotic War*, Moscow: Voenizdat, 1968, p.200.

Chapter 15

The Luftwaffe's last futile efforts

The New Luftwaffe offensive

In April 1943, taking advantage of the lull at the front, German aviation suspended activities to support its ground forces. Instead, the Kampfgeschwaderen launched large-scale strategic air attacks against Russian rear areas. The object of their close attention were large railway junctions and stations, maritime ports, plants and other important objects. These raids were carried out on the entire vast Eastern Front, stretching from the Baltic to the Black Sea.

The front sector around Leningrad was no exception. Hitler feared a new Russian offensive in this area and wanted to prevent the concentration of Red Army troops and their supply. In addition, massive air attacks in the Army Group North sector were supposed to misinform the Russians about the Wehrmacht offensive plans for the summer of 1943. The reason for this was the preparation of the Germans for Operation Citadel. The Wehrmacht High Command understood that it would not be possible to hide large-scale preparations from the enemy, but hoped to confuse the narrow-minded Stalin and his generals regarding the location of the main strike of the German army. Thus, one of the goals of simultaneous massive air attacks in different sectors of the Eastern Front was an attempt to disorientate the Soviets and prevent them preparing for new offensives.

At the beginning of May 1943, the Luftflotte 1 headquarters received another categoric order from Hitler's headquarters. The bombers were to destroy the port infrastructure on the shores of Lake Ladoga, as well as railway junctions and stations through which Leningrad and Leningrad Front troops were supplied.

In May 1943, Luftflotte 1 had the following forces:

- six He 111 H-6/H-14s from Staff Staffel and thirty-six He 111 H-16s from I./KG 53 (Korovye Selo Air Base);
- thirty-five He 111 H-16s from III./KG 53 (airbase Pleskau-Süd (city of Pskov);

- thirty Ju 87 B/D-3s from I./StG 5 (Gorodec airfield; 24km south of town Luga);
- thirty-five Fw 190 A-4/A-5s and three Bf 109 G-2s from I./JG 54, thirty-six Bf 109 G-2/G-4s and eighteen Fw 190 A-4/A-5s from II./JG 54 (Krasnogvardeysk airfield and Siverskaya Air Base).

In addition, in May 1943, the combat training Gruppe (II./KG 101) Oberst Albert Bohm arrived at the Pleskau-Süd (city of Pskov) from Germany. It was equipped with Ju 88 A and Do 217 E-4 bombers. There were only two Staffeln in its composition, as the third Staffel had already been formed at Pleskau-Süd (city of Pskov). Most of the German crews of this unit had no combat experience.

Goal selection

In late April–early May 1943, German reconnaissance planes again began to appear frequently in the vicinity of Lake Ladoga and produced aerial photography of railways, bridges, lake ports and ships. There were also night reconnaissance planes that used photoflash bombs for aerial photography. Such activity naturally caused the Russians alarm, since they knew well what actions followed after such flights. Soon these fears were fully realised.

Volkhov was chosen by the Germans as the main target for Luftwaffe attacks. This choice shows that the Luftflotte 1 headquarters did not act under the influence of emotions and political expediency, but on the basis of an objective analysis of the weaknesses of the Soviet transport and energy infrastructure. In the Volkhov area there was the major railway junction at Volkhovstroy, the Lenin hydroelectric plant, a thermal power station and a three-span railway bridge across the Volkhov. Thus, the most important transport and energy facilities, which played a key role for the supply of Leningrad, were concentrated on a small territory. In 1942–early 1943, the Luftwaffe periodically bombed Volkhov, but only in May 1943 did their attacks became massive. The Soviets, realising the vulnerability of these important facilities, constantly increased air defence around Volkhov. In May 1943, this crucial function was carried out by eight Separate Anti-aircraft Divisions (OZAD): 1, 25, 37, 69, 214, 251, 253 and 432. These anti-aircraft units had ninety-five anti-aircraft guns, including seventy-two medium calibre and twenty-three small calibre, as well as twenty-eight anti-aircraft machine guns and forty-four searchlights.

AIR BATTLE FOR LENINGRAD, 1941–1944

Aerial battle for Volkhov

On the night of 12–13 May 1943, the first bombing attack was carried out on Volkhov after German planes approached the target from the south, along the River Volkhov. The pathfinders were the first to appear over the city at 23.41 and they dropped photoflash bombs. However, the 'chandeliers', which descended slowly on parachutes, were blown away by the wind and only illuminated the southern part of Volkhov and its surroundings.

The main target of the German bombing was the Lenin hydroelectric plant. This important energy facility was located in the city centre, 600m south of the three-span railway bridge across the river. The length of the hydroelectric dam was 215m, and the width of its upper edge was only 10m. The engine room at the hydroelectric plant had dimensions of 230 by 40m. Keeping at an altitude of 4,500–5,000m, German planes dropped bombs into the riverbed, aiming at the hydroelectric dam. Huge columns of water rose above the surface of the river, and explosions thundered on both banks and in the city. However, the accuracy of bombing was low and just a few bombs exploded in the target area. Near the hydroelectric plant, the warehouse, the dam lock wooden booth, the water supply system and the electric power transmission lines were damaged. However, the main hydroelectric plant facilities were not affected and the generation and transmission of electricity did not stop during the air attack.[246]

On the night of 15–16 May, the Luftwaffe repeated its massive raid on Volkhov. This time, the main targets were the railway bridge and the major Volkhovstroy railway junction. The Germans dropped 500 high-explosive and fragmentation bombs on these objects. As a result of the air attack, several sections of railway tracks were destroyed and seventeen railway wagons were damaged. The railway traffic was completely stopped for five hours. Eleven wooden houses burned down in Volkhov. Twenty-one railway workers were killed and twenty-four other people were injured.

The Soviets tried to counteract the German raid. Two P-40 night fighters from the 630th Fighter Aviation Regiment (630th IAP) were scrambled from Plehanovo airfield (2km north of Volkhov) to intercept the German aircraft. This aviation regiment was specially relocated from Valdai Hills to strengthen the air defence of the town's important facilities. One of the P-40s was flown by an experienced pilot, Major Vasily Shapochka. At 01.15, he found an He 111 at an altitude of 3,800m. Major Shapochka approached from below and opened fire from all six machine guns. After that, the air gunner of the German bomber opened fire in return. The Soviet fighter was forced to carry out a sharp manoeuvre to avoid the

---

246. TSAMO RF. Foundation 13642. Inventory 0020244. Case 0061. Sheets 203–205.

THE LUFTWAFFE'S LAST FUTILE EFFORTS

firing, but then launched a new attack. Major Shapochka got close to the bomber at a distance of 50m, after which he again opened fire with six machine guns. This time the bullets hit the target. According to Soviet information, a burning He 111 crashed 10km south of Volkhov. After that, at 01.56 Major Shapochka intercepted another enemy bomber and pursued it to the front line. The pilot claimed that he shot down the plane. According to his report, an enemy bomber crashed on German territory in the Kirishi area. Another aerial victory was claimed by Major Artemiy Astapov, the pilot of the second P-40.[247]

On the night of 20–21 May, fifty He 111s carried out a third raid on Volkhov when about 200 bombs were dropped on the town. Important facilities in the area again sustained only minor damage.

On 22 May, between 07.10 and 10.10, Bf 109s from JG 54 attacked the three-span railway bridge across the River Volkhov three times. They approached the target at a high altitude, then dived at it from the direction of the sun and each fighter-bomber dropped one 250kg bomb. Russian anti-aircraft gunners opened fire in time and managed to hit one of the Bf 109s. The enemy plane did not have time to drop the bomb and, continuing to dive, crashed near Volkhovstroy railway junction and exploded. According to German data, it was Bf 109 G-2 W.Nr. 13744 'Gelbe 9' of 4./JG 54, piloted by Unteroffizier Johannes Runge. The German pilot had six aerial victories on his account.

On the same day, at 12.30, twenty-seven Ju 87s from I./StG 5 appeared over Volkhov and also dropped bombs on the railway bridge. However, the Germans were unable to hit the target, although several bombs exploded near the bridge and access railway tracks were damaged.

LaGG-3 fighters from the 156th Fighter Aviation Regiment (156th IAP), which were defending the important facilities in Volkhov, could not prevent the Stukas' attack. One of 'Stalin's Falcons', Captain Romanov, reported that he shot down an Fw 190 from an escort group of enemy bombers in a dogfight. According to German information, Fw 190 A-5 W.Nr. 1501313 'Schwarze 9' of 5./JG 54 piloted by Feldwebel Walter Heck was seriously damaged by Russian fighter fire. The pilot was able to fly to German territory and made an emergency landing in the Mga area. The landing was unsuccessful, the plane turned over, and the broken armour backrest broke the pilot's neck. As a result of this severe injury, Feldwebel Heck was completely paralysed and died in hospital three days later. It was a heavy loss for JG 54. Feldwebel Heck had fought since March 1942 and had recorded thirty-two aerial victories.

On 31 May, a large group of Ju 87s from I./StG 5 attacked the Volkhov railway bridge twice. However, the Stukas' pilots were again unsuccessful.

---

247. TSAMO RF. Foundation 20157. Inventory 1. Case 30. Sheets 24–29.

AIR BATTLE FOR LENINGRAD, 1941–1944

'The enemy continues massive bombing raids'

In parallel with the raids on the town of Volkhov, the Luftwaffe continued to bomb Russian ports on Lake Ladoga. Due to the strengthening of the Soviet air defence, the Germans switched to night attacks. On the night of 25 May 1943, fifty-eight He 111s from KG 53 struck the oil storage facilities at Morier harbour. Berths in Osinovets, Golsman and Novaya harbours were also targeted. To maintain the effectiveness of their night attacks, the Germans had to use pathfinder aircraft. They were the first to appear over the western shore of the lake and dropped photoflash bombs to mark targets for the bombers flying behind. Due to the bright light of the German photoflash bombs, it became as bright as day. Some photoflash bombs, descending by parachute, did not work and dropped into the lake in different places. In the dark, the Russians mistook such defective 'chandeliers' for bottom mines. Soon the Russians heard the hum of the engines of a large group of bombers approaching from the south. The Luftwaffe planes dropped their bombs on Russian ports exactly according to plan. According to Soviet information, 15–20 per cent of the bombs dropped did not explode. However, those that did were enough for the port infrastructure on Lake Ladoga to be severely damaged. For example, in Osinovets harbour, two food warehouses burned down and the breakwater was damaged. Some of the bombs exploded on the positions of the 95th Separate Anti-aircraft Division (95th OZAD). As a result, one 45mm anti-aircraft gun was smashed and several gunners were killed.

The 5th Separate Railway Anti-aircraft Battery (5th OZJB) under the command of Senior Lieutenant Pavel Gagarin claimed three downed German bombers. Another enemy aircraft was claimed by gunners on the gunboat *Lakhta*. In fact, all the German bombers returned safely to their air bases after completing the combat mission.

On the evening of 24 May, six Fw 190 fighter-bombers attacked transport vessels on Lake Ladoga but all their bombs fell past the targets. The night of the same day, German bombers raided Morier harbour, dropping about 200 high-explosive and fragmentation bombs.

On 26 May at 20.40 thirty He 111s under the cover of twelve Fw 190s carried out an air attack against Osinovets harbour. A total of 170 bombs were dropped on the port infrastructure. As a result, two piers were destroyed and two railway wagons carrying ammunition exploded. The dredging vessel *Svir-2*, two boats and a barge carrying firewood were damaged. Eight railway wagons burned out on the shore. Some of the bombs again fell on the positions of the 25th Separate Anti-aircraft Division (25th OZAD), destroying two anti-aircraft guns. As a result of this air strike, the head of the port of Osinovets, Captain 1st Rank Mikhail Nefedov, was killed. He was directing the extinguishing of a

THE LUFTWAFFE'S LAST FUTILE EFFORTS

fire at a warehouse when a German high-explosive bomb fell nearby. The bomb did not explode, but when it hit the ground, it dislodged stonework which hit Nefedov in the head.

Russian anti-aircraft gunners claimed that during the repulse of the air attack they shot down an He 111 and an Fw 190.[248] These claims were close to reality. According to German information, Russian fighters shot down an He 111 from 9./KG 53. The entire crew, consisting of pilot Siegfrid Thomas, radio operator Harry Wermbter, flight engineer Fritz Romer and flight gunner Hubert Franz, died. Anti-aircraft fire also shot down Fw 190 A-5 W.Nr. 1501185 piloted by Leutnant Werner Lohmann from 6./JG 54. The pilot made an emergency landing on Russian territory near Osinovets village. Nothing is known about his subsequent fate.

On the night of 26–27 May and the whole of the next day, groups of He 111s again attacked the port infrastructure of Soviet shipping on Lake Ladoga. Novaya Ladoga, Morier and Osinovets harbours, the port of Kobona, Lednevo settlement, Shlisselburg Bay, Morozova village, Karedja sandspit and Sukho Island were bombed. Significant damage was caused to the ports' infrastructure, including the destruction of a ship repair workshop in Novaya Ladoga harbour. The Leningrad Front supply warehouse was destroyed in the port of Kobona.

On 27 May at 20.40 thirty He 111s accompanied by ten Fw 190 As and Bf 109 Gs attacked the town of Novaya Ladoga. About 200 high-explosive and heavy incendiary bombs were dropped and many buildings were destroyed as fire engulfed entire blocks of residential buildings. In the town's port area, wharves were destroyed and the submarine chaser *MO-206* was damaged. Anti-aircraft gunners of the 11th Separate Anti-aircraft Division (11th OZAD) located in the port claimed four downed German aircraft. Two more victories over the enemy were recorded by the sailors of the gunboats *Bira* and *Bureya*, in Novaya Ladoga harbour. Fighters of the 11th Fighter Aviation Regiment Air Force Soviet Baltic Fleet (11th IAP VVS KBF) also tried to resist the enemy attacks. 'Stalin's Falcons' performed thirty-two sorties 'to cover the ports of Novaya Ladoga and Kobona', but 'had no meetings with enemy aircraft'.[249]

On the night of 27–28 May, Luftwaffe aircraft carried out another air attack on the ports of Novaya Ladoga and Kobona and the Syasstroy settlement in which the ports suffered new destruction. For example, in Kobona, railway tracks, electric power transmission lines and a fuel storage facility were destroyed. Night fighters from the 11th IAP VVS KBF flew to intercept the German bombers and the commander of the 2nd Squadron, Captain Alexander

---

248. TSAMO RF. Foundation 13642. Inventory 0020244. Case 0061. Sheets 207–209.
249. *The Military Chronicle of the Soviet Navy, 1943*, Moscow: Voenizdat, 1993, p.164.

Troshin, attacked and shot down two He 111s. Major Vasily Shapochka from the 630th Fighter Aviation Regiment (630th IAP) also reported on the downed He 111 in the Syasstroy area.

According to German information, KG 53 lost two aircraft that day:

- He 111 piloted by Commander of III./KG 53 Major Hubert Monh. The entire crew of Karl-Anton van Volken, Paul Altrock, Helmut Stuhr and Friedrich Standing were missing;
- He 111 piloted by Unteroffizierr Karl Kestrel of 2./KG 53. The entire crew of Hans Gegner, Gunther Brandstatter, Wilhelm Otto and Hermann Kraft were missing.

The death of the Commander III./KG 53, Major Hubert Monh, proved to be a serious blow to the entire Kampfgeschwader 53 'Legion Condor'. The commander of 7./KG 53, Oberleutnant Ernst Ebeling, later recalled:

> In one of the missions we lost Major Monh. None of the crews of the bombers flying nearby saw an air battle or an explosion from a direct hit by an anti-aircraft shell. It was only in 1955 that we learned from his navigator, Hauptmann Volhen, that their plane had been shot down by Soviet fighters. Major Monh did not want to be in Russian captivity and refused to leave the plane, but gave this opportunity to his crew. Only Hauptmann Volhen managed to escape. Shortly after the parachute canopy opened, he saw that the plane had exploded. During the multi-day pedestrian crossings at night, Hauptmann Volhen tried to reach the positions of his troops, but was still noticed by Russian soldiers. Hauptmann Volhen stayed in Russian captivity until 1955, having experienced many difficulties. Before his release from captivity, his wife and five children lived in complete obscurity about his fate in the city of Halle, also occupied by the Russians.[250]

The air battle of 30 May 1943

The series of bombing raids on Lake Ladoga port infrastructure continued with unrelenting force. On 30 May 1943 at 14.37 forty He 111s from KG 53,

---

250. Kiehl, H., *Kampfgeschwader 'Legion Condor' 53*, Stuttgart: Motorbuch Verlag, 1996, p.399.

THE LUFTWAFFE'S LAST FUTILE EFFORTS

accompanied by eleven Fw 190 As, carried out a massive raid on the port of Kobona. As a result, the railway tracks, landing stage and Leningrad Front supply warehouse were destroyed again.

At 20.20 on the same day, Russian radar stations detected several groups of German aircraft. The bombers were again flying in the direction of Lake Ladoga. According to Soviet information, thirty-seven He 111s participated in the raid, and they were accompanied by ten Fw 190 A and Bf 109 G fighters.

Soviet fighters were scrambled to intercept the enemy aircraft. Six Yak-7Bs from the 86th Fighter Aviation Regiment (86th IAP), led by Senior Lieutenant Korotkov, attacked a group of fourteen He 111s at an altitude of about 5,500m. German air gunners opened fierce barrage of firing in response. A Yak-7B piloted by Junior Lieutenant Khoroshkov dived on one of the He 111s and hit the blades of his propeller on its tail. However, 'Stalin's Falcon' had no time to check the results of the ramming as his aircraft was attacked by an Fw 190. The Russian fighter caught fire, and Junior Lieutenant Khoroshkov jumped out using a parachute.

Meanwhile, German bombers continued to fly in the direction of Osinovets port, on the western shore. At 20.52 they were over Lake Ladoga, after which they split into two groups. One group of bombers headed for Osinovets harbour, while the other attacked Morier harbour. They dropped bombs from 5,400–5,800m using a Lotfe 7D high-altitude bombsight. Such tactics made it possible to avoid the fire of Soviet anti-aircraft artillery, which was ineffective at such an altitude. German bombs once again caused serious damage to port infrastructure, and a chemical warehouse was destroyed in Osinovets harbour. Boat *No. 122* was sunk off one of the berths. In Morier harbour, German bomb blasts destroyed access railway tracks and a fuel oil pipeline. As a result of the fire, two cisterns with fuel burned to the ground. The patrol boat *KM-42* was damaged by bomb fragments.

On the way back, the crews of German bombers from KG 53 again withstood numerous attacks by Russian fighters. To repel the German air raid on 30 May, 'Stalin's Falcons' flew seventy-nine sorties and participated in numerous dogfights. For example, eight P-40s fighters from the 191st Fighter Aviation Regiment (191st IAP) attacked a group of He 111s. The pilot of one of the Tomahawks, Major Mitrokhin, shot down two He 111s and an Fw 190 near town Shlisselburg. According to Soviet information, the pilot of a German fighter jumped out of a falling fighter by parachute and was captured. In total, Russian pilots claimed eighteen aerial victories on 30 May 1943 (seven bombers and eleven fighters). 'Stalin's Falcons' own losses amounted to three fighters. Thus, the numerous dogfights on this day turned into a real battle.

Russian anti-aircraft batteries conducted intensive barrage firing on 30 May and claimed the destruction of three enemy aircraft.[251] Another two downed enemy aircraft were claimed by anti-aircraft gunners of the 5th Separate Railway Anti-aircraft Battery (5th OZJB).

When comparing Soviet data on the results of the battle with German sources, it can be concluded that 'Stalin's Falcons' and Soviet anti-aircraft gunners once again greatly overestimated their successes. In fact, on 30 May, KG 53 lost only one He 111 from 1./KG 53 piloted by Oberfeldwebel Willi Pfluger. His crew, consisting of navigator Erich Zellner, radio operator Rudolf Braunschuh, flight engineer Otto Maak and air gunner Walter Muller, were posted missing. Several He 111s were damaged by fragments of anti-aircraft shells and the bullets of Soviet fighters, but they returned safely to base. During an attack by Soviet fighters on a bomber from 9./KG 53, air gunner Oberfeldwebel Gotz Warner was killed. The fighters from I./JG 54 covering the bombers did not suffer any combat losses on this day.

In total, during May 1943, German bombers, mainly He 111s from I. and III./KG 53, made six raids on the port of Kobona, seven raids on Osinovets harbour, seven raids on Morier harbour, three raids on the port of Novaya Ladoga, two raids on lighthouses on Karedja sandspit and one raid on Sukho Island, the harbour of the Spit of Lednevo and Shlisselburg Bay.

The first massive attack on the Volkhov railway bridge

Soon the Luftflotte 1 staff officers realised that it was not possible to destroy Volkhov railway bridge with just night bombing and daytime air attacks by small groups of bombers. It took extraordinary luck to hit such a difficult target during a brief raid, even more so in the face of opposition from numerous anti-aircraft artillery. After analysing the reasons for the failures, the Germans decided to change tactics. The Luftflotte 1 headquarters decided to prepare a series of daily massive raids, with the methodical conduct of which the probability of damaging the load-bearing structures of the bridge increased significantly. In turn, the Soviets also expected an increase in German air attacks and prepared for it in advance. Additional ammunition was brought to the positions of anti-aircraft artillery batteries. Fighters were constantly on duty at Soviet airfields in anticipation of a German attack.

On 1 June, at 05.13, radar stations detected German bombers over German territory, in the Schapki settlement area (70km south-west of Volkhov). Thanks

---

251. TSAMO RF. Foundation 13642. Inventory 0020244. Case 0061. Sheets 304–307.

to the effective work of these radar stations, the Soviets had about twenty minutes to prepare for an attack. Air-raid horns howled in Volkhov, anti-aircraft gunners prepared to fire, and fighters were preparing to scramble. At 05.18, four Yak-7B fighters from the 630th Fighter Aviation Regiment (630th IAP), led by Lieutenant Mikhailov, took off from Plehanovo airfield. Three minutes later, five more La-5 fighters took off, led by Captain Cibulkin. Having gained an altitude of 5,000m, the fighters prepared for a fierce dogfight. At 05.33, the first group of eighteen Ju 88 bombers appeared over the huge swamps stretching south-west of Volkhov. 'Stalin's Falcons' immediately rushed to attack the German planes. However, a large group of Bf 109 and Fw 190 fighters covering the bombers completely tied up the Russian fighters in battle and did not allow the 'Stalin's Falcons' to intercept the bombers. The dogfight lasted about forty minutes. The pilots of the 630th IAP claimed three downed Fw 190s, and several more aerial victories were recorded by the pilots of the 156th IAP.[252] However, in reality, the fighters from JG 54 did not suffer any losses.

The German pilots claimed eight aerial victories in this air battle. Oberleutnant Walter Nowotny from 1./JG 54 shot down LaGG-5 (La-5) and LaGG-3 fighters. Unteroffizier Hager and Feldwebel Heinz Wernicke, both from 6./JG 54, shot down LaGG-3s, while Unteroffizier Ulrich Wernitz and Feldwebel Hermann Schleinhage, both from Stab/JG 54, shot down Yak-1s. Oberleutnant Alfred Teumer from 5./JG 54 and Unteroffizier Hugo Broch from 6./JG 54 shot down LaGG-3s. All German aerial victories fully corresponded to reality. The 630th IAP lost four fighters. Junior Lieutenants Pyotr Zhuravlev, Vasily Prokopenkov and Ivan Lebedev were missing. Lieutenant Petrovichev's fighter made an emergency wheels-up landing, the plane was completely smashed, and the pilot was injured. The LaGG-3 of Captain Ivan Pastukhov from the 156th IAP was also shot down. He performed an emergency wheels-up landing and remained unharmed. Two more Soviet fighters (a La-5 and Yak-7B) received severe damage but were able to return to base.

At 05.35 the next group of German bombers attacked the Volkhov railway bridge from the north-east. He 111s entered the target in threes and dropped bombs from a height of 6,000m. For accurate bombing, they used the Lotfe 7D bombsight. Shortly after the first group completed its run, a second group of He 111s appeared and these attacked the target from the east.

At 05.41, two more groups of He 111s reached Volkhov and attacked the Volkhov railway bridge from the western direction. Five minutes later, the next group of bombers dropped bombs on the bridge from an altitude of 5,700m. By this time, the target was completely hidden by smoke from the explosions.

---

252. TSAMO RF. Foundation 20157. Inventory 1. Case 30. Sheets 31–36.

Twenty Ju 87s from I./StG 5 were the last to bomb the bridge that day. The Stukas alternately dropped bombs from 800–400m, after which they left, heading west.

As a result of the intense bombing on 1 June, the metal structures of the bridge were damaged. Two spans of an auxiliary wooden bridge, which served as a stand-in for the metal bridge, were also destroyed. In several places on the river bank, the railway track was destroyed.

Anti-aircraft artillery fired 3,000 shells while repulsing the raid. The anti-aircraft gunners reported to the higher command that it had downed nine downed German aircraft (six He 111s and three Ju 87s).

The second massive Luftwaffe attack on the bridge

Twenty minutes after the enemy bombers were detected, six Yak-7Bs led by Captain Khodakov appeared over the front line. Soon, 'Stalin's Falcons' saw twenty He 111s flying in two groups at an altitude of 4,000–4,500m. The Yak-7Bs tried to attack the bombers from the front. However, twelve Fw 190s covering the bombers prevented the 'Stalin's Falcons' and forced the Soviet fighters to join the fleeting dogfight.

At 16.35 German bombers attacked eight LaGG-3 fighters from the 156th IAP led by Captain Pastukhov. In their reports, the Soviet pilots recorded two downed He 111s.[253]

The attacks of 'Stalin's Falcons' failed to interrupt the mission of the German bombers. The first group of twenty-four He 111s bypassed the town of Volkhov from the south and reached the target from the south-east. At 16.53, the bombers were within line of sight of the Volkhov railway bridge. In response to the appearance of enemy aircraft, Soviet anti-aircraft gunners opened a frenzied barrage. Some of the anti-aircraft guns conducted barrage firing along the course of the German bombers, the rest fired into the sky over the railway bridge. The sky over Volkhov was covered with hundreds of black clouds of anti-aircraft shell explosions. Dodging the bursts of anti-aircraft shells, the He 111s divided into pairs and threes. Soon the navigators turned on the Lotfe 7D bombsights and the bomber pilots began to slowly enter the target area.

Gilbert Geisendorfer from 6./KG 53 recalled:

> Approaching the target in a straight line is a critical moment. The pilot needs to keep the plane absolutely straight. No fluctuations

---

253. TSAMO RF. Foundation 13642. Inventory 0020244. Case 0061. Sheets 210–214.

THE LUFTWAFFE'S LAST FUTILE EFFORTS

in height, roll and speed. Such a flight created ideal conditions for measuring the instruments of anti-aircraft batteries. Who will be faster: are we with our approach to the target or enemy anti-aircraft guns? It depended on how good the scorer was. In such situations, I have learned to appreciate the skill and calmness of my navigator-bombardier Schmauz. To understand each other, we needed only brief glances and nods of the head.[254]

The second group of sixteen He 111s reached the River Volkhov near the village of Gostinopolye. Turning left, the bombers attacked the railway bridge from the south. Dozens of bombs exploded near the target, and it completely disappeared in smoke and columns of water. As soon as the last He 111 passed horizontally over the target, a group of eighteen Ju 87s appeared from the south-east. They flew one after another in a long column, at an altitude of 4,500m. The anti-aircraft gunners did not have time to deploy their guns towards the Stukas, and the first group of Ju 87s began attacking the target without interference. The dive bombers, their sirens howling, dropped their bombs from a height of about 1,000m. The bridge disappeared again in clouds of smoke and water columns. Amid the roar of the explosions, there was also a metallic crackling and grinding. It was clear that the bridge could not survive after so many attacks. However, when the smoke cleared and the river water calmed down, the metal structure still continued to stand on its supports. Three and a half hours later, at 20.30 on 1 June, the 98m span of the railway bridge collapsed into the river with a deafening screech and roar. When it fell, it raised huge waves that swept along the banks of the Volkhov, like a tsunami.[255]

After the German bombers flew away, Russian anti-aircraft gunners and Soviet fighter pilots began to compile reports on their 'victories'. The gunners, having fired 3,500 shells at the enemy, reported to their superiors they had seven downed enemy aircraft. 'Stalin's Falcons' proudly announced thirteen victories in air battles on the evening of 1 June. In fact, Luftwaffe losses turned out to be minimal. Fw 190 A-5 W.Nr. 7119 of 1./JG 54 was damaged in air combat, while another German fighter made an emergency landing at Mga airfield. He 111 W.Nr. 8500 of 2./KG 53 was also damaged and pilot Oberleutnant Martin Vollmer and navigator Feldwebel Heinz Fritche were injured. However, the bomber also flew safely back to base.

---

254. Kiehl, H., *Kampfgeschwader 'Legion Condor' 53*, Stuttgart: Motorbuch Verlag, 1996, pp.389–391.
255. TSAMO RF. Foundation 13642. Inventory 0020244. Case 0061. Sheets 215–216.

In the air battles that took place on the evening of 1 June, the pilots of JG 54 won six victories, with Oberleutnant Walter Nowotny the most successful. He shot down two LaGG-3s and one MiG-3. These claims by the Luftwaffe pilots again turned out to be very close to reality. The 86th Guards Fighter Aviation Regiment Air Defence (86th GIAP PVO) suffered the greatest losses, losing five Yak-7Bs in one battle at once. Two pilots, Captain Hodakov and Captain Manov, were missing. Junior Lieutenant Marchenko jumped out with a parachute and survived, while Lieutenant Manulin and Senior Lieutenant Korotkov performed wheels-up emergency landings.

'There were signs of destruction everywhere ...'

On 2 June 1943, as a result of artillery shelling, the new railway bridge across the Neva near the town of Shlisselburg was severely damaged. It was erected to replace the temporary bridge that the Soviets built in February 1943 after breaking the land blockade.

On 8 June, at 16.55, after a week-long break, the Luftwaffe conducted a new air attack on Volkhov. It involved eighteen Ju 88s and five Do 217 E-4s from II./KG 101, which took off from Pleskau-Süd (city of Pskov). Soon they were joined by an escort of fighters from JG 54, which took off from Siverskaya. The tactics and objectives of the air raid were the same. The bombers entered the target simultaneously from three directions: the south-west, south-east and north-east. From a height of 5,000–5,200m, they dropped high-explosive bombs and cluster bombs. As a result of the air raid, the newly restored railway infrastructure was damaged again and electric power transmission lines and residential buildings were destroyed. However, the critical facilities were not affected. The Lenin hydroelectric plant was promptly covered with a smokescreen. The measures taken by the Soviets proved effective, and only one bomb fell on the plant, the explosion of which did not lead to serious damage.

The Russians scrambled sixty fighters to intercept the German bombers. However, 'Stalin's Falcons' again failed to achieve worthwhile successes. The shooting of Soviet anti-aircraft gunners turned out to be more effective. The Do 217 E-4 W.Nr. 210 was heavily damaged by anti-aircraft fire. Its crew included pilot Leutnant Steer, navigator Obergefreiter Karl Gemzal, radio operator Unteroffizier Heinrich Peter and flight engineer Obergefreiter Wilhelm Steiner. The plane made an emergency wheels-up landing on Russian territory. The crew of the German bomber survived, but was captured by the Russians. During their interrogation, the German pilots showed a desire to actively cooperate with the Soviet special services. The pilots from the bomber crew

THE LUFTWAFFE'S LAST FUTILE EFFORTS

gave the Soviets detailed information about their Kampfgeschwader, locations, commanders, tactics and types of bombs used. The Germans admitted that the purpose of their mission was a wooden railway bridge across the Volkhov.[256]

On 17, 18, 19 and 21 June, bombers targeted Volkhov again. During this period, about 1,500 bombs of various types were dropped on the town. The Luftwaffe managed to damage the allegedly restored Volkhov railway bridge and the dam at the Lenin hydroelectric plant again. A train carrying ammunition was destroyed at Volkhovstroy junction. Despite the high intensity of the air attacks, the Germans suffered minimal losses. Several He 111s from III./KG 53 were damaged, but all of them were able to return to base. There were also isolated losses among the crews of German aircraft. On 18 June, air gunner Unteroffizierr Heinrich Klare from 7./KG 53 was killed. On 21 June, flight engineer Unteroffizierr Eugen Merz from 9./KG 53 was killed by the return fire of Russian anti-aircraft gunners.

During a series of massive Luftwaffe raids by the standards of the Eastern Front, the railway infrastructure of Volkhov, used to supply Leningrad, was severely destroyed. Railroad worker Yakov Mayorov recalled:

> There were traces of destruction everywhere. The earth gaped with craters. Here and there lay the mangled explosions, burnt skeletons of railway wagons, bridge trusses. Groups of Red Army men picked up and loaded stumps of rails, sleepers onto hand carts, stacked rusted fastenings in piles ... Volkhovstroy railway junction and Tikhvin railway station lay in ruins. Not a single building, not a single railway structure was left intact here.[257]

By destroying railway communications, the Germans tried to indirectly restore the land blockade of Leningrad. As already noted above, such global tasks could not be implemented by the Luftwaffe and artillery without a significant advance of the German land forces. The distance from the town of Kirishi, where German troops held a bridgehead on the eastern bank of the River Volkhov, to Volkhov was only 50km. However, in 1943, the Wehrmacht in this area no longer had the strength to advance even what was such an insignificant distance by the scale of the Eastern Front.

There is no doubt that such persistent attempts to block supplies to Leningrad were initiated from Hitler's headquarters. Despite the obvious senselessness of

---

256. TSAMO RF. Foundation 13642. Inventory 0020244. Case 0061. Sheet 221.
257. Mayorov, Y.M., *Highways of Courage*, Moscow: Voenizdat, 1982, p.76.

these actions, the Luftwaffe bombing attacks proved to be very painful for the Russians. The Soviets tried in every possible way to hide and downplay the serious damage they had suffered. In particular, the false Stalinist propaganda, recognising the loss of the Volkhov railway bridge, claimed that Russian railway workers and military sappers had restored the bridge in just two weeks. However, in reality, rail traffic through Volkhov was significantly limited for several months.

Luftwaffe raids on the port infrastructure on Lake Ladoga continue

On the afternoon of 5 June, sixty-six He 111s under the cover of sixteen Fw 190s bombed the town of Novaya Ladoga and the nearby port infrastructure. Many buildings were destroyed, an ammunition depot exploded and the communication lines of the main base of the Soviet Ladoga Military Flotilla failed. Dozens of people were killed and injured. After completing the mission, the German bombers turned around and quietly flew back to their airfields.

Russian fighters carried out ninety sorties to intercept the German bombers. 'Stalin's Falcons' claimed eleven aerial victories (seven He 111s, three Fw 190s and one Bf 109). The Soviets' own losses amounted to two fighters. Three more downed He 111s were recorded on their combat account by the anti-aircraft gunners of the Separate Anti-aircraft Division (11th OZAD) Lieutenant Colonel Ivan Ryzhenko.[258]

In fact, during that mission, KG 53 lost only one He 111 H-16, piloted by Leutnant Karl-Heinz Andreesen from 1./KG 53. His crew, consisting of navigator Werner Zollner, radio operator Werner Zorn, flight engineer Paul Zilinka and air gunner Eugen Danielowski, were killed. During the attacks of Soviet fighters on one of the 8./KG 53 aircraft, air gunner Unteroffizierr Erwin Seeber was killed. Several German bombers received minor damage from fragments of anti-aircraft shells and bullets of Soviet fighters.

On 11 and 12 June, Fw 190 fighter-bombers from JG 54 bombed Osinovets harbour three times, dropping twenty high-explosive bombs. As a result, piers and the water supply system were damaged.

On the evening of 22 June, thirty-four He 111s from KG 53, accompanied by Fw 190s and Bf 109s from JG 54, made another raid on Osinovets and Morier harbours. The bombers dropped about 130 bombs weighing from 50 to 250kg

---

258. TSAMO RF. Foundation 13642. Inventory 0020244. Case 0061. Sheets 309–312.

THE LUFTWAFFE'S LAST FUTILE EFFORTS

on the port infrastructure. The liquid fuel pipeline and several other facilities were damaged.

On 23 June, the Luftwaffe again launched a series of air attacks against Soviet harbours and transport communications in the Lake Ladoga area. At 10.30 (Moscow time), thirty Ju 87s from I./StG 5 raided Voibokalo and Pupyshevo railway stations and the tracks were destroyed. The movement of transport in the area was only restored by 19.00. A train was destroyed on a section of track between Pupyshevo and Novyi Byt and seventeen railway wagons and ten flat wagons were destroyed. During the air raid, nine people were killed and seventeen others were injured.[259]

German air attacks continued throughout the day. At 11.05 six Fw 190s dropped bombs on the port of Osinovets. Powerful explosions destroyed the railway tracks and pier.

At 13.15 four German planes attacked and sank the Lake Ladoga railway ferry, which was carrying eight railway wagons loaded with pyrite. Minesweeper *TSCH-63*, towing a railway ferry, received minor damage.

In the evening of 23 June at 21.00, another massive raid was made on Osinovets and Morier harbours in which German planes dropped about 350 high-explosive bombs. At Morier harbour, two steam locomotives, a pumping station and a pier were destroyed, while railway tracks and oil pipelines were damaged. The fuel oil storage caught fire and burned until morning. The flames and smoke of the fire rose hundreds of metres above Lake Ladoga. Several bombs exploded on the positions of Separate Anti-aircraft Battery No. 194. However, the human cost was small: one person was killed and three were wounded.

In the port of Osinovets, seven railway wagons were destroyed and one barge sank. Two piers were severely damaged, and the railway tracks leading to them were also destroyed.

On 23 June, Soviet fighter aircraft in the Lake Ladoga area carried out 102 sorties, including fifty-nine to cover lake ports. 'Stalin's Falcons' claimed thirteen aerial victories (five Fw 190s, four Ju 88s, two Bf 110s, one Do 215 and one He 111). The Red Army Air Force's own losses in this sector of the front amounted to three fighters. Soviet anti-aircraft artillery announced the downing of six Ju 87s.[260]

Despite the ability to quickly repair damage to their primitive port infrastructure, the Soviets were clearly frightened and puzzled by such prolonged Luftwaffe activity. Leningrad Front headquarters complained to

---

259. Ibid., Sheets 319–324.
260. Ibid., Sheets 332–337.

Joseph Stalin in its report: 'The enemy continues massive bombing raids on our railway and water communications, seeking to disable railway bridges through the river Volkhov, destroy railway stations and ports on Lake Ladoga.'[261]

It seemed to the Soviets that there would be no end to the German air attacks and the destruction that followed them. However, the very next day there was a sudden lull in the Leningrad sector. As it turned out, 23 June was the last day of Luftflotte 1's operation to destroy Russian transport communications. Hitler was preparing a new adventure on the Eastern Front, Operation Citadel, and was forced to shift the attention of his 'flaming Eye' from Leningrad to another Russian city, Kursk.

According to Soviet information, sixty-seven planes were shot down by anti-aircraft artillery and fighters during the repulse of the Luftwaffe raids in May–June 1943. This data, as usual, was a wild exaggeration of the real German losses. According to German information, during these two months, the combat losses of KG 53 amounted to twenty-one He 111s. Only five bombers were shot down during the air attacks described above.

The serious damage caused by German bombing and the complete inability of the Soviet air defence to protect the port infrastructure on Lake Ladoga is evidenced by the fact of personnel changes in the command of the Soviet air defence. In June 1943, the Commander of the Ladoga Divisional Air Defence Area, Major General Sergei Prokhorov, was removed from his post and replaced by Colonel Nikolai Travin. However, personnel changes in command also took place on the other side of the front. The Luftwaffe command, and more importantly Hitler, did not appreciate the merits of Commander of Luftflotte 1 Generaloberst Alfred Keller. Immediately after the end of the operation to destroy the port infrastructure at Lake Ladoga – on 26 June – he was removed from his post and transferred to the reserve.[262] The reason for Generaloberst Keller falling out of favour with the Führer is obvious: he did not follow Hitler's idiotic orders well. Generaloberst Keller could not create the miracle that Führer expected from him. Despite all the efforts of the crews of German bombers, Soviet communications on Lake Ladoga continued to function. This mission was fundamentally impossible for the Luftwaffe.

---

261. Ibid., Sheet 361.
262. After some time, Generaloberst Keller received the honorary position of Korpsführer National Socialist Flyers Corps (NSFK). It was a paramilitary organisation engaged in mass primary training of German pilots.

THE LUFTWAFFE'S LAST FUTILE EFFORTS

On the Leningrad Front again without changes

On 5 July, the Germans launched Operation Citadel. After that, the Russian command finally understood Hitler's plans and stopped being afraid of the offensive on Leningrad. Soon the Soviets themselves decided to attack on this section of the Eastern Front. On 22 July, the Red Army launched Operation Brusilov, the purpose of which was the defeat of the German 18th Army and the complete removal of the blockade of Leningrad.

Fierce Russian attacks continued for a month. The Soviets threw all their forces into battle, but were unable to break through the German defensive lines. These battles were reminiscent of the events of the First World War, when the two sides unsuccessfully attacked kilometres of barbed wire trenches and wood-earth blockhouses, each time suffering huge losses and rolling back. At the same time, the numerous swamps in the vicinity of Leningrad became a more serious obstacle for the Red Army than the machine gun and artillery fire of the Germans.

The Head of the Engineering Department of the Leningrad Front, General Boris Bychevsky, recalled:

> Who of the soldiers who fought in the summer of 1943 near Leningrad does not remember the marshes of Sinyavino! Even at night you feel sick from the fetid fumes, from the stench of continuously smouldering peat. Due to the constant humidity, the soldiers' uniforms become unusable in just a week. The narrow paths between the squares of peat recesses are targeted by enemy mortars. It is not uncommon for paramedics to die here, carrying out the wounded. They can't run fast with such a load. Gunners had to move their guns with their hands. I saw one of the artillery pieces go four metres into the swamp.[263]

The cruel Stalin and his incompetent commanders never spared their soldiers, considering them expendable material for the realisation of their goals. This battle was no exception. A gunner of the 63rd Guards Rifle Division, Nikolai Myasoedov, recalled:

> In these battles, from July 22 to August 4, 1943, we lost half of the people. And the infantry generally lost eighty per cent of the personnel. Cooks, scribes, locksmiths were gathered from

---

263. Bychevsky, B.V., *The City is the Front*, Leningrad: Lenizdat, 1967, p.228.

artillery units and all were sent to the infantry ... It was the most brutal, bloody operation.

Having lost 80,000 soldiers in these suicidal attacks – 20,000 of them were killed – on 22 August 1943, the Soviet troops again went on the defensive.

The air battle for Leningrad is over

In response to Operation Brusilov, the Luftwaffe resumed air attacks against Leningrad. On the night of 28–29 July, air raid sirens howled in the city and at At 01.50 numerous photoflash bombs hung in the sky. That night, Do 217 E-4 bombers from II./KG 101 dropped 800 incendiary bombs of various types on Leningrad. Among them were a large number of Brand C50 and Brand C250, bombs filled with a mixture of petrol, rubber and phosphorus. The incendiary bombs, caused many fires throughout the city. However, after two years of war, the city's residents and employees of the Soviet Local Rescue Service (MPVO) had extensive experience in dealing with this danger. Most of the fires were extinguished quickly, which prevented significant damage. Only five residential buildings and several outbuildings were partially destroyed.

Two more night attacks by small groups of Luftwaffe aircraft were carried out on 8 and 9 August. As a result, one residential building was destroyed and three people were injured. A fire broke out in the upper part of the Pyatiletka dormitory building in which seven people were burned.

The last air attack against Leningrad was registered on the night of 31 August to 1 September 1943, that is, two years after the beginning of the land blockade of the city. A single German bomber dropped five high-explosive bombs on the city. They exploded in a vacant lot and caused no damage. The German long-range artillery continued to shell Leningrad for another four months, until January 1944.

Since the second half of the summer of 1943, Luftwaffe activity in the Leningrad sector had decreased noticeably. First, Ju 87s from I./StG 5 flew to Norway. On 1 July, bombers from KG 53 relocated to Olsufievo airfield (near the city of Bryansk). Then, in August 1943, the last bomber Gruppe, II./KG 101, went back to Germany. Fighters from I./JG 54 and II./JG 54 also flew to other sectors of the front.

Soon, the situation on the fronts began to change rapidly. In August 1943, a large-scale Soviet offensive began on the front from Lake Ilmen to the Sea of Azov. In the Mediterranean, the Americans and the British landed first on Sicily, and then in southern Italy. Under these conditions, the Luftwaffe command no longer had the opportunity to keep bomber and fighter Geschwaders in secondary sectors of the front. As a result, in August 1943, only one Gruppe, IV./JG 54 under Hauptmann Rudolf Sinner, remained in the Leningrad area. It was formed in the early summer of 1943 and equipped with Bf 109s. Now this Gruppe had to fight Soviet aviation alone. Also, various Luftwaffe reconnaissance Staffeln remained in the Leningrad sector, which were sometimes involved in bombing attacks. However, their impact did not have a significant effect on the overall situation around Leningrad. Meanwhile, the number of Soviet aircraft in this sector of the front, on the contrary, was constantly increasing. For example, on 1 July 1943, the Air Force Soviet Baltic Fleet (VVS KBF), 13th Air Army (13th VA) and 14th Air Army (14th VA) had 718 aircraft, including 304 fighters.

Having given all its strike aviation units to other sectors of the front, the few Luftflotte 1 units took up a blind defence and no longer tried to actively influence the enemy. This decision meant that the air battle for Leningrad was over.

End of Army Group North

Despite the rapidly deteriorating situation on other sections of the Eastern Front, Wehrmacht units in the Leningrad area continued to hold their positions firmly. Apart from individual local movements and regroupings, almost nothing changed at the Leningrad Front until the beginning of 1944. For example, on the night of 3–4 October 1943, the Germans suddenly left the town of Kirishi. Moreover, the Russians noticed this only after the Germans blew up the bridge over the River Volkhov. Kirishi, on the eastern bank of the Volkhov, was in the hands of the Germans for exactly two years. It was captured by them back in October 1941 during the offensive on Tikhvin.

On the morning of 14 January 1944, Soviet troops launched Operation January Thunder. From Oranienbaum Bridgehead units of the 2nd Shock Army went on the offensive. A day later, near the village of Pulkovo on the outskirts of Leningrad, German positions were attacked by Soviet 42nd Army troops. The immediate goal of this Red Army offensive was the final relief of the Leningrad blockade. Further, Stalin's generals planned to encircle and defeat the main forces of the German 18th Army and create conditions for a rapid invasion of the Baltic States.

Despite a long and thorough preparation, in the first days of the offensive, the Red Army units achieved only minor successes. The advance of the Soviet troops was hindered by the stubborn defence of L Army Corps and III (Germanic) SS Panzer Corps. On 20 January 20, after fierce fighting, the Russians captured Ropsha settlement. After that, under the threat of encirclement, the German XXVI Army Corps began to retreat from the Mga area. Finally, after two years of attempts and huge losses at Sinyavino, this German 'enchanted stronghold' ended up in the hands of the Soviets.

On 26 January, Leningrad Front troops liberated the town of Krasnogvardeysk, and four days later they reached the River Luga, capturing a bridgehead on its western bank. On 29 January, the Moscow–Leningrad railway and the highway to Moscow were completely liberated. Thus, the land blockade of Leningrad was finally lifted.

By March 1944, Army Group North withdrew to the northern section of the Panther–Wotan line (between Lake Peipus and the Baltic Sea at Narva) and again took up a stubborn defence there. After a series of fierce and dramatic battles, the military formations of Army Group North were cut off by the Russians from the main German forces in Courland (450km south-west of Leningrad). There, Army Group North, created to capture Leningrad, and renamed by Hitler into Army Group Courland, ended its combat journey, and the remnants of its units were captured by the Russians.

Chapter 16

Mission impossible

Luftwaffe as ersatz of the Heer (land forces)

Large-scale conflicts of the twentieth century from the First World War to Operation Desert Storm became the heyday of military aviation. However, as practice has shown, even the most advanced aircraft remain only a powerful factor in supporting the ground forces. Despite the optimism of aviation enthusiasts, which periodically flashes brightly when another innovation in the field of military aircraft appears, the ability of this kind of weaponry to win even local wars alone raises many doubts. Nevertheless, attempts to use aviation as a key force in warfare have not stopped throughout the twentieth century. A striking example of such an aspiration is the use of German aviation in the region of Leningrad. After the failure of plans to capture the city by ground forces and the establishment of a land blockade of the city, the 'high honour' of forcing Leningrad to surrender fell to Luftwaffe.

What could the German Air Force, represented by Luftflotte 1, do to fulfill such an ambitious mission? Bomb all the buildings? Burn down the city? Kill all the inhabitants? Destroy the leadership of the defence of the city? Destroy the military industry? Bomb food and fuel supplies? Interrupt the power supply and destroy the water supply and sewerage system? Destroy transport communications and supply routes? Terrorise the residents? Break the morale of the defending troops? Hitler, who actually determined the strategy of German aviation in this sector of the front, believed that the Luftwaffe should perform all these tasks simultaneously and in the shortest possible time.

Let us consider what opportunities German aviation had to fulfill the mission assigned to it. By 1941, the Luftwaffe had extensive experience of bombing major cities. The culmination of this use of bomber aviation was the continuous months-long bombing of London. In addition, after the attack on the Soviet Union, the Germans were able to gain extensive experience in using bombers to attack large cities on the Eastern Front. For example, on 21 July 1941, the Luftwaffe made the first massive attack (195 bombers) on Moscow. Further raids on the capital of the USSR were carried out quite regularly. However, as readers already know, the first Luftwaffe raid on Leningrad took place only on 8 September 1941. The priority targets of the German bombers in autumn 1941 were important military facilities in the Leningrad area: port infrastructure, hydraulic structures, power plants, factories and ammunition depots. In total, during the entire period of the bombing of the city (8 September 1941–1 September 1943), sixty-three air raids on Leningrad were recorded. In 1941 there were thirty-eight, in 1942 fifteen and in 1943 twenty.

As readers already know, the bombing in autumn 1941 was the most intense. In total, from 8 September to 30 December 1941, German aircraft dropped 3,509 high-explosive bombs and over 66,000 small incendiary bombs on Leningrad. However, the effect of such raids was mainly psychological. Even the destruction of thousands of houses and hundreds of administrative and industrial buildings could not have any significant impact on a huge city with a population of millions. The most terrible consequences of the blockade – hunger and a lack of water supply and electricity – were exclusively the result of the actions of the ground forces, and not the Luftwaffe. Even the air attacks on industrial plants Leningrad in 1941 did not lead to a significant reduction in military production. Similar problems were caused by the cessation of supplies of raw materials and fuel to some military factories and the death of workers from starvation. In addition, Leningrad's industrial plants were so numerous that with the small number of bombers that Luftflotte 1 had at its disposal, decades of regular bombing would have been needed to destroy all the city's industrial facilities.

When analysing the intensity of the Leningrad bombing in the period from 1941 to 1943, one can notice a clear trend. The high intensity of attacks in autumn 1941 was associated with the offensive of the German ground forces. During this period, when the Soviet leadership was almost reconciled to the loss of the city, the Luftwaffe bombing had military significance, since it could really weaken the defence of the city. However, in 1942 and 1943, when the Wehrmacht did not have enough forces for an offensive, the effect of the Leningrad bombing was exclusively psychological. The attacks of German aircraft were carried out in Hitler's name in order to show that the Luftwaffe was still present in this sector of the front and was able to act. Single German planes could not burn or destroy the city. Thus, the raids did not have any strategic impact on the course of the battle on this section of the Eastern Front. In terms of the scale of the impact on the city, the effectiveness of aerial bombing was comparable or even inferior to the damage caused by the shelling of the German long-range artillery.

However, Luftflotte 1 units did have the capability to enhance the psychological effect of air strikes. Even single German bombers could easily destroy the historical sights of Leningrad, which are of great cultural value. In one of these buildings, the Smolny Institute, was the office of the Bolshevik Party of Leningrad, where the political leadership of the defence of the city was located. Thus, in case of total destruction of this building, the effect could be not only psychological. However, if we exclude the accidental close hits of bombs during attacks by warships, the Germans did not do this. The fact that cultural heritage sites were not considered as targets for air attacks was not an accident. This was probably a consequence of the tactics of the Luftwaffe commander in this sector of the front.

Hitler, von Küchler or Keller?

One can argue for a very long time about who determined the successes and failures of the Luftwaffe in the air battle for Leningrad. There is no doubt that Hitler and the Commander of Army Group North, Generaloberst Georg von Küchler, had a significant influence on the use of aviation in the area blockaded by the Germans. However, formally, from the beginning of the invasion of Russia until his resignation on 26 June 1943, Generaloberst Alfred Keller commanded all German aviation on the front line around Leningrad. This supreme Luftwaffe commander deserves special attention, so it is instructive to conduct a detailed analysis of his biography.

Keller was born on 19 September 1882 in the ancient German city of Bochum into the family of a minor civil servant. After receiving a high-quality education, the young man had no doubts when choosing a life path. In 1897, Alfred entered the cadet school. In a country where an atmosphere of frenzied militarism reigned for many years, a military career opened up broad prospects for the ambitious son of an official.

On 22 November 1902, after graduating from military school, Keller began military service in Pionier-Bataillon Nr. 17. In 1903, he received his first officer rank, Leutnant. The next nine years of his life were not marked by great career growth. In accordance with strict Prussian military traditions, he had to serve patiently for a long time in all officer positions in his native regiment. He received the next military rank, Oberleutnant, only in 1911. The turning point in Keller's fate happened in 1912, when he witnessed the demonstration flights of the first military aircraft. In the same year, he was trained as an observer pilot. In 1913, after completing his training at the experimental flight school Niederneuendorf, located north-west of Berlin, Keller qualified as a pilot. It was service in this new form of the German armed forces, Luftstreitkräfte der Deutschen Kaiserreiches, that determined his entire future life.

AIR BATTLE FOR LENINGRAD, 1941–1944

The beginning of the First World War, expected by the whole of Europe, found Keller at Darmstadt air base, where he was engaged in pilot training. In November 1914, he was promoted to Hauptmann and appointed commander of the Feldfliegerabteilung 27. The long-awaited war provided the commander of one of the first bomber aviation units with incredible opportunities to use his talents. From the very first days, Keller proved himself to be a commander of initiative, brilliantly aware of the technical capabilities of the first German bombers. Despite the modest strength of the unit, he managed to achieve very impressive results by the standards of aviation at that time.

Every year of the war was marked by the successes of the units commanded by Hauptmann Keller. In 1914, under his leadership, air attacks were carried out on Paris. In 1915, Keller's bombers participated in the Battle of Verdun. In 1916, his aviation units excelled in night bombing in the Battle of the Somme.

In early 1917, Keller was appointed commander of the Bombengeschwaders der Obersten Heeresleitung (Bogohl 1). In this important post, he continued to develop the tactics of night bombing and soon became the principle specialist in night operations in German aviation. At the beginning of 1918, the Geschwader under Keller's command made the first night air attack on Paris.

The success of Keller's activity as an organiser and commander of German bomber aviation was confirmed by the highest awards of the German Empire. In addition to many other orders, Keller was awarded the Iron Cross I. and II. Class. The culmination of the recognition of the merits of the bomber aviation enthusiast was his receipt at the end of 1917 of the highest Order of Prussia, Pour le Mérite.

Iron Keller

The reasons for the outstanding success of the actions of bomber units under the command of Hauptmann Keller are related to the peculiarities of his character. Unlike many of his colleagues in the First World War and the future Luftwaffe, such as Hermann Göring and Ernst Udet, Keller met the war as an accomplished 31-year-old professional. He perceived military service not as a fun and dangerous adventure, but as a harsh job. In addition, he did not seek to attract attention with circus tricks and jousting in the sky. This desire of the young hysterical aces of fighter aviation was deeply alien to him. Keller performed his service very carefully and demanded the same professionalism from his subordinates as from himself. Accurate aerial reconnaissance, high-quality planning of operations and gruelling practical training in bombing became the main distinguishing feature of his tactics using bombers.

Keller was distinguished not only by his personal bravery, which he repeatedly demonstrated in risky flights over enemy territory, but also by his undoubted organisational talent. He understood that such a complex weapon as a bomber requires pilots to have the appropriate abilities, the implementation of which requires long training. Therefore, he created favourable conditions for the selection and training of the first bomber pilots. Before allowing his pilots to carry out a combat mission, Keller carefully trained them to interact at the crew and Staffel levels. In the course of this organisational activity, Keller laid the foundations of the methodology for training pilots of German bombers. This showed his undoubted pedagogical talent.

The drive for success demonstrated by Keller since the beginning of his military career was balanced by a reasonable approach to the price of such military success. There is no doubt that Keller took care of his people. When conducting combat missions, he sought to achieve the maximum accuracy of bombing strikes in the absence of losses of crews. In response to the minimal losses that are inevitable in the conditions of the unpredictably changing fortunes of war, Keller developed new, safer tactics for crews. His actions lacked the haste and adventurism so characteristic of many fighter aviation aces. He preferred to spend time on additional training and developing new tactics than to rely on the favour of 'military fate'. Due to this character trait, Keller was the author of many tactical techniques for using bomber aircraft. In particular, he was the first to carry out the bombing of cities and ports, and night missions. Some of the attacks prepared and carried out under his command had a significant impact on the course of hostilities. For his strong-willed character and demanding attitude towards his subordinates, he soon became known in German aviation units by the nickname Iron Keller.

Thus, awareness of the capabilities and limitations of the new type of weapons allowed this competent commander to find the most effective ways to use his bombers. Although the Kaiser's new miracle weapon did not help Germany win the war, it became obvious to all belligerents and neutral observers that aviation, especially bombers, was an extremely promising branch of the armed forces. It was thanks to such innovators as Keller that many military leaders around the world realised the enormous potential of the emerging bomber aviation. Later, enthusiasts appeared predicting that aviation would completely change the strategy and tactics of future wars.

A lucky director

Alfred Keller took the defeat of Germany in the First World War in 1918 and the liquidation of German aviation in 1920 more calmly than many of his colleagues. At the end of 1918, with the rank of Major, he left the military service. Prudence and a balanced character allowed Keller to prepare well for a peaceful life. Soon he took a fairly high managerial position at Deutsche Luft-Reederei (DLR), which was the first German airline and the predecessor of the world-famous Lufthansa. At the initial stage, DLR operated military aircraft, which were flown by former military pilots. Thus, Keller, despite leaving military service, continued to be in his familiar element of aircraft and their pilots. Moreover, in a civilian position, he was as effective as in the war.

In 1923, Keller joined the airline Junkers Luftverkehr, founded by the German inventor and businessman Hugo Junkers. At that time, mail transportation became a promising source of income for airlines. It was in this direction that Keller headed, taking the post of director of Danziger Luftpost (Danziger air mail).

In 1925, Keller became the head of the Deutsche Verkehrsfliegerschule (German school of transport pilots) at Staaken, located on the western outskirts of Berlin in the Spandau district. In 1928, he moved his pilot school away from prying eyes to Broitzem airfield on the outskirts of Braunschweig. Here, in the time of the Reichswehr, Keller's started the secret training of new military pilots. The same type of military schools, under the cover of training pilots for transport aircraft, opened in many places in Germany. Every year Keller and his colleagues in the former Luftstreitkräfte had more and more work to do. Supporters of German military revenge gradually became more and more influential. Unlike his former boss Hugo Junkers, Keller was not a pacifist, but on the contrary, was an ardent supporter of the revival of German military aviation.

An important specialist in the training of military pilots

After the Nazis came to power, Hitler instructed his faithful servant Hermann Göring to secretly restore the German air Force, banned by the Versailles Treaty. The self-proclaimed Führer considered combat aviation an important tool for intimidating Western powers and the main weapon of future conquests in Europe. For this reason, the primitive psychopath Hitler demanded from his servant that hed ensure the reliability and highest efficiency of the new type of armed forces. Göring took up the execution of his Führer's order with maniacal zeal. However, his 'organisational abilities' in choosing people were limited by his personal preferences. Incompetent, but completely loyal friends, whom Göring put in all the key positions in the Luftwaffe, had no chance of coping with such an extremely difficult task. Organisational and technical problems had to be solved by inviting military specialists from infantry and artillery. Although these people sympathised with the Nazis, they were deeply unpleasant to such a lover of incoherent chatter and bright uniforms as Göring.

Grandiose plans to increase the number of aircraft required the accelerated training of an entire army of pilots. Due to the limitations of the Versailles Treaty, there was an acute shortage of specialists in training military pilots in Germany. Thus, Alfred Keller, who had been secretly engaged in such work for a long time, was among the first people invited by Göring to help create the Luftwaffe. In 1934, Keller resumed military service and received the military rank of Oberst. After some bureaucratic manipulations, common for that time due to the still-valid restrictions of the Versailles Treaty, he was transferred from the ground forces to the Luftwaffe. While waiting for a position worthy of his experience, Keller continued to lead his pilot school. Finally, on 1 May 1934, the first bomber squadron of Kampfgeschwader 154 'Boelcke' was created and Alfred Keller was appointed its commander. Despite the formidable name, in fact, this Kampfgeschwader was a training unit designed to test new types of German bombers and train pilots. After serving as commander for less than a year, Keller received a new position as commander of air formations in Luftkreis IV (4th Air District). The acute shortage of professionals in the rapidly developing Luftwaffe accelerated the career of this outstanding specialist in the field of pilot training and the tactics of bomber aviation. On 1 April 1936, Keller received the title of Generalmajor. At the beginning of 1938, he was appointed commander of Luftkreis II (Berlin) (2nd Air District) with the simultaneous assignment of the rank of Generalleutnant. Then he consistently held a number of other high command positions for a short time. On 1 April 1939, Keller received the title of General der Flieger.

At war again

Shortly after the start of the Second World War, on 11 October 1939, Alfred Keller was appointed commander of IV. Fliegerkorps and he again had the opportunity to prove his effectiveness under the conditions of military operations. Aviation units of IV. Fliegerkorps mainly operated over the Netherlands and Belgium, in particular, on 10 May 1940, they carried out air attacks on airfields. Moreover, the commander of IV. Fliegerkorps organised and controlled the activities of his subordinates not only on the ground, but also in the air. During the Battle of France, the 57-year-old Keller personally flew fifty-eight sorties in the Dunkirk area.

AIR BATTLE FOR LENINGRAD, 1941–1944

On 22 June 1940, France was forced to sign an armistice, which meant the victory of the Wehrmacht and the complete domination of Germany in continental Europe. Soon, inspired by his armed services' successes, Hitler began to distribute awards and titles to his military. On 19 July, Keller received the rank of Generaloberst der Flieger, which turned out to be the highest in his military career. On 24 June 1940, he was awarded the Ritterkreuz des Eisernen Kreuzes (Knight's Cross of the Iron Cross) for the successes of the IV. Fliegerkorps units subordinate to him and his personal contribution to the victory in the West. On 28 August 1940, Keller was appointed the Commander of Luftflotte 1 and Commander of the Luftwaffenbefehlshaber Ost (Commander of the Air Force in the East).

Convinced of his invincibility, Hitler continued to seize land across Europe and actively used the Luftwaffe units that proved their effectiveness to achieve his goals. He needed professionals like Keller. In turn, many of the Kaiser's old soldiers, who did not want to notice that Hitler was leading Germany to the grave, were very enthusiastic about the victorious promotion of the Wehrmacht in Europe. One of them, Keller, very energetically led Luftflotte 1 in the Balkans campaign, and then in Operation Barbarossa. During the invasion of the USSR, Luftflotte 1 aviation units mainly supported Army Group North. The further course of events is already known to the reader from the previous chapters of this book.

By the summer of 1943, the failure of the war strategy had become obvious to many sober-minded senior German officers. Even indirect hints from the military about the difficult situation at the front caused the Führer to have fits of furious rage. Hitler was unhappy with the old soldier Keller, who did not share his optimism about the state of affairs in the war, and sent the 61-year-old Generaloberst into honourable retirement. The vacant post of Commander of Luftflotte 1 was taken by the henchman of Generalfeldmarschall Erhard Milch, General der Flieger Günther Korten, who was more optimistic about the future of the Third Reich.

Embellishment or the justification of errors leads to incorrect assessment

The authors have an interesting report by the Commander of Luftflotte 1 Generaloberst Alfred Keller dated 15 March 1942, in which he analyses the results of combat missions carried out by German bombers to support the ground forces. This document is an example of what requirements Keller put forward for the professionalism of his subordinates. It said the following:

MISSION IMPOSSIBLE

The evaluation of the target images makes it clear that the hit of the bombs is partially very bad. Comparison with reports of success received from units shows that the actual effect achieved has no relation to the reported effect. This poor use of precious resources is unacceptable and, in addition, can shake the confidence of the troops in the skill of the bomber crews and in the reliability of their reports of success. I require all crews to increase the effectiveness of their weapons to the maximum level, that is, not only to fly well, but also to attack targets well.

The following three points should be made by the commanders:

1) Bombing, depending on the task or weather conditions, should be carried out mainly from the height most favourable for targeting and accuracy;
2) The difficulty in recognising targets requires particularly careful aiming and bombing. Constant training and guidance is required;
3) Success reports should be given in accordance with the facts. Embellishment or justification of error leads to an incorrect assessment of the actions and misconceptions. You should report what you actually saw, not what you would like to see.[264]

It can be assumed that approximately such an idea of Hitler's actions as commander-in-chief had formed in Keller's head by 1943.

Luftwaffe as ersatz of the Kriegsmarine

Based on the rather vague directives of Operation Barbarossa, the Germans did not plan to use Kriegsmarine ships to destroy the Soviet Baltic Fleet. The exceptions were torpedo boats, patrol ships and other small ships that operated in the Gulf of Finland. It was assumed that the ground forces during the Blitzkrieg would seize all the bases of the Soviet fleet, and the Luftwaffe would sink the large ships with bombs. It must be admitted that this very risky and presumptuous plan was brilliantly implemented as long as the ground forces were moving forward. As a result, in just over two months, the Wehrmacht captured all the advanced bases of the Soviet Fleet. Such a rapid advance of

---

264. Boelcke Archiv.

AIR BATTLE FOR LENINGRAD, 1941–1944

German troops to Leningrad completely paralysed the actions of the Russian fleet. On 28 August 1941, the main naval base of the Soviet Baltic Fleet at Tallinn fell.[265] From that day on, only two old naval bases located in the western part of the Gulf of Finland remained at the disposal of the Soviets: Kronstadt and Leningrad. However, thanks to Hitler's incompetence, the further advance of German troops was stopped, and the Soviets were able to save their ships from immediate total destruction. After stopping the Wehrmacht near Leningrad in the autumn of 1941, the Luftwaffe was forced to fight alone to sink the surviving Soviet Baltic Fleet ships. Luftflotte 1 had two effective means to destroy Russian ships: aerial bombs and parachute mines. The Germans only used aerial torpedoes on this sector of the front a few times.

Bottom mines as an offensive weapon of Luftwaffe in 1941

The Luftwaffe war in the Baltic Sea began with the use of mine weapons in the Kronstadt Naval Base area. Moreover, the Germans made an attempt to use bottom mines as an offensive weapon. It can be assumed that the idea of the operation, developed by the Luftflotte 1 staff officers, was based on a combination of several factors conducive to the success of this particular method of using this type of weapon.

Firstly, the special natural conditions in this part of the Baltic Sea restricted the movement of large ships strictly to the alignment of narrow fairways, which narrowed the mining target area.

Secondly, unpunished flights of German reconnaissance aircraft during the several pre-war weeks allowed the collection of extensive information about the most profitable sites for installing bottom mines in fairways near Kronstadt Naval Base.

Thirdly, the crews from 1./KGr. 806 and 1./KGr. 506 were well trained and had sufficient experience in carrying out mining missions in water areas.

Fourth, Hitler's new 'wonder weapon', bottom mines, could use innovative contactless types of sensors and magnetic or acoustic fuses. The Soviets did not know anything about these 'wonder weapon' features for a long time, which means they did not have effective methods of mine clearance.

Fifthly, the potential high accuracy of installing bottom mines in the places of the most intense ship traffic, namely at the exit from the harbours of

---

265. It should be noted that the details and results of attacks by Luftwaffe aircraft on ships during the escape of the Soviet Baltic Fleet from Tallinn Naval Base to Kronstadt are not covered in this book. These events will be the subject of description and analysis in other books by these authors.

Kronstadt Naval Base, allowed the literal locking up of numerous Soviet ships in narrow harbours. This could make them a convenient target for subsequent bombing attacks by Luftwaffe aircraft.

Sixth, the Germans counted on the effect of surprise and the general passivity of Soviet air defence, which they observed during the pre-war flights of German reconnaissance aircraft over the territory of the USSR.

The implementation of the first mission on 22 June 1941 seemed to fully confirm these advantages. At the initial stage, the German bombers acted almost as if they were on an exercise. The planes were able to approach the planned target areas without hindrance and maintain the optimal altitude for the most accurate discharge of bottom mines. Orientation in space in the twilight conditions of the midnight sun was facilitated by lighthouses functioning in a peaceful mode. Brightly burning lighted beacons clearly marked fairways, which greatly facilitated aiming when dropping bottom mines. However, when in the process of completing the first mission, the conditions for the actions of German bombers deteriorated significantly. The Soviets overcame their initial indecision and opened fire on the German planes. Although the anti-aircraft fire of the Russians did not lead to any losses of the attacking side, it created significant interference for the accurate installation of bottom mines.

The second fairways mining mission near Kronstadt Naval Base turned out to be a complete failure for the German crews.

The staff officers planning this mission underestimated the capabilities of the Russian air defence and repeated the original route of the approach of the bombers to the target area. The effect of surprise was completely lost and concentrated anti-aircraft fire was waiting for them. As a result, despite the fulfillment of the combat mission, the bombers suffered significant losses. On the scale of the Luftwaffe's operations on the Eastern Front, the destruction of four aircraft in one mission was an excessive fee. Fortunately for the Germans, three of the four bomber crews survived and were able to continue participating in the war. Realising the excessive danger of continuing missions in such unfavourable conditions, Luftwaffe staff officers showed prudence and stopped the fairways mining operation.

Based on the above reasons, the minelaying carried out by the Luftwaffe in June 1941 was very modest in scale. In its two missions, the Germans installed about seventy bottom mines from the air. Although mine clearance caused the Soviets a lot of problems, it was impossible to block all the fairways around Kronstadt Naval Base with so few mines. As the reader already knows, the only real consequence of this operation for the Soviet Baltic Fleet was the death of the minesweepers *T-208 Schkiv* and *TSCH-39 Petrozavodsk*. It is unlikely that the Germans, using such hi-tech and expensive weapons, counted on such modest results. Thus, the effectiveness of the use of mine weapons in June 1941 in the fairways around Kronstadt Naval Base turned out to be minimal.

The authors have no information about the extent to which the Luftflotte 1 command was free to choose weapons for the first attack on a large naval base in Kronstadt. As noted earlier, it is possible that when making a decision, they were directly or indirectly influenced by Hitler's conviction in the special effectiveness of the new 'wonder weapon'. Such false conclusions could have been broadcast in the directives of the Oberkommando der Luftwaffe to Luftflotte 1. In addition to the bewildering choice of bottom mines as offensive weapons, the failure of the operation was due to two main reasons.

The first reason is the template use of such a universal weapon as the Bombenmine (BM1000) when there were other possibilities of using this powerful weapon. Bombers from 1./KGr. 806 and 1./KGr. 506 could drop universal Bombenmine as bombs on ships in the harbours of Kronstadt Naval Base or on the port facilities of Kronstadt. Probably, the effect of an almost simultaneous explosion of 50 tons of explosives contained in seventy bottom mines would have been much more significant than two sunk minesweepers. However, the Germans acted in this situation in a formulaic manner and preferred to leave the 'wonder weapon' to rust on the seabed and wait for a lucky chance in the form of a large Russian ship passing nearby. Thus, when planning the operation in June 1941, Luftwaffe staff officers clearly overestimated the possibilities of using the BM1000 as naval bottom mines.

The second reason for the failure, apparently, lay in the insufficiently careful planning of the operation. Despite extensive intelligence information, Luftwaffe staff officers did their job poorly. In particular, they significantly overestimated the advantages described above for the precise installation of bottom mines in the Kronstadt Naval Base area. For example, the effect of surprise created favourable conditions for the effective work of the bomber crews only at the initial stage of the mission. And the main factor of counteraction to the operation, namely the ability of the Soviets' air defence, was significantly underestimated. As reality showed, the low accuracy of their barrage firing was compensated for by its high density. The choice of the night, or rather midnight sun, for the attack, although it created difficulties for the Soviet anti-aircraft gunners, did not help to avoid losses. If in the first mission the Russian fire only significantly reduced the accuracy of setting mines, then in the second it led to significant losses by the attacking side. Thus, the staff officers did not provide additional measures that could increase the safety of their bombers, which were very vulnerable to anti-aircraft fire at the time of aiming and dropping mines.

At the end of August 1941, the Luftwaffe resumed minelaying in fairways in the Kronstadt area. This time the task was performed by He 111 Hs from II./KG 4 under Oberstleutnant Gottlieb Wolff. The planes took off from Korovye Selo Air Base, about 14km south of Pskov. The authors of this book have no information about the details of these combat missions. It was probably a very limited-scale operation, during which the German bombers did not suffer any losses. Also, the authors do not have data on any significant successes of minelaying in August 1941. Most likely, there were simply no results from these actions.

Steen, Kupfer and Rudel get down to business

By the autumn of 1941, the well-worn Soviet Baltic Fleet was concentrated at the Kronstadt Naval Base. After the Wehrmacht captured the advanced fleet bases in the Gulf of Finland, Russian ships no longer posed a danger to German shipping in the Baltic Sea. However, at the moment when all the efforts of the Germans were focused on the capture of Leningrad, the Soviet Baltic Fleet suddenly reminded them about itself by firing large-calibre, long-range guns. This happened because the German troops and their Finnish allies advanced so deeply that the Russian ships could support their troops directly from the harbours of Kronstadt Naval Base. At this moment, Hitler was full of optimism about the capture of Leningrad, so he ordered his faithful 'Nazgûl' Generalmajor Wolfram von Richthofen eliminate a minor obstacle in the form of Russian ships on the way to the complete victory of German weapons.

The best crews of Ju 87 Rs from III./StG 2, terrifying with their heart-rending howl and monstrous efficiency, got down to business without delay. The staff officers of StG 2 did not have enough time for the planning and preparation of the first raids on the Soviet Baltic Fleet ships. The reason for the rush was too obvious; Russian shells fired from large-calibre naval guns were constantly falling on the heads of their comrades in the ground forces. For this reason, the German pilots began to carry out the order of the Führer in the spirit of Blitzkrieg, hoping for their combat experience, determination and luck.

On 16 September 1941, a group of Ju 87 Rs from III./StG 2 performed the first combat mission against the battleship *Marat* in bad weather conditions. The attack on this large target, motionless at anchor, was successful. Despite the frenzied fire of anti-aircraft guns, several large bombs hit the battleship. It is known that one of the bombs was dropped by the commander of 7./StG 2, Hauptmann Ernst Kupfer, and the other by Oberleutnant Hans-Ulrich Rudel. Rudel, who later became the best Stuka pilot, at that time held the position of Technical Support Officer with III./StG 2 and flew as a wingman of his commander, Hauptmann Ernst-Siegfried Steen. However, the target chosen by the desperate Luftwaffe pilots turned out to be too tough for their 500kg bombs. The old Russian dreadnought had well-armoured decks that withstood powerful blows. A much more powerful weapon was needed to destroy *Marat*.

AIR BATTLE FOR LENINGRAD, 1941–1944

It was from this episode that the competition for performance began between the three best Stuka pilots: the Commander of III./StG 2, Steen, and his two subordinates, Kupfer and Rudel. Two of this desperate trio already had extensive experience of successful ship attacks. On the combat account of Hauptmann Steen was the English destroyer HMS *Hereward*, which he sank together with his subordinates in 1941 near the island of Crete. Several more British destroyers and cruisers were seriously damaged by his bombs. In the same area of the Mediterranean Sea on 22 May 1941, his comrade Ernst Kupfer, leading a group of Ju 87s, sank the English light cruiser *Gloucester*. By September 1941, only Oberleutnant Hans-Ulrich Rudel had no enemy ships sunk on his combat account. An unfortunate combination of circumstances made his path to the status of an elite Stuka pilot an extremely long one. While his senior comrades were sinking British ships in the Battle of Crete, Rudel was forced to stay on the ground. However, his great desire to surpass his senior comrades and teachers did not cause anyone to doubt.

The sinking of a warship was considered the highest valour among the desperately brave pilots who overcame great difficulties to get into the famous Sturzkampfgeschwader 2 (StG 2) 'Immelmann'. Anyone who wanted to be awarded this honour had to enter into a game with death itself. There were few such desperate braves, even in StG 2. The stake in this dangerous game was the life of the pilot and his gunner/radio operator, but the title of the best Stuka pilot justified the deadly risk.

It was Steen, Kupfer and Rudel who challenged death, which means they became the leaders of the dive bomber pilots' teamwork, on which the success of the attacks depended. Perhaps, never on the Eastern Front in one Gruppe were three pilots of Ju 87s to be found who were so outstanding in skill and bravery. Like the Scandinavian berserkers, thanks to desperate fearlessness and fighting rage, Steen, Kupfer and Rudel dived their Stukas almost to the deck of the enemy ship. It was they who determined the course and result of the air attack. The other members of the group, not endowed with such exceptional qualities, dropped bombs on the target from a safer height. In parallel, their teammates tried to create optimal conditions for the berserkers to attack and registered the results of the fall of their bombs.

There should be only one 'berserker' left

Several attacks carried out by Luftwaffe aircraft in the period from 19 to 22 September 1941 caused a lot of damage to Soviet Baltic Fleet ships and the infrastructure at Kronstadt Naval Base. However, the main goal was never achieved. The long-range guns of large Soviet ships continued to fire at German and Finnish troops. Realising the impossibility of destroying battleships with the bombs at their disposal, dive bombers from III./StG 2 focused on smaller, unarmoured targets. This tactic again brought success.

On 21 September, Oberleutnant Hans-Ulrich Rudel sank the destroyer *Steregushchy* and was the first to open a combat account in this operation. On the same day, the commander of 7./StG 2, Hauptmann Ernst Kupfer, hit the destroyer *Grozyashchiy* with a bomb. However, he could not match the effectiveness of Oberleutnant Rudel, since the target of his attack was under repair in the dry dock and could not sink. The commander of III./StG 2, Hauptmann Ernst-Siegfried Steen, was both pleased with the brilliant results of his subordinates and at the same time annoyed by the fact that his bombing was not so effective.

Meanwhile, senior officers of the StG 2 staff, who usually did not undertake risky sorties, also joined the race to sink Russian ships. Among them was the commander of Sturzkampfgeschwader 2, Oberstleutnant Oskar Dinort. While in the cockpit of his Ju 87, he personally dropped a bomb on Russian ships, but, however, missed. There is no doubt that the atmosphere of rivalry among pilots was created by the Commander of VIII. Fliegerkorps, Generalmajor Wolfram von Richthofen. He received detailed reports on all the attacks of Soviet Baltic Fleet ships and stimulated his subordinates to take decisive action in every possible way. However, none of the Stukas pilots could even come close to the effectiveness of the fearless 'berserkers'.

The culmination of the dive bombers' actions was a series of attacks carried out on 23 September. At the disposal of III./StG 2, finally, there was an adequate weapon for the destruction of Soviet battleships. Prior to its introduction, the Stuka's standard armament was a set of one 250kg or 500kg bomb under the fuselage and two 50kg bombs under each wing. The new 'wonder weapon' had become cylindrical, armour-piercing explosive PC1000 bombs equipped with a delayed-action fuse. The exact number of battleship-killer bombs that arrived at the III./StG2 base in Tirkovo is unknown, but most likely there were no more than ten of them. Based on the special rarity of these weapons, only 'berserkers' got the opportunity to use them. As readers already know, on 23 September, the battleship *Marat* was, at last, destroyed. This was done by Oberleutnant Rudel, for whom it was the second Russian ship sunk in a few days.

The less fortunate Hauptmann Steen had the opportunity to prove his worth as the best Stuka pilot on the same day. Despite suffering two damaged aircraft during his attempts to take off, he still went on what was to be the last combat mission of his life. He flew the Ju 87 of Oberleutnant Rudel, leaving his subordinate not only without an aeroplane, but without a permanent comrade rear gunner. As readers already know, Hauptmann Steen and Feldwebel

Scharnowsky died while trying to destroy the cruiser *Kirov* with a PC1000. After this tragic loss III./StG 2 had only two 'berserkers' left: Kupfer and Rudel.

Their rivalry ended in favour of Rudel, who on 27 September struck his second battleship, *Oktyabrskaya Revolutsiya*, with a PC1000. Kupfer was seriously injured that day and was out of the game for a long time. The unpredictable 'military fate' turned out to be most favourable to Rudel. A year and a half later, Kupfer, who by that time had become the commander of StG 2, died in a plane crash. In August 1944, Rudel became commander of StG 2 and throughout the war he flew 2,530 sorties. For his impressive achievements, he received the status of the best Stuka pilot and a special award, which had to be made especially for him. The main thing was that Rudel became the only 'berserker' who lived to the end of the war.

A clear indicator of the effectiveness of the Luftwaffe attacks in September 1941 was a significant reduction in the intensity of artillery fire and, finally, the flight of Russian ships to Leningrad. However, in 1941, the problem of the complete destruction of the Soviet Baltic Fleet was not solved. Moreover, after a few months, the combat capability of some ships that were severely damaged by the berserkers was partially restored. For example, the destroyer leader *Minsk*, sunk by Oberleutnant Rudel in September 1941 and lying in shallow water, was raised by the Soviets on 25 August 1942. On 5 November, after a hasty and poor-quality repair, *Minsk* re-joined the Soviet Baltic Fleet. The main reason that the remnants of Stalin's fleet survived was the inability of the German ground forces to capture Kronstadt and Leningrad.

Führer's order

After overcoming the Wehrmacht crisis of the winter of 1941–42, the situation on the Eastern Front stabilised. Hitler blamed the failure of Operation Barbarossa on German military leaders and dismissed many of them. He attributed the retention of positions by German troops solely to his 'iron' will. Convinced of his infallibility, Führer moved to a new level of intervention in military matters. Leningrad and the remnants of the Soviet Baltic Fleet became the object of the application of his 'brilliant' military leadership abilities again. The Bolshevik stronghold, although it suffered the harsh conditions of the land blockade, resisted and was not going to surrender to the Germans. Based on this, Hitler chose for the upcoming attack an easier, and as it seemed to him, quickly achievable goal – Russian warships.

If the air attacks on the Soviet Baltic Fleet in September 1941 were due to the objective reason of helping the ground forces, then the decision to launch new attacks in 1942 was based solely on Hitler's irrational fears, issued by him in the form of categorical orders. The remnants of the Soviet Baltic Fleet, driven into the mouth of the Neva, did not pose any objective threat to the Germans. Meanwhile, the risks of losing valuable crews carrying out attacks on such well-protected targets had increased significantly. The Russians coped with the confusion of the first months of the war and strengthened the air defence of the surviving twelve warships. Based on these risks, the Luftflotte 1 command, citing objective reasons, repeatedly postponed the execution of Hitler's directive. When it became clear that the stubbornness of the intellectually limited Führer was winning, the Luftflotte 1 command did everything possible to reduce the risks of losing its people and aircraft. Based on a significant array of intelligence information, staff officers very carefully prepared Operation Eisstoss (Breaking ice). They used the experience of attacks on ships in 1941 and prepared weapons that proved their effectiveness in destroying well-armoured targets. Thus, in 1942, Luftwaffe pilots in the Leningrad area had no shortage of PC1000 armour-piercing explosive bombs.

A well-planned failure

As part of the implementation of Operation Eisstoss in April 1942, the Luftwaffe conducted two air attacks on Leningrad Naval Base. As already noted above, the Luftflotte 1 staff officers had enough time to carefully plan an air strike on the surviving Soviet Baltic Fleet ships. The location of the large ships that became the target of the attack was accurately determined by aerial reconnaissance. Tactical techniques and weapons were chosen optimally. Thus, provided that the capricious 'military fate' did not interfere in the case, the German pilots in this mission had every chance of success.

In the first evening attack, carried out in good weather conditions and normal illumination, the Germans managed to achieve the effect of surprise. Although the density of anti-aircraft fire over the target was high enough, the Russians could not prevent the crews of the German bombers from dropping bombs on the selected targets. Additional confusion among the Soviets was caused by the German long-range artillery, which opened a powerful fire on the positions of anti-aircraft batteries and airfields where the fighters were based.

However, the results of the first attack, carried out in favourable conditions using the optimal number of bombers, were disappointing. Despite nearby explosions, the battleship *Oktyabrskaya Revolutsiya* avoided any direct hits and did not suffer significant damage. Such a result was impossible to imagine in 1941, when the famous 'berserkers' Steen, Kupfer and Rudel participated in StG 2 missions. However, there were no 'berserkers' left among the dive bomber crews, and none of the pilots of the thirty Ju 87s involved in the attack tried to dive almost to the deck level of the Russian warships. The reason for the attack's failure was not only the low morale of the dive bomber crews, but also objective circumstances. After the difficult winter campaign of 1941–42, there was an acute shortage of aircraft and experienced crews in many Luftwaffe units. For example, in March 1942 Hans-Ulrich Rudel was appointed an instructor at Gruppe StG 2, based in the Austrian city of Graz. Instead of sinking Stalin's ships, the sole survivor of the berserkers was engaged in the routine combat training of the graduates of aviation schools. Most of the Ju 87 pilots who flew combat missions in Operation Eisstoss had only recently left such training units. They had never attacked such complex targets as warships, especially with strong air defence opposition. Thus, the level of training and experience of pilots who participated in the attacks on the Russian fleet in 1942 was significantly lower than in 1941. As a result, the probability of hitting such point targets as ships turned out to be significantly lower than had been calculated.

The planned nature of the attack also left the bomber crews vulnerable. The first mission on 4 April 1942, instead of being one sudden and lightning raid, turned into a long, time-stretched chain of events. As a result, the usually careless command of the Russian air defences had enough time to put all its assets on alert. The strikes on the ships were carried out at too long intervals, which allowed the anti-aircraft gunners to transfer fire from one group of German bombers to another in time.

An unexpected and unwelcome surprise was presented by the weapon that had given the greatest success to the Germans in 1941. Although the pilots managed to put one PC1000 armour-piercing explosive bomb into the cruiser *Kirov*, the result of its impact on the ship turned out to be very weak. This 'wonder weapon' suddenly showed complete inefficiency in defeating this large but weakly armoured target. If an ordinary 500kg high-explosive bomb had been used instead, the consequences could have been much more serious for *Kirov*.

The absence of the planned results of the mission on 4 April was partially compensated for by the phenomenal level of safety for the bomber crews who took part in the attack. All the fanatical attempts of the Russians to organise an effective counteraction to the air attack failed, and they failed to shoot down a single German bomber.

During the preparation of the second raid, the tactical skill of the Luftflotte 1 staff officers was again manifested. The effect of surprise was lost, but the Germans were again able to present an unpleasant surprise to the Soviets by conducting a night attack using photoflash bombs. Dive bombers certainly did not participate in this attack and bombs were dropped conventionally by He 111s. Despite the extremely small target for this method of bombing, a battleship, the crews achieved phenomenal accuracy. At least nine PC1000s fell next to *Oktyabrskaya Revolutsiya*, and one at a distance of only 20m from the side. However, all the bombs exploded at the bottom of the Neva without causing any damage to the battleship. If we imagine that instead of PC1000s, the Germans had dropped Bombenmine (BM1000) with the same accuracy, then the close explosion of almost 9 tons of powerful explosives would probably have caused fatal damage. Having completed the combat mission, all the He 111s from KG 4 that participated returned safely to Riga-Spilve airfield.

Thus, the careful planning of the operation by the Luftflotte 1 staff officers fully justified itself only in terms of ensuring the safety of the crews. However, the military objective of Operation Eisstoss completely failed. At the same time, Luftflotte 1 staff officers cannot be blamed for the obvious mistakes in choosing tactics or the type of weapons. The authors have no doubt that they had done their job brilliantly. However, a certain amount of improvisation and a departure from the template in the choice of weapons could have significantly changed the result of Eisstoss.

'Iron fist' of the Luftwaffe against Stalin's warships

Important circumstances forced the leadership of I. Fliegerkorps to interrupt the operation to destroy the remnants of the Soviet Baltic Fleet. As soon as the situation on the Eastern Front changed in a favourable direction for the Germans, the Luftwaffe finally had sufficient forces to complete the execution of the Führer's order. The 'Iron Fist', which would break through the armoured decks of Russian ships and send them to the bottom of the Neva, was again supposed to be dive bombers.

During the implementation of Operation Götz von Berlichingen, the first raid, which was carried out on 24 April 1942, turned out to be the most effective. In order to ensure optimal conditions for bombing and the safety of the crews, all tactical techniques that had previously proved their effectiveness were applied. Before the raid, the Russian anti-aircraft batteries were suppressed by the fire of the German long-range artillery. During the attack, some bombers periodically dropped bombs on the positions of Russian anti-aircraft gunners. To counter the air defence fighters, Ju 87 Ds were accompanied by German Bf 109 Fs.

The fighting spirit of the German pilots was noticeably higher, although the skill was still inferior to the level of September 1941. Three main targets were attacked: the battleship *Oktyabrskaya Revolutsiya* and the cruisers *Maxim Gorky* and *Kirov*. Again it was not possible to achieve hits on the battleship by PC1000s. *Maxim Gorky* also avoided direct hits, but was damaged by nearby explosions. In addition, the cruiser received new damage from close bursts of about a hundred heavy shells fired by German long-range artillery.

However, during the attack on the third-priority target, *Kirov*, the Germans were more successful. At the cost of the loss of one Stuka, it was possible to achieve hits by three heavy bombs at once. Another hit of a large-calibre projectile was achieved by German long-range artillery. Despite the blows of bombs and shells, the ship remained afloat. A feature of the design of *Kirov* was the presence of partial reinforcing of the most important parts of the ship. In particular, the armoured deck with a thickness of 50mm protected the central part of the cruiser, although the bow and stern did not have such protection. Ironically, the Germans used conventional high-explosive bombs in this attack, which hit the armoured centre of the ship. The deck withstood the blows, but many rooms located above it in the middle part were destroyed or severely damaged.

Summing up the results of Operation Götz von Berlichingen, it can be noted that the Luftflotte 1 command had learned lessons from Operation Eisstoss. The tactics of the raids were better adapted to the conditions of attacks on such complex single targets as warships. This immediately produced significant results: not as brilliant as in September 1941, but still better than in early April 1942.

During four raids – on 24, 25, 27 and 30 April – conducted by relatively small groups of Ju 87 Ds, it was possible to sink the hulk *Voroshilov*, the unfinished training ship *Svir* and the transport ship *Vakhur*. *Kirov* had been heavily damaged and took several months to repair. Various damage was received by *Oktyabrskaya Revolutsiya* and *Maxim Gorky*, the destroyers *Silnyi* and *Grozyashchiy*, submarine *M-90*, two minesweepers and five patrol boats. At the same time, the losses of the Luftwaffe during these raids amounted to only two Ju 87 Ds.

To call such results a great success would, of course, be an exaggeration. However, to declare Operation Götz von Berlichingen a 'collapse of Luftwaffe efforts' or a 'failed Pearl Harbor', as some Russian historians do, goes too far the other way. We should not forget that the repair, even if insignificant, of a warship in the conditions of a besieged city, which had barely survived the terrible winter of 1941–42, turned into a big problem. In addition, the sinking of three large ships, albeit auxiliary ones, had a strong psychological effect, which affected the fighting spirit of the Soviets.

In essence, Götz von Berlichingen was carried out at a tactical level by small forces in a very limited, local area. It did not have, and could not have, any strategic significance, as the Soviet side wanted to see it in order to attach excessive importance to its successes. These raids were in fact no different from many other raids on the positions of land artillery batteries. Only in this case, the batteries were floating, because they were the ships that stood with cold engines at berth embankments, at factory or improvised wharves and moved along the Neva only with the help of tugs.

It is possible to evaluate the results of the April Luftwaffe strikes in different ways. However, they clearly showed that the large Soviet Baltic Fleet ships could survive only by continuing to remain under the protection of coastal anti-aircraft batteries. In the event of their going to the open sea, the chances of survival would fall rapidly. This was clearly confirmed on 6 October 1943 on the Black Sea, when a group of Ju 87 Ds from III./StG 3 sank the destroyer leader *Kharkov* and the destroyers *Besposchadnyi* and *Sposobnyi* during four sorties. This incident prompted Stalin to issue an order prohibiting the commander of the Soviet Black Sea Fleet from using ships the size of destroyers and larger without his direct permission. After that, the Soviet Black Sea Fleet ships no longer participated in the war.

Bottom mines for mass use of the Luftwaffe in 1942

As readers already know, Operation Froschlaich was initiated in the spring of 1942 personally by Hitler, who was still afraid of the Soviet Baltic Fleet. The Führer completely ignored the fact that by this time the large Russian warships had been completely deactivated by the joint actions of the ground forces and the Luftwaffe.

In 1942, the Germans could no longer count on the effect of surprise, so when planning the operation, Luftflotte 1 staff officers took into account the strong opposition of the Soviet air defence. In this regard, during the preparation, rather difficult ways of aircraft approaching the target area were chosen. In addition, in 1942, the fairways sites selected by the Germans for the installation of bottom mines were further from the entrance to the harbours than in June 1941. These measures were supposed to reduce the risks for bomber crews. Thus, the factor of the powerful anti-air defence of Kronstadt Naval Base initially lowered the chances of successfully mining the fairways. An additional difficulty was the great remoteness of Prowehren airfield, KG 4's base, which was almost 800 km from the target area. Flying such distances caused excessive fatigue in the pilots, which, combined with the mental stress of the threat of the Russian air defences, could interfere with accurate aiming when dropping bottom mines.

The implementation of Operation Froschlaich generally went according to plan and during twelve night missions, bombers from KG 4 laid at least 600 bottom mines around Kronstadt. Despite all the air defence forces involved, the Soviets were unable to interrupt the operation. Measures to ensure the safety of the bomber crews also showed sufficient effectiveness. This is evidenced by the relatively small losses of the Germans: three aircraft in twelve missions in 1942 and four aircraft in two missions in 1941.

However, despite the devastation of the German reserves of bottom mines and low losses of bombers, the real effectiveness of this type of weapon turned out to be extremely low. The reason for the failure of Operation Froschlaich was a combination of many factors, the existence of which Luftflotte 1 staff officers knew even during the planning of the operation. Here are a few of them:

- the absence of lit beacons, turned off for blackout purposes, made it difficult to detect narrow fairways;
- the counteraction of anti-aircraft artillery and night fighters created extra stress for pilots when aiming in addition to being tired after a long flight;
- low motivation of crews forced to make routine sorties under the fire of Soviet anti-aircraft guns and drop bottom mines into the dark waters of the Gulf of Finland without visible results.

The combination of such unfavourable factors led to the fact that only individual Luftminen fell directly into fairways and created a potential threat to Soviet warships. The accuracy of dumping bottom mines, and, consequently, at least some effectiveness of this type of weapon was sacrificed to the formal execution of Hitler's idiotic order.

A factor in an even greater decrease in the effectiveness of German mine installation was the attempt to clear fairways, undertaken by the Soviets immediately after the end of Operation Froschlaich. The Russians, already informed by the Allies of all the secrets of the German 'wonder weapon', again made titanic efforts to eliminate this new threat to their shipping. During this operation, two wooden minesweepers, *Voronin* and *Piksha*, were blown up on the German bottom mines. Even taking into account the poor quality of the mine clearance conducted by the Soviets, the mines remaining at the bottom of the fairways could not significantly affect the capabilities of the Soviet Baltic Fleet. The temporary result of Operation Froschlaich was only the delay to submarines in going to sea, which the Soviets sent from Kronstadt Naval Base for a suicidal breakthrough into the Baltic Sea. Thus, despite their massive use, most of the bottom mines dropped by the Germans lay in shallow water outside the fairways and posed no threat to Russian warships.

The Germans again ignored the possibility of using bottom mines as superpowerful high-explosive bombs. Considering that each Bombenmine (BM1000) could destroy an entire city block, it is possible to imagine the scale of destruction in Leningrad with a hypothetical dropping of 600 such mines containing approximately 400 tons of powerful explosives. With this method of using these weapons, Hitler's dream of destroying 'the cradle of the of Bolshevism' could be much closer to realisation. However, the Germans, with a tenacity worthy of a better application, followed the failed plan of minelaying fairways around Kronstadt Naval Base. Valuable resources were literally scattered across the sea, and the lives of qualified crews, whose training took a lot of time, were put at unnecessary risk. The low losses of German bombers during Operation Froschlaich are explained by the monstrous inefficiency of the Soviet air defence. If the Germans had dared to carry out such an operation against a naval base on the Western Front then their losses would probably have been very high. Thus, it can be confidently stated that the massive use of bottom mines against Russian military shipping in May–June 1942 ended in a complete failure for the Luftwaffe. That is, literally the mountain brought forth a mouse. It must be emphasized once again that the Russians no longer had any combat-ready fleet. As readers already know, the surviving large ships were standing in the River Neva and as a result of damage from German bombs were unable to move independently. For this reason, they simply could not swim to the Kronstadt Naval Base, where the bottom mines installed by the Germans were waiting for them. The only tangible result of Operation Froschlaich were the multi-page reports by the headquarters of the Luftflotte 1, specially prepared for the Führer. In them, staff officers indicated detailed quantitative indicators of minelaying and concluded that it was completely impossible for Soviet ships to enter the Baltic Sea. Such optimistic reports about the power of German weapons, sent from different places on the huge Eastern Front, became pleasant evening reading for the psychopath Hitler hiding from the whole world in a bunker.

Bottom mines as weapons of despair of the Luftwaffe in 1943

In April 1943, staff officers took into account all their previous experience and flawlessly planned the third operation to mine the fairways around Kronstadt Naval Base. In turn, the crews of the Ju 88 A-4 bombers from III./KG 1 masterfully completed four missions, using the entire arsenal of effective tactical techniques to counter Soviet air defences, namely:

- covert approach to the target at minimum altitude to counter detection by Soviet radar stations;
- suppression of anti-aircraft artillery with a preventive bombing strike;
- active manoeuvring to avoid attacks by Russian night fighters.

It is safe to say that the tactics of reducing losses during the dumping of bottom mines in 1943 were brought to perfection by the Germans. This is clearly evidenced by the fact that not a single aircraft was lost during the four missions. However, it is worth noting that the scale of the operation in 1943 was a quarter of that in 1942.

In total, in April 1943, about a hundred bottom mines were dropped by German bombers around Kronstadt Naval Base. However, the results of mining the fairways were again negligible. The only result of four risky missions to install bottom mines was the accidental destruction of the submarine *Shch-323*. As a result of a control error, the submarine went beyond the fairway and was blown up on a bottom mine that lay beyond the safe area. Thus, in April 1943, the situation of 1942 was repeated, when the accuracy of the bottom mines was sacrificed to the safety of the crews. It can be assumed that almost all the bottom mines dropped by the Germans were lying on the bottom, but not in Russian fairways. Consequently, if the ships stayed strictly within the fairways, then the mines posed no threat to them.

In a sense, this operation on minelaying fairways around Kronstadt Naval Base turned out to be the last desperate demonstration of the melting Luftwaffe forces in this sector of the front. In 1944, the situation around Leningrad changed dramatically, and Luftflotte 1 no longer had the strength to mount such demonstrations.

The failure of the use of mines around Kronstadt Naval Base

At the time of the attack on the Soviet Union, Germany possessed a new universal weapon, the BM 1000 parachute mine. The Germans also had a reliable instrument of delivery of this 'wonder weapon' to the target area, He 111 and Ju 88 bombers. Their crews were well trained in the effective use of this weapon. There was also sufficient experience in using bottom mines against warships. In particular, as a result of the use of these weapons against the ships of the British fleet in November 1939, the destroyer *Gipsy* was sunk and the cruiser *Belfast* was severely damaged. These results caused unjustified optimism about the effectiveness of bottom mines in two completely incompetent, but very influential people: Hermann Göring and Adolf Hitler.

In June 1941, the Germans had a new target for using bottom mines against warships. Hitler, who was terrified of the Soviet Baltic Fleet, in the period from 1941 to 1943, demanded several times that the Luftwaffe destroy it. It is clear that only Hitler, who was completely incompetent in military matters, believed he could count on the destruction of all or even part of the

Soviet Baltic Fleet ships with this type of weapon. Therefore, Luftflotte 1 staff officers planned to use bottom mines to implement a more modest task. They wanted to blockade Russian naval bases or at least create significant difficulties for large ships to go to sea. However, even these modest hopes, due to the above reasons, were completely unjustified.[266] Meanwhile, between 1941 and 1943, minelaying operations around Kronstadt Naval Base were persistently repeated three times. The authors have no doubt that the Luftflotte 1 staff officers were aware of the utter uselessness of such use of bottom mines in this area. They had been on this sector of the front for the third year and had the opportunity to receive accurate intelligence information. The authors also have no reason to doubt the level of competence of Luftflotte 1 staff officers. Based on this, such persistent disregard by the Germans of the complete inefficiency of minelaying in this area requires a rational explanation: the belief that reason for this was the need to carry out direct orders from an incompetent Führer. Stubborn Hitler did not want to hear alternative proposals about other important goals, on the destruction of which valuable Luftwaffe resources could be spent. Thus, the Luftflotte 1 staff officers had no choice but to take all possible measures to reduce the harm to the bomber crews from following the stupid orders of the Führer. In this area, the Luftflotte 1 management, thanks to a rational approach and tactical skill, undoubtedly achieved success. They managed to minimise losses in 1941 and 1942 and even prevent the death of their crews in 1943 during minelaying missions.

Thus, due to Hitler's rude intervention, the Luftflotte 1 command acted extremely formulaically and did not use many opportunities to increase the efficiency of using bottom mines. For example, the Germans did not put mines in the way of the ships' departure from Kronstadt to Leningrad. Finally, there was no minelaying in the mouth of the Neva, where the surviving Soviet Baltic Fleet ships were located for a long time.

So was Hitler's directive to destroy the Soviet Baltic Fleet, which he repeated several times, fulfilled? Formally, the fleet was not destroyed. Despite numerous damages, some of the large ships survived. However, in essence, the Soviet Baltic Fleet was unable to have any significant impact on the course of the war and actually stood throughout it in ports in the eastern part of the Gulf of Finland. Large surface ships were completely disabled, and the submarines

---

266. The Luftwaffe operations at Kronstadt Naval Base described in this book were not the only cases of the use of bombers for minelaying the waters of the Gulf of Finland. In 1941, other naval bases of the Soviet Baltic Fleet, in particular Triigi, were subjected to minelaying from the air.

that had been reduced in number by half were completely locked up in the Gulf of Finland as a result of the installation of extensive anti-submarine networks and German and Finnish minelaying.

Hitler's suicidal strategy against the brilliant tactics of Luftflotte 1

If we analyse the battle for Leningrad as an isolated combat area, considering it essentially as a separate war, then all the possibilities and limitations of the use of military aviation are clearly visible. However, the realisation of the advantages and the acceptance of restrictions of the use of this kind of warfare was completely ignored by the incompetent German high command. A procrustean bed of compliance with Hitler's directives led the Luftwaffe to waste forces and valuable weapons on the routine execution of tasks that had very little connection with the real situation on this section of the Eastern Front. Instead of solving military problems, the officers and management of Luftflotte 1 directed their intellectual and organisational efforts to turn insane political directives caused by the irrational fears of the Führer into combat tasks. Hitler's brutal intervention completely deprived the leadership of Luftflotte 1 of independence at the strategic level. The payback for this was the rejection of the flexible and maximally efficient use of limited resources. Before 1943 some freedom of decision-making was found at the operational level, but only the tactical level, that is, the organisation and conduct of specific combat missions, was the full prerogative of the leadership and staff officers of Luftflotte 1. However, even excellent tactical skills and competent planning could not compensate for strategic mistakes in the choice of targets and the means of their destruction.

As the situation on the Eastern Front worsened, the degree of Hitler's intervention grew, and the degree of independence of the Luftflotte 1 command and staff officers decreased. In the end, this disastrous trend for the Germans became one of the reasons for the soft resignation of Generaloberst Alfred Keller in the summer of 1943. His merits and age prevented the Führer from bringing his destructive interference in the affairs of German aviation to the maximum level. The new commander of Luftflotte 1, fanatically devoted to Hitler, no longer allowed himself any independence in decision-making, even at the tactical level. After Keller's removal and the appointment of Korten in his place, Hitler had his hands free for the unlimited and absolutely meaningless sacrifice of Luftwaffe pilots. As a result of such actions, by August 1943, of all the Luftflotte 1 units in the Leningrad area, only one fighter Gruppe remained.

Thus, it can be stated that in 1943 the Germans lost the air war on this section of the Eastern Front. This was not due to the skilful actions of the Soviets, but because of the failed German strategy. However, one should not go to the other extreme and assert the success of Stalin's strategy. The military competence and intelligence level of the 'Red Lord' and the 'Brown Lord' were at an equally low level. Concrete examples of Stalin's failed military strategy are presented in this book in sufficient quantity.

Despite the strategic defeat in the air Battle for Leningrad, the Luftwaffe operated successfully at the operational and especially tactical level. The significant numerical advantage of the Red Army Air Force in 1941 and the huge resources that the Russians spent on the deployment of air defence were not a serious obstacle to the successful actions of Luftflotte 1. The technical superiority and the quality of Luftwaffe pilots' training remained at an unattainable level for the Soviets until the end of the war. The entry into Soviet Air Force service of well-designed and well-made British and especially American aircraft did not help Russian pilots to surpass the Germans or at least fight them on equal terms. Even recent graduates of German aviation schools without combat experience could well resist the famous 'Stalin's Falcons'.

Chronicle of a successful disaster

As noted above, the most efficient use of the Luftwaffe resources was in the summer and autumn of 1941. It was then that aviation was a powerful factor in complementing the offensive abilities of the ground forces. This was facilitated by a brilliantly organised collaboration between these branches of the armed forces. The versatility of German aviation units made it possible to use their capabilities flexibly to sometimes simultaneously solve several combat tasks. In addition to minelaying fairways and undertaking air strikes on Soviet Baltic Fleet ships and their bases, German bombers were used for the following combat missions:

- isolation of the combat area by bombing railway stations and disrupting communications;
- provision of supplies to Wehrmacht units in difficult situations due to bad roads;
- striking at Soviet troops to provide direct support to the advancing Wehrmacht.

In 1942, when the German Army in the Leningrad area went on the defensive, the effectiveness of the Luftwaffe decreased significantly. This was due not only to the improper use of this kind of resource, but also to the setting of tasks that the Luftwaffe could not perform without the participation of ground forces. An example was a pathetic attempt to force Leningrad to surrender by bombing and the disruption of transport communications on Lake Ladoga. In the case of joint actions with the Wehrmacht, the effectiveness of the Luftwaffe again reached a high level. For example, when there was a real need to stop the offensive of Soviet troops, Luftwaffe units brilliantly coped with this mission at a tactical level. For this they did not need petty guardianship and stupid orders from Hitler.

In 1943, until the retirement of Commander of Luftflotte 1 Generaloberst Alfred Keller, Luftwaffe units were mainly engaged in demonstrating their presence and the effect of their actions was more psychological than physical.

In the autumn of 1943, only a pitiful shadow remained of the very modest Luftwaffe forces in the Leningrad area. In Hitler's hands, the versatility of German bombers turned from a virtue into a disadvantage. The incompetent Führer used valuable aviation as a fire brigade to plug numerous holes in the Wehrmacht defences. Valuable aviation specialists died en masse in stupid missions, such as supplying numerous pockets, which became Hitler's mania at the end of the war.

Greetings to Stalin from Hitler from hell

The episode looks somewhat curious when the Führer's hopes for the destruction of large Soviet ships in the Kronstadt Naval Base area with the help of mines paradoxically began to be realised after his suicide and the collapse of the Third Reich. This happened because, despite all the efforts of Soviet minesweepers, the problem of bottom mines was not completely solved even after the end of the war. On 17 October 1945, the cruiser *Kirov* blew up on a bottom mine with a magnetic fuse. On this day, the cruiser was conducting artillery training near Kronstadt and was severely damaged. Boiler room No. 5, control devices to fire guns of the main calibre and the diesel generator were destroyed, while turret No. 2 of the main calibre was jammed. Boiler room No. 1, powder chambers of two artillery turrets, the central navigation post, the central artillery post, the energy and survivability post and the dry provisions storeroom were all flooded. The ship completely lost the ability to move independently and received a strong roll and draft on the bow. At the time of the explosion, five crew members were killed (all in the central navigation post). The proximity of the rescue infrastructure and the help of nearby ships made it possible to avoid the death of the cruiser. The emergency teams sent from Kronstadt Naval Base were able to stop the flow of water and stabilise the ship in a few hours of hard work. *Kirov* was towed to Kronstadt Harbour and delivered to a dry dock on 28 October 1945. After a long repair, which lasted until December 1946, Stalin's beloved cruiser was once again restored. However, the cost of the work amounted to about 200 million rubles.

Conclusion

The Battle of Leningrad became one of the most brutal of the war. The war was waged with the use of all branches of the armed forces: ground forces, navy and aviation. The duration of the confrontation between the Wehrmacht and the Red Army in the battles in the area of Leningrad is also impressive. Fierce battles lasted for almost two and a half years. But, for a long time, neither side could achieve a strategic breakthrough in this sector of the Eastern Front. However, the events that developed near Moscow, Stalingrad and Kursk pushed the battle for Leningrad into the background.

The authors have tried to focus their attention on the actions of aviation in this section of the Eastern Front. However, it turned out to be impossible to completely ignore the land battles, the actions of the fleet, the organisation of supplies and the humanitarian aspects associated with the blockaded city. In addition to the actual historical understanding of the events in the area of Leningrad, to one degree or another, the authors needed to reveal the psychological, social and economic aspects of the bloody confrontation between the two totalitarian states.

The main sources of factual information for writing the book were archival data and memories of eyewitnesses of the events from the two opposing sides. The main problem of the study of these materials was the comparison of quantitative and qualitative data on military events, taking into account the incompleteness and direct distortions of information from the German and Soviet sides. In addition to the most complete description of historical facts, the authors attempted to interpret them and establish the relationship of the events around Leningrad with the general course of the war. The main method of such interpretation was a critical analysis of all sources of information at the disposal of the authors. The generalisation of the results of such work allowed the authors to draw conclusions about the effectiveness of both individual operations in the air and, in general, the activities of the opposing sides' aviation in the Leningrad sector.

In addition, to study and evaluate historical events, the authors used an original psychological approach based on the study of the motives of the leaders of the

CONCLUSION

two totalitarian empires. This created conditions for a better understanding of the reasons for making certain decisions by specific people who determined the course of military operations, and ultimately were responsible for victories and defeats in the Leningrad area and the entire Eastern Front. In our opinion, the specificity of the Eastern Front lies in the special significance of the qualities of the character of Hitler[267] and Stalin,[268] who concentrated huge political and, most importantly, military power in their hands. These people determined the military strategy and managed the troops not only through the generals appointed by them, but also personally. The authors have not avoided moral assessments of the actions of the two tyrants, but on the contrary, considered a detailed analysis of the crimes of Hitler and Stalin one of the key factors in understanding the danger of totalitarian regimes for human civilisation. For a more complete perception of this position, readers are advised to pay attention to other books by authors who are interconnected and complement the overall picture of the war on the Eastern Front in the Second World War.

The authors do not pretend to fully disclose the topic stated in the book, and many of the interpretations set forth can undoubtedly be the subject of discussion and reasonable criticism.

---

267. A psychological portrait of Adolf Hitler can be found in Degtev, D., and Zubov, D., *The Luftwaffe's Secret WWII Missions*, Barnsley, UK: Air World/Pen & Sword Books, 2020.
268. A psychological portrait of Joseph Stalin can be found in Zubov, D., *Stalin's Falcons: Exposing the Myth of Soviet Aerial Superiority over the Luftwaffe in WW2*, Barnsley, UK: Air World/Pen & Sword, 2023.

References and Sources

Bychevsky, B.V., *The City is the Front*, Leningrad: Lenizdat, 1967.
Cherokov, V.S., *For You, Leningrad!*, Leningrad: Leninzdat, 1988.
Golubev, V.F., *Second Wind*, Leningrad: Lenizdat, 1988.
Golubev, V.F., *Wings Grow Stronger in Battle*, Leningrad: Lenizdat, 1984.
Grishchenko, P.D., *Fight Under Water*, Moscow: Molodaya Gvardiya, 1983.
Gundelach, K., *Kampfgeschwader 'General Wever' 4*, Stuttgart: Motorbuch Verlag, 1978.
Halder, F., *From Brest to Stalingrad: A war diary. Daily records of the Chief of the General Staff of the Ground Forces 1941–1942*, Rusich, 2001.
Held, W., Trautloft, H., Bob, E., *JG 54. A Photographic History of the Grunherzgeschwader*, Schiffer Military History, USA, 1990.
Keskinen, K., Stenman, K., *German Aircraft in Finland 1939–1945*, Tampere, Finland: Apali Oy, 1998.
Khazanov, D.B., *The Battle for the Sky. 1941: from the Dnieper to the Gulf of Finland*, Moscow: Yauza, 2007.
Kiehl, H., *Kampfgeschwader 'Legion Condor' 53*, Stuttgart: Motorbuch Verlag, 1996.
Krasnaya Zvezda newspaper, No. 196, 21 August 1941.
Ladinsky, Y.V., *Military Watchstanding*, Moscow: Voenizdat. 1983.
Ladinsky, Y.V., *On the Fairways of the Baltic*, Moscow: Voenizdat, 1973.
Ladoga Native (Memoirs of veterans of the Red Banner Ladoga Flotilla), Leningrad: Lenizdat, 1984.
Ladoga: Photo album, Moscow: Planeta, 1989.
Majorov, Y.M., *Highways of courage*, Moscow: Voenizdat, 1982.
Manstein, E., *Lost Victories*, Smolensk: Rusich, 1999.
Military Chronicle of the Navy. 1941–1942, Moscow: Voenizdat, 1992.
Morozov, E., *The failed Pearl Harbor, or Why Operation 'Eisstoss' Failed*, Moscow: AviaMaster, 2001. No. 3.
Novikov, A.A., *In the sky of Leningrad (Notes of the Commander of aviation)*, Moscow: Nauka, 1970.

REFERENCES AND SOURCES

On the road of life: memories of the front-line Ladoga, Moscow: Voenizdat, 1980.
Panteleev, Y.A., *Sea Front*, Moscow: Voenizdat, 1965.
Pavlov, D.V., *Leningrad is Under Siege*, Leningrad: Lenizdat, 1985.
Rudel, H.U., *Stuka Pilot*, Moscow: Centerpoligraph, 2009.
Rusakov, Z.G., *Our Sea was Ladoga*, Leningrad: Lenizdat, 1980.
The air defence forces of the country in the Great Patriotic War, Moscow: Voenizdat, 1968.
The blockade of Leningrad in the documents of declassified archives, Moscow: AST, 2004.
The military chronicle of Soviet Navy. 1943, Moscow: Voenizdat, 1993.
The Red Banner Soviet Baltic Fleet in the Battle for Leningrad. 1941–1944, Moscow: Nauka, 1975.
Waiss, W., *Chronic Kampfgeschwader Nr. 27 'Boelcke'*, Part 3. 01.01.1942–31.12.1942, Aachen: Helios Verlag, 2005.
Weal, J., *Jagdgeschwader 54 'Grunherz'*, Oxford: Osprey Aviation, 2001.

Archives

Central Archives of the Ministry of Defence of the Russian Federation (TSAMO RF)

TSAMO RF. Foundation 3. Inventory 11556. Case 1. Sheet 71.
TSAMO RF. Foundation 3. Inventory 11556. Case 10. Sheet 23.
TSAMO RF. Foundation 148a. Inventory 3763. Case 103. Sheets 253–254.
TSAMO RF. Foundation 204. Inventory 89. Case 181. Sheets 16–18.
TSAMO RF. Foundation 204. Inventory 89. Case 181. Sheets 51, 54.
TSAMO RF. Foundation 217. Inventory 1221. Case 174. Sheets 58–69.
TSAMO RF. Foundation 217. Inventory1221. Case 1594. Sheets 161–163.
TSAMO RF. Foundation 217. Inventory 1221. Case 103. Sheet 203.
TSAMO RF. Foundation 217. Inventory 1221. Case 103. Sheet 217.
TSAMO RF. Foundation 217. Inventory 1221. Case 103. Sheet 238.
TSAMO RF. Foundation 217. Inventory 1221. Case 103. Sheet 284.
TSAMO RF. Foundation 217. Inventory 1221. Case 103. Sheet 204.
TSAMO RF. Foundation 217. Inventory 1221. Case 103. Sheets 216–217.
TSAMO RF. Foundation 217. Inventory 1221. Case 103. Sheets 284–285.
TSAMO RF. Foundation 217. Inventory 1221. Case 103. Sheet 320.
TSAMO RF. Foundation 217. Inventory 1221. Case 103. Sheets 326–327.

AIR BATTLE FOR LENINGRAD, 1941–1944

TSAMO RF. Foundation 217. Inventory 1221. Case 301. Sheets 357, 361.
TSAMO RF. Foundation 217. Inventory 1221. Case 301. Sheet 364.
TSAMO RF. Foundation 217. Inventory 1221. Case 301. Sheet 366.
TSAMO RF. Foundation 217. Inventory 1221. Case 191. Sheet 16.
TSAMO RF. Foundation 217. Inventory 1221. Case 189. Sheets 566–567.
TSAMO RF. Foundation 217. Inventory 1221. Case 103. Sheet 414.
TSAMO RF. Foundation 217. Inventory 1221. Case 103. Sheet 415.
TSAMO RF. Foundation 217. Inventory 1221. Case 103. Sheet 428.
TSAMO RF. Foundation 217. Inventory 1221. Case 103. Sheet 429.
TSAMO RF. Foundation 217. Inventory 1221. Case 103. Sheet 429.
TSAMO RF. Foundation 217. Inventory 1221. Case 103. Sheets 430–431.
TSAMO RF. Foundation 217. Inventory 1221. Case 103. Sheets 475–476.
TSAMO RF. Foundation 217. Inventory 1221. Case 1594. Sheets 181–184.
TSAMO RF. Foundation 217. Inventory 1258. Case 125. Sheet 148.
TSAMO RF. Foundation 217. Inventory 1221. Case 1594. Sheets 190–193.
TSAMO RF. Foundation 217. Inventory 1221. Case 3141. Sheets 7–11.
TSAMO RF. Foundation 217. Inventory 1221. Case 3141. Sheets 13–27.
TSAMO RF. Foundation 217. Inventory 1221. Case 3141. Sheets 32–39.
TSAMO RF. Foundation 217. Inventory 1221. Case 3141. Sheet 40.
TSAMO RF. Foundation 217. Inventory 1221. Case 3141. Sheets 42–43.
TSAMO RF. Foundation 217. Inventory 1221. Case 3141. Sheets 43–46.
TSAMO RF. Foundation 249. Inventory 1544. Case 112. Sheet 144.
TSAMO RF. Foundation 344. Inventory 5554. Case 402. Sheets 302–303.
TSAMO RF. Foundation 362. Inventory 0006169. Case 0106. Sheets 300–304, 318–340.
TSAMO RF. Foundation 5678. Inventory 19877. Case 13. Sheets 5–7.
TSAMO RF. Foundation 13642. Inventory 0020244. Case 0061. Sheets 210–214.
TSAMO RF. Foundation 13642. Inventory 0020244. Case 0061. Sheets 215–216.
TSAMO RF. Foundation 13642. Inventory 0020244. Case 0061. Sheet 221.
TSAMO RF. Foundation 13642. Inventory 0020244. Case 0061. Sheets 304–307.
TSAMO RF. Foundation 13642. Inventory 0020244. Case 0061. Sheets 309–312.
TSAMO RF. Foundation 13642. Inventory 0020244. Case 0061. Sheets 319–324.
TSAMO RF. Foundation 13642. Inventory 0020244. Case 0061. Sheet 361.
TSAMO RF. Foundation 13642. Inventory 0020244. Case 0037. Sheet 34.
TSAMO RF. Foundation 13642. Inventory 0020244. Case 0037. Sheet 37.

REFERENCES AND SOURCES

TSAMO RF. Foundation 13642. Inventory 0020244. Case 0061. Sheet 13.
TSAMO RF. Foundation 13642. Inventory 0020244. Case 0037. Sheets 56–59.
TSAMO RF. Foundation 13642. Inventory 0020244. Case 0061. Sheets 203–205.
TSAMO RF. Foundation 22020. Inventory 0445249s. Case 0001. Sheet 21–22.
TSAMO RF. Foundation 22020. Inventory 0445249s. Case 0001. Sheet 24–29.
TSAMO RF. Foundation 22020. Inventory 0445249s. Case 0001. Sheet 30–41.
TSAMO RF. Foundation 22020. Inventory 0445249s. Case 0001. Sheet 56–57.
TSAMO RF. Foundation 22020. Inventory 0445249s. Case 0001. Sheet 59.
TSAMO RF. Foundation 20157. Inventory 1. Case 30. Sheets 24–29.
TSAMO RF. Foundation 20157. Inventory 1. Case 30. Sheets 31–36.
TSAMO RF. Foundation 20249. Inventory 1. Case 5. Sheet 6.
TSAMO RF. Foundation 20249. Inventory 1. Case 5. Sheet 8.
TSAMO RF. Foundation 20249. Inventory 1. Case 5. Sheet 11.
TSAMO RF. Foundation 20249. Inventory 1. Case 5. Sheet 13.
TSAMO RF. Foundation 20249. Inventory 1. Case 5. Sheet 14.
TSAMO RF. Foundation 20249. Inventory 1. Case 5. Sheet 15.
TSAMO RF. Foundation 20249. Inventory 1. Case 5. Sheet 17.
TSAMO RF. Foundation 20249. Inventory 1. Case 5. Sheet 18.
TSAMO RF. Foundation 20249. Inventory 1. Case 5. Sheet 19.
TSAMO RF. Foundation 20249. Inventory 1. Case 5. Sheet 20.
TSAMO RF. Foundation 20249. Inventory 1. Case 5. Sheet 21.
TSAMO RF. Foundation 20506. Inventory 1. Case 129. Sheet 15.
TSAMO RF. Foundation 20506. Inventory 1. Case 129. Sheets 16–17.
TSAMO RF. Foundation 20506. Inventory 1. Case 129. Sheet 24–26.
TSAMO RF. Foundation 20506. Inventory 1. Case 129. Sheet 67.
TSAMO RF. Foundation 20506. Inventory 1. Case 132. Sheets 19–21.
TSAMO RF. Foundation 20506. Inventory 1. Case 132. Sheet 40.
TSAMO RF. Foundation 20506. Inventory 1. Case 132. Sheets 41–43.
TSAMO RF. Foundation 20506. Inventory 1. Case 40. Sheet 21–25.
TSAMO RF. Foundation 22753. Inventory 0105884s. Case 0004. Sheet 51.
TSAMO RF. Foundation 22753. Inventory 0105884s. Case 0004. Sheet 52.
TSAMO RF. Foundation 22753. Inventory 0105884s. Case 0004. Sheet 53.
TSAMO RF. Foundation 22753. Inventory 0105884s. Case 0004. Sheet 68.
TSAMO RF. Foundation 22753. Inventory 0105884s. Case 0004. Sheet 72.

Central Naval Archive (TSVMA), Russian Federation
TSVMA. Foundation 216. Case 12490. Sheet 246.
TSVMA. Foundation 219. Case 134567. Sheets 77–79.
TSVMA. Foundation 399. Case 32. Sheet 60.

TSVMA. Foundation 401. Case 401879. Sheets 2–3.
TSVMA. Foundation 704. Case 5016. Sheet 14.
TSVMA. Foundation 704. Case 5016. Sheets 29–31.
TSVMA. Foundation 1003. Case 546. Sheets 288–301.
TSVMA. Foundation 1003. Case 546. Sheets 304, 318–320.
TSVMA. Foundation 57681. Case 4. Sheets 41–43.
TSVMA. Foundation 57681. Case 4. Sheets 48–50.
TSVMA. Foundation 57681. Case 4. Sheet 55.
TSVMA. Foundation 57681. Case 4. Sheet 56.
TSVMA. Foundation 57681. Case 4. Sheets 57–58.

Index

XXXXI Army Corps (mot.), 12, 23
LVI Army Corps (mot.), 12
7th Fighter Aviation Corps Air Defence (7th IAC PVO), 17–18, 20, 27, 42, 91, 105, 108, 135, 142, 145, 153, 244

Abwehr, 14
Air Force Soviet Baltic Fleet (VVS KBF), 5, 39–40, 105, 129, 139, 142, 277
anti-aircraft artillery, 28, 47, 71, 72, 80–81, 90, 95, 97, 107, 110, 114–115, 123, 137–138, 142, 147, 172, 174, 175, 178, 182, 210–212, 222–223, 235, 250, 265, 266, 268, 273–274, 300–301
Army Group B, 201
Army Group Centre, 61, 126
Army Group Courland, 278
Army Group North, vii, 12, 14, 21–23, 30, 38, 61, 122, 126, 128, 130, 139, 154, 205, 229, 242, 258, 277–278, 281, 286
Army Group South, 23

Baltic Sea, 3, 14, 38, 47, 168, 183, 190, 250, 252, 278, 288, 291, 300–301
Barbarossa, Operation, vi, 4, 12, 15, 20, 23, 38, 115, 128, 130, 286, 287, 294
Bell P-39 Airacobra, 212–213

Beriev,
  MBR-2, 88, 105, 139, 194, 219
Blitzkrieg, vi, 23, 88, 90, 287, 291
Bombenmine (BM1000), 3, 7, 40, 89, 168, 171–172, 184, 290, 297, 300
Brazil, Operation, 216, 220–221, 223, 224–225, 227
British Royal Navy, 8

Caucasus, 201
Citadel, Operation, 229, 258, 274–275
cruiser *Kirov*, 46–47, 49, 53, 58, 61, 128, 130, 135, 143, 144–145, 148–150, 294, 296, 297–298, 306–307
cruiser *Maxim Gorky*, 46–48, 128, 135, 143, 147–149, 297–298
cruiser *Petropavlovsk* (heavy cruiser *Lützow*), 47–48
Curtiss P-40 Tomahawks, 142, 164–165, 244–245, 260–261, 265

Demyansk, 126–128, 139–141, 169
destroyer *Besposchadnyi*, 299
destroyer *Engels*, 70
destroyer *Gordy*, 52, 61
destroyer *Grozyashchiy*, 51, 58, 61, 143, 148, 293, 298
destroyer *Karl Marx*, 70, 81
destroyer leader *Kharkov*, 299
destroyer leader *Leningrad*, 47–48, 129
destroyer leader *Minsk*, 47–48, 58, 59, 294
destroyer *Opytnyi*, 48
destroyer *Serdityi*, 70

destroyer *Silnyi*, 53, 61, 143–144, 149, 298
destroyer *Slavnyi*, 53
destroyer *Sposobnyi*, 299
destroyer *Steregushchy*, 50–52, 293
destroyer *Stoiky*, 135
destroyer *Strashnyi*, 70
destroyer *Strogyi*, 48
destroyer *Stroinyi*, 48
destroyer *Surovyi*, 61, 70
destroyer *Svirepyi*, 135
DFS 230, 135
Dornier,
Do 17, 29, 35
Do 215, 3, 15, 130, 136, 165, 273
Do 217, 259, 270, 276

'Eastern Ferry Operations Staff' (Einsatzstab Fähre Ost), 191, 220
Eisstoss, Operation, 126, 132, 137, 139, 141, 172, 295–298
East Prussia, 3, 14–17, 26, 37, 169, 173

Focke-Wulf,
Fw 190, 244–245, 255, 259, 261–263, 265–269, 272–273
Fw 200, 33
Förster, Commander of I. Fliegerkorps, General der Flieger Helmuth, 126–128, 141

Go 242, 169
Göring, Reichsmarschall Hermann, 29, 191–192, 282, 284–285, 302
Götz von Berlichingen, Operation, 140–141, 297–298
Gulag, 62–63
Gulf of Finland, 1, 3, 4, 17, 38, 43, 49, 60, 70, 88–89, 91, 106–108, 110, 117, 121, 126, 131, 133–134, 142, 168–170, 179, 181, 187, 190, 201, 202, 248, 250–251, 254, 287–288, 291, 300, 303, 304
gunboat *Bira*, 62, 70–71, 160–162, 166, 224, 233, 256, 263

gunboat *Bureya*, 62, 77, 160, 203, 256, 263
gunboat *Lakhta*, 154, 203, 262
gunboat *Nora*, 62, 69, 160–161, 166, 203–204, 218–219, 224–225, 256
gunboat *Olekma*, 62, 70
gunboat *Pioner*, 53, 59
gunboat *Selemdzha*, 25, 62, 66, 68, 160–161, 199, 203–204, 224, 225, 227, 234, 256
gunboat *Sheksna*, 62, 154

Halder, Chief of the General Staff of the Army High Command (OKH) Generaloberst, Franz, 26, 94, 101, 113, 114
Hawker Hurricane, 244
Heinkel,
He 59, 4, 53
He 111, 26, 36, 37–38, 41, 49, 74–75, 79, 80, 83–86, 90, 92, 99, 100, 108, 113, 120, 128, 133, 136–138, 156, 169, 172–173, 177–181, 184–186, 205, 229–233, 239, 244–245, 247–248, 250, 258, 260–269, 271–274, 290, 296–297, 302
He 115, 4
Henschel,
Hs 126, 28, 98, 146, 208
Hitler, Adolf, vi, 1–2, 7, 11–12, 22–23, 25–26, 31, 38, 46–48, 60, 79, 85–86, 88, 101, 104, 111, 113, 115–116, 119–120, 123, 126–128, 139, 149, 151, 154, 166–168, 189–192, 201–202, 206, 228–229, 239–240, 242–243, 245, 247–248, 258, 271, 274–275, 278–281, 284, 286–288, 290–291, 294–295, 299–304, 306, 309
hulk *Voroshilov*, 298

Ice Road, 103–104, 113–114, 116–119, 120–122, 125–126, 151, 236–237, 245

INDEX

Ilyushin,
  DB-3, 105
  Il-2, 28, 33, 39, 42–43, 87, 211, 214, 226, 244, 245
Iskra, Operation, 239, 242–243, 245, 247

JG 27, 28, 45, 52
JG 52, 28, 29
JG 54 'Grunherz', 4, 28, 34, 39, 42, 54, 72, 83, 87, 98, 108, 114, 117, 121, 128, 133, 140, 142–143, 149, 155, 157–158, 163–165, 188, 193–195, 199, 204, 212, 214–215, 236, 244–245, 255, 259, 261, 263, 266, 267, 269–270, 272, 276–277
Junkers,
  Ju 52, 33, 87, 209
  Ju 86, 29
  Ju 87, 20, 28, 33, 48, 49–53, 55, 58–60, 66, 127–128, 130, 133, 134, 136, 140–148, 160, 163–165, 183, 192, 205, 232–233, 244, 259, 261, 268–269, 273, 276, 291–293, 295–299
  Ju 88, 3–5, 15–19, 28, 33, 35, 39, 40, 44–45, 52–54, 58–59, 69, 70–73, 77–79, 83, 87, 98, 101, 107–108, 114, 117, 120, 128, 130–131, 133, 136, 140, 142, 156–158, 160–165, 172, 177–178, 180–181, 183, 192, 204, 211, 214–215, 223, 231, 244, 250–251, 259, 267, 270, 273, 301–302

Kampfgeschwader, 37–38, 117, 169, 186, 205, 258, 264, 271, 285
Keller, Commander of Luftflotte 1 Generaloberst Alfred, 61, 86, 119, 126, 130, 154, 188, 190, 247–248, 274, 281–287, 304, 306
KG 1 'Hindenburg', 39–40, 83, 101, 128, 156, 160, 164, 172, 177–178, 192, 204, 215, 223, 250, 252, 259, 270, 276, 301
KG 3, 29, 128
KG 4 'General Wever', 8, 26, 35–39, 41, 49, 74, 79–80, 83–84, 86, 92, 99, 100, 113, 116, 120–121, 128, 137–138, 168–169, 172–173, 177–178, 180, 183–184, 186, 290, 297, 299
KG 27 'Boelcke', 128, 135, 137
KG 53 'Legion Condor', 128, 205, 229, 232, 245, 247–249, 255, 258, 262, 263–266, 268–269, 271, 274, 276
KG 77, 38, 44–45, 52–54, 57–59, 77, 79, 83, 87, 117
KG 100 'Viking', 128
KG 101, 259, 270, 276
KGr. 506, 3, 4, 288, 290
KGr. 806, 3–5, 8, 70–72, 79, 83, 87, 117, 288, 290
Kriegsmarine, 47, 191–192, 287
Kronstadt Fortress, 171, 178, 251
Kronstadt Naval Base, 3–7, 52, 53, 170–172, 174, 176, 178, 182, 184, 186, 250–252, 288–292, 299–303, 306–307
Kupfer, Hauptmann Ernst, 51, 53, 60, 291–295
Kursk, 6, 274, 308
Kuznetsov, Nikolai, Admiral People's Commissar (Minister) of the Navy, 13, 155

Ladoga flotilla of the Axis powers, 189–190, 192, 198, 219, 220
Ladoga Military Flotilla, 13, 25, 28, 30, 62–64, 70, 73, 76, 78, 94, 153, 158, 160, 191–193, 196, 203–204, 217–219, 221, 223–225, 227, 233, 256, 272
Lahdenpohja harbour, 190–193, 200
Lavochkin,
  La-5, 245, 267

Lavochkin-Gorbunov-Gudkov,
LaGG-3, 19–20, 27–29, 33–34, 39–40, 42, 45, 71, 105, 135, 136, 142–143, 146, 164–165, 183, 213–214, 226, 261, 267–268, 270
Lisunov,
Li-2, 97–98
Luftflotte 1, 4, 15, 26, 28–29, 44, 61, 70, 73, 79, 83, 86, 94, 96, 111, 117, 119, 120, 126–132, 137, 139, 150, 154, 166, 168–169, 188–193, 198, 204, 216–217, 229, 234, 244–245, 247–248, 250, 258–259, 266, 274, 277, 279–280, 286, 288, 290, 295, 296–306
Luftmine A (LMA), 7
Luftmine B (LMB), 7, 26
Luftmine F (LMF), 7
Luftwaffe, vii, 7–9, 14, 23, 28–29, 31, 35, 38–41, 44–46, 48–49, 54, 59–60, 65–67, 71, 73, 78, 79, 81, 83, 89–90, 92, 95–99, 101, 104–109, 111, 116–118, 120–122, 126–133, 135, 137, 139, 141, 143–145, 147–150, 159–160, 164–169, 173–174, 179, 181, 184, 188, 191–192, 194–196, 198–199, 204–206, 208–211, 214–217, 220, 222–223, 226, 229–231, 233–234, 236, 238, 243–248, 252, 255, 257, 258–260, 262–263, 268–274, 276–277, 279–282, 284–292, 294–299, 301, 302–306

Meretskov, Commander of the Volkhov Front, General of the Army, Kirill, 202, 208, 210
Messerschmitt,
Bf 109, 4, 19, 27–29, 33–34, 39–40, 44–45, 52, 71–72, 83, 87, 98, 101, 108, 114, 117, 120–121, 128, 130–131, 133, 136, 140, 142, 146–149, 155–157, 162–165, 183, 188, 193, 194–195, 199, 204, 208, 212–216, 229–232, 236–237, 244–245, 259, 261, 263, 265, 267, 272, 277, 297
Bf 110, 18–20, 33, 45, 98, 136, 273
Mikoyan-Gurevich,
MiG-3, 16–20, 27–29, 33, 39, 42, 45, 72, 87, 105, 140, 142, 146, 148, 156, 158, 165, 270
Milch, Generalfeldmarschall Erhard, 286
Military Road No. 101 (VAD No. 101), 103, 117, 125
Military Road No. 102 (VAD No. 102), 103, 117
mine boat *KM 3*, 191, 218
mine boat *KM 4*, 191, 218
mine boat *KM 8*, 191
mine boat *KM 22*, 191, 218
minelayer *Marti*, 52, 128, 130, 142, 145, 269
minesweeper *TSCH-33*, 60
minesweeper *TSCH-39 Petrozavodsk*, 6, 289
minesweeper *TSCH-63*, 273
minesweeper *TSCH-82*, 229–230
minesweeper *TSCH-100*, 223
minesweeper *TSCH-122*, 68–69
minesweeper *TSCH-126*, 216
minesweeper *TSCH-127*, 71
minesweeper *TSCH-175*, 194
minesweeper *TSCH-206*, 53–54
minesweeper *T-208 Schkiv*, 6, 289
minesweeper *TSCH-304*, 183
minesweeper *TSCH-317*, 183
Moscow, vi, 22–23, 25, 36–38, 41–42, 61, 73, 81, 88, 112, 115–116, 150, 152, 210, 278–279, 308

'Natural coffee', Operation, 188–199
NKVD, 29, 62, 102, 125, 208
Nordlicht, Operation, 201–202

Oberkommando der Luftwaffe (OKL), 14, 168–169, 290

INDEX

Panzer Group 4, 12, 23
patrol ship *Constructor*, 63, 66, 71–72, 75–76, 256
patrol ship *Purga*, 63, 65, 76, 192, 203, 204, 225
Pearl Harbor, 7, 298
Petergof, 4, 17, 43, 47, 172, 252
Petlyakov,
   Pe-2, 42–43, 87, 193, 213, 215, 236, 245
Polikarpov,
   Po-2 (U-2), 245, 256
   I-15, 226
   I-15bis, 5, 226, 251
   I-153, 5, 18, 20, 29, 34, 40, 61, 84–85, 87, 105, 136, 138, 140, 173–174, 178–180, 245, 251
   I-16, 5, 18–20, 27, 34, 42, 61, 105, 108, 121, 136, 138, 145–146, 155–158, 162–165, 173–174, 181, 199–200, 245, 251
   I-180 ('Super Rat'), 199–200

Red Army, vi, vii, 2–3, 9–13, 20, 22, 26, 28–29, 32, 39, 42, 72, 74, 87–88, 99, 101, 115, 119, 122, 126, 139, 151, 189, 199, 201, 203, 205, 206, 207, 209, 210, 226, 231, 239, 241–245, 250, 255–256, 258, 271, 273, 275, 277, 305, 308
Red Fleet, 13, 145
Reinhardt, General der Panzertruppen Georg-Hans, 12, 23
Road of Life, 65–6, 73, 116, 118
Rudel, Oberleutnant Hans-Ulrich, 65–66, 73, 116, 118
RUS-2 'Redut' radar stations, 37, 83, 129, 133, 142, 147, 170, 257

Shlisselburg, 25–26, 28–30, 36, 113, 117, 121, 164–165, 192, 202, 204, 236, 240–244, 256, 263, 265–266, 270

Siebel ferry, 191–193, 198–200, 217–227, 256
Soviet Baltic Fleet, vii, 1–7, 9, 12, 14, 23, 39, 40, 46–48, 54, 57, 60–61, 70, 73, 93, 104–105, 127–131, 141, 144, 149, 168, 170, 172, 175, 182, 187, 252–255, 287–289, 291–295, 297, 299–300–303, 305
Soviet Local Rescue Service (MPVO), 31, 41, 44, 81, 84, 91, 96–97, 106, 122, 138, 246, 276
Stalin, Joseph, vi, 1–3, 11–12, 20–22, 24–25, 32–33, 43, 47, 60, 87–89, 102, 111–112, 123–125, 128, 133, 137, 139, 149–151, 153, 201–202, 206–210, 239, 242–244, 251–252, 258, 274–275, 299, 305–306
'Stalin's Falcons', 10, 18, 20, 27, 28–29, 33–35, 39–40, 82, 105, 108, 121, 135–136, 140, 143, 145, 148, 154, 156, 158, 162, 164–165, 173, 179, 181–182, 212–215, 244, 261, 263, 265–270, 272–273, 305
Stalingrad, vi, 201, 229, 239, 243, 308
Steen Hauptmann Ernst-Siegfried, 44, 48–49, 55, 56, 58, 291–293, 295
StG 1, 127–128, 130, 144, 160, 164, 192
StG 2 'Immelmann', 23, 28, 44, 48, 50–51, 53, 58–60, 66, 127–128, 130, 143, 148, 291–296
Stoergruppe L.Fl.1, 256
submarine *K-51*, 142
submarine *L-3*, 56
submarine *L-55*, 254
submarine *M-77*, 256
submarine *M-79*, 256
submarine *M-90*, 149, 298
submarine *P-2*, 135
submarine *Shch-302*, 53

submarine *Shch-323*, 253–254, 302
submarine *Shch-406*, 253

Tallinn Naval Base, 46
Tikhvin, 10–11, 74, 93, 98–99, 101, 104, 110, 115–116, 118, 122, 153, 216, 271, 277
torpedo boat *MAS 526*, 190–191, 222
torpedo boat *MAS 527*, 190, 199
torpedo boat *MAS 528*, 190, 199
torpedo boat *MAS 529*, 190
training ship *Svir*, 145, 148, 298
Trautloft commander of JG 54 Oberstleutnant, Hannes, 28, 42, 142, 155, 157, 163, 166
Tributs, Commander of the Soviet Baltic Fleet Vice Admiral, Vladimir, 60, 153, 158, 252
Triigi Naval Base, 61
tugboat *Buy*, 153
tugboat *Gidrotechnik*, 153–154, 231
tugboat *Krasnyi flot*, 49
tugboat *Morskoi lev*, 153
tugboat *Nikulyasy*, 77, 153–154, 232
tugboat *Orel*, 67–69, 153
tugboat *Podolsk*, 216
tugboat *Uzbekistan*, 216
Tupolev,
   SB high-speed bomber, 42, 105
   TB-3, 97

Udet, Luftwaffe Chief of Procurement and Supply for the Luftwaffe Generaloberst, Ernst, 282

Velikiye Luki Pocket, 243
von Küchler, Commander of Army Group North, Generaloberst, Georg, 139, 154, 242–243, 281

von Leeb, Generalfeldmarschall, Wilhelm Ritter, 12, 23, 61
von Manstein, Generalfeldmarschall, Erich, 12, 115, 201–202, 208–209, 228–229, 240
von Richthofen, Generaloberst der Flieger, Wolfram, 23, 48, 61, 119, 149, 229, 291, 293
Voroshilov, Marshal of the Soviet Union, Kliment, 26, 30, 36

Wehrmacht, vi, 12–13, 22, 24, 30–31, 61, 74, 87–88, 99, 101, 115–116, 119, 149, 167, 190, 201, 229, 239–240, 243, 245, 247, 258, 271, 277, 280, 286–288, 291, 294, 305–306, 308

X-Gerät radio navigation equipment, 92

Yakovlev,
   Yak-1, 16, 20, 27, 42, 71, 105, 136, 166, 213, 214, 245, 267
   Yak-7UTI, 27–28, 33–34
   Yak-7, 210-213, 245,265, 267-268, 270

ZG 26 'Horst Wessel', 19–20, 23, 44
Zhdanov, First Secretary of the Leningrad Regional Committee of the Communist Party, Andrei, 24, 29–30, 32, 36, 41–42, 102–103, 133, 137, 150
Zhukov, Commander of the Leningrad Front General of the Army General of the Army, Georgy, 42–43